T0220758

Communications in Computer and Information Science   1080

Commenced Publication in 2007
Founding and Former Series Editors:
Phoebe Chen, Alfredo Cuzzocrea, Xiaoyong Du, Orhun Kara, Ting Liu,
Krishna M. Sivalingam, Dominik Ślęzak, Takashi Washio, Xiaokang Yang,
and Junsong Yuan

Editorial Board Members

Simone Diniz Junqueira Barbosa🆔
*Pontifical Catholic University of Rio de Janeiro (PUC-Rio),
Rio de Janeiro, Brazil*
Joaquim Filipe🆔
Polytechnic Institute of Setúbal, Setúbal, Portugal
Ashish Ghosh
Indian Statistical Institute, Kolkata, India
Igor Kotenko🆔
*St. Petersburg Institute for Informatics and Automation of the Russian
Academy of Sciences, St. Petersburg, Russia*
Lizhu Zhou
Tsinghua University, Beijing, China

More information about this series at http://www.springer.com/series/7899

Christian Esposito · Jiman Hong ·
Kim-Kwang Raymond Choo (Eds.)

Pervasive Systems, Algorithms and Networks

16th International Symposium, I-SPAN 2019
Naples, Italy, September 16–20, 2019
Proceedings

 Springer

Editors
Christian Esposito
University of Naples Federico II
Naples, Napoli, Italy

Jiman Hong
Soongsil University
Seoul, Korea (Republic of)

Kim-Kwang Raymond Choo
The University of Texas at San Antonio
San Antonio, TX, USA

ISSN 1865-0929   ISSN 1865-0937   (electronic)
Communications in Computer and Information Science
ISBN 978-3-030-30142-2   ISBN 978-3-030-30143-9   (eBook)
https://doi.org/10.1007/978-3-030-30143-9

© Springer Nature Switzerland AG 2019
This work is subject to copyright. All rights are reserved by the Publisher, whether the whole or part of the material is concerned, specifically the rights of translation, reprinting, reuse of illustrations, recitation, broadcasting, reproduction on microfilms or in any other physical way, and transmission or information storage and retrieval, electronic adaptation, computer software, or by similar or dissimilar methodology now known or hereafter developed.
The use of general descriptive names, registered names, trademarks, service marks, etc. in this publication does not imply, even in the absence of a specific statement, that such names are exempt from the relevant protective laws and regulations and therefore free for general use.
The publisher, the authors and the editors are safe to assume that the advice and information in this book are believed to be true and accurate at the date of publication. Neither the publisher nor the authors or the editors give a warranty, expressed or implied, with respect to the material contained herein or for any errors or omissions that may have been made. The publisher remains neutral with regard to jurisdictional claims in published maps and institutional affiliations.

This Springer imprint is published by the registered company Springer Nature Switzerland AG
The registered company address is: Gewerbestrasse 11, 6330 Cham, Switzerland

Preface

On behalf of the Organizing Committee, it is our pleasure to present the 16th International Symposium on Pervasive Systems, Algorithms and Networks (I-SPAN 2019), held in Napoli, Italy, during September 16–20, 2019. The papers included in the proceedings present novel ideas or state-of-the-art perspectives regarding the topics of interest of the conference.

Pervasive systems, intelligent algorithms, and networks are emerging fields of research and revolutionary paradigm for next-generation IT applications. I-SPAN 2019 aimed to establish an international forum for engineers and scientists to present their excellent ideas, latest innovations, and experiences on Pervasive Systems, Algorithms, and Networks.

I-SPAN 2019 followed the tradition of previous successful I-SPAN conferences, I-SPAN 1994 (Kanazawa, Japan), I-SPAN 1996 (Beijing, China), I-SPAN 1997 (Taipei, Taiwan), I-SPAN 1999 (Perth/Freemantle, Australia), I-SPAN 2000 (Dallas/Richardson, USA), I-SPAN 2002 (Manila, Philippines), I-SPAN 2004 (Hong Kong, SAR China), I-SPAN 2005 (Las Vegas, USA), I-SPAN 2008 (Sydney, Australia), I-SPAN 2009 (Kaoshiung, Taiwan), I-SPAN 2011 (Dalian, China), I-SPAN 2012 (San Marcos, USA), I-SPAN 2014 (Chengdu, China), I-SPAN 2017 (Exeter, UK), and I-SPAN 2018 (Yichang, China).

In this edition the value, overall quality, and scientific and technical depth of the I-SPAN conference continued to strengthen and grow in importance for both the academic and industrial communities. Such strength was evidenced this year by having a significant number of high-quality submissions resulting in a highly selective program. All submissions received at least three reviews according to a high-quality peer review process involving about 50 Program Committee members and several additional reviewers. On the basis of the review results, 22 papers were selected for presentation at the conference, with an acceptance rate below 37%. In addition, the conference also featured two invited talks and three workshops.

- IW-HPCA 2019 (Chairs: Che-Lun Hung, Chun-Yuan Lin, Chih-Hong Chang) - The goal of this workshop was to provide a forum for researchers and practitioners to discuss and share their research and development experiences and outputs on the high performance computing technologies including software frameworks and algorithms and the applications which adopt high performance computing technologies. In the past few years, high performance computing has been utilized to accelerate the research domains including: image processing, molecular dynamics, astrophysics, financial simulation, computer tomography, quantum chemistry, bioinformatics, and many others. Especially, General Purpose Graphic Process Units (GPGPUs) have become popular to lot of scientific computing domains. Leveraging computing power of GPGPUs, the computational cost of many applications are able to be significantly decreased.

- IW-ConSec 2019 (Chairs: Andrea Bruno, Luigi Catuogno) - Nowadays, the growing complexity and widening capabilities of consumer ICT based devices and services, increasingly threaten end user's ability to control them, their actions, and related consequences. Moreover, the raising pervasiveness, ergonomics, and "intelligence" of such commodities are making the perception of their presence slide towards the threshold of unawareness. Within this scenario, consumers are often exposed to the risks introduced by the improper use of such technologies, both due to the lack of skillfulness and the unfair and deceptive intents. This workshop aims to investigate issues and trends of technologies and practices, pursuing the enhancement of security and privacy preservation in the consumer IT arena, adopting a multidisciplinary approach. To this end, the workshop brings together different approaches, experiences, and sensitivities involved in the field of IT security into a multidisciplinary discussion on the state-of-art consumer IT security technologies and practices, goals, and forthcoming challenges. In particular, IW-ConSec 2019 was open to contributions by researchers and operators from academia, industry, and governmental institutions involved in research on IT security and privacy, human-computer interaction, computer science education, and law enforcement.
- IWVT 2019 (Chairs: Shih-Yang Lin, Dong Guo) - The role of this workshop was to provide a forum for focused, intensive scientific exchange among researchers and practitioners interested in the specific topic. The workshop was the primary venue for the exploration of emerging ideas, as well as for the discussion of novel aspects of relevant research topics including autonomous driving, vehicles platooning, advanced driving, extended sensors, remote driving, advanced ITS, etc. In the past few years, intelligent and connected cars have been developed to accelerate the research of autonomous driving, which includes image processing, environment perception, data fusion, decision making, and control mechanism. Technical progress in autonomous driving and connected vehicles enables automated control mechanism and cooperative interaction of traffic participants. The key concern is the exchange of information and/or the negotiation of driving plans via V2X communications between automated vehicles, infrastructure, conventionally driven vehicles, and road users. The purpose of this workshop was to bring together people researching various aspects of autonomous driving and connected cars. Participants presented and discussed relevant problems and solutions.

The support and help of many people are needed in order to organize an international event. We would like to thank all authors for submitting and presenting their papers. We also greatly appreciated the support of the Program Committee members and the external reviewers who carried out the most difficult work of carefully evaluating the submitted papers.

We sincerely thank all the chairs and technical Program Committee members. Without their hard work, the success of I-SPAN 2019 would not have been possible.

Last but certainly not least, our thanks go to all the attendees that contributed to the success of the conference. Finally, we are confident that the beautiful location and the relaxing atmosphere of the venue provided the perfect ingredients for a successful international event, and created a unique opportunity for both researchers and technologists to present, share, and discuss leading research topics, developments, and future directions in their area of interest.

September 2019   Christian Esposito
                                                    Jiman Hong
                                                   Raymond Choo

Organization

Steering Chairs

Frank Hsu	Fordham University, USA
Chung-Ming Huang	National Cheng Kung University, Taiwan

General Chairs

Christian Esposito	University of Napoli Federico II, Italy
Jiman Hong	Soongsil University, South Korea
Raymond Choo	The University of Texas at San Antonio, USA

Workshop Chair

Christian Esposito	University of Napoli Federico II, Italy

Program Chairs

Chang Choi	Chosun University, South Korea
Ching Hsien (Robert) Hsu	Chung Hua University, Taiwan
Marcello Cinque	University of Napoli Federico II, Italy

Publicity and Proceedings Chairs

Xin Su	Hohai University, China
Andrea Bruno	University of Salerno, Italy

Local Organizers

Christian Esposito	University of Napoli Federico II, Italy
Marcello Cinque	University of Napoli Federico II, Italy

Treasurer

Tina Marcella Nappi	Istituto Internazionale per gli Alti Studi Scientifici (IIASS), Italy

Track Chairs

Track 1 – Big Data Analytics and Applications

Vincenzo Moscato	University of Napoli Federico II, Italy
Massimiliano Albanese	George Mason University, USA

Track 2 – Cloud, Fog, and Edge Computing

Ping Mao   Fordham University, USA
Massimo Ficco   University of Campania Luigi Vanvitelli, Italy

Track 3 – Health and Biomedical Informatics

Antonio Coronato   Institute for High Performance Computing and
                                 Networking, National Research Council of Italy
                                 (ICAR-CNR), Italy
Md Zakirul Alam Bhuiyan   Fordham University, USA
Christina Schweikert   St. John's University, USA

Track 4 – Parallel, Distributed Algorithms, and Graph Computing

Florin Pop   University Politehnica of Bucharest, Romania
Hoon Ko   Chosun University, South Korea

Track 5 – Mobile Computing and Communication

Luca Foschini   University of Bologna, Italy
Gianluca Rizzo   University of Applied Sciences of Western Switzerland
                                 (HES-SO Valais), Switzerland

Track 6 – Artificial Intelligence and Nature-Inspired Computing

Hongmou Zhang   German Aerospace Centre (DLR), Germany
Goreti Marreiros   Institute of Engineering, Polytechnic of Porto
                                 (ISEP/IPP), Portugal

Track 7 – Cyber Security

Francesco Palmieri   University of Salerno, Italy
Zhe Liu   University of Luxemburg, Luxemburg
Yu Yong   Shaanxi Normal University, China

Track 8 – Multimedia Communication and Computing

Marek Ogiela   AGH University of Science and Technology, Poland
Brij B. Gupta   National Institute of Technology Kurukshetra, India

Track 9 – Internet of Things, Smart City, and Cyber-Physical Systems

Xin Su   Hohai University, China
Oumaya Baala   Université de Technologie de Belfort Montbéliard,
                                 France

Contents

Cloud Fog and Edge Computing

Communication Solutions

1st International Workshop on High Performance Computing and Applications (IW-HPCA 2019)

1st International Workshop on Consumer Cyber Security (IW-ConSec 2019)

1st International Workshop on Vehicular Technology (IWVT 2019)

Big Data Analysis and Machine Learning

Automatic Maritime Traffic Synthetic Route: A Framework for Route Prediction

Lisa Natswi Tafa[1] , Xin Su[1(✉)] , Jiman Hong[2] ,
and Chang Choi[3]

[1] College of IOT Engineering, Hohai University, Changzhou 213022, China
lisatafa5@gmail.com, leosu8622@163.com
[2] School of Computer Science and Engineering,
Soongsil University, Seoul, Korea
jiman@ssu.ac.kr
[3] IT Research Institute, Chosun University, Gwangju 61452, South Korea
enduranceaura@gmail.com

Abstract. Ship movement information is becoming increasingly available, resulting in an overwhelming increase of data transmitted to human operators. Understanding the Maritime traffic patterns is important to Maritime Situational Awareness (MSA) applications in particular, to classify and predict trajectories on sea. Therefore, there is need for automatic processing to synthesize the behavior of interest in a simplified, clear, and effective way without any loss of data originality. In this paper, we propose a method to calculate route prediction from a synthetic route representation data once the picture of the maritime traffic is constructed. The synthetic route knowledge based on Automatic Identification System (AIS) is used to classify and predict future routes along which a vessel is going to move. This is in agreement with the partially observed track and given the vessel static and dynamic information. The prediction results do not only reduce data storage space in the database but can also supply data support for traffic management, accident detection, and avoidance of automatic collision and therefore promote the development of maritime intelligent traffic systems. Finally, the simulation results shows a good tradeoff between the predicted and the actual observed vessel routes.

Keywords: Route prediction · Maritime route extraction · AIS · MSA · Maritime traffic representation

1 Introduction

Maritime surveillance represents a challenging research field due to the broadness of the coverage area and the variety of monitoring activities, e.g. piracy, irregular migration and traffic monitoring. Based on AIS network, ships can automatically exchange navigation information, such as their unique identification, position, course, and speed, with nearby ships and terrestrial AIS receivers to facilitate the tracking and monitoring of ships' location and movement. AIS database is a valuable data source for maritime traffic and gives opportunity used for discovering the traffic knowledge from

© Springer Nature Switzerland AG 2019
C. Esposito et al. (Eds.): I-SPAN 2019, CCIS 1080, pp. 3–14, 2019.
https://doi.org/10.1007/978-3-030-30143-9_1

historical AIS trajectories. In [6], the authors considered a route in maritime to be a line generated from a series of sequential points through which vessels navigate their way to a desired destination. Information about time, speed, direction, and other vessels details generated by the AIS can be applied in route prediction to determine or predict the highest possible navigation. Therefore, the major purpose of trajectory prediction of vessels is to calculate the future trajectory of vessels, which is a highly valuable piece of information because it facilitates the provision of important information on warnings related to traffic conditions, traffic control and planning, and others. With the explosive growth of maritime traffic data, more and more data forms are now available to people. However, some problems still occur, such as data loss, errors, diversity, and so on. Thus, there is an increasing interest in performing data analysis over AIS data and develop many applications for maritime traffic management, route prediction and collision risk [14]. Thus, methods that solve these problems and exploit huge amounts of the data stream must be developed to predict the trajectories of vessels. Presently, information on the movement of vessels are increasingly detected, collected, and stored in the database. Hence, one of the important applications based on the big data is prediction [5]. Some authors proposed an intelligent model to solve the issue of the trajectory prediction of vessels based on machine learning methods but has a drawback on huge data space storage. Diverse technologies are being deployed for maritime surveillance enhancement, such as vessel positioning systems [16] or meteorological and oceanographic sensors [17]. As a result, a large amount of heterogeneous data sources feed the maritime surveillance systems. The fusion of such data sources enables the creation of a real-time picture of the situation at sea and enlarges the available knowledge.

In this paper, we analyze the application of synthetic route detection algorithm to a simple, yet complex, case study where environmental (e.g., sea status) conditions are considered. The main aim of the paper is to be able to predict the future route along which a vessel is going to move, in agreement with the partially observed track and given the vessel static information. The synthetic analysis is compared with the historical behavior of the existing state-of-art system in order to prove the outperformance of the proposed synthetic model. The results derived from the model show efficiency in dealing with real-time data with simplicity and accuracy.

The rest of the paper is organized in the following manner. Section 2 presents the geographical area under analysis. Section 3 explains the related works with respect to the project and research area on maritime traffic representation. In Sect. 4, the proposed Maritime Traffic Route Prediction knowledge is detailed. Section 5 will introduce the simulation results. Section 6, the paper ends drawing some conclusions, remaining challenges and future lines of exploitation.

2 Geographical Analysis

The geographical area of study in this research is based on the East China Sea, which is a part of the Pacific Ocean and covers an area of roughly 1,249,000 square kilometers [18]. United Nations Conference on Trade and Development (UNCTAD) estimates it, roughly 80% of global trade by volume that is transported by sea. Out of that volume,

60% of maritime trade passes through Asia, with the South and East China Sea carrying a relatively large part of global shipping. Most studies have mainly focused on the Baltic Sea but in this research, we tended to focus on East China Sea since it is also characterized by intense traffic as shown in Fig. 1. Due to the increasing ship presence enlarging the risk of accidents, threatening the East China Seas ecosystem and its population safety and security.

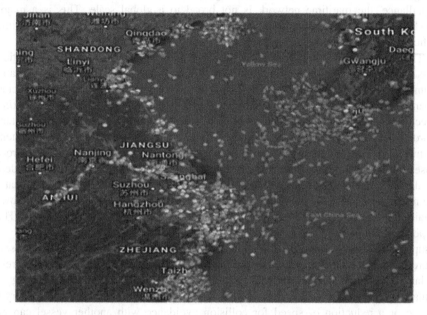

Fig. 1. Geographic view of the East China Sea showing traffic density.

3 Related Works

The current literature encompasses many solutions for the representation of maritime traffic by means of self-reporting data. These solutions can be grouped in two district classes, based on the adopted criteria: spatial grid techniques and spatiotemporal techniques. The solutions in the first class mainly segment the area of interest in a number of cells forming a grid, where each cell characterized by the traffic of the traversing maritime vessels [9, 10]. These solutions are very simple and easy to build in order to realize traffic detection and visualization from low-level maritime data obtained from on-board navigation equipment [19]. However, they are affected by two main weakness factors. Firstly, the increase in the scale of the monitored area implies a considerable computational overhead to their construction and use, making the relative analysis of maritime traffic complex or intractable on global scale. Secondly, the aggregation and manipulation make the identification and prediction much more difficult to be implemented.

The report in [4] shows a methodology to extract a geographical network repre-sentation of maritime ship traffic by analyzing historical self-reporting data. The approach was applied in representing traffic routes over an area of interest in a compact approximation as well as a reference to perform anomaly detection, situation prediction and track reconstruction [2]. The authors stated that different levels of granularity of the demonstration could be achieved by operating a trade-off between system complexity and goodness of fit. In the generation of geographical networks for maritime traffic surveillance, the maritime network is not broad to a global scale. This is a major drawback since other challenging scenarios such as open sea areas where maritime traffic is also highly dense are not analyzed.

The work described in [1] describes the application of data clustering and detection so as to identify traffic flows, group them and find possible from AIS trajectory data in an unsupervised manner. In this study real AIS data has been used and the conducted experiments proved that the proposed framework could effectively discover conflicting trajectories. The study of the found set of conflicting trajectories is extremely important in order to provide useful knowledge for maritime traffic monitoring and its consequent optimization. The authors in this paper did not address the problem of defining the root causes for the raising of conflicts from discovered clusters of trajectories, hence hinders the alertness of maritime near-collision behaviors discovered from AIS trajectory data. The researchers in [7, 12] analyzed maritime vessels as a collective entity that follows certain traffic patterns within the sea fragment of interest based on certain criteria. The proposed methodology constructs inferred knowledge on the maritime traffic in an unsupervised way, so as to identify low-likelihood behaviors and to predict vessels future positions. The subsequent low-likelihood behavior detection was entirely explained through an object-oriented representation, with vessels corresponding to virtual object interacting among each other's. For example, an unexpected trajectory's change or a reduction of speed for collision avoidance with another vessel can be represented as in interaction of the two objects. By using such a representation, the authors were able to generalize a set of behavioral patterns so as to understand vessel behavior and intent. Such an approach exhibits a serious limitation when applied to the context of the detection of turning points in unregulated areas, where the behavior of vessels is much more complex and, therefore, difficult to be categorized. Most of the current applications to support maritime traffic management is not based on historical traffic data, but only rely on past/current experience of operators/captains. Moreover, compressed representations, which visualize maritime traffic to easily enable maritime traffic monitoring, are also strongly needed.

The authors in [3] took as a representative example of complex maritime traffic scenario a portion of the Baltic Sea, known to be characterized by a dense traffic, and proposed an analysis in order to detect de-facto routes, with the consequent intent of modelling the traffic. This led to a highly compressed representation of the traffic in that area, capable of offering the needed visualization capability and the knowledge for real-time monitoring, anomaly detection and situation prediction, enhancing the MSA [13]. Their performance analysis resulted in a reduction of the needed capacity to store data related to each route, equal to more than a 99%, while keeping the same representation accuracy. Specifically, it reduces 1,842,298 geographical points to 2,095 tracklets.

However, the authors did not discuss the compressed maritime representation foundations to other real time maritime monitoring applications such as route prediction.

The work in [15] presents the design of a standard AIS database for keeping, predicting and mining data on maritime trajectory. Extreme Learning Machine (ELM) was exploited for path prediction and consequently validated by using an AIS database. The obtained results showed that such a solution could be used as a standardized benchmark for assessing different prediction algorithms and easily integrated so as to build more advanced AIS applications.

4 Maritime Traffic Route Prediction

The proposed Maritime Traffic Route Prediction aims at the analysis of vessels simple and precise synthetic representation of maritime traffic from self-reporting positioning data in order to easily determine the highest probable route to be taken by a vessel. Synthetic route is a light and structured trajectory of the maritime traffic, setting the foundations of real-time traffic monitoring and prediction.

4.1 Synthetic Route Representation

Prior to synthetically represent maritime traffic, waypoints and raw maritime routes are detected [8]. There are three types of entry points to be considered in maritime traffic, which are entry points, exit points and ports. Entry/Exit points are created and updated when a vessel enters/leaves the area of interest. Ports (reference points invariant with respect to the monitored area) identify local ports, offshore platforms and stationary points, detected by speed gating. Both Ports and Entry/Exit points are generated, enriched with more information and/or merged according to an incremental Density-Based Spatial Clustering approach [10, 11], where the clustering parameters are set based on specific traffic density, intensity and regularity in the area of interest. Exits, entries and ports are used as the main nodes in the creation of the maritime traffic network. Once the waypoints are derived, the positions of the vessels transiting between these waypoints are clustered resulting in the construction of routes by connecting the formed waypoints. These detected waypoints are later used as the main nodes in the Synthetic Maritime Network Generation.

An algorithm used to construct synthetic route is mainly based on a method where the route is unfolded on the temporal dimension [3]. An algorithm based on latitude/longitude computation and position prediction is used in the computation of a synthetic route. During the first phase of latitude/longitude computation a starting point is initialized, *Pini* where the algorithm searches for all points within the temporal state sequence cell, $\bar{S}$ centered in *Pini* and with radius (r). The size of the temporal state sequence cell is important; it should not be too large hence $r < R$. If the radius is too large, it leads to biasing the motion characterization of the relevant observation neighborhood, thus, the route classification due to the distinct local direct distributions, which could be included into the same state cell in Fig. 2.

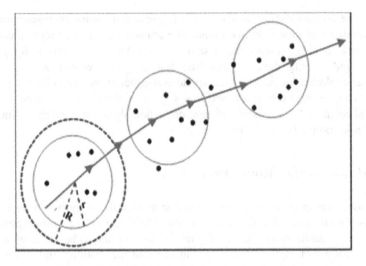

Fig. 2. Synthetic route unfolding over temporal axis.

As soon as the neighboring points are found, their mean is computed ($Psynth_m$) and that point is assigned to the synthetic route together with the estimated bearing. The computed ($Psynth_m$) and the estimated bearing is used to compute the next position, $Pnext$, then $Pini$ is updated with $Pnext$ and perform latitude/longitude computation for the updated $Pini$, continuing until reaching other route waypoint. Lastly all points associated to $Psynth_m$ are concatenated, resulting in the temporal construction of synthetic route $\overline{R}$.

$$\overline{R} = \left((Pj, COGj, tj)_{j=1}^{L} \right)_{m=1}^{X} \tag{1}$$

where Pj is the $j - th$ point associated to the $i - th$ route within the search area. $COGj$ is the Course Over Ground, tj is the vector determining the timestamp when the vessel enter/exit the area of interest, L is the total number of neighboring points within a search cell, $(Pj, COGj, tj)_{j=1}^{L} \rightarrow Psynth_m$, and X is the total number of points within a synthetic route. The sum of the points associated to each $Psynth_m$ is equal to the total number of points of the route under analysis outlined as follows:

$$\sum_{j=1}^{L} Psynth_m = \sum_{m=1}^{X} L_m \tag{2}$$

4.2 Vessel Synthetic Route Prediction

The route prediction method proposed in this paper is based on the exploitation of Maritime Traffic Network Generation algorithm, which analyses decomposed routes, towards the discovery of vessels behavioral patterns in an attempt to synthetically and accurately represent the maritime traffic in the monitored area [7]. Once the picture of the synthetic maritime traffic is constructed, there is need to find the highest possible route, $R_c^{-N^*}$, to which a vessel is going to move using the vessels static and dynamic information obtained from the a previously observed track. This problem can be outlined as shown in Eq. (3), where, N, is the number of compatible routes of vessel type, c, $\bar{S}$ is the state sequence cell region and V is the vessel track of observed state vectors.

$$R_c^{-N^*} = \arg_N \max P(\bar{R}_c^N \mid V, \bar{S}) \tag{3}$$

Following Bayes rule procedure indicated in [20], Eq. (3) is further decomposed as follows:

$$P(\bar{R}_c^N \mid V, \bar{S}) \alpha P(V, \bar{S} \mid \bar{R}_c^N) P(\bar{R}_c^N) \tag{4}$$

Using a variation of the probabilistic approach in Hidden Markov Model (HMM) and spatiotemporal trajectory mining technique [21, 22], the joint probability, $P(V, \bar{S} \mid \bar{R}_c^N)$, and the vessel track, V, and the state sequence, $\bar{S}$, given the synthetic route, $\bar{R}_c^N$, is shown below:

$$P(V, \bar{S} \mid \bar{R}_c^N) = P(V \mid \bar{S}, \bar{R}_c^N) P(\bar{S} \mid \bar{R}_c^N) \tag{5}$$

Lastly, the probability of each compatible route is assigned based on the posterior probability that the vessel belongs to that route. Given the state sequence, $\bar{S}$, and the synthetic route, $\bar{R}_c^N$, the time window and the later positions of the vessels is predicted as follows:

$$P(V \mid \bar{S}, \bar{R}_c^N) = \prod_{t=1}^{T} P(v_t \mid \bar{s}_t, \bar{R}_c^N) \tag{6}$$

Figure 3a and b below shows the area under study and the vessel destination prediction given a set of compatible routes. The probability of vessel location is computed based on Eq. (6) and conditioned to the distribution of vessel types within each route. The extracted synthetic routes give enough information to effectively predict the vessel position even in complex routing systems. For the considered vessel, there are initially three compatible routes. The reported percentage represents the probability that the vessel is expected to move along each route based on equation. It clearly shows in Fig. 3a that the trajectory with the highest probability of 58.2% is the desired route that the vessel under observation is expected to follow. The trajectory with probability of 48.9% is the least likely expected route that the vessel follows.

(a)

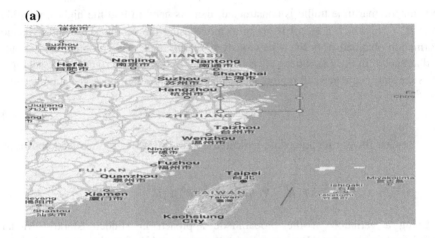

(b)

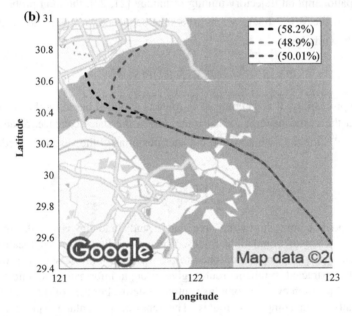

Fig. 3. a. Study coverage area. **b.** Destination prediction probabilities. **(a and b).** The probabilistic vessel track prediction of the East China Sea

5   Simulation Results

Figure 4 shows the estimation of transition probabilities. The blue line shows the actual route after observation and the red dotted line shows the predicted distributions of the distances, in miles between vessels in Shanghai Sea. The time lag is the range from 10 to 80 min, with an increment of 10 min. The figure shows how to derive the transition probability from the distance between the new observation and the predicted position given the previous position. This gives a measure of match between the routes and the observed sequence. Looking at the simulation result, the vessel transition probability is decreasing with increase in distance. There is a good tradeoff between the predicted and the actual observed route that the vessel followed, and shows the precision of the probabilistic synthetic route approach.

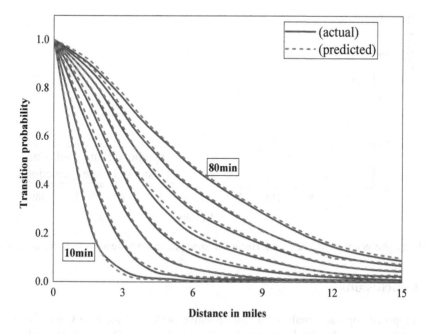

Fig. 4. Comparison of transition probability estimation. (Color figure online)

Figure 5 compares the accuracy of the synthetic route prediction and historical route prediction directly from analyzing historical self-reporting data. Due to the compressed, light and structured representation of the synthetic route, prediction algorithm presents relatively high accuracy and consistency regardless of the vessel traffic density.

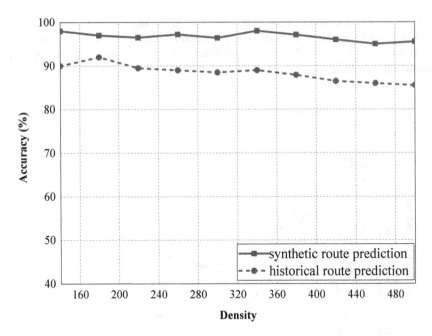

Fig. 5. Accuracy of Synthetic and Historical route prediction in relation to traffic density

6 Conclusions

The proposed approach analyzed a representative portion of the East China Sea maritime traffic to model the traffic on this heavily transited area. The results show that in a highly compressed representation, it is capable to visualize the maritime traffic, and to provide the necessary knowledge for real-time maritime route prediction, and thereby enhancing the MSA. The model can address real-time traffic data and provide accurate predictions of real-time trajectories. The prediction results can also supply data support for traffic management, accident detection, and avoidance of automatic collision and therefore promote the development of maritime intelligent traffic systems.

Most maritime applications rely on systems built over end-user knowledge. It could be of more benefit if they are to be combined with edge computing to increase the rate at which computations are done therefore reducing the possibility of delay. The fusion of maritime route prediction with weather forecast could also make maritime diversify maritime applications.

Acknowledgements. This work was supported in part by the National Natural Science Foundation of China under Grant 61801166, in part by the Fundamental Research Funds for the Central Universities under Grant 2019B22214, and in part by the Changzhou Sci. and Tech. Program under Grant CJ20180046. This work was supported by Institute for Information and communications Technology Promotion (IITP) grant funded by the Korea government (MSIT) (2017-0-00255, Autonomous digital companion framework and application).

References

1. Lei, P., Tsai, T., Wen, Y., Peng, W.: A framework for discovering maritime traffic conflict from AIS network. In: 2017 19th Asia-Pacific Network Operations and Management Symposium (APNOMS), Seoul, pp. 1–6 (2017)
2. Brandsæter, A., Manno, G., Vanem, E., Glad, I.K.: An application of sensor-based anomaly detection in the maritime industry. In: 2016 IEEE International Conference on Prognostics and Health Management (ICPHM), pp. 1–8. IEEE, June 2016
3. Arguedas, V.F., Pallotta, G., Vespe, M.: Maritime Traffic Networks: from historical positioning data to unsupervised maritime traffic monitoring. IEEE Trans. Intell. Transp. Syst. **19**(3), 722–732 (2017)
4. Arguedas, V.F., Pallotta, G., Vespe, M.: Automatic generation of geographical networks for maritime traffic surveillance. In: 17th International Conference on Information Fusion (FUSION), pp. 1–8. IEEE, July 2014
5. Qi, L., Zheng, Z.: Trajectory prediction of vessels based on data mining and machine learning. J. Digit. Inf. Manage **14**(1), 33–40 (2016)
6. Lei, P.R., Li, S.C., Peng, W.C.: QS-STT: QuadSection clustering and spatial-temporal trajectory model for location prediction. Distrib. Parallel Databases **31**(2), 231–258 (2013)
7. Pallotta, G., Vespe, M., Bryan, K.: Vessel pattern knowledge discovery from AIS data: a framework for anomaly detection and route prediction. Entropy **15**(6), 2218–2245 (2013)
8. Bomberger, N.A., Rhodes, B.J., Seibert, M., Waxman, A.M.: Associative learning of vessel motion patterns for maritime situation awareness. In: 2006 9th International Conference on Information Fusion, pp. 1–8. IEEE, July 2006
9. Arguedas, V.F., Pallotta, G., Vespe, M.: Unsupervised maritime pattern analysis to enhance contextual awareness. In: Context-Awareness in Geographic Information Services (CAGIS 2014), p. 50 (2014)
10. Ester, M., Kriegel, H.P., Sander, J., Xu, X.: A density-based algorithm for discovering clusters in large spatial databases with noise. In: KDD, vol. 96, no. 34, pp. 226–231, August 1996
11. Ester, M., Wittmann, R.: Incremental generalization for mining in a data warehousing environment. In: Schek, H.-J., Alonso, G., Saltor, F., Ramos, I. (eds.) EDBT 1998. LNCS, vol. 1377, pp. 135–149. Springer, Heidelberg (1998). https://doi.org/10.1007/BFb0100982
12. Chang, S., Hsu, G., Yang, J., Chen, K., Chiu, Y., Chang, F.: Vessel traffic analysis for maritime intelligent transportation system. In: 2010 IEEE 71st Vehicular Technology Conference, Taipei, pp. 1–4 (2010). https://doi.org/10.1109/vetecs.2010.5493942
13. Douglas, D.H., Peucker, T.K.: Algorithms for the reduction of the number of points required to represent a digitized line or its caricature. Cartogr. Int. J. Geogr. Inf. Geovisual. **10**(2), 112–122 (1973)
14. Batty, E.: Data analytics enables advanced AIS applications. In: Doulkeridis, C., Vouros, George A., Qu, Q., Wang, S. (eds.) MATES 2017. LNCS, vol. 10731, pp. 22–35. Springer, Cham (2018). https://doi.org/10.1007/978-3-319-73521-4_2
15. Mao, S., Tu, E., Zhang, G., Rachmawati, L., Rajabally, E., Huang, G.B.: An automatic identification system (AIS) database for maritime trajectory prediction and data mining. In: Cao, J., Cambria, E., Lendasse, A., Miche, Y., Vong, C. (eds.) Proceedings of ELM 2016, pp. 241–257. Springer, Cham (2018)
16. Ma, S., Wang, J., Meng, X., Wang, J.: A vessel positioning algorithm based on satellite automatic identification system. J. Electr. Comput. Eng. 1–4 (2017)

17. Sendra, S., Parra, L., Lloret, J., Jiménez, J.M.: Oceanographic multisensor buoy based on low cost sensors for posidonia meadows monitoring in Mediterranean Sea. J. Sens. 1–23 (2015)
18. http://www.shiptraffic.net/2001/04/east-china-sea-ship-traffic.html
19. Ducruet, C. (ed.): Maritime Networks: Spatial Structures and Time Dynamics. Routledge, New York (2015)
20. Giannotti, F., Nanni, M., Pinelli, F., Pedreschi, D.: Trajectory pattern mining. In: Proceedings of the 13th ACM SIGKDD International Conference on Knowledge Discovery and Data Mining, pp. 330–339. ACM, August 2007
21. Emrich, T., Kriegel, H., Mamoulis, N., Renz, M., Zufle, A.: Querying uncertain spatio-temporal data. In: 2012 IEEE 28th International Conference on Data Engineering, Washington, DC, pp. 354–365 (2012)
22. Bayes' theorem. https://en.wikipedia.org/wiki/Bayes%27_theorem

A Reinforcement Learning Based Intelligent System for the Healthcare Treatment Assistance of Patients with Disabilities

Antonio Coronato[1] and Muddasar Naeem[2(✉)]

[1] ICAR-CNR Naples, Naples, Italy
antonio.coronato@ocar.cnr.it
[2] Universita' Degli Studi di Napoli 'Parthenope', Naples, Italy
muddasar.naeem@icar.cnr.it, muddasar.naeem@uniparthenope.it

Abstract. Nowadays, one of the clinical challenge is the realization of personalized treatments, which falls into the more general paradigm of the precision medicine. On the other hand, over the last years we have assisted the rising of technologies able to assist people at home during their daily activities. In this paper we present an intelligent system, which is able to self-adapt to user's skills aiming at assisting her/him in the healthcare treatment. The system adopts the Reinforcement Learning paradigm to adapt the way to communicate with the patient. By this way, in case of patients with physical disabilities (e.g. auditory or visual impairments) or cognitive disabilities (e.g. mild cognitive impairments), the system automatically searches for the most effective way to communicate and remind the daily treatment plan to the patient.

Keywords: Artificial Intelligence · Reinforcement Learning · Healthcare · Pill reminder

1 Introduction

Improvement in patient treatment and care is important for all healthcare stakeholders in order to provide a higher level of satisfaction to patients [2]. Medical assistance depends on various factors such as trained personal, quality care centers, medical and nuclear examination equipment, use of suitable medication [3], pervasive computing [43] and use of modern technologies; e.g. Artificial Intelligence (AI) and Machine Learning (ML). AI is radically improving the quality and effectiveness of healthcare services. In fact, almost all sectors of the medicine and clinical practice and tools are affected: diagnostic systems (e.g. [5]), personalized treatments (e.g. DTR [22]), medical imaging ([10]), dialogue systems and

The AMICO project has received funding from the National Programs (PON) of the Italian Ministry of Education, Universities and Research (MIUR): code ARS01_00900 (Decree n.1989, 26 July 2018).

© Springer Nature Switzerland AG 2019
C. Esposito et al. (Eds.): I-SPAN 2019, CCIS 1080, pp. 15–28, 2019.
https://doi.org/10.1007/978-3-030-30143-9_2

chat-bots (e.g. [12]), virtual environments [47], social-technical systems [48], risk management (e.g. [13]), control systems (e.g. [15]), Ambient Assisted Living (e.g. [1]) and rehabilitation (e.g. [17]).

RL is a ML approach much more focused on goal-directed learning from interaction, than other approaches of machine learning i.e. supervised and unsupervised learning [20]. Finding an optimal policy is the central objective of any RL algorithm, which is similar to a clinical scenario where doctors try to find an optimal sequence of treatments for a patient. Byt is way, RL has achieved considerable success to help clinicians in optimizing and personalizing sequences of clinical treatments (e.g. [25,26]).

The conventional way to assist patients and elderly persons in their activities of daily living (ADL) was based on cues, signals and verbal reminders by caregivers. Later computer based solutions, such as 'Cognitive Ortosis for Assisting activties in the Home (COACH)' [35], have been developed for assistance. Some works to assist elderly people using computer vision technology are: [37–40]. We have also seen implementation of mobile health monitoring systems for ill and elderly peoples [44, 45]. However, we may have some failure modes and effects of 'mobile health monitoring systems' [46]. Then we witnessed the use of AI and ML for the development of intelligent robotic caregivers [36]. Other interesting projects are the assisted cognition project [31], aware home project [30], adaptive house [33], nursebot project [32] and automated hand-washing assistance [34]. Most of these works assist elderly people and patients with dementia in one of ADL like, as an example, hand washing.

The focus of this work is to provide assistance to elderly patients having any mental or physical disability. In particular, we devised a pill reminder for the suggestion and tracking of healthcare daily treatment. According to our knowledge, there is no such study is present in literature till date and this will be the first system which help patient through a suitable type of message. We modeled the problem as a Markov Decision Process (MDP) and provided solutions by using dynamic programming and actor critic algorithms. The proposed intelligent system first sends reminders to patients according to ones treatment plan and then guides the patient to the assumption of a specific medicine through an appropriate type of message. The message type is very critical and the choice of the message is performed by considering the patient person skills i.e. physical and mental. After learning, the RL Reminder is able to choose a suitable type of audio or visual or textual message depending upon ones physical and mental abilities.

The next part of the paper is organized as follows. Background section presents a brief introduction to RL. Next, the system model is described. Results and discussion concludes the paper.

2   Background

Most of the RL problems are based on the Markov Decision Process (MDP). A MDP model is defined by the following components:

-Set of states: $S = \{s_1, s_2, s_3, ...s_n\}$
-Set of actions: $A = \{a_1, a_2, a_3, ...a_n\}$
-Transition model: $T(s_t, a, s_{t+1})$
-Reward R.

Reward and transition depend upon the current state, chosen action and next resulting state.

The goal of RL is to interact with a given environment without any prior knowledge and learn the characteristics of the environment based by means of many repetitive interactions. The part of the RL algorithm who does interactions and learns is known as an **agent**. The target of the RL agent is to find an optimal **policy**, which is a set of couples <**state, action**> that will allow to maximize the rewards collected over the time.

The working framework of RL is shown in Fig. 1. The main difference between RL and MDP is that a RL agent does not know all elements of the MDP i.e. probabilistic model and reward function. The parameters which are stationary in an MDP framework may vary in RL environment when an agent take actions. So RL tries to find a solution of the MDP without having information about the model. An RL agent has to try different actions to learn a policy by interacting with world.

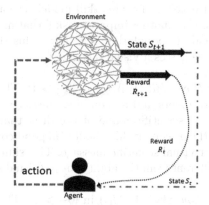

Fig. 1. The Reinforcement Learning problem.

Besides learning a sequence of actions, an agent should maintain a balance between exploitation and exploration. That is a equilibrium between maximizing reward from already known actions or to explore new actions -never selected before- that (hopefully) will lead to improve the finally reward. In exploitation, the agent prefers to take best action based on his current knowledge. On the other hand, in exploration, an agent attempts new actions in a stochastic way to improve his experience and learning in order to get more knowledge and better rewards.

RL algorithms may be categorized into two branches i.e. model free (direct learning) and model based (indirect learning). Model based algorithms learn the model dynamics and major model based approaches are policy search, return function, value function and transition model [27]. Sampling (Monte Carlo) and bootstrapping also known as Temporal Difference (TD) are used to learn value function and are model free approaches. Temporal difference is further divided into on-policy (State-Action-Reward-State-Action) and off-policy (Q-learning) algorithms.

3 System Model

This section presents the proposed approaches based on RL to assist patients and elderly persons at home having one or combination of more than one disabilities. In this work we consider audio and visual disabilities, and some cognitive impairments affecting the patient working memory and attention. For this reason we modeled five skills as follows:

Auditory Perception

- *Audio Skill* (AU_s) in $[0- > 1]$: This skill models the ability of the patient to listen audio messages. It plays an important role in the treatment process of any patient and reduces dependency on caregivers.

Visual Perception

- *Visual Skill* (VS_s) in $[0- > 1]$: This skill models the ability of the patient to view visual messages. It is another important skill that must be consider when assisting patients and elderly population. The lower this skill is, the lower the probability that the patient sees a visual message is.

Working Memory

- *Working Memory High Skill* (WM_{hs}) in $[0- > 1]$: The lower the skill, the lower the probability to understand a "complex" message. A complex message may ·be, for example, the scientific name of the drug that the patient has to assume. If patient's working memory high skill is in good condition, then she/he can understand audio or visual scientific message. This skill concerns the ability to understand and is different from the ability to see (visual skill) or listen (audio skill).

- *Working Memory Low Skill* (WM_{ls}) in $[0- > 1]$: The lower the skill, the lower the probability to understand even a "simple" audio or visual message. This skill is related to critical mental conditions.

Attention

- Attention Skill (AT_s) in $[0- > 1]$: The lower the skill, the higher the probability to ignore the message. The level of attention of the patient is a critical factor in successful completion of the task.

The purpose of the RL based Reminder is to provide assistance to patients about their treatment plans through effective messages depending on their disabilities. One relevant characteristic of the reminder is that it is not pre-programmed and customized based on the actual patient skills. Instead, it is able to learn the capabilities of the actual patient by means of an Rl approach that relies on an interactive phase during which the reminder explores several kinds of basic messages and their combinations to find the most effective for the patient.

To do that, we defined six types of basic messages as shown in Table 1 and all possible combinations are shown in Fig. 2. For instance, if the condition of a patient audio and working memory is good, then the reminder can send him/her an audio "scientific" message to take the 'TACHIPIRINA 1000 mg' pill; whereas, in case of a minor working memory disability, a "simpler" message to take the pill from the "red box" may be more effective. The agent may optionally send an image of a particular box when the patient does not have reasonable audio hearing abilities. Moreover, in some cases, it may opt to send images of both pill and box. The tutor has total sixty three choices (actions) in order to remind the patient whose choice depends upon his/her given working memory, attention and disabilities condition.

Table 1. Basic messages

Label	Message type
C1	Audio scientific message
C2	Audio simple message
C3	Visual pill-box image
C4	Visual pill-box and pill image
C5	Scientific textual message
C6	Simple textual message

No	Message	No	Message	No	Message
1	C1	2	C2	3	C3
4	C4	5	C5	6	C6
7	C1C2	8	C1C3	9	C1C4
10	C1C5	11	C1C6	12	C2C3
13	C2C4	14	C2C5	15	C2C6
16	C3C4	17	C3C5	18	C3C6
19	C4C5	20	C4C6	21	C5C6
22	C1C2C3	23	C1C2C4	24	C1C3C4
25	C1C2C5	26	C1C3C5	27	C1C4C5
28	C1C2C6	29	C1C3C6	30	C1C4C6
31	C1C5C6	32	C2C3C4	33	C2C3C5
34	C2C4C5	35	C2C3C6	36	C2C4C6
37	C2C5C6	38	C3C4C5	39	C3C4C6
40	C3C5C6	41	C4C5C6	42	C1C2C3C4
43	C1C2C4C3	44	C1C3C4C5	45	C1C2C3C6
46	C1C2C3C5	47	C1C2C4C6	48	C1C3C4C6
49	C1C3C5C6	50	C1C4C5C6	51	C2C3C4C5
52	C1C2C5C6	53	C2C3C4C6	54	C2C3C5C6
55	C2C4C5C6	56	C3C4C5C6	57	C1C2C3C4C5
58	C1C2C3C4C6	59	C1C2C3C5C6	60	C1C2C4C5C6
61	C1C3C4C5C6	62	C2C3C4C5C6	63	C1C2C3C4C5C6

Fig. 2. All available actions at message interpretation state (message choices) (Color figure online)

The work-flow of proposed tutoring system is given in Fig. 3. The objective of the reminder (the RL Agent) is to suggest the drug to assume (depending on the treatment plan) by sending a pill reminder through the most appropriate type of message for the patient condition. The role of the Observer from one hand is to check that the patient is assuming the right pill, from the other hand is to generate the reward for the Rl Agent that has by this way the means to learn and improve its performance. The possible responses of the patient to a reminder is to take either the right pill-box (in this case the Reminder receives a rewarded as a numerical number equal to 1) or the wrong pill-box (in this case the Reminder receives no reward), as graphically shown in Fig. 4.

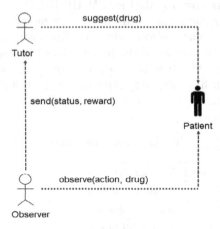

Fig. 3. The proposed model

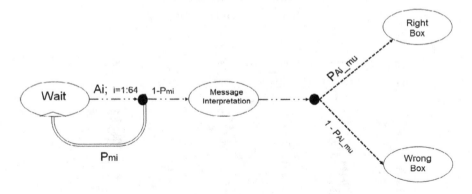

Fig. 4. The Reinforcement Learning block

The agent first takes account of a patient's attention before sending message. In case of low attention skills it stays at wait state and sends repetitive alerts to catch the attention of the patient. Once the patient improves his attention, then the agent sends the reminder. In Fig. 4, large open circles are states and small solid circles are action nodes for each state-action pair. This is the finite MDP model [20] we defined for this application and the resulting destination state depend on the probability of the current state-action pair. The probability that a patient will understand a message or ignore a message is calculated as:

$$\text{Probability that the message is understood } = P_{mu} = f\left(AU_s, VS_s, WM_{hs}, WM_{ls}\right) \quad (1)$$

$$\text{Probability that the message is ignored} = P_{mi} = f\left(AT_s\right) \quad (2)$$

Equations 1 and 2 indicate the probability that the patient understands the message. It is a function of the audio, visual and working memory abilities of that patient. Similarly, the probability that the patient will ignore the message depends on her/his attention status. This can be further elaborated in Eqs. 3 and 4.

$$P_{mu} = \min(1, C1 * AU_s * WM_{hs} + C2 * AU_s * WM_{ls} + C3 * VS_s * WM_{hs} \quad (3)$$
$$+ \ C4 * VS_s * WM_{ls} + C5 * VS_s * WM_{hs} + C6 * VS_s * WM_{ls})$$

$$P_{mi} = 1 - AT_s \quad (4)$$

3.1   Algorithm 1

First of two algorithms used for learning in our work is Dynamic Programming (DP), introduced by Richard Bellman in 1950 [19,42]. It is a model based technique which requires the full knowledge of the environment; i.e. the transition model and rewards and is used to find optimal value function or policy by using value iteration or policy iteration. We used value iteration algorithm for our pill reminder system. The state value and action value function for a RL problem using Bellman equation can be written as shown in Eqs. 5 and 6 respectively.

$$V^\pi\left(s'\right) = \sum_a \pi\left(s, a\right) \sum_{s'} p\left(s' \mid s, a\right) \left[R\left(s, s', a\right) + \gamma V^\pi\left(s'\right)\right] \quad (5)$$

$$Q^\pi\left(s, a\right) = \sum_{s'} p\left(s' \mid s, a\right) \left[R\left(s, s', a\right) + \gamma Q^\pi\left(s', a'\right)\right] \quad (6)$$

The target of value function approaches is to calculate state and action value function and then drive optimal policy through maximum value function in every states. Optimal state value function using Bellman optimality Eq. 7 is given as:

$$V^{\pi*}\left(s'\right) = \max_{a \in A(s)} \sum_{s'} p\left(s' \mid s, a\right) \left[R\left(s, s', a\right) + \gamma V^{\pi*}\left(s'\right)\right] \quad (7)$$

By using Eq. 7, we can write optimal equation for our model. For example, the Bellman optimality equation at wait and message selection states abbreviated as w and MS respectively, may be written as shown in Eqs. 8, 9 and 10.

$$V_*\left(w\right) = \max_a \left\{p\left(w \mid w, a\right) \left[r\left(w, a, w\right) + \gamma V_*\left(w\right)\right]\right.$$
$$\left. + p\left(MS \mid w, a\right) \left[r\left(MS, a, w\right) + \gamma V_*\left(MS\right)\right]\right\} \quad (8)$$

$$V_*\left(w\right) = \max_a \left\{P_{mi}\left[r\left(w, a, w\right) + \gamma V_*\left(w\right)\right] + \left(1 - P_{mi}\right)\left[r\left(MS, a, w\right) + \gamma V_*\left(MS\right)\right]\right\} \quad (9)$$

$$V_* (MS) = \underset{a}{\max} \{P_{mu} [r (RB, a, MS) + \gamma V_* (RB)]$$

$$+ (1 - P_{mu}) [r (WB, a, MS) + \gamma V_* (WB)]\} \tag{10}$$

Similarly, the optimality equation for action value function may be written as in Eq. 11 and the complete pseudo code for tutoring system using the Bellman optimality equation according to [20] is given in Algorithm 1.

$$Q^{\pi*} (s, a) = \sum_{s'} P \left(s' \mid s, a\right) \left[R \left(s, s', a\right) + \gamma * \underset{a'}{\max} Q^{\pi*} \left(s', a'\right)\right] \tag{11}$$

Algorithm 1. Value iteration algorithm

Emulate
$AU_s, VS_s, WM_{hs}, WM_{ls}$
Emulate AT_s
Initialize
Rewards for all state-action pairs, $R_{s,a}$
Q to zero,
γ, the learning rate $= 0.9$
Calculate
P_{mu}, P_{mi}
repeat
    Initialize s
    repeat
      Choose a' $\epsilon - greedily$
      Take action a, observe R, s'

$$Q(s, a) = \sum P \left(s' \mid s, a\right) \left[r + \gamma \underset{a}{\max} Q_* \left(s', a'\right)\right]$$

      $s \leftarrow s'$
    until s is terminal
until convergence

3.2   Algorithm 2

Second methodology for current work is the well known actor-critic RL algorithm [28]. It is a hybrid method consisting of value function and policy [29]. The critic part of the algorithm estimates the state value 4 or action value function 5, while the actor updates the policy in accordance with critic feedback. This type of method stands between policy based methods and value based methods; i.e. it estimates both policy and value function. It is applicable to small state-action spaces such as our model as well as to large action-state spaces. For the first case, the critic is estimated through Q-function while Boltzmann policy or $\epsilon-$ greedy may be used for actor policy estimation.

The working flow of actor critic algorithm is given in Fig. 5 and pseudo code in Algorithm 2.

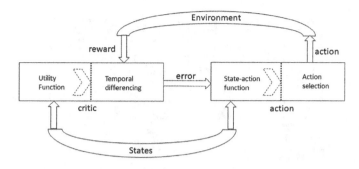

Fig. 5. Actor critic algorithm

4   Results and Discussion

This section presents some results obtained in a simulation environment.

At the end two learning curves for tow algorithms are shown in Figs. 10a and b respectively. We can see that actor critic method takes greater number of iteration for convergence.

For example, Figs. 6 and 7 shows the results of a first experiment for a group of people with different range of audio skills. Some of those have very good hearing ability, some with average audio skills and some have a bad hearing conditions. We evaluate results for these patients (one with a specific audio ability) by considering other variable skills like: VS_s, WM_{hs}, WM_{ls} and AT_s. We also consider the cases when few patients have good working memory conditions while others have poor working memory. In general, the experiment has

---

Algorithm 2. Actor critic algorithm

Emulate
AU_s,VS_s,WM_{hs},WM_{ls}
Emulate AT_s
Initialize
Rewards for all state-action pairs, $R_{s,a}$
Q to zero,
γ, the learning rate $= 0.9$
Calculate
P_{mu}, P_{mi}
   Initialize s
1. Select action a_t in the present state s_t.
2. Get the next state s_{t+1}
3. Get the reward.
4. Update state s_t utility function (critic).
     $U(s_t) \leftarrow U(s_t) + \alpha \left[r_{t+1} + \gamma U(s_{t+1}) - U(s_t) \right]$
5. Update the probability of the action using error (actor).
     $\delta = r_{t+1} + \gamma U(s_{t+1}) - U(s_t)$
until terminal state

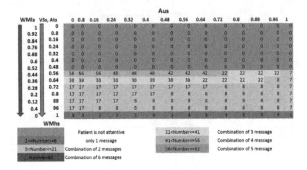

Fig. 6. Results for different skill levels of VS_s, WM_{hs}, WM_{ls} and AT_s against AU_s; WM_{hs} increases while WM_{ls} decreases

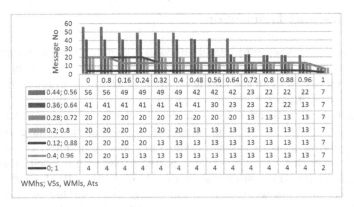

Fig. 7. Results for different skill levels of VS_s, WM_{hs}, WM_{ls} and AT_s against AU_s; WM_{ls} increases while WM_{hs} decreases

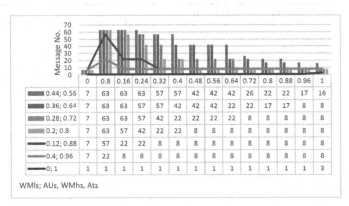

Fig. 8. Results for different skill levels of AU_s, WM_{hs}, WM_{ls} and AT_s against VS_s; WM_{hs} increases while WM_{ls} decreases

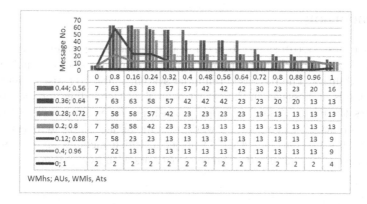

	0	0.8	0.16	0.24	0.32	0.4	0.48	0.56	0.64	0.72	0.8	0.88	0.96	1
0.44; 0.56	7	63	63	63	57	57	42	42	42	30	23	23	20	16
0.36; 0.64	7	63	63	58	57	42	42	42	23	23	20	20	13	13
0.28; 0.72	7	58	58	57	42	23	23	23	23	13	13	13	13	13
0.2; 0.8	7	58	58	42	23	23	13	13	13	13	13	13	13	13
0.12; 0.88	7	58	23	23	13	13	13	13	13	13	13	13	13	9
0.4; 0.96	7	22	13	13	13	13	13	13	13	13	13	13	13	9
0; 1	2	2	2	2	2	2	2	2	2	2	2	2	2	4

WMhs; AUs, WMls, Ats

Fig. 9. Results for different skill levels of AU_s, WM_{hs}, WM_{ls} and AT_s against VS_s; WM_{ls} Increases while WM_{hs} decreases

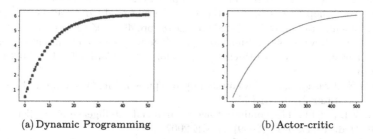

(a) Dynamic Programming   (b) Actor-critic

Fig. 10. Learning curves

demonstrated that the choice of the kind of message depends not only on one singular skill of the patient, but the agent choose a suitable message by considering all the physical and mental abilities of a particular patient.

In a second case study, we consider a group of patients with different levels of visual perceptions such that poor, below average, average, above average and good skills. For each patient belong to such a second case study, we examine other skills level i.e audio and working memory as shown in Figs. 8 and 9.

From the results, we can firstly demonstrate that the agent only start sending messages when the patient attention is at a good level. Secondly, the agent has not selected full or partial scientific messages for patients who have weak working memory (so that it adapts its behavior to patient's conditions). Only a single message has been chosen when either patient has very good hearing ability or visual perception. For example in Fig. 6, the message number one, which is an audio scientific message, is chosen when patient audio and working memory are in very good state. Similarly, in Fig. 7, message number two, which is a simple audio message, is the choice of agent. The reason to choose different types of audio message i.e. scientific and audio for a patient with good hearing ability is that in the first case (Fig. 6), patient's working memory high skill to understand a complex message is good while not in the second case (Fig. 6).

5 Conclusion

We have proposed a tutoring system using actor critic and dynamic programming algorithms to provide clinical support to patients having audio or visual or some mental disabilities. The RL based reminder system is able to assist patients with different kinds of messages in their treatment plan. Depending upon the patient disabilities, the RL agent sends an appropriate type of message according to schedule time of treatment. In our future work, we will validate the system against real patients within the national AMICO projects, which includes an experimental work package to be conducted at home of patients with hypertension.

References

1. Paragliola, G., Coronato, A.: A reinforcement-learning-based approach for the planning of safety strategies in AAL applications. In: Intelligent Environments 2018 - Workshop Proceedings of the 14th International Conference on Intelligent Environments, Rome, Italy, 25–28 June 2018, pp. 498–505 (2018)
2. Ross, C.K., Steward, C.A., Sinacore, J.M.: The importance of patient preferences in the measurement of health care satisfaction. Med. Care, **31**, 1138–1149 (1993). JSTOR
3. Rao, G.N., Prasad, L.V.: How can we improve patient care? Community Eye Health **15**(41), 1–3 (2002). NCBI-PMC
4. Patel, V.L., et al.: The coming of age of artificial intelligence in medicine. Artif. Intell. Med. **46**(1), 5–17 (2009). AIME 2007
5. Ling, Y., et al.: Diagnostic inferencing via improving clinical concept extraction with deep reinforcement learning: a preliminary study. In: Proceedings of the 2nd Machine Learning for Healthcare Conference, pp. 271–285 (2017)
6. Ling, Y., et al.: Learning to diagnose: assimilating clinical narratives using deep reinforcement learning. In: IJCNLP (2017)
7. Schleidgen, S., Klingler, C., Bertram, T., Rogowski, W.H., Marckmann, G.: What is personalized medicine: sharpening a vague term based on a systematic literature review. BMC Med. Ethics **14**, 55 (2013)
8. Petersen, B.K.: Precision medicine as a control problem: using simulation and deep reinforcement learning to discover adaptive, personalized multi-cytokine therapy for sepsis, CoRR, abs/1802.10440 (2018)
9. Sahba, F., Tizhoosh, H.R., Salama, M.M.A.: A reinforcement learning framework for medical image segmentation. In: The 2006 IEEE International Joint Conference on Neural Network Proceedings (2006)
10. Maicas, G., Carneiro, G., Bradley, A.P., Nascimento, J.C., Reid, I.: Deep reinforcement learning for active breast lesion detection from DCE-MRI. In: Descoteaux, M., Maier-Hein, L., Franz, A., Jannin, P., Collins, D.L., Duchesne, S. (eds.) MICCAI 2017. LNCS, vol. 10435, pp. 665–673. Springer, Cham (2017). https://doi.org/10.1007/978-3-319-66179-7_76
11. Kearns, M.J., Litman, D.J., Singh, S.P., Walker, M.A.: Optimizing Dialogue Management with Reinforcement Learning: Experiments with the NJFun System, CoRR, abs/1106.0676 (2011)
12. Odom, P., Natarajan, S.: Active advice seeking for inverse reinforcement learning. In: Proceedings of the 2016 International Conference on Autonomous Agents & Multiagent Systems, AAMAS 2016, pp. 512–520 (2016)

13. Paragliola, G., Naeem, M.: Risk management for nuclear medical department using reinforcement learning. J. Reliab. Intell. Environ. **5**(2), 105–113 (2019)
14. Coronato, A., Paragliola, G., Naeem, M., De Pietro, G.: Reinforcement learning-based approach for the risk management of e-health environments: a case study. In: 14th International Conference on Signal Image Technology & Internet Based Systems, Las Plamas Spain, 26–29 November 2019
15. Prasad, N., Cheng, L.-F., Chivers, C., Draugelis, M., Engelhardt, B.E.: A reinforcement learning approach to weaning of mechanical ventilation in intensive care units, CoRR, abs/1704.06300 (2017)
16. Pilarski, P.M., Dawson, M.R., Degris, T., Fahimi, F., Carey, J.P., Sutton, R.S.: Online human training of a myoelectric prosthesis controller via actor-critic reinforcement learning. In: 2011 IEEE International Conference on Rehabilitation Robotics, pp. 1–7 (2011)
17. Reinkensmeyer, D.J., Guigon, E., Maier, M.A.: A computational model of use-dependent motor recovery following a stroke: optimizing corticospinal activations via reinforcement learning can explain residual capacity and other strength recovery dynamics. Neural Netw. Off. J. Int. Neural Netw. Soc. **29**, 60–69 (2012)
18. Peters, J., Schaal, S.: Reinforcement learning of motor skills with policy gradients. Neural Netw. **21**(4), 682–697 (2008)
19. Russell, S., Norvig, P.: Artificial Intelligence: A Modern Approach. Prentice Hall Press, Upper Saddle River (2009)
20. Sutton, R.S., Barto, A.G.: Reinforcement Learning: An Introduction. MIT Press, Cambridge (1998)
21. Lavori, P.W., Dawson, R.: Dynamic treatment regimes: practical design considerations. Clin. Trials **1**(1), 9–20 (2004)
22. Chakraborty, B., Moodie, E.E.: Statistical Methods for Dynamic Treatment Regimes. Springer, New York (2013). https://doi.org/10.1007/978-1-4614-7428-9
23. Arjas, E., Saarela, O.: Optimal dynamic regimes: presenting a case for predictive inference. Int. J. Biostat. **6**(2) (2010)
24. Robins, J.M.: Optimal structural nested models for optimal sequential decisions. In: Lin, D.Y., Heagerty, P.J. (eds.) Proceedings of the Second Seattle Symposium in Biostatistics, vol. 179, pp. 189–326. Springer, New York (2004). https://doi.org/10.1007/978-1-4419-9076-1_11
25. Thall, P.F., Wathen, J.K.: Covariate-adjusted adaptive randomization in a sarcoma trial with multi-stage treatments. Stat. Med. **24**, 1947–1964 (2005)
26. Murphy, S.A., Oslin, D.W., Rush, A.J., Zhu, J.: Methodological challenges in constructing effective treatment sequences for chronic psychiatric disorders. Neuropsychopharmacology **32**, 257–262 (2006)
27. Polydoros, A.S., Nalpantidis, L.: Survey of model-based reinforcement learning: applications on robotics. J. Intell. Robot. Syst. **86**(2), 153–173 (2017)
28. Konda, V.R., Tsitsiklis, J.N.: Actor-critic algorithms. In: Advances in Neural Information Processing (2000)
29. Patacchiola, M.: A Developmental Model of Trust in Humanoid Robot, University of Plymouth (2018)
30. Mynatt, E.D., Essa, I., Rogers, W.: Increasing the opportunities for aging in place. In: Proceedings on the 2000 Conference on Universal Usability, CUU 2000 (2000)
31. Kautz, H., Arnstein, L., Borriello, G., Etzioni, O., Fox, D.: An overview of the assisted cognition project. In: Proceedings on the: Conference on Universal Usability, Caregiver: The Role of Intelligent Technology in Elder Care, Edmonton (2000)

32. Pineau, J., Montemerlo, M., Pollack, M., Roy, N., Thrun, S.: Towards robotic assistants in nursing homes: challenges and results. Robot. Auton. Syst. **42**, 271–281 (2003)
33. Mozer, M.C.: Lessons from an adaptive home. Smart Environ. **12**, 271–294 (2005)
34. Hoey, J., Poupart, P., von Bertoldi, A., Craig, T., Boutilier, C., Mihailidis, A.: Automated handwashing assistance for persons with dementia using video and a partially observable Markov decision process. Comput. Vis. Image Underst. **144**(5), 503–519 (2010)
35. Mihailidis, A., Fernie, G.R., Barbenel, J.C.: The use of artificial intelligence in the design of an intelligent cognitive orthosis for people with dementia. Assist. Technol. **13**(1), 23–29 (2001)
36. Suresh, H., Hunt, N., Johnson, A.E.W., Celi, L.A., Szolovits, P., Ghassemi, M.: Clinical Intervention Prediction and Understanding using Deep Networks, CoRR (2017)
37. Wren, C.R., Azarbayejani, A., Darrell, T., Pentland, A.: Pfinder: real-time tracking of the human body. IEEE Trans. Pattern Anal. Mach. Intell. **19**, 780–785 (1997)
38. Oliver, N., Garg, A., Horvitz, E.: Layered representations for learning and inferring office activity from multiple sensory channels. Comput. Vis. Image Underst. **96**, 163–180 (2004)
39. Llorca, D.F., Vilarino, F., Zhou, J., Lacey, G.: A multi-class SVM classifier for automatic hand washing quality assessment. In: Proceedings of the British Machine Vision Conference (2007)
40. Llorca, D.F., Parra, I., Sotelo, M.Á., Lacey, G.: A vision-based system for automatic hand washing quality assessment. Mach. Vis. Appl. **22**(2), 219–234 (2011)
41. Russell, S.J., Norvig, P., Canny, J.F., Malik, J.M., Edwards, D.D.: Artificial Intelligence: A Modern Approach. Upper Saddle River, Prentice Hall (2003)
42. Sutton, R.S., Barto, A.G., Reinforcement Learning: An Introduction, 2nd edn., in progress, p. 2. The MIT Press Cambridge (2014, 2015)
43. Bakhouya, M., Campbell, R., Coronato, A., de Pietro, G., Ranganathan, A.: Introduction to special section on formal methods in pervasive computing. ACM Trans. Auton. Adapt. Syst. (TAAS) **7**(1), 6 (2012)
44. Cinque, M., Coronato, A., Testa, A.: Dependable services for mobile health monitoring systems. Int. J. Ambient. Comput. Intell. (IJACI) **4**(1), 1–15 (2012)
45. Coronato, A., De Pietro, G., Sannino, G.: Middleware services for pervasive monitoring elderly and ill people in smart environments. In: 2010 Seventh International Conference on Information Technology: New Generations (2010)
46. Cinque, M., Coronato, A., Testa, A.: A failure modes and effects analysis of mobile health monitoring systems. In: Elleithy, K., Sobh, T. (eds.) Innovations and Advances in Computer, Information, Systems Sciences, and Engineering, vol. 152, pp. 569–582. Springer, New York (2012). https://doi.org/10.1007/978-1-4614-3535-8_48
47. Coronato, A., De Pietro, G., Gallo, L.: An agent based platform for task distribution in virtual environments. J. Syst. Arch. **54**(9), 877–882 (2008)
48. Coronato, A., De Florio, V., Bakhouya, M., Di Marzo Serugendo, G.: Formal modeling of socio-technical collective adaptive systems. In: 2012 IEEE Sixth International Conference on Self-Adaptive and Self-Organizing Systems Workshops, pp. 187–192 (2012)

Saliency Guided Data Association Measure for Multiple-Object Tracking

Syeda Fouzia[1(✉)], Mark Bell[2], and Reinhard Klette[1]

[1] School of Engineering, Computer and Mathematical Sciences,
Department of Electrical and Electronic Engineering, Auckland University
of Technology, Auckland, New Zealand
syeda.fouzia@aut.ac.nz
[2] Crown Lift Trucks Ltd., Auckland, New Zealand

Abstract. The association of correct object locations to its respective track over time is vital for robust tracking results when employing a detection-based tracking approach. It is important for handling object track identity switches which is one of the limiting issues when designing multiple-object trackers. This paper expresses an object model by its saliency-colour histogram. Dissimilarity between a reference track model and input candidate detection (obtained by an object detector) is quantified by a measure derived from the Bhattacharyya coefficient. The Bhattacharyya distance measure is used for validating the confidence in tracks based on an adaptively obtained threshold value. This approach results in improved tracker results under a track-identity loss scenario, especially under short-term partial or full occlusions, clutter or scale variations. The suggested method for track assignment, combined with a state-of-art real-time object detector YOLO (i.e. "You only look once") led to improved online results by reducing the number of miss-assignments within tracks.

1 Introduction

Detection-based tracking is a widely used method for tracking multiple objects especially driven by recent progress in object-detection deep learning frameworks. This method involves the application of an object detection algorithm individually in every frame and associates the detections across multiple frames to form trajectories. Certainly, the robustness of resulting tracks depends heavily on the detection quality of the employed detector and also the *data association* algorithm used for associating the detected outputs to the corresponding target tracks.

Multiple methods have been used in literature for the computation of cost affinity, for the task of assigning candidate detections outputs to corresponding tracks in online tracking applications. Traditionally, a cost assignment matrix is generated by using various distance measures based on cues such as motion, appearance, colour, *saliency*, texture, or a combination of them. The popular

© Springer Nature Switzerland AG 2019
C. Esposito et al. (Eds.): I-SPAN 2019, CCIS 1080, pp. 29–42, 2019.
https://doi.org/10.1007/978-3-030-30143-9_3

Hungarian method has been used quite often for solving such an assignment in a *multiple-object tracking* (MOT) paradigm [23].

In detection-based tracking frameworks, rather than employing features beyond the detection component, object bounding box geometry (i.e. its position and size) is often being used for motion estimation and data association.

The *simple online and real-time tracker* (SORT) is an example of such an approach. This is a Kalman-filter-based tracking algorithm [29] with frame-to-frame data association being done based on the *intersection over union* (IOU) measure. This measure expresses the bounding-box overlap-ratio, and gives most effective tracking outputs at higher frame rates. SORT uses the Hungarian algorithm for solving the cost assignment problem. Its recent version is *SORT with a deep association metric* (DeepSort); see [15].

In DeepSort, for data association both motion and appearance cues are combined to form a cost affinity matrix. It has an improved *multiple-object tracking accuracy* (MOTA) compared to its predecessor. It mainly improves the problem of identity switches in tracks. This is being achieved by adding a deep *convolutional neural network* (CNN) that has been trained offline to classify pedestrians on a large scale person re-identification dataset. The *cosine distance* between detected pedestrians and their tracks in appearance space is being used to re-identify them. This deep distance metric, in combination with the Mahalanobis distance, is used to compute detection-to-track affinity for assigning multiple detections to their corresponding tracks [15].

Also, the complex *joint probability data association based filter* (JPDAF) tracker has been revisited, in a tracking-by-detection paradigm. It is based on weighing object measurements by their association likelihoods for generating state hypotheses [11]. In a multiple hypothesis tracking approach (MHT) [17], every possible state hypothesis is tracked. For both these approaches, their computational complexity grows exponentially with an increase in the number of objects to be tracked which makes them impractical for online real-time tracking applications.

This paper proposes that an *appearance-saliency-map guided data association measure* could be an advantage to verify the track identity especially in cases of occluding tracks or multiple bounding boxes on the same target.

A visual saliency map of the *region of interest* (ROI) could be an important feature in validating the track assignment problem. A saliency distribution dissimilarity measure between a detected ROI and predicted candidate track locations is described by the Bhattacharyya coefficient. It could be a useful association metric if used in conjunction with the Mahalanobis distance. Though it is used earlier in the mean shifting track framework [9], here is it re-purposed for validating confidant tracks. It is an optimal assumption due to its link to Bayesian errors; although there are other distance measures like the Kullback distance measure (but this violates one of the distance axioms) or the histogram intersection measure (which is scale variant).

In order to improve the robustness of the tracker, we combine both colour and saliency features here, weighting their respective contribution automatically to the cost likelihood function, making this a more informed metric for data associations. Colour histogram feature incorporation makes the tracker robust to the scenes where objects seem to be less salient than background and saliency cues seem to be less informed measures for association. The resulting strategy will improve the *mostly tracked trajectories* (MOT) metric and decreases *identity switches* between tracks.

Fig. 1. *Left.* Saliency detection example. *Right.* Identity switch scenario for short term occlusion (Color figure online)

See Fig. 1. The left figure outlines a saliency detection example and the right depicts a scenario for a short term occlusion. It can be seen that two tracks are partially occluded by each other for a short time. We argue that the IOU distance measure [14], between detections and predicted bounding boxes from the existing track targets, is a non-optimum measure here. Track identity is lost only because the IOU distance measure validates the red track but is actually the yellow track interfering with the target, causing the track miss-assignment here (in the third frame, detection belonging to the yellow track being assigned to the red track).

It is proposed that the corresponding detection will not be assigned to the red track if the *Bhattacharyya distance* validation fails (dissimilarity between colour-saliency distribution between predicted red track location and corresponding detection) outlining that it is just *occluding another track* and not the original tracked object. We suggest that the Mahalanobis distance will solve the Kalman motion uncertainty problem; a saliency distribution similarity measure of candidate detection and tracking, quantified by the *Bhattacharyya distance measure* bdist, will solve the short-term occlusion problems. It will make the tracker more robust to occlusions.

The paper is structured as follows. Section 2 outlines related work on saliency-based tracking methods. Section 3 describes the algorithm, YOLO model training and implementation, also providing dataset details. Section 4 explains the method for associating the detection obtained by a trained YOLO detector, with corresponding target tracks. Section 5 outlines the quantitative evaluation for the tracking approach proposed. Section 6 concludes the discussion.

2   Related Work

Track association is a vital challenge in designing multiple-object tracking algorithms. The robustness of such assignments is very important for seamless tracking results. Such an association is mainly classified into two broad categories. Local methods employ a pair of frames for data association; this is fast, but irrelevant factors like camera motion or pose variations likely pose a track miss-assignment problem. Global techniques perform the same association using a batch of frames. Moreover, a few global association techniques consider this association as a constrained network flow problem and a k-shortest path algorithm is used for associating the tracks [1].

Tracking partially occluded, closely located targets suffers from shortcomings incurred by object detectors, especially when following the tracking-by-detection paradigm. Bochinski et al. [2] employed the IOU measure and predefined threshold values for the association of targets in frames; authors depicted acceptable tracking performance at 100 fps for tracking. Chen et al. [17] proposed a multiple hypothesis tracking method by exploiting detection correlation across video frames. This method claims to handle close objects. In a few other techniques, dense detections are also being used without non-maximum suppression for tracking, mainly to handle scenarios where targets are in close proximity [5].

Tracking methods employing deep learning frameworks are used to model the target of interest appearance using networks pre-trained for other tasks (transfer learning) and to associate these target objects over multiple frames. A network trained for learning data association in the context of MOT is employed in [4]. A Siamese network is modified to learn deep features for multiple-object tracking with object association [3]. A multipurpose CNN for both detection and tracking under common region-based fully convolution neural network (R-FCN) is proposed [7]. A model for person tracking using head-joints is employed based on human pose estimation; it failed to deliver desired results under occlusions [6]. Associations of objects in consecutive pairs of frames is jointly modelled and associations are learnt in an end-to-end manner. Object affinities are estimated in frame-pairs using a deep affinity network [8]; it is suggested to handle occluded scenes.

Despite the rich literature regarding deep learning-based target tracking, results still suffer from the lack of robust track association strategies especially for close proximity and partially occluded objects. A detailed study on the significance of saliency-based trackers depicts the usefulness for using saliency feature advantages over various other cues such as motion, texture, gradient or colour. An object is represented and tracked based on human attentive mechanism using visual saliency maps. Such methods have been seen to work better for occluded and cluttered scenes.

A combination for features like colour-texture, colour-saliency, or colour-orientation is studied under a mean-shift tracking framework [13]. Tracking the targets of interest employed a simple saliency visual descriptor which counts the number of similar pixels lying in the local neighbourhood named *local similarity number* (LSN). It was used to model the amount of saliency in corresponding target patches. It is being used in a mean-shift tracking framework with a saliency-colour histogram model [16]. Spatio-temporal discriminative saliency maps were used to track non-rigid objects; this outputs accurate regions occupied by the targets as tracking results. A *tailored fully convolutional neural network* (TFCN) is developed to model the local saliency of regions of interest. Latter local saliency maps are generated with the help of a multi-scale multi-region mechanism that takes into account the visual perceptions with varying spatial layouts and scales. Finally, these local saliency maps are fused with a weighted entropy method, resulting in a final discriminative saliency map [10].

Improvement in discrete correlation filters-based trackers with saliency-based filter responses helped to handle tracking in challenging scenes. Filter weights are selected adaptively based on temporal consistency of visual saliency maps [12]. Particle filters suffer from tracking artefacts in occlusions, clutter and illumination variations. Saliency information incorporated in the framework aided to improve tracking results in complex scenes. A bottom-up saliency based tracker that tracked any salient target in the scene used colour features and sparse optical flow [19].

Static and motion features based on saliency are first extracted from the frames of videos locally, regionally or globally. Then they are combined in a conditional random-field fashion. The salient region in the frame is tracked using a particle filter. Tracking is robust w.r.t. changes of illumination and shape and can track any object category as long as it is salient in the scene [21]. A smooth pursuit tracking algorithm is proposed that uses three kinds of saliency maps. These were appearance, location and motion saliency maps. Appearance saliency maps use deep CNN-based features along with gnostic fields. A location map predicts where the object location will be in the next frame and motion saliency maps show which objects are moving in the scene. All three maps are fused together in a smooth pursuit fashion. The resulting map is used to generate bounding boxes for the tracked targets [22].

This work is inspired by various recent multiple-target tracking algorithms which have employed visual saliency maps for robust tracking outputs.

3   Tracking Framework

An *object* is being modelled based on its appearance and motion features. The displacement of a specific object in the next frame is modelled by a linear velocity assumption using a Kalman filtering framework. The camera is assumed to be static and uncalibrated.

The tracking problem is defined in 8-dimensional state space $(u, v, \gamma, h, \dot{x}, \dot{y}, \dot{\gamma}, \dot{h})$ which combines bounding box centre coordinates (u, v), their aspect ratio γ, height h and velocities in image space. An object state at any time instance t is defined directly by its bounding box coordinates (u, v, γ, h).

3.1 YOLOv3 Object Detector

Many recent methods for object detection are employing deep learning based techniques such as *Faster-RCNN* [27], SSD [28] or YOLO [18]. Few make use of sliding-window approaches or region-proposal methods, to generate region hypotheses, and then to generate objectness scores. Thus, deep learning-based methods proved to be more robust for detection for varying scales of objects [18]. The YOLO architecture for detection has been released in two versions: v2 and v3.

The reason for employing a deep learning framework like YOLO is getting *reliable*, i.e. accurate and real-time detection quality for tracking. YOLO is an end-to-end single convolutional neural network (CNN) architecture which detects the object's ROIs based on their bounding box predictions and class probabilities. It divides the input image into an $S \times S$ grid. Moreover, if the centre of an object is located within that grid, then the grid will detect the object of interest. Each grid predicts the bounding boxes and a confidence score, where the confidence score quantifies how confident the model is that the bounding box certainly contains a specific class of objects.

Algorithm 1: Saliency-guided data association for computing track assignment

Input   : A new frame at time t with detections set from YOLO detector D^t and track set T^{t-1}

Output: The new track set T^t

1 For each detection candidate from set D^t;

2 **if** *Mahalanobis-distance* $< \tau_m$ **then**

3   **if** *Bhattacharyya-distance* $< \tau_{bdist}$ **then**

4   Assign the corresponding detection to a track;

5   Obtain assigned track set $T^{t-1}_{assigned}$ matched detection set $D^t_{matched}$, Unassigned track set $T^{t-1}_{unassigned}$ and unmatched detection set $D^t_{unmatched}$;

6   Predict first track subset by Kalman Filtering based on successful association in previous step: $Trackset^t_1$;

7   Predict second track subset from unassigned track set or remove the ones who crossed the max track age threshold $\tau_{max-age}$ i.e. output is $Trackset^t_2$;

8   Create third track subset from unmatched detection set $D^t_{unmatched}$ i.e. $Trackset^t_3$;

9   Combine the three track subsets to form new candidate track set $T^t_{candidate}$;

10     $T^t_{candidate}$ formed new input for the algorithm at time t+1 with detections set D^{t+1} For each detection candidate from set D^{t+1}, find Mahalanobis-distance b/w each detection and corresponding track mean and Bhattacharyya-distance quantifying degree of similarity in their saliency distributions, go to Step 3 if condition is met.

11   **end**

12 **end**

The intersection over union (IOU) between a predicted box and ground truth is used to calculate confidence for a detection. It outputs 1 for a perfect match case, and the opposite if a predicted box is not present in the grid.

YOLO is a sliding window-based method; but, unlike a model based ACF detector, it examines the entire image during training. It learns the context of the object with respect to its surroundings as well.

YOLO version 3 (YOLOv3) is an improved version of its earlier version YOLOv2, now using multi scale training, a better classifier and image patches of 320×320; it runs in 22 ms at 28.2 mean average precision (mAP). The trade-off between speed and accuracy of the network is checked during training by changing the size of the network.

3.2 Datasets

The *YOLOv3* object detector is trained for two categories which are significant for warehouses, i.e. *pedestrians* and *forklift trucks*. The detection outputs are employed to track pedestrians and trucks in occluded and cluttered warehouse environments (tracking by detection approach).

Our self-collected warehouse image dataset, including 3,077 training images with manually labelled ground truth bounding boxes for forklift trucks and pedestrians, defining 8,242 ROIs was annotated. Each image contains 1–7 labelled instances of a forklift truck or pedestrian. Subsets of image data from the Caltech pedestrian and INRIA pedestrian datasets are also added to get enough training samples for pedestrians.

The pedestrians, present in these subsets, with different degrees of occlusion, wearing different costumes, have many kinds of scales and changing postures. GeForce GTX 1080 Titanium GPU with compute capability 6.1 and 12 GB memory is used for model training. Table 1 summarises the number of training images and ROIs used for every image subset.

Table 1. Datasets

Dataset	Caltech pedestrian subset [24]	INRIA person subset [25]	Our dataset
Training images	10,000	614	3,077
ROIs	22,000	1,237	8,242

3.3 YOLO Training and Evaluation

For training, CNN weights that are pre-trained on the ImageNet dataset are used, i.e. weights from the *DarkNet53 model*. DarkNet model inputs a text file for each image and every ground truth object in the image in the format $x, y, width, height$ where these parameters are relative to the image's width and height. A text file with names and paths of the images to be trained was supplied to DarkNet to load the images to be trained on. A test text file for testing and validation text file for validation images is also created.

After training the pretrained *DarkNet53 model* for about $20k$ iterations ($13,500$ images), a validation accuracy of 91.2 and a testing accuracy of 90% is obtained. This was without any data augmentations or other transformations. Random flag parameters for multi-scale training were enabled in script, resulting in robustness for detecting objects in different image resolutions. The input image size by default was set to a resolution of (416×416), but was altered every 10 batches. Resulting test accuracy was good enough for this work. The details of the training are not included as the focus for this paper is on tracking methodology.

4   Data Association

The Mahalanobis distance, which is the squared distance between predicted object states (by a Kalman filter) and, can be written as follows:

$$\mathbf{d}^1 (i, j) = (d_j - y_i)^T \mathbf{S}_i^{-1} (d_j - y_i) \tag{1}$$

where (y_i, S_i) denotes the projection of the i-th track distribution into measurement space and d_j denotes the j-th bounding box detection. It provides information about possible object locations based on motion that helps in short term prediction of track a state. It eliminated unlikely assignments by thresholding at 95% confidence interval, computed from the inverse χ^2 distribution $\tilde{\chi}^2$ [15].

We denote by $\mathbf{p}^*$ the reference track saliency-colour model; $\mathbf{p}(x_t)$ is the candidate detection model. Then, the distance between the two is described by the Bhattacharyya distance (bdist) [19]:

$$\mathbf{d}^2 (i, j) = \text{bdist} \left[\mathbf{p}^*, \mathbf{p}(x_t) \right] = \left[1 - \sum_{u=1}^{M} \sqrt{\mathbf{p}_u^* (x_o) \, \mathbf{p}_u (x_t)} \right]^{\frac{1}{2}} \tag{2}$$

For this work, the degree of saliency of a region with respect to its neighbourhood is described by the Euclidean distance between the pixel vector and the average vector of the input detection in the *Lab* colour space [20]. It is described by:

$$S(x, y) = \left\| I_\mu^* - I_\sigma^* (x, y) \right\| \tag{3}$$

where I_μ^* is the mean image feature and I_σ^* is the Gaussian blurred image, using a 5×5 separable binomial kernel.

Also, the colour or saliency distribution of a region of interest, described by detection, centred at location x, is given by:

$$\mathbf{p}_u (x) = C \sum_{i=1}^{N_p} k \left(\left\| \frac{x_i - x}{h} \right\|^2 \right) \delta \left[b(x_i) - u \right] \tag{4}$$

where C is a normaliser, δ is the Kronecker function, k is a kernel with bandwidth h, N_p is the number of pixels in the ROI and $b(x_i)$ is a function that assigns one of the m bins to a given colour or saliency at location x_i. The kernel k is used to consider spatial information for adaptively lowering the values for far pixels [19]

The influence of each distance measure on the combined association cost can be controlled through a hyperparameter Λ. Colour and saliency will be weighted automatically according to its value for deciding the final affinity for corresponding detections. The cost optimisation is being solved optimally through the Hungarian algorithm:

$$\mathbf{c}_{i,j} = \Lambda \mathbf{d}^1 (i,j) + (1 - \Lambda) \mathbf{d}^2 (i,j) \tag{5}$$

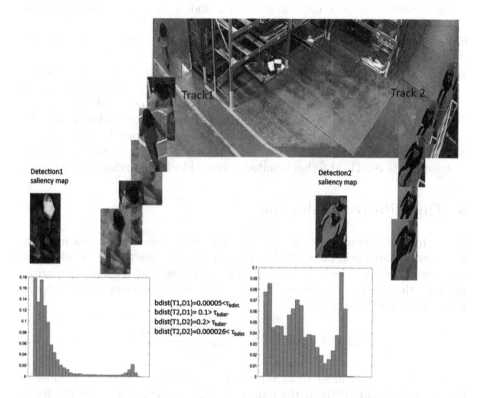

Fig. 2. Saliency guided data association

Refer to Fig. 2 for visualising the concept. It can be seen that for detection 1, bdist between detection 1 and track 1 fulfils the bdist criterion and also lies within the Mahalanobis distance threshold, so it is being assigned to track 1. The distance of detection 1 to track 2 violates the bdist threshold. The same principle applies for the detection 2 assignment here:

1. For the task of assigning detections to current track targets, every target's bounding box geometry is predicted by the Kalman filter.
2. The tracker is initialised by using the geometry of the object bounding box, with the initial velocity set to value zero.

3. Covariance of the velocity component is initialised with a large value to model uncertainty in assumption.

4. When a detection is associated to a target, target state is updated by this detection and Kalman filter is used to solve the velocity components optimally. But if the detection is not associated to the target identity, then its state is predicted rather than corrected by the filter using the respective motion model.

5. A threshold is imposed to reject assignments where the detections lies beyond that region of assignment both for *Mahalanobis* and *Bhattacharyya* distance, i.e. should lie within the thresholds τ_m and τ_{bdist} (These thresholds are selected adaptively based on scenario).

6. For creating trackers, we consider any detection that violates both distance criterion, to signify the existence of an untracked object.

7. Tracker has to undergoes a trial period where the target needs to be associated with detections to have enough evidence in order to prevent tracking of false positives. Tracks are terminated if they are not detected for $\tau_{max-age}$ frames. This ensures to prevent an increase in number of trackers caused by predictions over longer durations without corrections from the detector.

8. In all experiments $\tau_{max-age}$ is set to 30 frames contrary to max age of one frame (as in SORT) [14] that resulted in many identity switches among tracks.

5   Quantitative Evaluation

To evaluate tracking performance, two important evaluation measures are employed in this work, i.e. *multiple object tracking accuracy* (MOTA) and *multiple object tracking precision* (MOTP). MOTA includes all configuration errors made by the tracker i.e. false-positives, false negatives, number of ID switches, averaged over all frames:

$$\text{MOTA} = 1 - \frac{\sum_t (FN_t + FP_t + IDSW_t)}{\sum_t GT_t} \qquad (6)$$

where FN_t is the number of false-negatives or misses, FP_t is the number of false-positives, and IDSW is the number of ID switches, where t is the frame index and GT is the number of ground truth objects.

The multiple object tracking precision (MOTP) is the average dissimilarity between all true-positives and their corresponding ground truth targets:

$$\text{MOTP} = \frac{\sum_{t,i} d_{t,i}}{\sum_t c_t} \qquad (7)$$

where c_t denotes the total number of matches in frame t and $d_{t,i}$ is the bounding box overlap of target i with its assigned ground truth object.

We conducted experiments with the proposed improvement in data association metric. We use detections for pedestrians and trucks with confidence threshold of .25 or higher from YOLO for our work. Refer to Fig. 3. Tracking

Fig. 3. *Left.* Occluded forklift tracking *Right.* Multiple occluded pedestrian tracking

Fig. 4. Example of a challenging scene from the TUD-Stadtmitte sequence showing pedestrians with similar looking appearance and different poses [26]

Table 2. Tracking metric results improvement depicted by increase in value of *MOTP, MOTA* and *MT* (mostly tracked trajectories).

Quantitative evaluation		
Metrics	With IOU measure	With saliency guided bhattacharyya distance measure
MOTP	71.1	73.9↑
MOTA	61.3	63.7↑
FAF	0.1	1.3
MT	13.2	20.1↑
ML	15.4	43.1
FP	267	345
FN	401	325
ID SW	25	19
Fragment	27	82

results from our warehouse data is shown for pedestrians and trucks, partially occluded by each other. It can be seen that there is no identity switching due to use of distinct colour-saliency map validation step.

Table 3. Quantitative comparison with [14,15]. Last column lists results for a forklift-pedestrian sequence from warehouse data

Sequence: TUD Crossing				
Metrics	[14]	[15]	Ours	Results
MOTP	63.1	71.9	72.3	73.3↑
MOTA	35.3	53.7	56.2	75.1↑
FAF	2.3	1.3	1.1	1.6
MT	12.5	38.2	41.2↑	55.3↑
ML	25.4	14	21	23.1
FP	762	1062	833	513
FN	401	325	256	1056
ID SW	442	245	331	254
Fragment	186	102	142	317

We also tested it on the TUD-Stadtmitte sequence from the MOT challenge 2015 dataset [26]. It is recorded with a static camera placed at 2 m height showing people walking on the street. It is an outdoor sequence with 179 frames, 10 tracks, 1,156 bounding boxes, 640 × 480 resolution and 25 fps. Pedestrians are shown partially occluded with low illumination in background and object contrast is minimal. Figure 4 is a shot from the sequence.

Check Table 2 for quantitative results improvement by incorporation of the proposed saliency guided data association method.

Table 3 outlines the comparison with other state of art multiple objects trackers [14,15]. Our implementation runs at around 20 frames/second. Hence, given a modern GPU, the system will operate in real time. Since for the forklift tracking category, public ground-truth detections and tracks is not available, we formulated ground-truth dataset for evaluation.

6   Conclusions

We aimed at a deep exploration into an algorithm for robust multi-object tracking, for further limiting problems known from testing previous trackers. Besides track identity switches, the other tracking challenge that needs to be addressed is track re-identification. Incorporating the appearance information for tracks and finding the track deviations in appearance space should contribute to solve these tracking issues. We anticipate various trade-offs when solving such issues. An offline CNN-trained model for pedestrian re-identification has already shown improved results under track-identity switch scenarios [15]. Used appearance-space distance measures can be extended to other object categories such as trucks in warehouses or cars on roads.

References

1. Berclaz, J., Fleuret, F., Turetken, E., Fua, P.: Multiple object tracking using k-shortest paths optimization. IEEE Trans. Pattern Anal. Mach. Intell. **33**(9), 1806–1819 (2011)
2. Bochinski, E., Eiselein, V., Sikora, T.: High-speed tracking-by-detection without using image information. In: Proceedings of IEEE International Conference on Advanced Video Signal Based Surveillance, pp. 1–6 (2017)
3. Bae, S.H., Yoon, K.J.: Confidence-based data association and discriminative deep appearance learning for robust online multi-object tracking. IEEE Trans. Pattern Anal. Mach. Intell. **40**(3), 595–610 (2017)
4. Schulter, S., Vernaza, P., Choi, W., Chandraker, M.: Deep network flow for multi-object tracking. In: Proceedings of IEEE Conference on Computer Vision Pattern Recognition, pp. 6951–6960 (2017)
5. Tang, S., Andres, B., Andriluka, M., Schiele, B.: Subgraph decomposition for multi-target tracking. In: Proceedings of IEEE Conference on Computer Vision Pattern Recognition, pp. 5033–5041 (2015)
6. Insafutdinov, E., et al.: Arttrack: articulated multi-person tracking in the wild. In: Proceedings of IEEE Conference Computer Vision Pattern Recognition, pp. 6457–6465 (2017)
7. Hershey, S., et al.: CNN architectures for large-scale audio classification. In: Proceedings of IEEE International Conference on Acoustics Speech Signal Processing, pp. 131–135 (2017)
8. Sun, S., Akhtar, N., Song, H., Mian, A., Shah, M.: Deep affinity network for multiple object tracking. arXiv preprint arXiv:1810.11780 (2018)
9. Comaniciu, D., Ramesh, V., Meer, P.: Real-time tracking of non-rigid objects using mean shift. In: Proceedings of IEEE Conference on Computer Vision Pattern Recognition, vol. 2, pp. 142–149 (2000)
10. Zhang, P., Wang, D., Lu, H., Wang, H.: Non-rigid object tracking via deep multi-scale spatial-temporal discriminative saliency maps. arXiv preprint arXiv:1802.07957 (2018)
11. Hamid Rezatofighi, S., Milan, A., Zhang, Z., Shi, Q., Dick, A., Reid, I.: Joint probabilistic data association revisited. In: Proceedings of IEEE International Conference on Computer Vision, pp. 3047–3055 (2015)
12. Aytekin, C., Cricri, F., Aksu, E.: Saliency-enhanced robust visual tracking. arxiv.org/pdf/1802.02783.pdf (2018)
13. Alikhani, I., Tavakoli, H.R., Rahtu, E., Laaksonen, J.: On the contribution of saliency in visual tracking. In: Proceedings of VISIGRAPP, vol 4: VISAPP, pp. 17–21 (2016)
14. Bewley, A., Ge, Z., Ott, L., Ramos, F., Upcroft, B.: Simple online and realtime tracking. In: Proceedings of IEEE International Conference on Image Processing, pp. 3464–3468 (2016)
15. Wojke, N., Bewley, A., Paulus, D.: Simple online and realtime tracking with a deep association metric. In: Proceedings of IEEE International Conference on Image Processing, pp. 3645–3649 (2017)
16. Tavakoli, H.R., Moin, M.S., Heikkilä, J.: Local similarity number and its application to object tracking. Int. J. Adv. Robot. Syst. **10**(3), 184 (2013)
17. Kim, C., Li, F., Ciptadi, A., Rehg, J.M.: Multiple hypothesis tracking revisited. In: Proceedings of International Conference on Computer Vision, pp. 4696–4704 (2015)

18. Redmon, J., Farhadi, A.: YOLOv3: An incremental improvement. arXiv preprint arXiv:1804.02767 (2018)
19. Sidibé, D., Fofi, D., Mériaudeau, F.: Using visual saliency for object tracking with particle filters. In: Proceedings of European Signal Processing Conference, pp. 1776–1780 (2010)
20. Achanta, R., Hemami, S., Estrada, F., Süsstrunk, S.: Frequency-tuned salient region detection. In: Proceedings of IEEE International Conference on Computer Vision Pattern Recognition, pp. 1597–1604 (2009)
21. Zhang, G., Yuan, Z., Zheng, N., Sheng, X., Liu, T.: Visual saliency based object tracking. In: Zha, H., Taniguchi, R., Maybank, S. (eds.) ACCV 2009. LNCS, vol. 5995, pp. 193–203. Springer, Heidelberg (2010). https://doi.org/10.1007/978-3-642-12304-7_19
22. Yousefhussien, M.A., Browning, N.A., Kanan, C.: Online tracking using saliency. In: Proceedings of IEEE Winter Conference on Applications Computer Vision (WACV), pp. 1–10 (2016)
23. Kuhn, H.W.: The Hungarian method for the assignment problem. Nav. Res. Logist. Q. **2**(1–2), 83–97 (1955)
24. Caltech pedestrian detection benchmark. www.vision.caltech.edu/Image_Datasets/CaltechPedestrians/
25. INRIA person dataset. http://pascal.inrialpes.fr/data/human/
26. Multi-object tracking benchmark. motchallenge.net
27. Ren, S., He, K., Girshick, R., Sun, J.: Faster R-CNN: towards real-time object detection with region proposal networks. In: Proceedings of Advances Neural Information Processing Systems, pp. 91–99 (2015)
28. Liu, W., et al.: SSD: single shot MultiBox detector. In: Leibe, B., Matas, J., Sebe, N., Welling, M. (eds.) ECCV 2016. LNCS, vol. 9905, pp. 21–37. Springer, Cham (2016). https://doi.org/10.1007/978-3-319-46448-0_2
29. Broida, T.J., Chellappa, R.: Estimation of object motion parameters from noisy images. IEEE Trans. Pattern Anal. Mach. Intell. **1**(1), 90–99 (1986)

A Document Visualization Strategy
Based on Semantic Multimedia Big Data

Antonio M. Rinaldi[1,2(✉)]

[1] Department of Electrical Engineering and Information Technologies,
University of Naples Federico II, Naples, Italy
`antoniomaria.rinaldi@unina.it`
[2] IKNOS-LAB Intelligent and Knowledge Systems,
University of Naples Federico II, LUPT, Naples, Italy

Abstract. The integration of semantic web and big data is a key factor in the definition of efficient model to represent knowledge and implement real world applications. In this paper we present a multimedia knowledge base implemented as a semantic multimedia big data storing semantic and linguistic relations between concepts and their multimedia representations. Moreover, we propose a document visualization strategy based on statistical and semantic analysis of textual and visual contents. The proposed approach has been implemented in a tool, called Semantic Tag Cloud, whose task is to show in a concise way the main topic of a document using both textual features and images. We also propose a case study of our approach and an evaluation from a user perception point of view.

Keywords: Knowledge base · Semantic big data · Ontology ·
WordNet · ImageNet · graphDB · Semantic tag cloud

1 Introduction

In the big data years, the use of approaches to capture, store and analyze data is a crucial factor in the implementation of knowledge based systems and smart applications. In this context, user oriented system use formal knowledge representations based on different symbols to easily interact with humans and, if it is represented using well know formalism like ontologies [26], it can be used by machines. On the other hand, novel technologies as Big Data give useful tools to manage high volume of data together with other dimensions related to changing data velocity and variety [16]. In the last years, a novel research area was arising from the Big Data paradigm and the Semantic Web vision called Semantic Big Data [35]. The union of these approaches give use novel strategies for managing and analyzing the large amount of data and useful tools to transform data in information and knowledge.

Our approach is based on the retrieval of knowledge represented in different multimedia forms [3] linked with semantic and linguistic relationships. The semantic information is extracted from a knowledge base in which concepts are

© Springer Nature Switzerland AG 2019
C. Esposito et al. (Eds.): I-SPAN 2019, CCIS 1080, pp. 43–57, 2019.
https://doi.org/10.1007/978-3-030-30143-9_4

represented in various multimedia forms and it is implemented by means of a big data. Our semantic multimedia big data (SMBD) is used to implement a the implementation of a visual smart interface.

Generally speaking, it is a visual semantic tag cloud where concepts have both a text and visual representations. The textual view uses a set of terms in which their characteristics are used (e.g. size, color and font) to indicate the important relations between terms and documents [44]. On the other hand, the visual representation shows the multimedia form (i.e. images) related to a concept. Tag clouds derive from the collaborative tagging paradigm [27] used in many social networks, forums and users' communities. In [6] the authors argue that if terms for tagging are recognized only in according to their frequency, several issues related to high semantic density because few topics will tend to dominate the entire visualization and less important terms will vanish. Tag clouds synthesize document collections by providing a brief summary of their information content. The purpose of summarization is to reduce the length of a document by creating a summary that preserves the most important points in the original document. In this way a user can preliminary understand the main topic of retrieved documents and decide if it is relevant or not for his/her research purpose [45,46].

In our paper, a novel method based on the combination of a textual and visual analysis of the original document to better understand the document content is presented.

The paper is organized as follows: in Sect. 2 we present an analysis of works related to semantic big data and document visualization; Sect. 3 is focused on the SMBD model and it implementation and the proposed strategy for document visualization is described in Sects. 4 and 5 shows a use case example of our strategy; eventually, Sect. 6 is devoted to the presentation of conclusion and future works.

2   Related Work

The evolution of Big Data research in the last years has followed different lines. In this section, we highlight some novel directions for the integration between Big Data and semantic web technologies. Moreover, some works related to document visualization using tag clouds also are presented.

A first formal definition of Big Data is given in [23]. In this paper the authors define Big Data as an information resource with specific dimensions related to a high *Volume*, *Velocity* and *Variety* of data. This asset requires specific techniques, methodologies and technologies to analyze data and transform it into *Value*. The Big Data dimensions can be extended with another one if we consider the *Veracity* [7]. Several surveys have been proposed in literature tho give a comprehensive classification of big data components both from a theoretic and technological point of view [17,34]. *Volume* and *Velocity* dimensions have been extensive studied during the last years but a methodological attention to *Variety* is arose only lately. In [35] a process called Big Data "Semantification" is presented and it is based on a methodology to manage heterogeneous Big Data using semantic technologies. In this way, a non-semantic Big Data is annotated by means of RDF vocabularies. The need of merging Big Data technologies in legacy systems using semantic-based approaches is very important issue and it emerges in different contexts [25]. In [1] a chain of NLP modules within virtual machines integrated in a distributed architecture for scaling up text analysis is proposed. Great efforts to enable social applications are based on the use of semantic and ontologies approaches to implement social multimedia big data [7,18]. The authors describe an online news management system [52] implemented following a link network model. An extract-transformation-load system to integrate different data sets by means of ad hoc semantic model is presented in [5]. It produces semantic linked data complied with the data model. A framework to query big data sources using Resource Description Framework (RDF) representation is presented in [8]. The authors consider semantic heterogeneity and URI-based entity identification solved by a semantic entity resolution method based on inference mechanism using rules to manage the misunderstanding of data. A formal knowledge structure based on a conceptualization represented by semantic web approach [48], is a basic approach to reduce *Variety* issue and align different heterogeneous repositories [42] in complex scenario as the financial domain. In this context the use of Big Data sanctification give us new tools for classifying information based on specific knowledge structures. The MOUNT system is presented in [43]. It aims at representing and processing a large-scale heterogeneous big data generated from multiple sources using multi-level semantic annotation and query processing.

Focusing on the specific task related to document visualization using tag clouds, our approach uses a keywords extraction technique to construct a summary through tag clouds. The quality of the extracted keywords depends on the algorithms used and various methods have been proposed in the literature [51]. Artificial intelligence techniques in addition to semantics [30] and co-occurrence [37] were extensively used for extracting keywords from a single document. In [4] different information is used based on the VSM and genetic algorithms to compute a grade of similarity between sentences and weights associated to the features. In [29] the authors use linguistic features to represent the relevance of the term, also based on the position in the document. In [53], a tag-oriented approach based on a linear transformation to measure the tag relevance is discussed. Cluster-based algorithms have also been proposed, for example in [28] k-means has been used to semantically group similar tags. Another interesting method based on the co-occurrences of tags with the aim of comparing the structure of the folksonomies network is proposed by [20] in which the authors have analyzed the similarities between the tags and the documents to enrich semantic and hierarchical aspects. In [38] a model for the union of ontologies and social networks with the use of tags mechanisms has been presented. In [21] the authors present a technique to support collaborative semantic understanding of generated tags. Their approach gathers tags in different semantic groups and the relations among tags is expressed through the visual distance between them.

The proposed strategy presents several novelties. Our framework offers a high level of generalization compared with the presented literature where the discussed approaches and frameworks face the issue of the *Variety* dimension in specific domains or without considering multimedia information. Following our approach, we design and implement a formal semantic-based model to fully represent and manage specific and general knowledge domains. Moreover, we consider some standard multimedia descriptors to give a possible solution to the question of heterogeneity. In addition, we propose a different strategy based on the dynamic extraction of networks from our SMBD and use a metric for the generation of tags based on a combination of textual and visual analysis.

3   The Semantic Multimedia Big Data

The SMBD implemented in this paper is based on a model proposed in [49]. A general concept can be represented in various multimedia forms (i.e. signs) such as text, images, gestures, sounds and any way in which information can be communicated as a message. Each type of representation has properties that distinguish them. The model structure consists of a triple $< \mathbf{S}, \mathbf{P}, \mathbf{C} >$ defined as: (i) S: the set of signs; (ii) P: the set of properties used to relate signs with concepts; (iii) C: the set of constraints on the P collection.

We use two types of representations (MM): *word* (i.e. text), and the *visual* (i.e. images). The properties are linguistic relations and the constraints contain validity rules applied to properties with respect to the considered multimedia. Knowledge is conceptual represented by an ontology and by a *Semantic Network* (SN) from a logic point of view. It is a graph structure where nodes are concepts and arcs are linguistic relation between them. The concept is a set of multimedia data representing an abstract idea. The language chosen to describe this model is the DL version of OWL. It consents the declaration of disjointed classes to state, for example, that a word can belong to a syntactic category. It is also possible to declare union classes used to specify domains, ranges and properties to relate concepts and multimedia nodes. The connections in the semantic network are represented as *ObjectProperties* and have constraints that depend on the syntactic category or type of property (semantic or lexical). Some examples are described in the Table 1.

As examples of constraints, the hyperonomy property can only be used between nouns and nouns or between verbs and verbs. Each multimedia is linked to the represented concept by the ObjectProperty *hasConcept* and vice versa with *hasMM*. They are the only properties that can be used to link concepts with multimedia. The other properties are used to link multimedia to multimedia or concept to concepts. The attributes of Concept and Multimedia classes are also described. The concept has as attribute: *Name* which represents the name of the concept and the field *Glossary* which contains a short description of it. The common attributes of the MM subclasses are *Name* and *ID*. Each subclass has its own set of features depending on the nature of the media. In the visual case we use the PHOG [9] global feature descriptor which has good

Table 1. Properties

Property	Domain	Range
hasMM	Concept	MM
hasConcept	MM	Concept
hypernym	Nouns and Verbs	Nouns and Verbs
holonym	Noun	Noun
Entailment	Verb	Verb
Similar	Adjective	Adjective

Table 2. Properties constraints

Constraint	Class	Property	Constraint range
AllValuesFrom	Noun	Hypernym	Noun
AllValuesFrom	Adjective	attribute	Noun
AllValuesFrom	Verb	also see	Verb
AllValuesFrom	Noun	Hyponym	Noun

performance with respect to other descriptors [41]. This descriptor consists of a histogram of orientation gradients over each image subregion at each resolution level. The distance between two PHOG image descriptors reflects the property of images to contain similar shapes in corresponded spatial layout. The use of union classes simplify the domain rules but at the same time the model does not exhibit perfect behavior. For example, the property of hyperonymy allows the relationship between nouns and verbs. In this context, we have to define different constraints to represent how the linguistic properties relate concepts and/or MM. Table 2 shows some of the these constraints.

In some cases, the existence of a property between two or more individuals involves the existence of other properties. For example, if a concept A is a hyponym of a concept B, the concept B is hyperonym for A. These features are described using properties features and some examples are in Table 3.

Our model and the related SN have been implemented in a SMBD using theNeo4j graph database and it has been populated using WordNet [39] and ImageNet [24]. Therefore, we can consider the same knowledge organization of these sources. The Fig. 1 is a macro visualization the resulting graph limited to 24271 nodes and 40000 relationships [10, 11].

The goal of this figure is to show the complexity of our SMBD.

4   The Visualization Framework

The visualization of the document summarization in described and discussed in the following of this section. It uses a Semantic Tag cloud where the task of

Table 3. Properties features

Property	Features
hasMM	Inverse of hasConcenpt
hasConcept	Inverse of hasMM
hyponym	Inverse of hypernym: transitivity
hypernym	Inverse of hyponym: transitivity
verbGroup	Symmetry and transitivity

tag recognition (i.e. the extracted keywords) is based on a Word Sense Disambiguation (WSD) step. The WSD is a basic action because the property of a term to express different meaning; this linguistic property is called polysemy. The implemented knowledge base (i.e. SMDB) is the used as support for the visualization and the WSD tasks and also to add semantic related terms to the recognized tags. We use our SMBD in the visualization process and both in the WSD step and to retrieve additional keywords. The system executes the WSD task to assign the right sense to each term. This step is based on the analysis of the term context. Therefore, each term sense is compared with all the senses of the other terms in a document. We use a semantic based similarity metric to measure the relatedness between terms and we assign to the considered term the sense with the high similarity score value. First of all we assign to the defined linguistic properties a weight σ_i, which represents the straighten of each relation from a expressive power point of view. In our opinion the linguistic relations have different power when they connect concepts or words. Also other authors support our intuition [19]. The weight assigned to each property is set following the measures defined in the work cited just now and we extend them to similar properties. They are real numbers in the $[0, 1]$ interval. The defined metric is composed of two components: the path length (l) between pairs of terms and the depth (d) of their subsumer, represented by the number of hops. This correlation is the semantic relatedness between the considered terms and it is computed through a nonlinear function. The use of this kind of function depends to different questions. The score of path length and depth may range from 0 to infinity due to their definition. On the other hand, the terms relatedness is represented with a number in the $[0, 1]$ interval. When the path length decreases toward 0, the relatedness should monotonically increase toward 1, on the contrary it should monotonically decrease toward 0 when path length goes to infinity. Moreover we have to consider a scaling effect regarding the depth, because a word in a high semantic hierarchy level expresses a more general concept than one in a lower level. A non linear function is able to scale down the contribution of subsumers in a upper level and scale up those in a lower one.

We are now in the position of present the metric components and later the our similarity function.

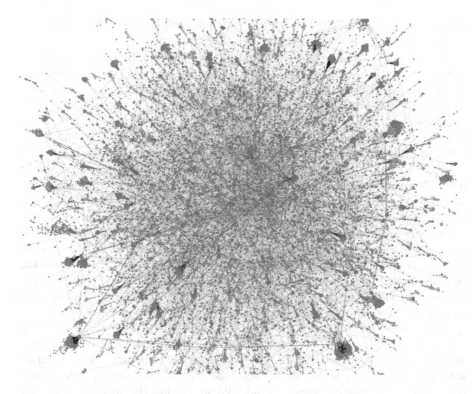

Fig. 1. Macro visualization of Neo4j db with Gephi

Given two words w_1 and w_2, the length l of the path between w_1 and w_2 is computed using our SMBD and it is defined as:

$$l(w_1, w_2) = \min_j \sum_{i=1}^{h_j(w_1, w_2)} \frac{1}{\sigma_i} \tag{1}$$

where j spans over all the paths between w_1 and w_2, $h_j(w_1, w_2)$ is the number of hops in the j-th path and σ_i is the weight assigned to the i-th hop in the j-th path in respect to the hop linguistic property.

We use our SMDB to measure the depth d of w_1 and w_2 subsumer. Te compute this measure we consider only the IS-A hierarchy (i.e. the hyponymy and hyperonymy structure). Moreover, the depth is measured as the number of hops from the subsumer of w_1 and w_2 to the root of the hierarchy. With this aim, we use an exponential function to solve the issues discussed above.

We define the *Semantic Similarity Score* (SSS) as:

$$SSS(v) = \sum_{(w_p} e^{-\alpha \cdot l(w_p)} \frac{e^{\beta \cdot d(w_p)} - e^{-\beta \cdot d(w_p)}}{e^{\beta \cdot d(w_p)} + e^{-\beta \cdot d(w_p)}} \tag{2}$$

where (w_p) are all pairs of words in the document v and $\alpha \geq 0$ and $\beta > 0$ are two scaling factors (i.e. $\alpha = 0.2$ and $\beta = 0.6$) [32].

The proposed function is used to compute the WSD for all the senses related to the extracted term. The WSD task is performed in a window of context and in our approach we use the entire document. The sense with the maximum score computed by our metric is associated as right sens to the considered term. This task returns a list of concepts represented with their terms and ordered by the SSS. Moreover, we use also visual information in the WSD task. The images are taken from the analyzed document to measure the similarity with respect to the our SMBD visual collection. An image is represented by the same global feature descriptor used in our big data (i.e. PHOG). This feature is compared with the ones in the SMBD through a distance metric which measures the proximity between two points belonging to the same metric space (i.e. the feature space). Since every visual node in the database is linked to a concept, the result is a list of concepts, sorted by the evaluated metric. We use the cosine metric to measure the similarity. In the whole WSD process we consider as good candidates the concepts in common between the textual and visual WSD. The combination of textual and visual analysis is combined using the SUM function [31] and the chosen sense represented by term/image is the one with the highest value.

The Visual Semantic Tag Cloud is built following a novel technique. It is based on a combination of term semantic properties and statistical information. We use the weight associated to the recognized keywords and their relations with the same terms in our knowledge base The importance of each term is measured considering its polisemy grade. We argue that the polysemy expresses the ambiguity in the use of a terms when it can have multiple meanings. This value is calculated using our knowledge base.

We called this measure *centrality* and it is calculate for a generic term i as:

$$\chi_i = \frac{1}{poly_i} \tag{3}$$

$poly_i$ is the associated number of senses of i.

Querying the knowledge base the word *lion* has, for example, four associated senses therefore its chance to represent a specific sense is equal to $1/4$.

The proposed metric uses statistic information based on term-weight function to better represent relevant document terms. Our approach takes into consideration two different normalized components [50]:

- *Term frequency*- the number of occurrences of a term in a document;
- *Document size factor*- it compensates for high term frequencies of terms in large documents.

We are now in the position of presenting our metric to visualize the summarized document:

$$V_{i,k} = \frac{(a + (1-a)(TF_{i,k}/TF_{max,k}))\chi_i}{\sqrt{\sum_{i \in k}(a + (1-a)(TF_{i,k}/TF_{max,k})(\chi_i))^2}} \tag{4}$$

where k is the set of terms representing to the j-th document, i is the i-th term, $TF_{i,k}$ represents the term frequency of i in k, $TF_{max,k}$ being the highest value of the term frequency in k, ϖ_i is the centrality of i, a is used as a smoothing factor to dump TF by the largest TF value in k related to the second metric component. The need is to not allow important changing of the normalized $TF_{i,k}$ for small variations of $TF_{i,k}$. The suggested line in literature is to set $a=0.5$ [36].

The proposed metric add statistical measures to efficiently visualize document summary also combining semantic information as centrality. In this way we can have an improving in the recognition of relevant terms.

These information are used to compute the font size in the visualization of the semantic tag cloud. Moreover, we add semantic related terms through our knowledge base. This information enrichment is performed by a semantic network extraction created by the recognized terms in the WSD step. Starting from the concepts represented by these terms we add other direct linked concepts considering all linguistic relations counting out hyperonym to avoid general concepts. These terms are visualize by the same original term font size with a scaling factor computed by Eq. 2.

In the following section we will present some experiments to show that the tag cloud enrichment with new terms semantically related to the ones extracted from the analyzed document but not present in it improves the perception of the document topic by users.

5   Case Study and Evaluation

This section is focused on the implementation of a Semantic Tag Cloud for document visualization. We describe the procedure for the generation of our document summary visualization tool considering a real document from Wikipedia in a general conceptual domain about *animal* and about a specific topic i.e. *lion* (http://en.wikipedia.org/wiki/Lion).

The web document has been preprocessed with the aim of transform in a basic form all the extracted terms. The WSD task is later performed to disambiguate the analyzed terms and have their right sense. The correct meaning is recognized using the process described in the previous section by means of visual and textual information measuring the semantic relatedness between all keywords in the document and visual features. An example of disambiguated term is *"lion"*.; we extract four senses from our knowledge base derived from the integration of WordNet and ImageNet in our SMBD. The glossary of these senses are:

1. lion, king of beasts, Panthera leo: large gregarious predatory feline of Africa and India having a tawny coat with a shaggy mane in the male;
2. lion, social lion: a celebrity who is lionized (much sought after);
3. Leo, Lion: (astrology) a person who is born while the sun is in Leo;
4. Leo, Leo the Lion, Lion: the fifth sign of the zodiac; the sun is in this sign from about July 23 to August 22.

Lion

From Wikipedia, the free encyclopedia

The **lion** (*Panthera leo*) is a species in the family Felidae; it is a muscular, deep-chested cat with a short, rounded head, a reduced neck and round ears, and a hairy tuft at the end of its tail. The lion is sexually dimorphic; males are larger than females with a typical weight range of 150 to 250 kg (330 to 550 lb) for males and 120 to 182 kg (265 to 400 lb) for females. Male lions have a prominent mane, which is the most recognisable feature of the species. A lion pride consists of a few adult males, related females and cubs. Groups of female lions typically hunt together, preying mostly on large ungulates. The species is an apex and keystone predator, although they scavenge when opportunities occur. Some lions have been known to hunt humans, although the species typically does not.

Male lion in Okonjima, Namibia

Typically, the lion inhabits grasslands and savannas but is absent in dense forests. It is usually more diurnal than other big cats, but when persecuted it adapts to being active at night and at twilight. In the Pleistocene, the lion ranged throughout Eurasia, Africa and North America but today it has been reduced to fragmented populations in Sub-Saharan Africa and one critically endangered population in western India. It has been listed as Vulnerable on the IUCN Red List since 1996 because populations in African countries have declined by about 43% since the early 1990s. Lion populations are untenable outside designated protected areas. Although the cause of the decline is not fully understood, habitat loss and conflicts with humans are the greatest causes for concern.

Female (lioness) in Okonjima

One of the most widely recognised animal symbols in human culture, the lion has been extensively depicted in sculptures and paintings, on national flags, and in contemporary films and literature. Lions have been kept in menageries since the time of the Roman Empire and have been a key species sought for exhibition in zoological gardens across the world since the late 18th century. Cultural depictions of lions were prominent in the Upper Paleolithic period; carvings and paintings from the Lascaux and Chauvet Caves in France have been dated to 17,000 years ago, and depictions have occurred in virtually all ancient and medieval cultures that coincided with the lion's former and current ranges.

(a) Wikipedia page

(b) Text Semantic Cloud

(c) Image Semantic Tag Cloud

Fig. 2. Semantic Tag Cloud Example

Only the first one has a high similarity with all the other word of analyzed terms and the images in the original document. The list of disambiguated terms has benn used to build a SN for each term and, following the strategy described before new terms have been found to enrich our visualization. A complete example of the Semantic Cloud generation process is in Fig. 2.

The number of shown terms and images can be set by the user. The semantic tag cloud shows the terms and images more similar to the representative concept for the analyzed document. On the other hand, the use of a semantic big data give us also a visual representation of the considered concept. Therefore, the visual cloud has been generated using the images related to the concepts recognized in the WSD. We explicit point out that some concepts haven't related images due to the knowledge source (i.e. ImageNet) used to populate our SMBD.

We have to highlight the improvements of the presented visualization approach with a proper evaluation of the proposed techniques. At this stage of our research, we want to measure the user perception in the using of our visualization tool. We are interested in this kind of evaluation due to intrinsic subjective nature of the understanding process of document topic. For this reason, we need to take into account specific indicators to measure the user perception.

We chose to use a general and well-known knowledge source as Wikipedia and fetch 500 web pages related to animal domain and generate the related summaries represented by semantic clouds. Therefore, they are analyzed by a questionnaire asked to a group of 100 users (MSc students and Ph.D. students of information science). In our experiments we present a comparison of our textual (**VC**) and visual (**VC**) techniques with common document term frequency counting (**TC**) for tag cloud generation.

Our approach has been evaluated using a methodological framework discussed in [40]. This methodology is devoted to the service evaluation and it is based on two different kinds of statements:

- **E** - a general evaluation on service category;
- **P** - an evaluation of a particular service.

A 7-point scale in a *strongly disagree* (**1**) to *strongly agree* (**7**) interval is used to measure each statement. Moreover, we evaluate our strategy using others measures [22,33] to put into account different features of our methodology:

- **PU** - Perceived Usefulness;
- **PEU** - Perceived Ease of Use;
- **PE** - Perceived Enjoyment.

The document test set and the related tag clouds have been randomly assigned to users and evaluated using these indicators.

The results are shown in Fig. 3 in terms of mean.

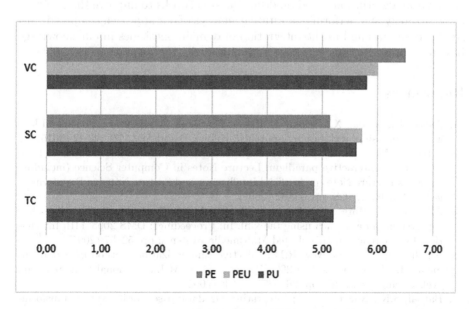

Fig. 3. Experimental results

The proposed textual and visual tag clouds visualization strategies shown better results in terms of topic document understanding compared with the standard frequency-based tag cloud. Moreover, the enrichment of our visualization structure with terms semantically related to the ones extracted from the analyzed documents gives an improvement of the user knowledge about the document topic.

6   Conclusion

Efficient approaches to analyze documents and represent their contents in an improved view can provide a solution for information overload. In this context the integration of semantic web vision and big data technologies represent an interesting way to organize and store data. Semantic analysis techniques and document visualization tools offer a concise way to represent huge volume of data and support people to recognize and understand information from the original sources [12,14]. In this paper a semantic multimedia big data has been presented. Information has been organized and stored using a multimedia model in which the concepts are represented in textual and visual form. The model has been implemented using a graph big data. Moreover, a strategy based on semantic tag cloud has been proposed to visualize key concepts related to analyzed documents A real case study on the semantic tag cloud generation and visualization has been presented to show the effectiveness of our approach. We are considering to extend our framework with other statistical components and implement novel browsing strategies by means of textual and visual tags to enhance basic tasks of the information retrieval process [2]. In addition, we are investigating on the use of other visual description based on deep neural networks to improve the accuracy of our strategy and perform quantitative analysis of our approach compared with similar base lines and in the integration of domain ontologies in our knowledge base to improve its topic coverage and multimedia representations [13,15,47].

References

1. Agerri, R., Artola, X., Beloki, Z., Rigau, G., Soroa, A.: Big data for natural language processing: a streaming approach. Knowl.-Based Syst. **79**, 36–42 (2015)
2. Albanese, M., Capasso, P., Picariello, A., Rinaldi, A.: Information retrieval from the web: an interactive paradigm. Lecture Notes in Computer Science (including subseries Lecture Notes in Artificial Intelligence and Lecture Notes in Bioinformatics), vol. 3665, LNCS, pp. 17–32 (2005)
3. Albanese, M., Maresca, P., Picariello, A., Rinaldi, A.: Towards a multimedia ontology system: an approach using tao xml. In: Proceedings: DMS 2005–11th International Conference on Distributed Multimedia Systems, pp. 52–57 (2005)
4. Alguliev, R.M., Aliguliyev, R.M.: Effective summarization method of text documents. In: Proceedings The 2005 IEEE/WIC/ACM International Conference on Web Intelligence, 2005, pp. 264–271. IEEE (2005)
5. Bansal, S.K., Kagemann, S.: Integrating big data: a semantic extract-transform-load framework. Computer **48**(3), 42–50 (2015)

6. Begelman, G., Keller, P., Smadja, F., et al.: Automated tag clustering: improving search and exploration in the tag space. In: Collaborative Web Tagging Workshop at WWW2006, Edinburgh, Scotland, pp. 15–33 (2006)
7. Bello-Orgaz, G., Jung, J.J., Camacho, D.: Social big data: recent achievements and new challenges. Inf. Fusion **28**, 45–59 (2016)
8. Benbernou, S., Huang, X., Ouziri, M.: Semantic-based and entity-resolution fusion to enhance quality of big RDF data. IEEE Transactions on Big Data (2017)
9. Bosch, A., Zisserman, A., Munoz, X.: Representing shape with a spatial pyramid kernel. In: Proceedings of the 6th ACM International Conference on Image and Video Retrieval, pp. 401–408. ACM (2007)
10. Caldarola, E., Picariello, A., Rinaldi, A.: Big graph-based data visualization experiences: the wordnet case study. In: IC3K 2015 - Proceedings of the 7th International Joint Conference on Knowledge Discovery, Knowledge Engineering and Knowledge Management, vol. 1, pp. 104–115 (2015)
11. Caldarola, E., Picariello, A., Rinaldi, A.: Experiences in wordnet visualization with labeled graph databases. Commun. Comput. Inf. Sci. **631**, 80–99 (2016)
12. Caldarola, E., Picariello, A., Rinaldi, A., Sacco, M.: Exploration and visualization of big graphs the dbpedia case study. In: IC3K 2016 - Proceedings of the 8th International Joint Conference on Knowledge Discovery, Knowledge Engineering and Knowledge Management, vol. 1, pp. 257–264 (2016)
13. Caldarola, E., Rinaldi, A.: An approach to ontology integration for ontology reuse. In: Proceedings - 2016 IEEE 17th International Conference on Information Reuse and Integration, IRI 2016, pp. 384–393 (2016)
14. Caldarola, E., Rinaldi, A.: Improving the visualization of word net large lexical database through semantic tag clouds. In: Proceedings - 2016 IEEE International Congress on Big Data, BigData Congress 2016, pp. 34–41 (2016)
15. Caldarola, E., Rinaldi, A.: A multi-strategy approach for ontology reuse through matching and integration techniques. Adv. Intell. Syst. Comput. **561**, 63–90 (2018)
16. Caldarola, E.G., Rinaldi, A.M.: Big data: a survey: the new paradigms, methodologies and tools. In: DATA 2015–4th International Conference on Data Management Technologies and Applications, Proceedings, pp. 362–370 (2015)
17. Caldarola, E.G., Rinaldi, A.M.: Big data visualization tools: a survey: the new paradigms, methodologies and tools for large data sets visualization. In: DATA 2017 - Proceedings of the 6th International Conference on Data Science, Technology and Applications, pp. 296–305 (2017)
18. Caldarola, E.G., Rinaldi, A.M.: Modelling multimedia social networks using semantically labelled graphs. In: 2017 IEEE International Conference on Information Reuse and Integration (IRI), pp. 493–500 (2017)
19. Castano, S., Ferrara, A., Montanelli, S.: H-match: an algorithm for dynamically matching ontologies in peer-based systems. In: In Proceedings of WebS, pp. 231–250 (2003)
20. Cattuto, C., Schmitz, C., Baldassarri, A., Servedio, V.D., Loreto, V., Hotho, A., Grahl, M., Stumme, G.: Network properties of folksonomies. Ai Commun. **20**(4), 245–262 (2007)
21. Chen, Y.-X., Santamaría, R., Butz, A., Therón, R.: TagClusters: semantic aggregation of collaborative tags beyond tagclouds. In: Butz, A., Fisher, B., Christie, M., Krüger, A., Olivier, P., Therón, R. (eds.) SG 2009. LNCS, vol. 5531, pp. 56–67. Springer, Heidelberg (2009). https://doi.org/10.1007/978-3-642-02115-2_5
22. Davis, F.D.: Perceived usefulness, perceived ease of use, and user acceptance of information technology. MIS Q. **13**(3), 319–340 (1989)

23. De Mauro, A., Greco, M., Grimaldi, M.: A formal definition of big data based on its essential features. Library Rev. **65**(3), 122–135 (2016)
24. Deng, J., Dong, W., Socher, R., Li, L.J., Li, K., Fei-Fei, L.: Imagenet: a large-scale hierarchical image database. In: IEEE Conference on Computer Vision and Pattern Recognition, 2009. CVPR 2009, pp. 248–255. IEEE (2009)
25. Emani, C.K., Cullot, N., Nicolle, C.: Understandable big data: a survey. Comput. Sci. Rev. **17**, 70–81 (2015)
26. Gruber, T.R.: A translation approach to portable ontology specifications. Knowl. Acquis. **5**(2), 199–220 (1993)
27. Hammond, T., Hannay, T., Lund, B., Scott, J.: Social bookmarking tools (i) a general review. D-lib Magazine **2**(4) (2005). http://www.dlib.org/dlib/april05/hammond/04hammond.html
28. Hassan-Montero, Y., Herrero-Solana, V.: Improving tag-clouds as visual information retrieval interfaces. In: International Conference on Multidisciplinary Information Sciences and Technologies, pp. 25–28. Citeseer (2006)
29. Hu, X., Wu, B.: Automatic keyword extraction using linguistic features. In: Sixth IEEE International Conference on Data Mining Workshops, 2006, ICDM Workshops 2006, pp. 19–23. IEEE (2006)
30. Hulth, A.: Improved automatic keyword extraction given more linguistic knowledge. In: Proceedings of the 2003 Conference on Empirical Methods in Natural Language Processing, pp. 216–223. Association for Computational Linguistics (2003)
31. Kittler, J., Hatef, M., Duin, R.P.W., Matas, J.: On combining classifiers. IEEE Trans. Pattern Anal. Mach. Intell. **20**(3), 226–239 (1998)
32. Li, Y., Bandar, Z.A., McLean, D.: An approach for measuring semantic similarity between words using multiple information sources. IEEE Trans. Knowl. Data Eng. **15**(4), 871–882 (2003)
33. Lin, C.S., Wu, S., Tsai, R.J.: Integrating perceived playfulness into expectation-confirmation model for web portal context. I&M **42**(5), 683–693 (2005)
34. Lv, Z., Song, H., Basanta-Val, P., Steed, A., Jo, M.: Next-generation big data analytics: state of the art, challenges, and future research topics. IEEE Trans. Ind. Inform. **13**(4), 1891–1899 (2017)
35. Mami, M.N., Scerri, S., Auer, S., Vidal, M.-E.: Towards semantification of big data technology. In: Madria, S., Hara, T. (eds.) DaWaK 2016. LNCS, vol. 9829, pp. 376–390. Springer, Cham (2016). https://doi.org/10.1007/978-3-319-43946-4_25
36. Manning, C.D., Raghavan, P., Schtze, H.: Introduction to Information Retrieval. Cambridge University Press, New York (2008)
37. Matsuo, Y., Ishizuka, M.: Keyword extraction from a single document using word co-occurrence statistical information. Int. J. Artif. Intell. Tools **13**(01), 157–169 (2004)
38. Mika, P.: Ontologies are us: a unified model of social networks and semantics. Web Semant.: Sci., Serv. Agents World Wide Web **5**(1), 5–15 (2007)
39. Miller, G.A.: Wordnet: a lexical database for english. Commun. ACM **38**(11), 39–41 (1995)
40. Parasuraman, A., Zeithaml, V.A., Berry, L.L.: Servqual: a multiple-item scale for measuring consumer perceptions of service quality. J. Retailing **64**(1), 12–40 (1988)
41. Purificato, E., Rinaldi, A.M.: Multimedia and geographic data integration for cultural heritage information retrieval. Multimedia Tools Appl. **77**, 1–23 (2018)
42. Quboa, Q., Mehandjiev, N.: Creating intelligent business systems by utilising big data and semantics. In: 2017 IEEE 19th Conference on Business Informatics (CBI), vol. 2, pp. 39–46. IEEE (2017)

43. Rani, P.S., Suresh, R.M., Sethukarasi, R.: Multi-level semantic annotation and unified data integration using semantic web ontology in big data processing. In: Cluster Computing (2017)

44. Rinaldi, A.: Improving tag clouds with ontologies and semantics. In: Proceedings - International Workshop on Database and Expert Systems Applications, DEXA, pp. 139–143 (2012)

45. Rinaldi, A.: Document summarization using semantic clouds. In: Proceedings - 2013 IEEE 7th International Conference on Semantic Computing, ICSC 2013, pp. 100–103 (2013)

46. Rinaldi, A.: Web summarization and browsing through semantic tag clouds. Int. J. Intell. Inf. Technol. **15**(3), 1–23 (2019)

47. Rinaldi, A., Russo, C.: A matching framework for multimedia data integration using semantics and ontologies. In: Proceedings - 12th IEEE International Conference on Semantic Computing, ICSC 2018, vol. 2018, pp. 363–368 (2018)

48. Rinaldi, A., Russo, C.: A semantic-based model to represent multimedia big data. In: MEDES 2018–10th International Conference on Management of Digital EcoSystems, pp. 31–38 (2018)

49. Rinaldi, A.M.: A multimedia ontology model based on linguistic properties and audio-visual features. Inf. Sci. **277**, 234–246 (2014)

50. Salton, G., Buckley, C.: Term-weighting approaches in automatic text retrieval. In: Sparck Jones, K., Willett, P. (eds.) Readings in Information Retrieval, pp. 323–328. Morgan Kaufmann Publishers Inc., San Francisco (1997)

51. Siddiqi, S., Sharan, A.: Keyword and keyphrase extraction techniques: aliterature review. Int. J. Comput. Appl. **109**(2), 18–23 (2015)

52. Xu, Z., Wei, X., Luo, X., Liu, Y., Mei, L., Hu, C., Chen, L.: Knowle: a semantic link network based system for organizing large scale online news events. Fut. Gener. Comput. Syst. **43**, 40–50 (2015)

53. Zhu, J., et al.: Tag-oriented document summarization. In: Proceedings of the 18th International Conference on World Wide Web, pp. 1195–1196. ACM (2009)

Improving Portfolio Performance Using Attribute Selection and Combination

Xiaoran Wang, James Ho-Shek[✉], Dominik Ondusko,
and D. Frank Hsu

Laboratory of Informatics and Data Mining, Department of Computer
and Information Sciences, Fordham University, New York, NY 10023, USA
{xwang312, jho9, dondusko}@fordham.edu,
hsu@cis.fordham.edu

Abstract. In portfolio management, stock selection and evaluation can be based on a variety of financial attributes over a period of time. It has been shown recently by Irukulapati et al. that long term portfolio management strategy using attribute selection and combinatorial fusion can not only achieve better results than individual attributes but also exceed the performance of the Russell 2000 index. In this paper, we propose a method to compute the attribute scoring system using weighted average by recency (AR) giving more weight to scores at the time closer to the present. We then show, by market testing, that our results perform better than that of Irukulapati et al. in a majority of cases as well as the Russell 2000.

Keywords: Information fusion · Portfolio management · Cognitive diversity · Rank-score characteristic (RSC) function

1 Introduction

Financial analysts and portfolio managers concern themselves with building an effective portfolio that grows over time. To achieve this goal, there have been various methods and approaches considered traditionally. They make key assumptions to make these models function properly. These models include Capital Asset Pricing Model (CAPM), which uses expected return on a security, also known as the risk-free return, plus a risk premium, which is based on the beta of the security, and a risk premium, the rate of return higher than the risk-free rate. Additionally, this method accounts for higher risk premium in order to allow investors seek a riskier approach [2]. Another approach is Arbitrage Pricing Theory (APT) which deals with theory of asset pricing. Asset pricing assumes that an asset's returns can be forecasted with the linear relationship of an asset's expected returns and the macroeconomic factors that affect the asset's risk. APT is considered as a more flexible and sophisticated alternative to the Capital Asset Pricing Model (CAPM). However, the APT approach takes a considerable amount of time to determine all the various risk factors that may influence the price of an asset. Although both approaches are still widely being used, there are many challenges to optimize the best approach. Due to many issues that cannot be accounted for in these models, it may be better to combine methods to build models.

© Springer Nature Switzerland AG 2019
C. Esposito et al. (Eds.): I-SPAN 2019, CCIS 1080, pp. 58–70, 2019.
https://doi.org/10.1007/978-3-030-30143-9_5

In past works, computational and algorithmic based methods have been applied to portfolio management. As early as 1995, attempts at using artificial intelligence has been applied to portfolio management see [12]. We have seen a movement towards pattern recognition and knowledge based systems. This methodology is also seen in [1] whereby genetic algorithm (GAs) techniques are applied to solve for issues of optimization. Results of implementing GAs has shown that positive returns can be achieved even in a bearish market. Lastly, data mining techniques have been applied to classify Indian stocks into clusters [10]. In this approach diversification of the portfolio reduces the risk of associated to the portfolio constructed.

In this paper, we continue the research in the lines of [7] and [13] which selects attributes using a sliding rule and combines these selected attributes using combinatorial fusion. Combinatorial fusion is a method for combining multiple scoring system using both rank and score combinations [3–6]. By using the rank-score characteristic (RSC) function of an attribute A and the cognitive diversity between two attributes A and B, we are able to define the diversity strength of an attribute. Then using this notion of diversity strength of an attribute and the attributes performance, we are able to perform attribute selection using a sliding rule on two ranks of diversity strength of an attribute and its performance. To compute the score function of the attribute scoring system, we use two approaches to aggregate stock performance across a temporal span of ten years with respect to (1) average by time (AT), and (2) average by recency (AR).

The paper is structured as follows. Section 2 describes our dataset and stock selection, financial attributes and computing the attribute scoring system, and attribute selection by sliding rule, the attributes we have, and the processing method. Section 3 covers combination of multiple attribute systems using three different methods: (a) average combination, (b) weighted combination by diversity strength, and (c) weighted combination by performance. Section 4 covers market test and compares our result with that of Irukulapati et al. Section 5 concludes the paper with further work.

2 Multiple Attribute Systems

2.1 Dataset and Stock Selection

The dataset used for this paper is sourced and pulled from Bloomberg. This was done on a built-in excel plug where we pulled US equity totaling 3,000 stocks from the month of February 2007 to December 2016. This dataset is the same as [7]. After we performed data cleaning to deal with missing values, we ended up with a set of 707 stocks all of which have full ten years of history with information for all attributes.

2.2 Financial Attributes

Our dataset contains 8 attributes each of which can be viewed as an indicator for portfolio buying, holding or selling. Each attribute is known for valuing different aspects of a stock. We briefly describe these eight attributes as follows: More details can be found in [8, 14].

Earnings per Share (EPS): One of the most important profitability measures for publicly listed firms. It refers to the share of net income of a company that is owned by common shareholders. It is used as an indicator of a company's future revenues.

Earnings before interest, tax, depreciation, and amortization (EBITDA): A company's revenue before back interest expense, taxes, depreciation & amortization expense to net income.

Profit Margin: The ratio of net income to the revenue, which tells the percentage of a company's revenues that are available to meet the operating and nonoperating expense.

Price to Earnings (P/E Ratio): is the ratio of the price of a stock to its earnings per share, described to the conventional logic that the P/E gauges the market's assessment of the firm's future.

Cash Flow per Share: The ratio of the sum of inflow and outflow cash related to a firm's day-to-day business activities, generated from the purchase and disposal of long-term investment and generated from issuance and repayment of capital. A positive value illustrates that cash is flowing into the company.

Price to Book Ratio: The ratio of a stock's market price to its book value. The premium to book value is attributable to two sources: the capitalized value of excess earnings on current book equity and the net present value of all anticipated future earnings from new investments.

Current Enterprise Value (EV): A measure of a company's total value, often used as a more comprehensive alternative to equity market capitalization.

Volume: Trading Volume, which represents how much amount of the security buy and sold in the market at a given duration of time. Large trade volumes may indicate that there is a significant news event.

2.3   Computing the Attributes Scoring System

Each attribute associated with each stock has data that spans 10 years. We use two approaches to construct a scoring system for each of the eight attributes. Both approaches take advantages of the temporal fashion. Approach 1 takes simple average by time (AT). However, approach 2 uses weighted average by recency (AR).

Average by Time (AT): The average by time approach was also used in [7]. Here a simple average is done across ten years worth of data and this average value is then used as a score to denote the stock score.

Weighted Average by Recency (AR). Our weighted average by recency approach uses a weight based on time with values closer to the present being weighed greater than values in the past. The data closer to 2016 takes a significant more effect on the score than earlier years. Since time becomes more important, we neglect those stocks with insufficient number of data in the past ten years. $w_i = \frac{i}{n}$ is used in calculating the weight, where i is the position of the data start from Feb 2007, and n is the total number of data across the time span. The weights are then normalize to 1 across the time span.

2.4   Attribute Selection by Sliding Rule

Before we combine these attributes we must address the issue of attribute selection using conventional wisdom, in finance and other areas [4, 6, 8, 15], which favors attributes that are diverse in formation and relevant in that it provides good performance.

Analysts who build models often use various measures and favor certain measures to decide how to pick a stock. Some common attributes as addressed above, include EPS, P/E ratio and Dividends per share. That being said, it is accepted that not a single indicator or attribute is the best method for portfolio building. Moreover, we have to address the problem of many attributes, some of which may be redundant. In this section, we conduct attribute selection using a sliding rule which involves performance and diversity strength of each of the eight attributes.

For measuring performance of attribute A, we use the attribute P/E ratio and obtain its top 100 stocks and use it as an evaluation method for performance of A by finding its average returns. We do this for all attributes to find the individual attribute's ability to find "good" stocks.

In order to calculate the diversity strength of the attribute A, we calculate the cognitive diversity (CD), d(A, B), between A and any other attribute B in the attribute set {A, B, C, D, E, F, G, H} as:

$$d(A,B) = d(f_A, f_B) = \sqrt{\sum_{i=1}^{707} \left([f_A(i) - f_B(i)]^2 \right)} \tag{1}$$

where $f_A(i) = s_A(r_A^{-1}(i))$ is the rank-score characteristic (RSC) function, $s_A: D \to R$ is the score function of A, $r_A: R \to N$ Nis the rank function of A, $D = \{d_1, d_2, \ldots, d_{707}\}$, $N = \{1, 2, \ldots, 707\}$, and R = set of real numbers [4–6].

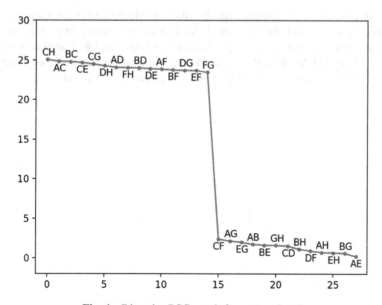

Fig. 1. Diversity RSC graph for approach AT

Since there are 28 points of the 8 attributes, we rank the 28 diversity scores (called Diversity RSC Graph) in Figs. 1, and 2 for approach AT and approach AR respectively. In Figs. 1 and 2, we see that the top 15 pairs have much higher diversity (point # 0 to #14) scores than other 13 points (#15 to #27). So, we define diversity strength of attribute A, ds(A), to be the number of A appearing in the top 15 pairs.

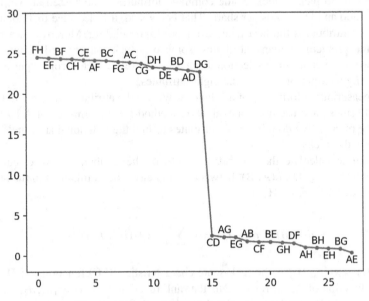

Fig. 2. Diversity RSC graph for approach AT

After obtaining the performance and the diversity strength of these 8 attributes, we use the sliding rule to pick the top 5 attributes that are both strong in performance and diversity strength. In both cases of approach AT and AR, the top 5 attributes selected are A, B, C, E, and H. We note that these five attributes are the same attributes but have different score functions due to different scoring approaches AT and AR.

3   Combination of Multiple Financial Attributes

In this section, we will combine the five selected attributes in both cases AT and AR, using combinatorial fusion. Combinatorial fusion, as proposed and studied by Hsu et al. [3–6], has been used in several domains such as on-line learning [11] and virtual screening [15]. It has been shown that combination of two or many scoring systems can perform better than each individual system only if they are relatively good and they are diverse. This technique has been used previously in financial analysis and portfolio building by Hsu et al. [7, 9, 13]. In the first paper by Vinod et al. [13], they showed that by using multiple scoring systems and cognitive diversity between them, one can improve portfolio management by selection of stock in a set of diverse and good performance attribute systems. In Luo et al. [9], we see that this technique can be extended to algorithmic combinations that select diverse stocks with good performance. Then in Irukulapati et al. [7], it is shown that this can be used for long term portfolio management. In this section, we combine the five attributes selected by sliding rule as it did in Irukulapati et al. [7], with combinations of the five attribute scoring systems constructed by the approaches AT and AR. As in [7] we also use three methods of combination average combinations, weighted combination by diversity strength, and weighted combination by performance.

3.1   Method of Combination

We use three types of combinations: simple average combination, weighted combination by diversity strength, and weighted combination performance. In all these methods, both rank and score combinations are conducted.

Average Combination: By adopting the average combination method, scores or ranks associated with different attributes have an equal weight during the combination. In all combinations, top 100 stocks based on combined scores/rank of the attributes are chosen and their performances' scores are averaged and evaluated.

Weighted Combination by Diversity Strength: Each and every attribute has a diversity strength as defined in Sect. 2. The diversity strength values are used as a weight of the feature. During combination, the score/rank of each attribute will multiply by the diversity strength. Top 100 stocks based on the combined scores/ranks are chosen and their performances' scores are averaged and evaluated.

Weighted Combination by Performance: For the individual attribute, top 100 scores (which is also the top 100 ranks) are evaluated. The average scores of the performance associated to the top 100 stocks are used as the weights of the attributes. During the combination, the score/rank of each attributes will multiply by the weights, and normalizing after combination. Top 100 stocks' performance scores are averaged and evaluated.

Sections B and C includes Figs. 3 and 4 simple average combination, weighted combination by diversity strength, and weighted combination performance as well as Figs. 5 and 6 simple average combination, weighted combination by diversity strength, and weighted combination performance for RSC function graph of the 5 attributes A, B, C, E, H and combinatorial fusion ($2^5 - 1 - 5 = 26$ cases of rank and score combinations) using three methods simple average combination, weighted combination by diversity strength, and weighted combination by performance corresponding to two approaches AT and AR respectively.

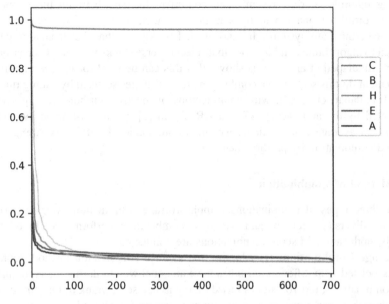

Fig. 3. RSC function graph of the 5 attributes A, B, C, E, H using approach AT

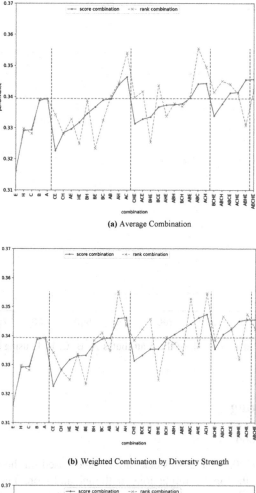

(a) Average Combination

(b) Weighted Combination by Diversity Strength

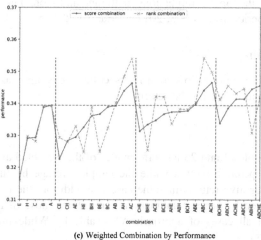

(c) Weighted Combination by Performance

Fig. 4. (a) Average combination (b) Weighted combination by diversity strength (c) Weighted combination by performance

3.2   Approach AR

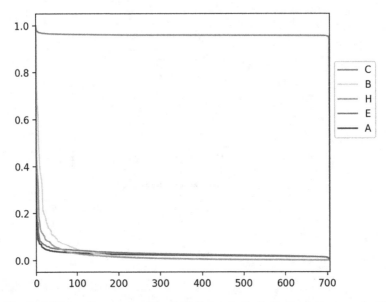

Fig. 5. RSC function graph of the 5 attributes A, B, C, E, H using approach AR

4   Market Testing

4.1   Testing Method

Portfolio size of 10, 20, 30 and 40 stocks are created based on the intersection of the top 100 stocks from the top 3 combinations (both rank and scores) in each methods and approaches. Time period from Jan 3, 2017 to Mar 19, 2018 is used for the testing.

4.2   Testing Results

For methods without the portfolio size of intersecting stocks, the maximum number of stocks are chosen and tested for the return.

4.3   Discussion

As we can see in Tables 1 and 2 that performance of the weighted average by recency approach AR give positive returns while the simple average by time approach AT provides us with negative returns in some cases. In addition, the performance of the stock portfolios given by score combinations outperform those of rank combination selection in almost all cases of approach AT (Table 1). While in the case of AR

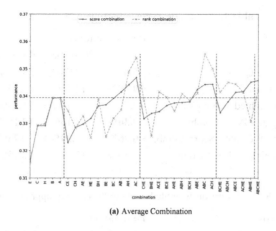

(a) Average Combination

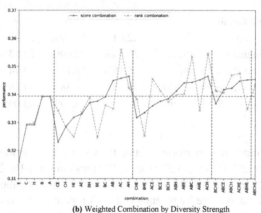

(b) Weighted Combination by Diversity Strength

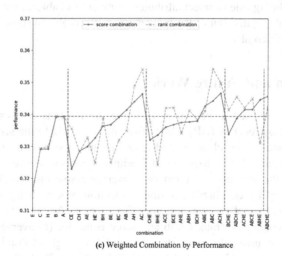

(c) Weighted Combination by Performance

Fig. 6. (a) Average combination (b) Weighted combination by diversity strength (c) Weighted combination by performance

Table 1. Return on average by time approach AT

(I) Approach AT	Portfolio returns			
	10 stocks	20 stocks	30 stocks	40 stocks
(a) Average Score Comb.	5.01%	**17.73%**	8.62%	6.03%
Average Rank Comb.	**−9.30%**	−12.15%	−12.15%	−12.15%
(b) Diversity Weighted Score Comb.	9.59%	13.77%	11.29%	**13.89%**
Diversity Weighted Rank Comb.	**−9.30%**	−12.15%	−12.15%	−12.15%
(c) Performance Weighted Score Comb.	−0.36%	**11.39%**	9.73%	4.66%
Performance Weighted Rank Comb.	**−9.30%**	−12.15%	−12.15%	−12.15%

Table 2. Return on weighted average by recency approach AR

(II) Approach AR	Portfolio returns			
	10 stocks	20 stocks	30 stocks	40 stocks
(a) Average Score Comb.	15.36%	17.85%	23.90%	**25.06%**
Average Rank Comb.	**22.01%**	19.79%	20.57%	21.41%
(b) Diversity Weighted Score Comb.	**30.96%**	22.69%	22.53%	22.53%
Diversity Weighted Rank Comb.	**29.18%**	18.73%	23.74%	23.69%
(c) Performance Weighted Score Comb.	10.88%	9.38%	11.19%	**13.86%**
Performance Weighted Rank Comb.	22.01%	19.79%	23.09%	**24.62%**

(Table 2), rank combination performs better than score combination in 8 of the 12 cases ((a) 10 stocks, 20 stocks, (b) 30 stocks, 40 stocks and (c) 10, 20, 30, 40 stocks). This also demonstrates the power of the approach to compute the attribute scoring system using weighted average by recency (AR). Compare to the results by Irukulapati et al. ([7], Table 3), where they use only the average by time to score attribute system, but also use the sliding rule to select attributes, our results (Table 2) are better than that of Irukulapati et al. [7] in 4 out of the 6 cases ((a) rank comb, (b) score comb and rank comb, and (c) rank comb).

5   Conclusion and Future Work

In the paper, we propose a method to compute the attribute scoring system using weighted average by recency (AR) which gives more weight to the scores at the time closer to the present. After cleaning and removing the stocks with missing data, we reduce the US equity 3,000 stocks to 707 with 8 financial attributes. Two scoring methods to score the attributes are conducted: average across time (AT), and weighted average by recency (AR). Then an attribute selection process using sliding rules is conducted to select a set of five attributes for each of AT and AR. Six kinds of combination are conducted (rank comb and score comb for (a) average combination, (b) weighted comb using diversity strength, and (c) weighted comb using performance). We demonstrate, by market testing (Table 1 and Table 2 for AT and AR respectively), that our results are better than that of Irukulapati et al. [7] in four out of six cases (rank comb, score comb and rank comb, and rank comb). Our results also perform better than the Russell 2000 index.

Our work suggests several issues worthy of further study in the future. We list the following:

In the paper, we use average combination and weighted combination by diversity strength and performance. Some other method of combination such as mixed group rank (see [4]) may be used.

In the paper, we use the US Equity 3000 stocks and reduce, after cleaning and deleting the ones with missing data, to 707. We started with scoring each stock by 8 attributes. In the future, we may use a larger data sets with more attributes involved.

In the future work, we will consider different industry sectors in the attribute selection and combination process.

Similar to [9], we will consider various machine learning algorithms to select attributes and combine the selected attributes. Then combinatorial fusion using cognitive diversity will guide us when to combine and how to combine (by rank or by score) [4–6].

References

1. Abdelazim, A.H.Y., Wahba, K.: An artificial intelligence approach to portfolio selection and management. Int. J. Financ. Serv. Manag. (2006)
2. Damodaran, A.: Equity Risk Premiums (ERP): Determinants, Estimation and Implications – The 2018 Edition, 14 March 2018
3. Hsu, D.F., Chung, Y.S., Kristal, B.S.: Combinatorial fusion analysis: methods and practices of combining multiple scoring systems. In: Advanced Data Mining Technologies in Bioinformatics, pp. 32–62. Idea Group Inc. (2006)
4. Hsu, D.F., Kristal, B.S., Hao, Y., Schweikert, C.: Cognitive diversity: a measurement of dissimilarity between multiple scoring systems. J. Interconnect. Netw. **19**(1), 1–42 (2019)
5. Hsu, D.F., Kristal, B.S., Schweikert, C.: Rank-score characteristics (RSC) function and cognitive diversity. In: Yao, Y., Sun, R., Poggio, T., Liu, J., Zhong, N., Huang, J. (eds.) BI 2010. LNCS (LNAI), vol. 6334, pp. 42–54. Springer, Heidelberg (2010). https://doi.org/10.1007/978-3-642-15314-3_5
6. Hsu, D.F., Taksa, I.: Comparing rank and score combination methods for data fusion in information retrieval. Inf. Retr. **8**(3), 449–480 (2006)
7. Irukulapati, J., Hsu, D.F., Schweikert, C.: Long-term portfolio management using attribute selection and combinatorial fusion. In: ICCI*CC, pp. 593–599 (2018)
8. Leibowitz, M.L.: Franchise Value and the Price/Earnings Ratio. Research Foundation Books, vol. 1994, no 1, January 1994
9. Luo, Y., Kristal, B.S., Schweikert, C., Hsu, D.F.: Combining multiple algorithms for portfolio management using combinatorial fusion. In: IEEE ICCI*CC, pp. 361–366 (2017)
10. Nanda, S.R., Mahanty, B., Tiwari, M.K.: Clustering Indian stock market data for portfolio management. Expert Syst. Appl. **37**(12), 8793–8798 (2010)
11. Mesterharm, C., Hsu, D.F.: Combinatorial fusion with on-line learning algorithms. In: FUSION, pp. 1–8 (2008)
12. Trippi, R.R.: Artificial Intelligence in Finance and Investing: State-of-the-Art Technologies for Securities Selection and Portfolio Management. McGraw-Hill, Inc. New York (1995)

13. Vinod, H.D., Hsu, D.F., Tian, Y.: Combinatorial fusion for improving portfolio performance. Adv. Soc. Sci. Res. Using R **196**, 95–105 (2010)
14. Wiley Study Guide for 2017 Level 1 CFA Exam: Volume 3: Financial Reports and Analysis, 1st edn., pp. 41–132. Wiley, Hoboken (2017)
15. Yang, J.-M., Chen, Y.-F., Shen, T.-W., Kristal, B.S., Hsu, D.F.: Consensus scoring criteria for improving enrichment in virtual screening. J. Chem. Inf. Model. **45**(4), 1134–1146 (2005)

Exploiting Recommender Systems
in Collaborative Healthcare

Daniela D'Auria[1], Mouzhi Ge[2(✉)], and Fabio Persia[1]

[1] Faculty of Computer Science, Free University of Bozen-Bolzano, Bolzano, Italy
{daniela.dauria,fabio.persia}@unibz.it
[2] Faculty of Informatics, Masaryk University, Brno, Czech Republic
mouzhi.ge@muni.cz

Abstract. With the development of new medical auxiliaries such as virtual reality and surgery robotics, recommender systems are emerged to interact with the medical auxiliaries and support doctor's decisions and operations, especially in collaborative healthcare, recommender systems can interactively take into account the preferences and concerns from both patients and doctors. However, how to apply and integrate recommender systems is still not clear in collaborative healthcare. Therefore, from practical perspective this paper investigates the application of recommender systems in three typical collaborative healthcare domains, which are augmented/virtual reality, medicine and surgery robotics. The results not only provide the insights of how to integrate recommender systems with healthcare auxiliaries but also discuss the practical guidance of how to design recommender systems in collaborative healthcare.

Keywords: Recommender systems · Medical auxiliaries ·
Collaborative healthcare

1 Introduction

Collaborative healthcare systems enable the patients and doctors work together and output the diagnosis and treatment plan efficiently and effectively [1]. In the last years there has been a more and more common trend to exploit recommender systems to significantly improve the process in the context of collaborative healthcare systems. For instance, in [15] the authors propose a collaborative filtering recommender system to match patients with doctors in primary care; more specifically, they model patient trust in primary care doctors using a large-scale dataset of consultation histories, and account for the temporal dynamics of their relationships, defined in a novel quantitative measure of patient-doctor trust. Moreover, Casino et al. [6] propose a context-aware recommender system offering personalized recommendations of exercise routes to people according to their medical condition and real-time information from the smart city; the authors also carried out experiments on both a simulated dataset and real data, which were able to verify the system's usefulness. Additionally, the authors in

© Springer Nature Switzerland AG 2019
C. Esposito et al. (Eds.): I-SPAN 2019, CCIS 1080, pp. 71–82, 2019.
https://doi.org/10.1007/978-3-030-30143-9_6

[4] designed and developed a new-drug recommender system that is targeted at healthcare professionals across the world; more specifically, users can search for the available drug in the market. Those supportive recommendations for new similar drugs are presented to the user in the subsequent login sessions. Their proposed system uses the feature-based recommendation algorithm and the ratings provided by various users to deliver appropriate recommendations. It also effectively overcomes the cold-start problem by grouping similar users based on their areas of specialization.

Despite the recent efforts, there is still no guideline about how recommender systems can be exploited in a general way to significantly enhance the system performance in the collaborative healthcare context. Thus, this paper proposes a model to integrate recommender systems in collaborative healthcare and further investigates three typical healthcare domains - *augmented/virtual reality*, *medicine*, and *surgery robotics* - where recommender systems can support processes in the healthcare treatment, decision and operations. We also provide concrete real-world scenarios and discuss how to design recommender systems in collaborative healthcare as well as the related challenges.

The remainder of the paper is organized as follows. In the next section we describe the general recommender system and how to integrate recommender systems in collaborative healthcare, while in Sect. 3 we clarify the main role of recommendations in collaborative healthcare, with reference to the *augmented/virtual reality*, *medicine*, and *surgery robotics* domains. Eventually, Sect. 4 concludes the paper and outlines future research.

2   Recommender Systems and Collaborative Healthcare

A recommender system can be formally presented as a set of users $U = \{u_1, u_2, ..., u_i, ..., u_m\}$ and a set of objects $O = \{o_1, o_2, ..., o_j, ..., o_n\}$. The relations between O and U can be further presented as a matrix [14]. The size of O and U can be very large such as thousands or even millions of users and items [12]. For each element (u_i, o_j) in the O and U matrix, a recommender can compute a score $r_{i,j}$ that matches the expected interest of the user u_i to object o_j or the expected utility of object o_j for user u_i. however, since the user's preference may change over time, it is also important to take into account how users' preferences change with context e.g. based on a knowledge base. In order to formulate the recommendation problem, for user $u \in U$, the recommender system is to find a set of objects in O that can maximize the utility for u in a given context. For most of the recommender systems, the utility is simplified to a rating value that can be specified by the user, or the utility can be expressed by a profit function, which can be defined as how the configuration of O can be best satisfy U. The configuration is a combination of item feature. While each object in O is also associated with a set of features, for example, consider O as a set of movies, each movie can be represented by its title, genre, director, year of release, main actors, etc, each user in U can be related with a profile that includes different features, such as age, gender, income, and marital status.

The utility function in recommender system is usually defined as a subset of $U \times O$ [13]. Therefore, when the utility is specified as user ratings r, the critical problem is to extrapolate the value of r for each pair $(u, o) \in U \times O$. For example, in a movie recommender system, such as the one at *MovieLens.org*, users initially rate movies they have already seen, with ratings specified on a likert scale from 1 to 5, where 1 is "Awful" and 5 is "Must See". MovieLens then uses the ratings of the community to recommend other movies each user might be interested in or to predict how each user might rate a movie. Estimating unknown ratings from known ratings can be usually done in two ways: one way to use heuristics to model the utility function and empirically validating their performance, whereas the way aims at estimating the utility function that optimizes certain performance criteria, such as the mean square error. Once the unknown ratings are estimated, actual recommendations are made by selecting the top-rated items.

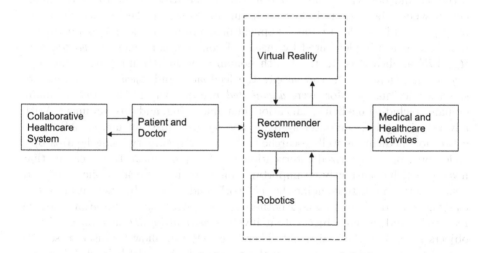

Fig. 1. Medical auxiliaries with recommender systems in collaborative healthcare

In order to show how recommender systems are positioned in collaborative healthcare, Fig. 1 describes the patient-doctor centered process of using collaborative healthcare systems. The initial collaborative healthcare systems are designed to facilitate the interactions between patient and doctors to carry out medical and healthcare activities. More recently, those activities are supported by different medical auxiliaries such as augmented/virtual reality or surgery robotics. Thus, the auxiliaries are developed between patient/doctors and their operations. One of the main goals of these auxiliaries is to provide decision support for patients and doctors, where recommender systems are used to interact with the medical auxiliaries and offer the patients and doctors with useful recommendations such as possible treatment plans. In this paper, we mainly focus on how recommender systems interact with the auxiliaries in collaborative healthcare.

3 Recommendations in Collaborative Healthcare

In this section we propose different domains where collaborative recommender systems can be effectively exploited to significantly improve the process or activities. More specifically, we identified *augmented/virtual reality, medicine,* and *surgery robotics* as interesting domains, quite unexplored from this perspective.

3.1 Augmented Reality/Virtual Reality

The initiative of using the computer and associated technologies in applications of the health area is extensively increasing. The essential features for the *medical 3D applications* are to generate presence sensations as follows: the first feature deals with the *3D objects* whose content of the virtual environment can dispose the images *similar to actual objects*, in relation to the colors, volumes, textures, activities and behaviors; the second feature is the *realistic control* of the interaction where the actions in the environments consider the physical behavior of objects and people. In these applications, *interaction* and *reaction* to the user actions are implemented by means of common equipment in *virtual reality (VR)* applications. In the health domain, the mostly used are *datagloves, haptic equipment,* which can supply the feedback, and *eyeglasses* to generate stereoscopic images. Moreover, *augmented reality (AR)* is also used in many domains including medicine, education, manufacturing, and entertainment. With advances in optics, computer systems, and surgical instruments, an AR application for medicine is well researched. Particularly, surgery using laparoscopy, endoscopy, or catheterized intervention has been significantly increased, that involves AR has currently an important role in many medical applications. AR denotes a technique to combine the real world and virtual objects that are artificially generated by computers. Another aspect of AR is the registration between real world and virtual objects, that involves *estimating 3D position* of virtual objects related to the real world. Therefore, AR can allow the user to see 3D virtual objects superimposed upon the real world. With the help of AR, a surgeon can see the hidden organs inside the body, and consequently improve the perception of treatment procedure by interacting with the real world.

While all these systems can help to make the best use of the cutting-edge technologies in our daily lives, meanwhile, they will also be exposing us to new *security threats*. As a result, there has been some augmented reality hack, in which attackers compromise the AR glasses or windshield to display non-existent content and lead doctors into making fatal mistakes. Moreover, when a doctor checks the patients' vital signs through an AR display, incorrect information can delay the immediate attention to a patient. AR can become an effective tool for deceiving users as one part of the social engineering scheme, since fake indications can misguide medical doctors into making mistakes.

Thus, *Virtual Reality (VR)* is more and more exploited in the last few years. Consequently, more brands are generating and even sharing different contents with VR, for instance, some of them are continuously generating and sharing VR content in real time on *social media*, such as Facebook or Instagram [18].

As a result, there is an increasing need for stable approaches on the one hand that can exploit VR in different domains as well as adaptable for the social media context; on the other hand, such approaches should still keep their *collaborative* features. For example, D'Auria et al. in [7,8] propose an interactive framework based on specialized sound. As a consequence, the authors designed and implemented a novel cloud application in the context of *cultural heritage*, where a personal guide was attracting the interest of tourists towards buildings or monuments, thus providing sound segments of augmented reality. More specifically, the developed system can interact with intelligent headphones; on the one hand, such headphones detect the orientation of the listener; on the other hand, it successfully produces an audio output, which intuitively takes into account the position and orientation of the listener in both indoor and outdoor environments. As a result, such novel headphones were designed and implemented in open-ear mode, with the aim of successfully identifying the user in the real-world context. Overall, we can deduce that the sharing of this framework in real time on a social media can be promising; in fact, being just connected to a social media, users from all around the world can easily observe how tourists interact with the environment and they might be more and more interested in the cultural heritage such as the monuments of a city.

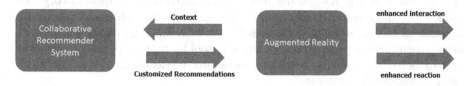

Fig. 2. Interaction between collaborative recommender system and augmented reality

Another scenario in the context of cultural heritage is given by the authors in [5]. They present a modular eye tracking system supporting art galleries fruition without diverting the attention of visitors. Thus, each time a visitor lingers on any detail of a painting, a hidden camera detects his/her gaze and the framework beams in real time the related illustrative contents on the wall region around it. As a result, the system developed in [5] significantly improves the gaze detection functionalities by means of an emotional analysis module. Since it is well-known that the pupil reflects the emotional arousal, the authors continuously check its size, with the aim to discover radius variations. As soon as the visitor completes the visit, the framework can effectively summarize the observed details and the emotional reactions in a report.

As shown in Fig. 2, recommender systems can enhance both the *interaction* of human beings with VR, and the effectiveness of the *reaction* of the augmented reality environment to the user inputs; this is achieved by grasping the context from the virtual environment, and providing it with customized recommendations.

In summary, recommender systems can be exploited to alleviate the issues mentioned in the beginning of this section, as an additional support to the collaborative approaches, for instance they could allow therapists and surgeons to automatically obtain all the patients' data crawled from social networks; on the other hand, recommender systems can quickly suggest data of interest for the context, such as patients' allergies or previous accidents. Additionally, the use of social networks will also allow us to exploit the efficient and effective techniques to identify potentially malicious attacks [2,3,17].

3.2   Medicine and Healthcare

In public health systems, there is not only an *information overload* problem, but also the one related to the fact that information comes from *different sources* and *formats*. Personal health record systems are meant to centralise and standardise an individual's health data and enhance the data sharing among authorised professionals or entities. Therefore, recent trends in research have focused on *health information retrieval*, and thus different approaches to health recommender systems can help the medical community. This system is a specialisation of a recommender system, where a recommendable item of interest is a piece of non-confidential, scientifically proven or at least generally accepted medical information, which in itself is not linked to an individual's medical history. We can identify those systems designed for different purposes such as a *diagnostic* or *educational tool* to assist physicians in the decision-making process when treating a patient or as a personal health advising tool for users, especially focused on healthy behavioural change, engaging users into physical activities or nutrition-based recommender systems.

People may present different conditions, and each of them will have different needs and interests. Thus, recommender systems ought to be able to determine these health conditions and which is the meaningful data from the patients' health record, in order to provide tailored, context-related, high-quality and trusted recommendations. Moreover, the development of recommender systems to predict the risk associated with individual diseases has been a topic of intensive research for some decades. Prediction should not only be accurate, however, but also helpful for physicians to define appropriate treatments and predict the risk to patients of undesirable outcomes. This is to assess individual patient risk, and to present that risk to patients in a personalized way with respect to their illnesses and possible undesirable outcomes of treatments. The motivation is to advise a consulting patient based on the medical records of patients with similar indications. Reasons to employ collaborative filtering techniques in searching medical databases are above all to *maximize* the *effectiveness* and *quality* of *medical care*. Collaborative filtering requires access to user profiles to identify user preferences and make recommendations. To transfer the recommender systems' methodology to medical applications, patients are identified with users, patterns containing data of medical histories, and physical examinations are identified with user profiles; additionally, for both users and patients a notion of similarity is employed, and patient diagnoses are identified with user ratings.

For instance, the authors of [11] provide a concrete example where collaborative approaches based on virtual reality could be potentially extended to the context of *medical domain*; in fact, they design and develop a low-cost system which exploits a haptic interface supported by a glove sensorized on the wrist; such a sensor on the glove allows the identification of the orientation of the wrist, with the aim to support patients during their wrist rehabilitation. Consequently, in this way, by exploiting virtual reality, the patient can perform some movements that are very helpful for his/her rehabilitation process; additionally, more specifically, by using the tracking of the wrist orientation, he/she can be trained and significantly supported to achieve different goals of increasing complexity. The extension of this application with the support of a smart collaborative recommender system can give a big contribution for making these games more and more interactive and educational for the communities of patients, medical doctors, and physiotherapists, especially for nursing complicated fractures, such as the compound fractures of the pelvis.

As a result, we can infer that the most extensive use of robotic technology for medical applications is in rehabilitation robotics, which traditionally includes assistive robots, prosthetics, orthotics, and therapeutic robots. Assistive robots provide greater independence to people with disabilities by helping them perform activities of daily living. For example, robot manipulators can assist individuals who have impaired arm or hand function with basic tasks, such as eating and drinking, or with vocational tasks, such as opening a filing cabinet. Assistive robotics also includes mobility aides such as wheelchairs and walkers with intelligent navigation and control systems, for individuals with impaired lower-limb function. Eventually, Fig. 3 shows an example of a medical robotic cyber physical system.

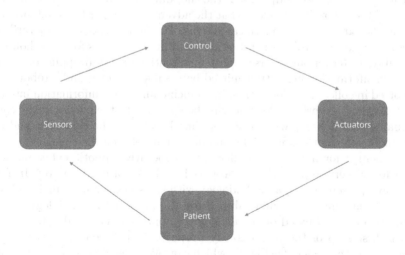

Fig. 3. Example of a medical robotic cyber physical system

In summary, knowledge-based systems have been critical in healthcare domains, as in most cases a first diagnosis screening is based on the gathered clinical data of the patient and the knowledge models. Data mining or ontology-based systems are two possible applications of artificial intelligence in this scope. The recommender system can base on a data mining system, using conditional probabilities to infer a recommendation or the design of a designed a pre-operative assessment decision support system also based on ontologies and on the patient's data, to deliver personalised reports, perform risk assessment and also clinical recommendations.

3.3 Surgery Robotics

In *medical robotics*, specifically in *surgery*, there is potential danger involved in the process of operating patients by instructing commands to robots. If there is no encryption or authentication mechanism driving the same, the system is prone to *"man in the middle" attacks*. The consequences may even cause that an unauthorized entity takes control of a surgical robot. These robots rely on available networks as well as temporary ad hoc wireless and satellite networks for transmitting sensitive information like video, audio and other sensory information between the surgeon and robots. Even though this technology has been contributing immensely to the medical world, the open and uncontrollable communication system encourages a variety of cyber security risks.

As most of the robots are governed by communication networks, they are highly *vulnerable* to *manipulation attacks*. A worm may be written to manipulate components in the robot and spread over the network without any human intervention. It is an attack wherein the adversary takes in control of the communication between two endpoints. If the endpoints were believed to be the controller and the robot, it is possible that the adversary disregards the intention of the controller and executes unethical actions. The hijacking may temporarily or permanently take control of the robot and disrupt the services for a few hours or irreversibly. Moreover, an adversary with an intention of eavesdropping or snooping on the information being transmitted between a controller and a robot, may be involved in collecting information, introducing unreliable information into the communication network, while appearing benign to both the parties at the ends. Eventually, an adversary who positions himself between the controller and the robot might intercept confidential communication between the ends.

An example for modeling an effective collaborative robotic cyber physical system for surgery applications is proposed by D'Auria et al. in [10]. In fact, the authors present a design methodology with the specific aim to make robotic surgery systems much less vulnerable. Since the proposed methodology is very flexible, generic, and based on a *collaborative* approach. This is due to the fact that the first step of the methodology proposed in [10] consists in collecting *patient/doctor requirements* (Fig. 4), which can take advantage of a social media structure. Additionally, on the other hand this first step could be easily supported by the use of *collaborative recommender systems*, that can continuously suggest the factors to be improved, based on the collected experience. More specifically, the proposed methodology begins with the analysis of a surgical scenario where all the patient/doctor requirements have to be inferred from. Examples of requirements collected via a collaborative approach are the *performance of a surgical task*, the *risk analysis*, the *patient safety distance*, the *alarm commands*, and the *control system*. Such requirements (that we can also consider as *indices*) are evaluated taking into account information collected both via *hardware* (thus, managing *sensor-level information*), and from some sophisticated software (for example, software managing complex vital information). As soon as an initial set of sensors is selected, the methodology looks for an optimized solution (the second step of the methodology in [10] involves the use of an *optimizer*) taking into account both the information collected via hardware/software, and all the requirements supported and processed via collaborative recommender systems. Then, the detected solution of the optimization algorithm is compared against the collected and analyzed specific requirements of the patient for the design of the collaborative robotic cyber physical system. Also this step is definitely essential, and can take an effective advantage of the *recommender systems*; in fact, both the new features to be integrated can significantly broaden the knowledge base, and, especially, eventually give the final suggestion to the designer about whether the initial patient/doctor requirements are met or not. In case the feedback given by the recommender system is negative (that means the optimized solution detected is not applicable), then the patient's requirements are updated accordingly. As a result, this cyclic model can be very accurate, since it aims at increasingly improve the first solution detected.

Use Case. Surgery Robotics significantly supports the surgeons during the surgical procedures. Such devices are very advantageous because they allow doctors to carry out major surgeries that are definitely much less invasive than traditional methods. They turn out to be much more precise and accurate in their methods. This allows for less recovery time and pain to the patient. With the use of these robots, the surgeon can potentially also perform the operation from across the room or even in a separate room.

Surgical robots, such as the *daVinci* by Intuitive Surgical Incorporated of Sunnyvale, CA, are being used for a growing number of surgeries. These robots allow surgeons to perform *Minimally Invasive Surgery (MIS)* by indirectly controlling MIS instruments using robotic manipulators. Thus, those next generation surgical robots will allow surgeons to perform robotic-based *MIS* remotely. Teleoperated surgical robots, or telesurgical robots, will allow highly trained medical personnel to provide skilled care from distant locations.

However, robotic surgical systems are definitely among the most complex medical cyber-physical systems. They allow to carry out minimally invasive procedures with better visualization and increased precision exploiting 3D magnified views of the surgical field and tele-manipulated arms and instruments that mimic human hand movements. As a consequence, past studies have emphasized the importance of security attacks in this field; attacks could take place, for instance,

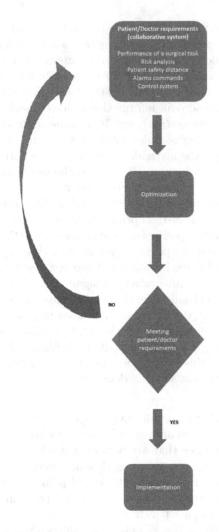

Fig. 4. A design methodology for the collaborative robotic healthcare system

on the network communication between the teleoperation console and the control system of a surgical robot.

For instance, one potential scenario in that context consists in a device getting a virus; that might cause an injury to a patient, and consequently it might happen as follows: (1) the robot cuts through a major artery during a minor surgery; (2) the patient gets too much insulin due to an insulin pump getting hacked; (3) the information about the hacked could not get through to the monitor; then it may lead to serious injury to the patient and even death. Moreover, there is the possibility of "a tablet being stolen from a traveling hospice nurse" or "data being transferred lead to the loss of sensitive data". One critical risk is that if a medical robot gets hacked while it is performing a surgery on a patient in the hospital, and the hacker begins taking over the operation. Finally, another risk is if a virus gets in the network, and shuts all the devices down while in the middle of surgery. Thus, these remarks about the vulnerability of robotic surgery systems allow us to understand how relevant the use of cyber physical systems, supported by collaborative recommender systems, is in this context.

In summary, collaborative recommender systems can be very helpful in this context for different reasons: first, because they can for instance immediately suggest how to carry out specific emergency procedures as soon as a robot makes a mistakes [8,9,16]; then, because they can help designers develop stable and effective robotic cyber physical systems for surgery application.

4   Conclusions

In this paper, we have proposed a new process model of integrating medical auxiliaries such as virtual reality and surgery robotics into collaborative health-care, where recommender systems and different medical auxiliaries are considered as a component to support and facilitate collaborative healthcare systems and medical activities. In order to demonstrate how to use recommender systems within healthcare auxiliary domains, we have chosen three typical collaborative healthcare application domains - augmented/virtual reality, medicine and surgery robotics, and investigated the interactions between recommedner systems and each of the selected domains. This paper has shown that how recommender systems can be integrated with healthcare auxiliaries collaborative healthcare. Also, as healthcare auxiliaries are still emerging technologies, this paper has discussed the practical guidance of how to design recommender systems in augmented/virtual reality, medicine and surgery robotics.

As future works, we plan to further formally refine the integration model and specify the exact interactions between recommender systems and auxiliaries. Further, the effectiveness of this model can be further tested by developing a real-world recommender system prototype by taking collaborative healthcare scenario into account.

References

1. Esposito, C., Ciampi, M., De Pietro, G.: An event-based notification approach for the delivery of patient medical information. Inf. Syst. **39**, 22–44 (2014)
2. Amato, F., Santo, A., Moscato, V., Persia, F., Picariello, A.: Detecting unexplained human behaviors in social networks, pp. 143–150 (2014)
3. Amato, F., et al.: Multimedia story creation on social networks. Future Gener. Comput. Syst. **86**, 412–420 (2018)
4. Bhat, S., Aishwarya, K.: Item-based hybrid recommender system for newly marketed pharmaceutical drugs. In: 2013 International Conference on Advances in Computing, Communications and Informatics, pp. 2107–2111 (2013)
5. Calandra, D., Di Mauro, D., D'Auria, D., Cutugno, F.: An emotional eye tracker for cultural heritage support, vol. 11, pp. 161–172 (2016). Cited by 9

6. Casino, F., Patsakis, C., Batista, E., Borràs, F., Martínez-Ballesté, A.: Healthy routes in the smart city: a context-aware mobile recommender. IEEE Softw. **34**(6), 42–47 (2017)

7. D'Auria, D., Di Mauro, D., Calandra, D.M., Cutugno, F.: Caruso: interactive headphones for a dynamic 3d audio application in the cultural heritage context. In: Proceedings of the 2014 IEEE 15th International Conference on Information Reuse and Integration (IEEE IRI 2014), pp. 525–528, August 2014

8. D'Auria, D., Di Mauro, D., Calandra, D., Cutugno, F.: A 3d audio augmented reality system for a cultural heritage management and fruition. J. Digit. Inf. Manag. **13**(4), 203–209 (2015)

9. D'Auria, D., Persia, F.: Automatic evaluation of medical doctors' performances while using a cricothyrotomy simulator. In: Proceedings of the 2014 IEEE 15th International Conference on Information Reuse and Integration, pp. 514–519 (2014)

10. D'Auria, D., Persia, F.: A collaborative robotic cyber physical system for surgery applications. In: 2017 IEEE International Conference on Information Reuse and Integration (IRI), pp. 79–83, August 2017

11. DAuria, D., Persia, F., Siciliano, B.: Human-computer interaction in healthcare: How to support patients during their wrist rehabilitation. In: 2016 IEEE Tenth International Conference on Semantic Computing (ICSC), pp. 325–328, February 2016

12. Ge, M., Persia, F.: A survey of multimedia recommender systems: challenges and opportunities. Int. J. Semantic Comput. **11**(3), 411 (2017)

13. Ge, M., Persia, F.: A generalized evaluation framework for multimedia recommender systems. Int. J. Semantic Comput. **12**(4), 541–557 (2018)

14. Gedikli, F., Bagdat, F., Ge, M., Jannach, D.: RF-REC: fast and accurate computation of recommendations based on rating frequencies. In: 13th IEEE Conference on Commerce and Enterprise Computing, CEC 2011, Luxembourg-Kirchberg, Luxembourg, 5–7 September 2011, pp. 50–57 (2011)

15. Han, Q., de Rituerto de Troya, M., Ji, M., Gaur, M., Zejnilovic, L.: A collaborative filtering recommender system in primary care: towards a trusting patient-doctor relationship. In: 2018 IEEE International Conference on Healthcare Informatics (ICHI), pp. 377–379, June 2018

16. Persia, F., D'Auria, D.: An application for finding expected activities in medical context scientific databases. In: 22nd Italian Symposium on Advanced Database Systems, pp. 77–88 (2014)

17. Persia, F., Helmer, S.: A framework for high-level event detection in a social network context via an extension of iseql. In: 2018 IEEE 12th International Conference on Semantic Computing, pp. 140–147 (2018)

18. Persia, F., Ge, M., D'Auria, D.: How to exploit recommender systems in social media. In: 2018 IEEE International Conference on Information Reuse and Integration, IRI 2018, Salt Lake City, UT, USA, 6–9 July 2018, pp. 537–541 (2018)

Advanced Methods to Extract Value from Scientific Datasets

Lucian Perju[1], Marius-Dorian Nicolaescu[1,2], Florin Pop[1,3(✉)],
Ciprian Dobre[1,3], and Sanda Maiduc[1]

[1] University Politehnica of Bucharest, Bucharest, Romania
lucianprj@gmail.com, {florin.pop,ciprian.dobre}@cs.pub.ro
[2] Executive Unit for Financing Higher Education, Research, Development and
Innovation (UEFISCDI), Bucharest, Romania
marius.nicolaescu@uefiscdi.ro
[3] National Institute for Research and Development in Informatics (ICI) Bucharest,
Bucharest, Romania
{florin.pop,ciprian.dobre}@ici.ro

Abstract. In these days the scientific community is times bigger comparing with the previous centuries. The need of powerful tools to aggregate and analyse the information about articles, books and other publications becomes greater with each published paper. In this paper we describe a solution for understanding and leveraging this data. The platform integrates the following requirements: data aggregation, data analysis (visualizations, dashboards, graphs), complex and simple searches, and support for data export. The platform brings value to its users due to various reasons such as quick identification of relevant data and in depth analysis on the provided input. Another key feature is the granularity, application being easily configurable for rigorous use cases: just one author, a group of authors or an entire scientific field.

Keywords: Data analysis · Data aggregation · Data retrival · Big Data · Elastic Search · Containerization

1 Introduction

The scientific community can be seen as a wide network composed of researchers, no matter their field of study: biophysics, cell biology, medicine, computer science and others [8]. The members are expected to give objective results and through their solutions push the humanity forward. Those fields are not separated, and interdisciplinary research is a common process which can be found these days.

The research presented in this paper is supported by the following projects: CRESCDI (25PFE/17.10.2018), StorEdge (GNaC 2018 ARUT - AU11-18-07), ROBIN (PN-III-P1-1.2-PCCDI-2017-0734), NETIO ForestMon/Tel-MONAER (53/05.09.2016, SMIS2014+ 105976), SPERO (PN-III-P2-2.1-SOL-2016-03-0046, 3Sol/2017) and UAV (1SOL/2017). We would like to thank the reviewers for their time and expertise, constructive comments and valuable insight.

ⓒ Springer Nature Switzerland AG 2019
C. Esposito et al. (Eds.): I-SPAN 2019, CCIS 1080, pp. 83–95, 2019.
https://doi.org/10.1007/978-3-030-30143-9_7

David Cahan said in 2003 that the modern scientific community emerged in the 19th century because the professionalization of science occurred: there has been for the first time a clear separation of sciences and people could say that they were scientists and felt as being part of a bigger image [2].

The progress of the scientific community is growing every year and the related publications tend to do the same thing. If in the beginnings there was not much information to start from, in the present, by virtue of the fast-increasing community and the internet support there is a great quantity of articles and research for any possible domain.

Even though this brings a lot of value to each researcher, looking for the right information can easily become a great issue considering the numerous data sources. Another problem is tracking the progress and how it is correlated with the work belonging to other scientists. Having many possible data sources, aggregating them rapidly becomes a burden for a person if it has to do this work manually.

A platform which has the capabilities of storing scientific data, analysing it and creating the means of exporting relevant parts of it would greatly improve the process of correlating the work of different researchers.

Based on the motivation, we would like to create a system which is capable of aggregating information or metadata about scientific work, no matter if we talk about an article, a book or a patent, briefly: anything that can be cited and can be used by a scientist while searching for information and tracing his or others work. The platform must integrate the following requirements: data aggregation; data analysis (visualizations, dashboards, graphs); complex and simple searches; and support for data export.

Another objective for data analysis is the customization flexibility. We would like to have the means for using the stored data at its full capacity in order to extract value from it. Standard visualizations and graphs bring value but keep it on low levels because the data is not used at its maximum potential.

The application is designed to handle the need of granular analysis of scientific papers. There are several use cases which provide reasons for such an objective: one user would like to analyse only his data, a group of researchers wants to see how the work of each individual is correlated, a university needs to track its progress or even an entire country may be interested in the local research. The application can be expanded further to bigger use cases such as entire continents, or why not, a global solution.

Data reduction capabilities are a mandatory requirement if we want to easily aggregate the data. The tools used to actually implement this should to be able to do such a thing, because we want to focus on the results. The results must be accurate, with as little as possible, preferably none, altered data.

When it comes to possible data sources, the application should have a versatile approach by supporting different file formats. The actual input may come from sources such as Google Scholar, DBLP, ORCID, ISI Clarivate and others like them [7]. Another important source of information which can be indexed and analysed comes directly from the user who wants to write its own files in a standard format.

Our personal contributions are the designing and the implementation of a platform which supports the following operations on scientific metadata: analysing, indexing, searching both with complex and simple queries, visualizing important connections using a graph and the possibility of creating custom visualizations and dashboards. It was designed with some key features: *modularity*, because we may want to add another file format which has to be processed and analysed; *fault tolerance*, we don't want to lose any important information; *ease of use* with intuitive graphical interfaces; *in-depth and accurate analysis* of existing data.

In the following sections we first analyse the existing solutions which have similar capabilities with the objective we are pursuing. We also get a glimpse of possible data sources and what technologies may fit with this task. After that an abstract architecture is analysed and how the process of its implementation went. Finally, we see how it behaves on different kinds of input and the generated results based on those.

2   Related Work

When we talk about data sources in the context of scientific publication, we can easily conclude that there are many possibilities to choose from, all of them with strong and weak points. Usually, most of them have approximately the same information but also something which makes them stand in front of the others. In this chapter we are going to describe few of them, analysing their key points [3].

In order to easily analyse and search for articles, all we need is a standard file format. Generally, when we search information for scientific papers, we are more interested in metadata associated with it, having attributes such as: the author, the title, where it was published, when it was published, maybe some keywords. If we had to search through the entire articles to find the desired information, we would need a lot of computing power and much time to spend waiting for the results. Another reason is the recognition of your community: the citations must be somehow structured and easy to read. Because all of the previously described reasons, the scientific community felt that there must be something faster and easier to comprehend [6].

There isn't just one accepted file format because each citations aggregator may define its own format, based on the scientific field they work and their needs. For example, a *.bib file has an associated unique entry key and all the data is saved as key-value pairs [9].

When working with different data sets which we would like to aggregate, we can certainly say that some challenges will occur. One of them is the ambiguity: even if we want to analyse the same article, but data is provided from different sources, the names for example may be different. The order of the first and last name may be different, they can also be in uppercase or in lowercase, and even more challenging when the same author has multiple names. If this is the case, we can talk about middle names and the first letter of their father's name.

Solution	Account needed	Semantic search	Customized search	Graph	Custom visualization	Export data
Google Scholar	No - analyse articles Yes - add articles	Yes	Advanced filtering	No	No	BibTex and others
Microsoft Research	No - analyse articles Yes - add articles	Yes	Advanced filtering	Correlations between relevant data	Yes	BibTex and others
AMiner	No - analyse articles Yes - add articles	Yes	No	No	No	BibTex and others
Web of Science	Yes - analyse articles Yes - add articles	Yes	Advanced filtering	No	No	BibTex and others
Brain Map	No - analyse articles Yes - add articles	No	No	No	No	No
Publish or Perish	No - analyse articles Yes - add articles	No	Advanced filtering	No	No	CSV and others
Our Solution	No - analyse articles No - add articles	No	Advanced filtering	Correlations between relevant data	Yes	CSV

Fig. 1. Summarized analysis of similar solutions.

The notation may be different if in one article they used their name shortened as for example just the first letter of their first name or maybe they used dashes and dots in their names. Sometimes, the processed input by an online data set aggregator may be not quite precise [11, 12]. It happens that an article wrote for example in 2015 to appear saved as wrote in 2016.

Another problem is the existence of wrong entries. Based on their names, a data aggregator may think that some articles belong to someone else. Usually, in order to solve such problems, the actual author or another person who finds out that the data source sustains he is the writer of some articles which do not belong to him, the person in case has to write an email to those who maintain the data set and let them know that there are some wrong entries. After that, those who are in charge of the data set must edit the wrong entries and ensure that everything is right. As it sounds, this process is very time consuming and unpleasant.

At this very moment we can find on the internet other solutions which have the same mindset as ours. We want to get a glimpse of their functionality and usability, so we defined a set of metrics to be used while doing this comparison. Those are based on our needs, matters as possibility to search, visualize, aggregate and export data as in the following:

– the user should create an account;
– semantic search;

- customised search - simple or advanced;
- visualize data - graph based;
- visualize data - qualitative and quantitative approach;
- export data.

We present in Fig. 1 an analysis of the most used online solutions. Our target is a platform which contains most of them and why not some additional features, such as classifying entries based on their geographical region, no matter if we talk about a city, a country or an entire continent.

The solution is designed to support all of these, given the fact that it can be instantiated in any university, company, city or country. It can export data in an user-friendly format as CSV, it can create custom visualizations, dashboards and graphs. Another important aspect is that it gives the power to those who are really interested in it because everything can be easily monitored either through an interface or logs.

3   Proposed Architecture

3.1   General View

The abstract architecture presented in Fig. 2 has the main purpose to give an insight over data about scientific papers and books, as seen from the following perspectives: a single user who is interested in correlating his work, a university who wants to have a local database with the articles of its researchers, a country which wants to analyse the national progress in science and other use cases like those mentioned earlier. Its main purpose is to give to users the correct output, in depth analysis of their data, a way to export in a friendly format the entries which may be of interest, all of this while being fault tolerant and capable of integrating new modules without lots of effort. The user will have access to the following features: uploading its files, seeing a graph of his work correlated with the one of his peers, export his data and analyse it using different custom visualizations and dashboards. The administrators will be capable of monitoring each piece of the architecture, either through an interface or a logging system [10].

3.2   Components Description

User Input. This component is part of the user interface. The user can upload his files here and if he wants to get a notification when his data is ready to be explored, he can give an email address. There are important aspects which have to be acknowledged: the interface must be responsive, in order to be usable in different environments such as: desktop browsers, mobile phones, tablets; the interface has to be clean and easy to understand; it also must ensure that if the user uploaded a wrong file, the work done in order to fix the error is as small as possible.

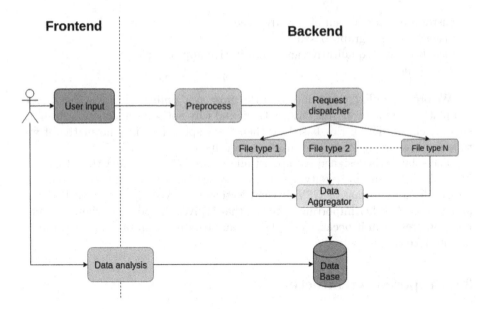

Fig. 2. Abstract architecture of the proposed platform.

Pre-process. This step checks if the input is correct based on the metadata associated with the request. The application can process only some file types, so if we want to be sure that no further effort is given for a request which will not give value, it will be dropped at this step. The request should have attached at least one file with a valid file type and the size of each file should be greater than zero. If one of the previous rules is not matched, the sender is going to know about his input problems and will receive an error message as response. Otherwise, he will receive a success code. If an email address was provided, a message is going to be sent when the data is ready. After the input was pre-processed and all the sanity checks were passed, the request will be forwarded to the request dispatcher.

Request Dispatcher. This component acknowledges the existence of all allowed file types. When it receives a request, it checks the type of the attached data. The request is sent to the processor specialized with that file type. The request dispatcher must contain a mapping of file types to servers. This should be easy to edit, in order to make sure that if one processor host changes or if there are going to be added or removed file types, the administrator can do this without modifying the structure of the request dispatcher. One of the most important aspects of this application is the modularity. As time passes, there are going to be new accepted formats associated with scientific data. This means that some of the older ones may disappear and the application should be able to handle such events.

Processing of Allowed File Types. For each accepted file type there is a separate processing unit. This processing unit must ensure that it implements a best effort policy. Even though the received file has the right type and is non zero sized, there may be some malformed entries. A malformed entry can mean anything from being un-parsable to not having some mandatory fields. Those are the title and the author name. There can also be fields which are not allowed, such as abstract. Given the purpose of the application, some of them will not bring any value to the final result. Another target of the parser is normalizing the data. There may be older and newer entries of the same file type. Some of the fields, even if they mean the same thing, have different names. This is inner normalization, the processes of ensuring the consistency of naming conventions of the same file type fields. Another type normalization is outer normalization. If inner normalization meant that the same format should always use always same naming conventions, outer normalization takes care of the final result which is actually indexed. There is a set of final allowed fields, such as: author, author-email, booktitle, title, journal, year, doi.

Each processor must guarantee that its final output will be in compliance with the global defined schema. After it processed each entry and normalized it, the result is going to be a JSON. There is going to be a mapping one to one: raw entry to JSON output. This applies only to correct inputs. Malformed ones are going to be dropped and the event will be logged in order to be analysed be an administrator and see if there any further actions to take.

This processor must be able to work with a messaging queue compliant technology. The question is now why we would need a messaging queue protocol. The answer is straightforward: later in the processing the time will increase considerably and we do not want to miss any processed information. A messaging queue will work like a buffer for parsed entries.

Data Aggregator. Data aggregator is a subsystem which ensures that there aren't duplicates in the final result and different entries associated with the same scientific paper of the same author will be merged in a single entry which contains all the known information. The actual processor is the Aggregator/Indexer. Parsed entries come from the messaging queue and everything starts with de-normalizing of data. A scientific paper may have multiple authors, so for each author the associated entry is going to be cloned. Now, each entry has just one author. Using the title of the article and the author name, an algorithm generates an unique key which will be used to search in the cache. The same key is going to be used to index later in the database. The cache is queried using that key, and, if there is not any match, the entry is indexed as it is in the database.

If there is a match it means that there are information's indexed in database about the same combination of author name and article title. The aggregator queries the database and fetches the data found with the previously calculated unique key. It checks content both on the already saved data and what we are processing at the very moment. If there is additional data, it will be added to the old data. An interesting thing is that some fields are of interest even though they exist in both entries: an article may have been presented in many conferences, it can be part of a book, so all this data must be kept. After the processing is finished, the improved entry is indexed with the same unique key.

Data Storage. The database is concerned with keeping the data safe for a long time, to answer queries as fast as possible, no matter what type of search is needed: a simple one or a complex one such as filtering. It is able to make aggregations of data based on different metrics. It is also capable to work very well with data which does not necessarily have the same structure all the time.

Data Analysis. The data analysis is part of the user interface component. In order to have the possibility to analyse and export data there must be a visual way to do that. Data analysis consists of two parts: what the user actually can see and the querier which handles the requests and brings to the frontend data which can be easily presented and understood. The user can filter all the data. He can select for which years he wants to visualize his scientific work, or the titles. It can also select a title of an article and see who the other authors were, if there were any. Finally, he can export all this data in a user-friendly format, such as CSV.

Another thing which data analysis offers a graph view of the data is. We can see how different authors worked together for articles, how they are connected. We can also see in what years they published the most articles, how many each year, with whom they collaborated in the past.

3.3   Workflow

The user must collect its interest files from different data sources such as Google Scholar, ORCID, ResearchGate and other as these. It can also write his own files, as long as the file type and content respects the application rules. It uploads files and writes its email address if he wants to be notified when the data is ready to be explored.

Now, the files are sent to the preprocessing unit, which takes care of the file type correctness and the size limits. The files are still untouched, all the information which exists right now is that the format and the file type are correct.

The request dispatcher will forward the request to the associated file type. Each file type processing unit will take care of all the conditions described earlier in this chapter and send the parsed entries to a messaging queue.

The aggregator will see that there are new entries on the messaging queue and will start to process them. It will check if they have been seen before and handle them accordingly. If it is the first time an entry was seen, it will be indexed, otherwise all the relevant information will be aggregated from the processed entry and from the one found in the database.

Until this point the user must have received his notification email. He now can go and analyse his data: applying filters, selecting years of interest, seeing his collaboration graph. If he wants to save some of the filtered data, he can export it as CSV.

4   Implementation Details

Figure 3 is a detailed schema of the backend architecture. Each component is going to be presented and where problems occurred, we will provide further explanations.

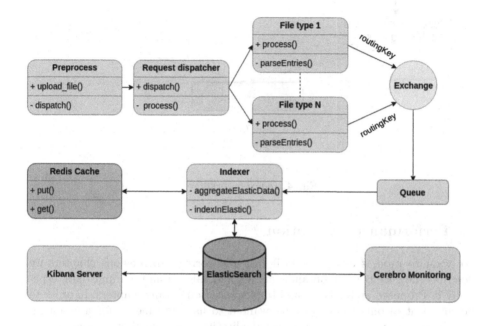

Fig. 3. Detailed architecture and implementation solutions.

The most important component is the Indexer that is subscribed to RabbitMQ with a routing key and each time there is new message on the queue, it will start to process it. Given the fact that an article may have several authors, for each author the entry is going to be replicated. After this step, based on author's name and article's title we create a unique key using the MD5 algorithm. Its workflow can be seen in Fig. 4.

Now we can see the crucial importance of Redis. We want to aggregate as much as possible information about articles and different data sources may have different field of interest for us. We want our final data to be as complete as possible. Redis will keep information about previously processed entries and based on them we will know if we have to aggregate the currently processed data with data already existent in the database. Some may say that caching was not mandatory, and it brings complexity without a legit purpose. This is not true because when indexing a lot of data, if we queried for each new entry the load on ElasticSearch would rapidly become tremendous. Caching will assure us that users who want to query their data will not encounter delayed responses and unresponsive services.

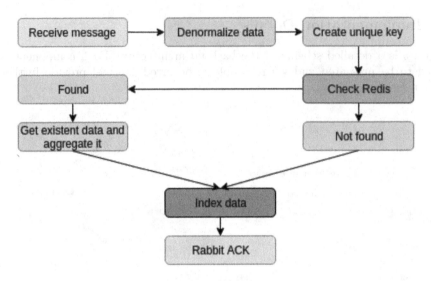

Fig. 4. Indexer workflow.

5   Performance Evaluation

We want to process data and do it fast and correct. In previous chapters we described how we tried to obtain accuracy and value from the input data, especially in Proposed architecture and Implementation details chapters. In order to be confident in our application, we wanted to have the means for a quantitative analysis of performance, not just qualitative. We are going to separate the benchmarking in the following categories: ElasticSearch performance, RabbitMQ performance and web page rendering.

In order to evaluate ElasticSearch we used the monitoring plugin offered by Kibana [5]. The index where our data is stored is called articles. The analysis will be focused on the events which are correlated with operations on this index: creating and searching documents.

Figure 5 represents the indexing rate in ElasticSearch when there is a bulk of entries. We can see the fast indexing rate, but we will see later in this chapter that is much lower than the RabbitMQ indexing rate, hence the reasons for buffering. Indexing happens sporadically and we are more interested in the search and aggregation capabilities of Elasticsearch, because we want a platform which is designed for analysing the data, not just for storage purposes.

Figure 6 shows a window of 15 min while we had 2 periods when we generated bulks of read requests. The first period had approximately 150 requests and the second one over 300. We can see that ElasticSearch gave us fast responses to our queries [4]. RabbitMQ acts like a buffer for us: the file type processors are the producers and the indexer is the consumer. Usually, were there aren't many messages to process the waiting queue doesn't store any messages and sends them directly to the Indexer. In order to try the maximum capacity, we assumed that

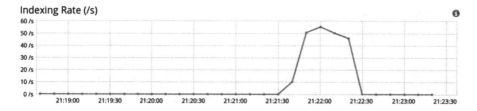

Fig. 5. ElasticSearch index rate.

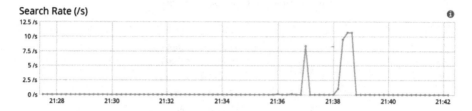

Fig. 6. ElasticSearch read rate.

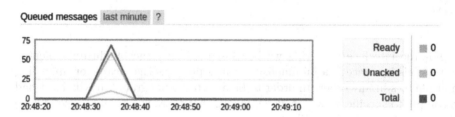

Fig. 7. RabbitMQ queued messages.

a normal user will upload at most 5 to 10 files at a time with approximately 100 entries each. We also tried to push this limitation and considered there are several users who are doing exactly the same thing.

The Fig. 7 shows as how many messages are actually queued because they couldn't be processed in real time by the Indexer. We can see that at peak, there are at most 70 to 75 messages waiting to be processed. Another thing revealed by this figure is the fact that the application works in spikes when it comes to indexing, because there are going to be much more people who want to analyse the existent data than those who upload information. In order to better present the spikes which appear during the processing we will provide the next figure.

In Fig. 8 we can observe the processing spikes which appear because of two main reasons: the first one is the processing power before a message actually appears in RabbitMQ because this is related to the upload speed and parsing. The other reason is the Indexer, it has to check the cache and index the data. We consider that the parsing power of the architecture can be seen in the two previous graphics, due to the direct correlation of parsing and pushing to the queue and fetching from RabbitMQ to index data [1].

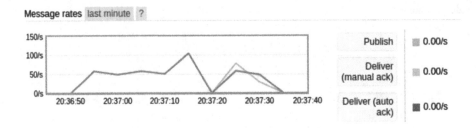

Fig. 8. Indexer processing spikes.

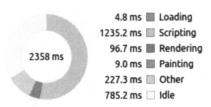

Fig. 9. Kibana plugin loading statistics for application startup (without Kibana deployment).

For the interface rendering we benchmarked only the plugin implemented by us. This interface is a minimalist one and provides the means for uploading multiple files in any order. In order to be able to be integrated in Kibana it had to comply to specific structure which means that there is actually backend code which is integrated in the Kibana server.

Figure 9 lets us now that most of the relevant loading time is spent scripting, process which presumes two things: one part of the scripting is done for the Kibana parts and the other one for our plugin. We can see that other relevant times are those spent for rendering, painting and Other operations. We ignored the others because their order size is much smaller.

6   Conclusion

We understood that the number of published articles grows faster each year and correlating them without any support from an automated solution can easily become a burden for any researcher. We analysed the common needs of a scientist encountered during the research process and brought to life a platform which has the capabilities to make its exploration easier.

We investigated different existing solutions and technologies, and based on those we designed a platform which can do complex searches, customized dashboards and visualizations. It also gives the possibility of correlating the existing data in a graph, feature which can make the users aware of how their work is related to other people's work. We gave a versatile solution which can be easily used by a single user, a group of researchers or why not, by an entire scientific field.

In the future we would like to introduce semantic search in order to reduce even more the efforts of any researcher who is interested in leveraging his work. This type of search will give better results for any researcher because it is context aware and makes in depth correlations of data, things such as what are the most popular articles for specific keywords, how the work of the current author is related and others.

References

1. Boschi, S., Santomaggio, G.: RabbitMQ Cookbook. Packt Publishing Ltd., Birmingham (2013)
2. Cahan, D.: Institutions and Communities. University of Chicago Press, Chicago (2003)
3. Custura, A.M., Bajenaru, L., Pop, F.: An automatic method for the analysis of scientific literature collection. Stud. Inform. Control **27**(4), 423–430 (2018)
4. Gormley, C., Tong, Z.: Elasticsearch: The Definitive Guide: A Distributed Real-time Search and Analytics Engine. O'Reilly Media, Inc., Sebastopol (2015)
5. Gupta, Y.: Kibana Essentials. Packt Publishing Ltd., Birmingham (2015)
6. Ifrim, C., Iuga, I., Pop, F., Wallace, M., Poulopoulos, V.: Data reduction techniques applied on automatic identification system data. In: Szymański, J., Velegrakis, Y. (eds.) IKC 2017. LNCS, vol. 10546, pp. 14–19. Springer, Cham (2018). https://doi.org/10.1007/978-3-319-74497-1_2
7. Ifrim, C., Pop, F., Mocanu, M., Cristea, V.: AgileDBLP: a search-based mobile application for structured digital libraries. In: Cardoso, J., Guerra, F., Houben, G.-J., Pinto, A.M., Velegrakis, Y. (eds.) KEYSTONE 2015. LNCS, vol. 9398, pp. 88–93. Springer, Cham (2015). https://doi.org/10.1007/978-3-319-27932-9_8
8. Kornfeld, W.A., Hewitt, C.E.: The scientific community metaphor. IEEE Trans. Syst. Man Cybern. **11**(1), 24–33 (1981)
9. Koulouri, X., Ifrim, C., Wallace, M., Pop, F.: Making sense of citations. In: Calì, A., Gorgan, D., Ugarte, M. (eds.) KEYSTONE 2016. LNCS, vol. 10151, pp. 139–149. Springer, Cham (2017). https://doi.org/10.1007/978-3-319-53640-8_12
10. Sanders, G.L., Shin, S.: Denormalization effects on performance of RDBMS. In: Proceedings of the 34th Annual Hawaii International Conference on System Sciences, p. 9. IEEE (2001)
11. Serbanescu, V., Pop, F., Cristea, V., Antoniu, G.: A formal method for rule analysis and validation in distributed data aggregation service. World Wide Web **18**(6), 1717–1736 (2015)
12. Talaş, A., Pop, F., Neagu, G.: Elastic stack in action for smart cities: making sense of big data. In: 2017 13th IEEE International Conference on Intelligent Computer Communication and Processing (ICCP), pp. 469–476. IEEE (2017)

A Business Reputation Methodology Using Social Network Analysis

Antonio Galli, Michela Gravina, Vincenzo Moscato, Antonio Picariello, Carlo Sansone, and Giancarlo Sperlí[✉]

University of Naples "Federico II", Via Claudio 21, Naples, Italy
{anto.galli,mi.gravina}@studenti.unina.it,
{antonio.picariello,carlo.sansone,giancarlo.sperli}@unina.it

Abstract. Nowadays, every facet of people's lifestyle is impacted by the continuous use of technologies and in particular the Internet. Social interactions have been radically changed since new technologies have removed communication barriers. The obstacles of time and space have been overcome, letting people from different places and cultures communicate. People tend to become part of a dense social network, where the distribution of information becomes an almost immediate process. This is the reason why companies, public institutions and business activities have opted for social networks as communication medium. As a consequence, people seem to incorporate information gained from the social networks into their decision-making processes.

In this paper we analyze how *what is said* in the social network could influence people's decisions. As social network, we consider YELP community, that is a user generated content platform based on 'word of mouth', in which users can share their opinions about news, product, community, businesses. We propose a methodology for reviews analysis with the aim to compute business attractiveness, combining user's sentiment and business reputation.

Our results show that reviews analysis should be performed because it may provide useful information to monitor how business public opinion changes over time.

Keywords: Natural language processing · Sentiment analysis · Social network analysis

1 Introduction

The proliferation of technology, especially the widespread use of the Internet, has completely changed people's life letting to overcome the obstacles of time and space. Undoubtedly, the major impact has been on social life where connections between people from different places and cultures have been made possible. As a consequence, people become part of a dense social network, encouraging the transfer and sharing of information. The development of technology has, then, enhanced OSN features, enabling users to share their life by describing

© Springer Nature Switzerland AG 2019
C. Esposito et al. (Eds.): I-SPAN 2019, CCIS 1080, pp. 96–106, 2019.
https://doi.org/10.1007/978-3-030-30143-9_8

multimedia content (text, audio, video, images) and interacting with such objects in order to provide feedback or comments or feelings compared to them. In the last years, several OSNs (such as Facebook, Twitter, and so on) provide several features to share and interact with multimedia contents (audio, video, images, texts). Social networks like Facebook are designed for social interaction, while others such as Flickr are designed for content sharing services, allowing people to improve their social connections. The analysis of these heterogeneous data assumes a key role for many companies. On one hand it represents the lifeblood for this company on other hand managing these information becomes more difficult. To gather knowledge from these raw data requires a new approach that involves the Big Data and related technologies. In fact using a simple 'click', it is possible to know people's thoughts, opinions, to send and receive messages, keeping in touch with anyone you want. This is the incredible power that has made businesses exploit social networks for marketing, advertising and for being more easily connected to their customers. In fact, it implies that it is easy to be 'influenced' by the others if the majority of people shares the same idea or if somebody who is well known in the network (the so called influencer) expresses an opinion about a topic, such as a business object. In this way, people's thought about a topic could be the result of what is extracted from the network.

In this paper we analyze the power of social networks, considering what people think about businesses. In particular we take into account people's reviews in order to evaluate a business reputation, that is its *public opinion*. In our opinion, reviews analysis can be useful to a business owner for realizing activities aimed at improving the performed services and for 'having a look' of what people think, getting an immediate feedback. Furthermore, reviews analysis should be performed because customers tend to opt for businesses with a *good public opinion*.

As case of study, we considered YELP Dataset Challenge[1], containing about 5 million reviews, more than one million users, about 150 thousand businesses. Yelp is a user generated content platform in which users feed a virtual community based on 'word of mouth'.

The rest of the paper is organized as follows: Sect. 2 outlines some related works; Sect. 3 introduces the proposed approach; Sect. 4 outlines system architecture; Sect. 5.1 introduces the dataset used and the experimental setup; Sect. 6 reports the obtained results, finally, Sect. 7 provides some conclusions.

2 Related Works

In last years with the advent of the Internet, Web 2.0 and the Online Social Network (OSN) the expression "social network" has become a common vocabulary. Their adoption has allowed people living in different parts of the world to establish different type of relationships and to share, comment and observe various types of multimedia content. OSN is often associated with the more general concept of "social media": it refers to online technologies and procedures that

---

[1] https://www.yelp.com/dataset/challenge.

social network users use to share textual contents, images, videos, and audios. The analysis of these heterogeneous data allowed to support different application, in particular related to marketing strategies. In fact, the interaction among firms and customers led to build brand loyalty through the promotion of products and services as well as the setting up of online communities of brand followers [4]. Furthermore, the interaction among customers allows firms to increase the trend reputation exploiting new means and channel [3]. Social media marketing campaign is also influenced by the type of industry and product. For instance, in the hotel industry Corstjens and Umblijs [2] show how the firm reputation impacts the effectiveness of social media efforts. Thus, Social media improves the relationships among customers and brand improving exposure time and spread of marketing campaign [8]. The aim of these marketing campaigns is to spread out the influence of a given product or technologies among users. The influence process is, then, a process where ideas or behaviors are spread with the initiator and the recipient unaware of any intentional attempt at influence by giving advice and recommendations, by serving as a role model that others can imitate, by persuading or convincing others, or by way of contagion [11]. Rogers [6] provides a definition based on the communication concept describing as a process in which participants create and share information with one another in order to reach a mutual understanding. In particular, Rogers defines the Diffusion as the process in which an innovation is communicated through certain channels over time among the members of a social system. For this reason the analysis of business attractiveness has grown in importance to identify main features of a given business object with respect to its competitors, as shown in [9], or to analyze how the users' ratings affect deal selection [10]. Social Media provide then useful information for computing business attractiveness because they provide different point of views about a given firms in terms of ratings, reviews, pricing and so on. In fact, in [12] the authors use Yelp to study human foraging patterns modern human food foraging patterns, with respect to both geography and cuisine. On-line reviews are also investigating by Bai et al. [1] for product marketing combining user's rating and useful score of its reviews. Zhao et al. [13] studies user's influence on local businesses using user sentimental deviations and the review's reliability. Nevertheless, the large amount and the heterogeneity of users' reviews led to define new challenges, as shown [7] that have to be address for properly supporting different applications. Furthermore, Li et al. [5] show how the Big Data methodologies can be used for supporting marketing analysis investigating also the connection between social media and marketing stocks.

The main novelties of the proposed approach are:

- The definition of new methodology for reputation computing in OSN based on the analysis of textual reviews;
- The adoption of a new strategy to evaluate business' attractiveness combining users' sentiment and business reputation;
- The implementation of the proposed approach on a scalable and parametrizable Big Data infrastructure.

3   Methodology

The aim of our approach is to combine user's sentiment and business object's reputation on the basis of users' reviews for computing business attractiveness. We analyze reviews written by different users who express their opinion using natural language assigning a star degree (from 1 to 5) to their experience in the business object. In particular our analysis is focused on the reviews expressed by users with the aim of extracting useful information to determine how much a business is appreciated. In the following we introduce some basic concepts to better explain the proposed methodologies as well as:

- the concept of review and the reason why it is important to analyze business reviews.
- the concept of *public opinion.*
- the concept of user and his main characteristics.

Review is a subjective opinion expressed by a user about a given business to judge its main features in both positive and negative terms. In particular a review is directed to potential customers, so its function should help them in the decision making process. For this reason, a review inevitably influences the user's thought, having an impact on what is considered *public opinion.*

On the other hand, reviews are useful for business owner who should be interested in improving business services and in fixing those that have not been successful.

Public Opinion is defined as the collective thinking of the business clients' majority. We argue that *user's opinion about a business, of which the user knows nothing, is strongly influenced by public opinion, that becomes the user's prejudice without direct experience of business services.* As a consequence, businesses with a 'good public opinion' are more likely to attract new customers, whereas a customer is unlikely to opt for a business with bad reviews.

User is someone who is able to make a review about a business or to provide feedback on reviews from other users, confirming or contradicting them. In Yelp community, each user has a personal page containing personal information and a set of attributes that allow to define how much the user is able to 'influence' the others.

In our opinion we can define an 'influencer' someone that respects the following characteristics:

- *Elite User* that is active in the Yelp community according to the number of well-written reviews, high quality tips, a detailed personal profile, an active voting and complimenting record. Yelp Elite is a privileged title granted to users by Yelp.
- *Large Number of fans*: this implies that the user is popular.
- *Large number of written reviews*: this means that he is active in the community.

- *Large number of friends*: this implies that the user is part of a wide social network.
- *Large number of compliments by other users*: this takes into account how 'useful', 'funny' and 'cool' the user's reviews have been and how many compliments the user has received by other users of the community.

Our purpose is to asses a business public opinion in a quantitative manner, taking into account different influence factors (i.e. opinion value, number of compliments and so on). In fact, we argue that public opinion may depend on both 'what' has been written in the reviews and who has written that.

Definition 1. *Let* r *and* u_r *be respectively a given review and user who has written the review* r, *we define the opinion value* $Ov(r,u_r)$ *according to the following relation:*

$$Ov(r, u_r) = f(R(r), U(u_r), S(r)) \tag{1}$$

where $R(r)$ *is the review value,* $U(u_r)$ *is the user value and* $S(r)$ *is the review success.*

More specifically, we better describe the meaning of the $R(r), U(u_r), S(r)$ concepts.

$R(r)$ takes into account the number of starts of the review r, indicated by s_r, which is an user evaluation metric expressed as a number between 1 and 5, and the review text tx_r that is the user's thought written in natural language. It is necessary to convert tx_r into a numeric value, processing it using Sentiment Analysis and Natural Language Processing *nlp* libraries. This step is referred by the notation $nlp(tx_r)$. Thus, $R(r)$ can be defined according to the following relation:

$$R(r) = g(s_r, nlp(tx_r)) \tag{2}$$

In turn, considering u a generic user, $U(u)$ is computed considering its attributes, including the number of friends, the number of written reviews, the number of received compliments, the number of fans and the title of Elite User. Then $U(u)$ can be computed according to the following equation:

$$U(u) = \sum_{i=1}^{n} w_i a_u^i \tag{3}$$

where w_i and $a_u = (a_u^1, a_u^2, ...a_u^n)$ are respectively the weight of the attribute a_u^i and the vector corresponding to the attributes of user u.

Finally, the review success $S(r)$ depends on how 'useful', 'funny' and 'cool' users consider the review r. It is possible to compute $S(r)$ according to the following equation:

$$S(r) = \beta us_r + \delta f_r + \gamma c_r \tag{4}$$

where β, δ, γ are the weights associated to us_r, f_r and c_r, us_r the number of times the review is found 'useful', with f_r the number of times the review is found 'funny' and with c_r the number of times the review is found 'cool'.

According to the Eq. (1), an *opinion value* is computed for each review. However, the *public opinion of a specific business* can be computed taking into account the *opinion value* $Ov(r,u_r)$ of all the reviews r related to the business. In particular the *public opinion of a specific business* changes over time depending on the reviews that have been written up to a specific time t. Furthermore, each review is weighted in proportion to when it has been posted; in fact the most recent reviews seem to influence the opinion of users more. Thus, considering a specific business b and indicating with r_t the review posted at t, its *public opinion at specific time t, BPO(b,t)* can be computed according to this recurrence relation:

$$BPO(b,t) = Ov(r_t, u_{r_t}) + \alpha BPO(b, t-1)$$

(5)

where α is the weight associated with public opinion generated by the reviews preceding the one at time t.

4   Architecture

In this section system architecture is described. As shown in Fig. 1, three main layerss have been selected:

- Data ingestion that has the aim to crawl data from different data sources as well as Yelp, Foursquare, TripAdvisor and so on;
- Data storage in which are stored the crawled reviews as document into the NoSQL document database;
- Data processing using Big Data methodologies to infer business object's attractiveness.

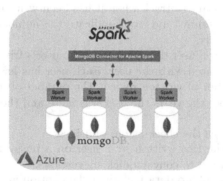

Fig. 1. System architecture

More in detail, we store users' reviews into the NoSQL database MongoDB[2] because it allows to easily manage each review as a document in conjunction with its metadata (i.e. title, number of compliments, business object and so on).

---

[2] https://www.mongodb.com/it.

The data processing layer is based on Apache Spark[3], an open-source distributed general-purpose cluster-computing framework, to process these large amount of hetereogenous data. Finally, we use Microsoft Azure platform as infrastructure as a service (IaaS) to support scalability of the proposed approach.

5   Experimental Evaluation

In this section we describe the evaluation results obtained according to the experimental protocol defined into the Sect. 5.1.

5.1   Experimental Protocol

Our evaluation concerns the following three types of analysis:

- Perform the Parameter estimation for identifying the best parameters for the computation of *Opinion value*;
- Evaluate the Natural Language Processing module with respect to the users evaluation (in terms of stars) about its reviews;
- Analyze how the business object reputation changes over the time.

We carried out our evaluation on YELP Dataset Challenge[4]. Yelp is a user generated content platform in which users feed a virtual community based on 'word of mouth'. Yelp Dataset Challenge[5] is composed of six json files:

- *business.json* contains business data including location data, attributes, and categories.
- *review.json* contains full review text data including the identifier of the user that wrote the review and the identifier of the business the review is written for. For each review the number of stars assigned by the user is given. The review date is necessary to track when it has been written. Furthermore, the attributes 'useful', 'funny' and 'cool' indicate the number useful, funny and cool votes respectively.
- *user.json* contains the user data including the user's friend mapping and all the metadata associated with the user. Each user has has several attributes, including the number of written review, the number of 'useful', 'funny' and 'cool' votes received, the years the user was Elite and the number of compliments received.
- *checkin.json* contains the checkins on a business.
- *tip.json* contains the tips written by a user on a business. Tips are shorter than reviews and tend to convey quick suggestions.
- *photo.json* contains photo data including the caption and classification (one of "food", "drink", "menu", "inside" or "outside").

Among al json files, only business.json, review.json, user.json have been taken into account during the analysis.

The evaluation has been performed on Microsoft Azure using a Linux virtual machine with the characteristics shown in Table 1.

---

[3] https://spark.apache.org/.
[4] https://www.yelp.com/dataset/challenge.
[5] https://www.yelp.com/dataset/challenge.

Table 1. Virtual machine characteristics

Operating system	Linux Ubuntu 17.04
CPU	Intel Xeon E5
RAM	16 GB

The presented methodology has been implemented using PySpark, a collaboration of Apache Spark and Python, that exploits the simplicity of Python and the power of Apache Spark.

5.2   Experimental Results

As aforementioned, the *public opinion at a specific time t of a business b* (Eq. 5) can be computed by taking into account equations (1), (2), (3) and (4). Equation (1) represents the opinion value which depends on *what* has been written (review value), *who* wrote it (user value) and *how* successful it was (review success). Review value $(R(r))$ is computed by processing the text with the Natural Language Toolkit (NLTK)[6], a suite of libraries and programs for symbolic and statistical natural language processing (NLP) for English written in the Python programming language . In Yelp Community, when writing a review, the user is used to assign a number of stars (form 1 to 5) that can be interpreted as his brief opinion. For this reason, the number of stars should be taken into account when computing the review value $R(r)$ that is the average of the number of stars normalized between -1 and 1 as shown in Table 2, and the value NLTK provides by processing the review text. User value $U(u)$ is computed to estimate the 'importance' of the user in Yelp Community. In this context, a user should have a great 'importance' if his opinion has a strong impact. This means that his reviews are likely to be considered by other users. User value $U(u)$ is computed by taking into account user attributes, giving a high value to 'influencer users' and a low value to 'fake users' that are likely to write 'fake reviews'. In this context a potential 'fake user' is someone who joins the community only to promote or disparage a particular business. He is identified by the characteristics of

Table 2. Normalized number of stars

Number of stars	Normalized value
1	-1
2	-0.5
3	0
4	0.5
5	1

---

[6] https://www.nltk.org/.

having no friends or fans, not being an Elite User and having few reviews related to the same business.

Review success $S(r)$ estimates how much the review r is taken into account by the various users. It depends on how many times the review has been evaluated cool, useful and funny.

Combining the Eqs. (1), (2), (3) and (4), the *opinion value of a review r written by the user u_r* can be computer according to the following equation:

$$Ov(r, u_r) = R(r)(1 + U(u_r))(1 + \beta us_r + \delta f_r + \gamma c_r) \qquad (6)$$

where $U(u_r)$ and review success $S(r) = \beta us_r + \delta f_r + \gamma c_r$ are normalized in range [0,10] and $R(r)$ is limited in range [−1,1]. The Eq. (6) shows that $R(r)$ is amplified by user value and review success and the sign of $Ov(r, u_r)$ is established by $R(r)$. The additive term +1 is introduced to avoid a *null opinion value* in particular situations where the user has a zero value and the review has not been successful. The value of β, δ and γ are set so that $\beta + \delta + \gamma = 1$. The choice of the parameters is based on a tuning phase in with the brute-force or exhaustive search is applied to find the values that maximize review success.

6   Results

In this section the results obtained by applying the presented methodology to a business are reported. In particular the following values are chosen for the parameters in Eqs. 5 and 6: $\alpha = 0.5$, $\beta = 0.7$, $\delta = 0.2$ and $\gamma = 0.1$.

Fig. 2 shows the percentage of stars associated with the reviews of the considered business, while Fig. 3 shows the percentage of Positive and Negative reviews.

As seen, Review Value $R(r)$ is computed as average of the number of stars and the value NLTK provides by processing the review text. Figure 4 confirms the strict correlation between review text processed by NLTK and the number of stars associated by the user, showing that 'what' users say corresponds to the stars of the reviews. Figure 5 illustrates how public opinion about the business changes with time. As expected by the analysis of the reviews, business public opinion remains positive over time.

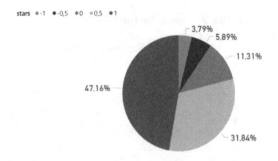

Fig. 2. Percentage of stars associated with reviews.

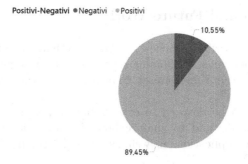

Fig. 3. Percentage of positive and negative reviews.

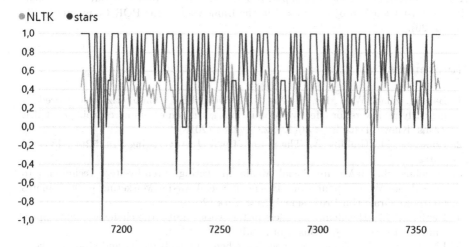

Fig. 4. Illustrates number of stars and NTLK value of each review. X-axis represents review identifier. The most recent reviews are considered.

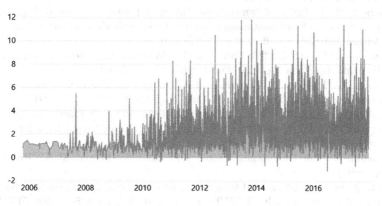

Fig. 5. Illustrates business public opinion over time.

7   Conclusion and Future Works

In this paper we describe a review analysis methodology with the aim to infer business attractiveness combining sentiment and business reputation. The obtained results on the Yelp Dataset Challenge show the effectiveness of the proposed approach.

Future works will be devoted to extend the proposed evaluation to other Online Social networks and to analyze how this approach can be useful for supporting several application as well as Viral Marketing, recommendation and so on.

Acknowledgment. This work is part of the Synergy-net: Research and Digital Solutions against Cancer project (funded in the framework of the POR Campania FESR 2014–2020).

References

1. Bai, T., Zhao, W.X., He, Y., Nie, J.Y., Wen, J.R.: Characterizing and predicting early reviewers for effective product marketing on e-commerce websites. IEEE Trans. Knowl. Data Eng. **30**(12), 2271–2284 (2018)
2. Corstjens, M., Umblijs, A.: The power of evil. J. Advertising Res. **52**(4), 433–449 (2012)
3. Gunelius, S.: 30-Minute Social Media Marketing: Step-by-step Techniques to Spread the Word About Your Business: Social Media Marketing in 30 Minutes a Day. McGraw Hill Professional, New York (2010)
4. Kaplan, A.M., Haenlein, M.: Users of the world, unite! the challenges and opportunities of social media. Bus. Horiz. **53**(1), 59–68 (2010)
5. Li, Q., Chen, Y., Wang, J., Chen, Y., Chen, H.: Web media and stock markets: a survey and future directions from a big data perspective. IEEE Trans. Knowl. Data Eng. **30**(2), 381–399 (2017)
6. Rogers, E.M.: Diffusion of Innovations. Simon and Schuster, New York (2010)
7. Shayaa, S., et al.: Sentiment analysis of big data: methods, applications, and open challenges. IEEE Access **6**, 37807–37827 (2018)
8. Tuten, T.L.: Advertising 2.0: Social Media Marketing in a Web 2.0 World: Social Media Marketing in a Web 2.0 World. ABC-CLIO (2008)
9. Valkanas, G., Lappas, T., Gunopulos, D.: Mining competitors from large unstructured datasets. IEEE Trans. Knowl. Data Eng. **29**(9), 1971–1984 (2017)
10. Wang, C.Y., Chen, Y., Liu, K.R.: Game-theoretic cross social media analytic: how yelp ratings affect deal selection on groupon? IEEE Trans. Knowl. Data Eng. **30**(5), 908–921 (2017)
11. Weimann, G.: The Influentials: People Who Influence People. SUNY Press, New York (1994)
12. Xuan, Q., et al.: Modern food foraging patterns: geography and cuisine choices of restaurant patrons on yelp. IEEE Trans. Comput. Soc. Syst. **5**(2), 508–517 (2018)
13. Zhao, G., Lei, X., Qian, X., Mei, T.: Exploring users' internal influence from reviews for social recommendation. IEEE Trans. Multimedia **21**(3), 771–781 (2018)

Cyber Security

Sensitive Data Encoding in Blockchain-Based P2P Trading System

Yiming Liu(ID), Xin Su$^{(\boxtimes)}$(ID), Ning Xu(ID), and Xiao Yao(ID)

College of IoT Engineering, Hohai University, Changzhou 213022, China
15995086362@163.com, leosu8622@163.com,
{20101832, 20141925}@hhu.edu.cn

Abstract. With the rapid development and application of information technology, blockchain technology has become one of the important means to promote the integration of the real economy and the digital economy. However, for the application of blockchain technology in P2P transactions, existing technology provide no reasonable framework. This paper proposes a framework of P2P trading system based on blockchain technology. The proposed framework can ensure the security of data and establish trust among entities. It can also reduce business divergence and costs. In order to prevent the leak of sensitive data in the trading process, we also propose an encoding method of sensitive data. This guarantees the data from being stolen or tampered. The calculations on matrixes of this method can use the computing resources of all nodes in the blockchain to calculate in parallel, and then summarize the results. This makes full use of massive GPU resources in the blockchain, and makes the calculation valuable. The proposed framework and method realize transactions without the intervention of a centralized platform. It not only establishes the trust relationship among entities well, but also realizes safe and reliable P2P transactions.

Keywords: Blockchain technology · P2P trading · Decentralization · Data encoding

1 Introduction

The world economy is entering a development period dominated by the information industry. With the development of information technology represented by blockchain technology and artificial intelligence, the global economy and industrial structure are undergoing deepening and adjustment. The digital, networked and intelligent trend of industrial development is becoming more and more obvious. In order to seize the opportunity, build a new pillar of the industrial system and advance to a high-end level of the global value chain, we should promote the deep integration of blockchain and other technologies with the real economy and develop the digital economy [1–3].

Based on the features of blockchain technology, such as decentralization and tamper-proof, blockchain technology can be applied to electronic commerce and smart contract to build a blockchain-based P2P trading system. Accordingly, ensuring data security and transparent, establishing trust relationship between entities and reducing commercial friction and trust cost has become the trend of current research.

© Springer Nature Switzerland AG 2019
C. Esposito et al. (Eds.): I-SPAN 2019, CCIS 1080, pp. 109–117, 2019.
https://doi.org/10.1007/978-3-030-30143-9_9

This paper proposes a framework of P2P trading system based on blockchain technology, and in order to prevent the leakage of sensitive data in the circulation process, we also give the corresponding encoding method of sensitive data. In this paper, the blockchain technology is applied to electronic commerce and smart contract, and the mechanism of association between digital asset and physical asset is also introduced. The method proposed not only establishes the trust relationship between entities well and realizes safe and reliable P2P transaction, but also promotes the integration of blockchain with the real economy and improves the efficiency of social and economic operation.

2 Blockchain Technology and Digitalization

The concept of blockchain originated from the article "Bitcoin: A peer-to-peer Electronic Cash System" published by *Satoshi Nakamoto* in 2008 [4]. Blockchain technology is a new distributed computing method that uses chained data block structure to verify and store data, uses cryptography to ensure data security, uses distributed consensus algorithm to generate and update data, and uses smart contract (automated script code) to program and operate data. Originally, blockchain was designed to record bitcoin transactions in a tamper-proof and publicly verifiable manner, and bitcoin was the first prototype of a blockchain-based cryptocurrency. Blockchain is an innovative application of distributed storage, consensus mechanism, P2P communication, encryption algorithm and other computer technologies in the information age. The blockchain is jointly maintained by all peer nodes, and each node has a local copy of a complete record, which can build a set of trust mechanism in the absence of a centralized institution, and guarantee the transparency, traceability and difficulty of illegal tampering of data [5, 6].

In the process of social digitization, information data is an important resource and factor of production, and the field of electronic transaction involves a large amount of information data. At present, the most common risks in electronic transactions are information leakage and data tampering, therefore, it is particularly important to prevent these problems during the trading process. In the traditional electronic transaction process, the main security problems are that order information, confirmation information, personal information of participants, etc., are intercepted, tampered with or maliciously destroyed in the transmission process; Bank accounts, passwords and bank identification numbers of participants were stolen; Via system vulnerability, criminals tamper with the data in the system and generate false information. In addition, the third-party payment institution, e-commerce platform, cloud computing center and other centralized platform have problems such as excessive collection of user data, disclosure of user information, low fault tolerance, poor anti-collusion and vulnerability to attacks, and in traditional electronic transactions, credit relies heavily on third-party platform, and the online transaction cost of both parties is high [7–9].

At present, smart contract are usually used for the exchange of virtual digital asset. However, for the application of blockchain in P2P electronic transactions, the existing technology does not provide a reasonable trading method and application framework. Therefore, the main purpose of this paper is to propose a P2P trading method based on blockchain technology to protect the information data in transactions, and solve the problem that traditional electronic trading credit relies heavily on third-party platform. Centralized platform may excessively collect user data and disclose user data, the method proposed in this paper make the transaction can bypass the third-party platform and save the transaction costs of both parties. The method proposed also introduces the mechanism of association between digital asset and physical asset in electronic transactions using blockchain technology. The method ensures the data security and transparency, establishes the trust relationship between the entities, reduces the commercial friction and reduces the trust cost [10–12].

3 Related Works and Our Proposed Framework

3.1 A Distributed, Tamper-Resistant Transaction Framework

In [13], the use of a blockchain based mechanism to secure the Internet BGP and DNS infrastructure is proposed. While the blockchain has scaling issues to be overcome, the key advantages of such an approach include the elimination of any PKI-like root of trust, a verifiable and distributed transaction history log, multi-signature based authorizations for enhanced security, easy extensibility and scriptable programmability to secure new types of Internet resources and potential for a built in cryptocurrency. A tamper resistant DNS infrastructure also ensures that it is not possible for the application level PKI to spoof HTTPS traffic.

3.2 A Blockchain Based Scheme for Secure P2P Cloud Storage

In [14], a blockchain-based security architecture for distributed cloud storage is proposed, where users can divide their own files into encrypted data chunks, and upload those data chunks randomly into the P2P network nodes that provide free storage capacity. A genetic algorithm is customized to solve the file block replica placement problem between multiple users and multiple data centers in the distributed cloud storage environment. Numerical results show that the proposed architecture outperforms the traditional cloud storage architectures in terms of file security and network transmission delay. On average, the file loss rate is close to 0% on this architecture while it's nearly 100% and 71.66% on the architecture with single data center and the distributed architecture using genetic algorithm. Besides, with the proposed scheme, the transmission delay on the proposed architecture is reduced by 39.28% and 76.47% on average on the user's number and the number of file block replicas, respectively, in comparison to the architecture with single data center. Meanwhile, the transmission delay of file block replicas is also reduced by 41.36% on average than that on the distributed architecture using genetic algorithm.

3.3 Peertrust: A Reputation-Based Trust Supporting Framework

Peertrust is a reputation-based trust supporting framework, which includes a coherent adaptive trust model for quantifying and comparing the trustworthiness of peers based on a transaction-based feedback system, and a decentralized implementation of such a model over a structured P2P network. Peertrust model has two main features. First, three basic trust parameters and two adaptive factors are introduced in computing trustworthiness of peers, namely, feedback a peer receives from other peers, the total number of transactions a peer performs, the credibility of the feedback sources, transaction context factor, and the community context factor. Second, a general trust metric is defined to combine these parameters [15].

3.4   The Proposed Framework of Blockchain-Based P2P Trading System

The overall framework of the system is shown in Fig. 1. The system will be developed and deployed within the blockchain that supports smart contract according to the framework proposed in this paper, and provides open transaction interface to enable blockchain users to conduct physical commodity transactions. The Web layer provides a visual interface for smart contract and data, so that users can visually check the trading products and the credit information of the trading participants. In addition, it provides a friendly human-computer interaction interface.

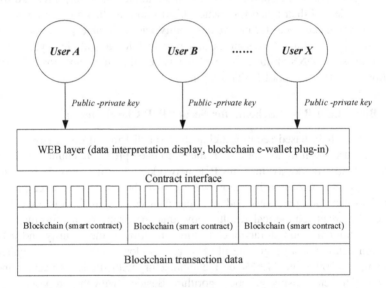

Fig. 1. The framework of blockchain-based P2P trading system

In this system, as there is no transaction record in the initial state, the two parties cannot obtain each other's credit information. Therefore, in order to ensure the establishment of the credit system, the credit deposit agreed by both parties in the contract is relatively large, but with the increase of the number of transactions, the searchable credit record also increases. Since in the blockchain, there is a cost to calling the contract interface (for example, a certain amount of gas is paid in Ethereum), the deducted deposit can be used to pay the cost of calling the contract interface for credit query, and can also be used to reward users with high credit values.

4 The Encoding Method for Sensitive Data in Blockchain-Based P2P Trading System

In the third section of this paper, we propose a framework of P2P trading system based on blockchain technology, which solves the problem of falsified data in electronic transactions. However, for the sensitive data related to transactions, such as bank accounts, order information, etc., we propose the corresponding encoding method. The method is used to encode the sensitive data generated in the transaction, so that the sensitive data is obtained by the final party, and the sensitive data is prevented from leaking in the circulation process.

We obtain the set of random numbers by the hash algorithm from the information data generated by the participants in the transaction, especially the sensitive data. The seed code is automatically generated by the system's smart contract, and the transformation function group of code generation is generated by combining the code generation algorithm in the contract with the set of random numbers and the seed code. The irreversible and reversible coding generation algorithms are detailed in Tables 1 and 2. Among them, the j in Table 1 is randomly selected from $[0, Z+1]$, k and b correspond to M-dimension vector. A_i is randomly selected from the random number set and split into a L-dimension variable, and then k and b are generated by selecting M bit from the L-dimension variable according to the $round(M/N + 1)$ step size. The time complexity of calculation mainly depends on X to the j power, and j is related to the number of packets of the seed code. The algorithm for randomly selecting the elements of set in the process can adopt linear congruential method and middle-square method. The operation of k and b can be calculated by matrix calculation. In the code-generation function group, the function is a polynomial function of X:

$$
\begin{cases}
F^1(X) = X^j \times k_1 + b_1 \\
\qquad \cdots \\
F^{Z-2}(X) = X^j \times k_{Z-2} + b_{Z-2} \\
F^{Z-1}(X) = X^j \times k_{Z-1} + b_{Z-1} \\
F^Z(X) = X^j \times k_Z + b_Z
\end{cases}
\tag{1}
$$

Each transformation function in Table 2 is associated with a random M-dimension number G, each dimension has a value range of $[0, M]$, 0 indicating that the corresponding code bit is not exchanged, and G is used for digital replacement of the corresponding code bit when the final code combination is used. Taking a decimal number as an example, in combination, the maximum number of digits for each calculation is up to 3 digits. For numbers less than 3 digits, 0 is added to the left. For the combined digits, exchange bit referenced G to obtain the final digits. For the final digits, verification is required, if it is repeated, a new G is generated to ensure that the number is not repeated. In the code-generation function group, the function is a linear monotone function of X (Fig. 2):

$$\begin{cases} F^1(X) = X \times k_1 + b_1 \\ \quad \cdots \\ F^{Z-2}(X) = X \times k_{Z-2} + b_{Z-2} \\ F^{Z-1}(X) = X \times k_{Z-1} + b_{Z-1} \\ F^Z(X) = X \times k_Z + b_Z \end{cases} \tag{2}$$

Table 1. The irreversible encoding algorithm for sensitive data

Algorithm	Irreversible sensitive data encoding method
Input:	1. The set of random numbers A: $\{A_1, A_2, \cdots\}$
	2. The seed code $Seed_N$ (automatically generated by the smart contract)
Output:	Sensitive data encoding
Step 1:	Compute the hash of transaction data (especially sensitive data) and convert it into numbers to obtain a set of random numbers A: $\{A_1, A_2, \cdots\}$.
Step 2:	Generate encoding of length M, seed code of length N ($M > N$), and a random number of length L.
	Divide $Seed_N$ into $Z = M - N$ groups, each with a corresponding code-generation function.
	Split each seed code into an N-dimensional variable and add 1 to the left of the seed until the M bit, denoted by X. X is the input of the corresponding code-generation function.
	The code-generation function is a polynomial function of X:
	$$F_{Z-i}(X) = X^j \times k_{Z-i} + b_{Z-i} \ (i = 0, \cdots, Z-1)$$
Step 3:	Calculate all $F_{Z-i}(X) = Y$, and modulate each dimension of Y according to the base number of scales. Combine each dimension of Y to generate the final number.

Based on the framework and the encoding method proposed in this paper, we simulate the blockchain by Golang. Part of the terminal result is shown in Fig. 3. It shows that every transaction or data information written into the blockchain contains a hash of the previous block, which ensures data security and establishes trust relationship between the entities.

Table 2. The reversible encoding algorithm for sensitive data

Algorithm	Reversible sensitive data encoding method
Input:	1. The set of random numbers $A: \{A_1, A_2, \cdots\}$
	2. The seed code $Seed_N$ (automatically generated by the smart contract)
Output:	Sensitive data encoding
Step 1:	Compute the hash of transaction data (especially sensitive data) and convert it into numbers to get a set of random numbers $A: \{A_1, A_2, \cdots\}$.
Step 2:	Generate encoding of length M, a seed code of length N, $M/3 > N$, and a random number of length L.
	Divide $Seed_N$ into $Z = M - N$ groups, each with a corresponding code-generation function.
	Split each seed code into an N-dimensional variable, denoted by X. X is the input of the corresponding code-generation function.
	The code-generation function is a linear monotonic function of X:
	$$F_{Z-i}(X) = X \times k_{Z-i} + b_{Z-i} \quad (i = 0, \cdots, Z-1)$$
Step 3:	Calculate all $F_{Z-i}(X) = Y$ and combine each dimension of Y to generate the final number.
	Associate each code-generation function with an M-dimensional random number G such that each dimension has a value range of $[0, M]$, where 0 indicates that the corresponding code bit will not be exchanged, and that the bit will be exchanged otherwise.

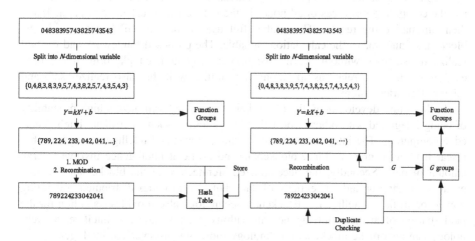

Fig. 2. The flow of encoding method for sensitive data in blockchain-based P2P trading system

Fig. 3. Part of terminal result of the blockchain simulated by Golang

5 Conclusions

This paper proposes a framework of P2P trading system based on blockchain technology. In order to prevent the leak of sensitive data in the trading process, we also propose an encoding method of sensitive data, where the blockchain technology is applied for enhancing the electronic commerce and smart contract. This guarantees the data from being stolen or tampered. The calculations on matrixes of this method can use the computing resources of all nodes in the blockchain to calculate in parallel, and then summarize the results. This makes full use of massive GPU resources in the blockchain, and makes the calculation valuable. The proposed framework and method realize transactions without the intervention of a centralized platform. It not only establishes the trust relationship among the entities well, but also realizes safe and reliable P2P transactions.

In the future development, the blockchain technology will have a high probability of being integrated with other information technologies, such as artificial intelligence, edge computing. The integration of blockchain and artificial intelligence is also a hot research topic at present. First, blockchain and artificial intelligence involve a large amount of data. Secondly, the decentralized architecture of the blockchain not only ensures the sharing and authenticity of data, but also provides distributed computing power for artificial intelligence. Blockchain technology also provides a solution for the paid sharing of artificial intelligence algorithms. Finally, artificial intelligence technology can also make blockchain technology more autonomous and intelligent.

Acknowledgements. This work was supported in part by the National Key Research & Development Program 2018AAA0100800, the Key Research and Development Program of Jiangsu under grant BE2018004-04; it was also supported by the Fundamental Research Funds for the Central Universities under Grant 2019B22214, and by the State Key Laboratory of Integrated Management of Pest Insects and Rodents under grant IPM1914.

References

1. Redondo, T.: The digital economy: social interaction technologies-an overview. IJIMAI **3**(2), 17–25 (2015)
2. Catalini, C., Gans, J.S.: Some simple economics of the blockchain. National Bureau of Economic Research (2016)
3. Huckle, S., Bhattacharya, R., White, M., et al.: Internet of things, blockchain and shared economy applications. Procedia Comput. Sci. **98**, 461–466 (2016)
4. Nakamoto, S.: Bitcoin: a peer-to-peer electronic cash system (2008)
5. Khalilov, M.C.K., Levi, A.: A survey on anonymity and privacy in bitcoin-like digital cash systems. IEEE Commun. Surv. Tutor. **20**(3), 2543–2585 (2018)
6. Schmitt, A.J., Sun, S.A., Snyder, L.V., et al.: Centralization versus decentralization: risk pooling, risk diversification, and supply chain disruptions. Omega **52**, 201–212 (2015)
7. Granjal, J., Monteiro, E., Silva, J.S.: Security for the internet of things: a survey of existing protocols and open research issues. IEEE Commun. Surv. Tutor. **17**(3), 1294–1312 (2015)
8. Sicari, S., Rizzardi, A., Grieco, L.A., et al.: Security, privacy and trust in Internet of Things: the road ahead. Comput. Netw. **76**, 146–164 (2015)
9. Crosby, M., Pattanayak, P., Verma, S., et al.: Blockchain technology: beyond bitcoin. Appl. Innov. **2**(6–10), 71 (2016)
10. Su, X., Liu, Y., Geng, Y., et al.: Semantic-based role matching and dynamic inspection for smart access control. Multimed. Tools Appl. **77**(14), 18545–18562 (2018)
11. Narayanan, A., Bonneau, J., Felten, E., et al.: Bitcoin and Cryptocurrency Technologies: A Comprehensive Introduction. Princeton University Press (2016)
12. Liu, Y., Cheng, Z., Wang, Z., Chen, S., Su, X.: Fine-grained data traffic management system based on VPN technology. In: Jung, J.J., Kim, P., Choi, K.N. (eds.) BDTA 2017. LNICST, vol. 248, pp. 19–25. Springer, Cham (2018). https://doi.org/10.1007/978-3-319-98752-1_3
13. Hari, A., Lakshman, T.V.: The Internet blockchain: a distributed, tamper-resistant transaction framework for the Internet. In: Proceedings of the 15th ACM Workshop on Hot Topics in Networks, pp. 204–210. ACM (2016)
14. Li, J., Wu, J., Chen, L.: Block-secure: blockchain based scheme for secure P2P cloud storage. Inf. Sci. **465**, 219–231 (2018)
15. Xiong, L., Liu, L.: PeerTrust: supporting reputation-based trust for peer-to-peer electronic communities. IEEE Trans. Knowl. Data Eng. **16**(7), 843–857 (2004)

A New Instance of a Lightweight Authentication Protocol Based on the LPN Problem

Paolo D'Arco and Marco Nilo[(✉)]

Universitá degli Studi di Salerno, Fisciano, SA, Italy
m.nilo@studenti.unisa.it

Abstract. Authentication is one of the most important issues in the information technology field and, primarily, in Cryptography. With the diffusion of devices for the Internet of things, the interest in efficient and with low computational loads authentication protocols, has increased more and more in the last few years. Indeed, traditional protocols, based on symmetric primitives and, in general, on pseudo-random functions, are not suitable for computationally constrained devices. On the other hand, one of the most interesting families of protocols for such devices seems to be the one based on the *learning parity with noise* problem. In this paper, building on some previous works, we propose a new instance of a lightweight authentication protocol constructed on this problem. We describe some optimizations which could be employed to improve the efficiency of an implementation, and we give also a look at the real world, discussing the applicability of our proposal to several devices available on the market.

1 Introduction

Authentication is a crucial issue in Cryptography and a preliminary step in almost every secure application. Basically, it is the process through which a party can convince another party that it is, in fact, who or what it declares itself to be. Along the years several techniques have been developed built on something the party *is*, *knows*, or on something the party *holds*. Currently, efficient and secure solutions for traditional network infrastructures are available. But the Internet of Things (IoT, for short) has extended the traditional infrastructures to a global heterogeneous environment, with a huge number of computational devices with very different capabilities. And if, from one hand, the IoT opens plenty of new possibilities, e.g., environmental monitoring, risk control, dangerous situations management, sensitive areas surveillance, domotic, smart applications, on the other hand it introduces also new challenges: heavily-constrained devices, like cheap sensors or tiny RFID tags, cannot afford the computational load required by protocols designed for traditional communication networks and devices. Lightweight tools and strategies, less demanding in terms of computational power and storage requirements, are needed. In order to deal with such a

© Springer Nature Switzerland AG 2019
C. Esposito et al. (Eds.): I-SPAN 2019, CCIS 1080, pp. 118–132, 2019.
https://doi.org/10.1007/978-3-030-30143-9_10

new environment, several solutions have been proposed. But some of them are highly questionable (see [1] for an overview of the ultralightweight approach).

Our Contribution. In this paper, starting from some previous works on authentication protocols based on the difficulty of the learning parity with noise problem, namely [8] and [4], we propose a new instance of the protocol proposed in [4], which essentially incorporates [8]. The protocol has a very small number of operations that would be considered burdensome on tiny devices[1].

We close the paper providing a preliminary analysis on the protocol applicability to some existing commercial products. The analysis is performed taking into account mainly the user memory, and verifying the compatibility with the resources required by the entire authentication protocol.

2   Notations and Background

In this section we provide the notation and some preliminary notions which will be used in the following sections. Our treatment is essentially the same of [8].

2.1   Notations

We use lower letters like x, bold letters like $\mathbf{x}$ and upper letters like X to, respectively, denote single elements, vectors and matrices over $\mathbb{Z}_q$. Moreover, for a vector $\mathbf{x}$, let $wt(\mathbf{x})$ denote the Hamming weight of the vector $\mathbf{x}$, i.e. the number of 1's in the vector, e.g., given $\mathbf{x} = 10100111$, then $wt(\mathbf{x}) = 5$. And, given a vector $\mathbf{x}$, let $\overline{\mathbf{x}}$ denote its bit-by-bit complement, i.e., $\overline{\mathbf{x}}[i] = 1 - \mathbf{x}[i]$ for all i. Then, given two vectors $\mathbf{x}$ and $\mathbf{y}$, let $\mathbf{x}_{\downarrow \mathbf{y}} \in \mathbb{Z}_2^{wt(\mathbf{y})}$ denote the vector $\mathbf{x}$, whose size is $wt(\mathbf{y})$, obtained by removing from $\mathbf{x}$ all the $\mathbf{x}[i]$ where $\mathbf{y}[i] = 0$, e.g., given $\mathbf{x} = 10100111$ and $\mathbf{y} = 11010011$, then $\mathbf{x}_{\downarrow \mathbf{y}} = 10011$.

Finally, we extend boolean operators to vectors. Precisely, given two vectors $\mathbf{x}$ and $\mathbf{y}$, let $\mathbf{x} \wedge \mathbf{y} = \mathbf{z}$ mean $\mathbf{z}[i] = \mathbf{x}[i] \wedge \mathbf{y}[i]$, for all i. Similarly, for the XOR $\oplus$ operator. We also use $\mathbf{x} \longleftarrow_{\$} \{\mathbf{y} \in \mathbb{Z}_2^{2\ell}\}$ to denote the uniformly random sampling of a vector $\mathbf{x}$ from $\{\mathbf{y} \in \mathbb{Z}_2^{2\ell}\}$.

2.2   Authentication Protocols

An authentication protocol is characterised by two main actors: a Prover P and a Verifier V. The Prover P tries to authenticate itself to the Verifier V. P and V are both ppt algorithms and share a secret $\mathbf{x}$, generated by a key-generation algorithm $K(1^\gamma)$, where γ is the security parameter. P and V can exchange

---

[1] As a side note, we stress that the learning parity with noise problem is considered appealing since it offers the possibility to design protocols with security reductions and, unlike other numerical problems used in Cryptography, it does not succumb to known quantum algorithms. Moreover, as stated, the protocols based on it are usually very efficient and suitable for devices with low computational power, e.g., RFID Tags.

several messages. An authentication protocol is correct if a legitimate P always authenticates itself to V. It could be vulnerable to different types of attack. Roughly speaking, we identify:

- **Passive Attacks.** In a passive attack we have two phases. In the first, the adversary eavesdrops a polynomial number of communications between P and V. In the second, the adversary tries to deceive V in authenticating itself as P, using all the information obtained in the first phase.
- **Active Attacks.** An active attack is similar to a passive attack, with the difference that, in the first phase, the adversary can interact with P.
- **MIM Attacks.** In a MIM attack an adversary can interact in the first phase with *both* P and V. Man-In-the-Middle attacks (MIM) are probably the most powerful attacks.

In this paper we focus only on passive and active attacks.

Definition 1. *An authentication protocol is (t, Q, ϵ)-secure against an active attack if, every adversary A of time t, making at most Q queries to P, has at most a negligible probability ϵ of deceiving V in authenticating itself as P.*

We consider also the privacy issue, and model it according to the common indistinguishability approach.

Definition 2. *An authentication protocol is (t, ϵ)-private if, for every two Provers P_1 and P_2, for a randomly chosen bit b, given the transcript of a protocol execution between P_b and V, every adversary A of time t has at most a negligible advantage ϵ of guessing b better that choosing it at random.*

3 Authentication Protocols Based on the Learning Parity with Noise Problem

3.1 The LPN Problem

The learning parity with noise problem (LPN, for short) can be described as follow: for $0 < \tau < 1/2$ and a vector $\mathbf{x} \in \mathbb{Z}_2^{\ell}$, define the distribution $\Lambda_{\tau,\ell}(\mathbf{x})$ on $\mathbb{Z}_2^{\ell} \times \mathbb{Z}_2$ by the pair $(\mathbf{r}, \mathbf{r}^T \mathbf{x} \oplus e)$, where $\mathbf{r} \in \mathbb{Z}_2^{\ell}$ is uniformly random and $e \in \mathbb{Z}_2$ is selected according to the Bernoulli distribution over $\mathbb{Z}_2$, with parameter τ. The $LPN_{\tau,\ell}$ problem consists in distinguishing an oracle returning samples from the distribution $\Lambda_{\tau,\ell}(\mathbf{x})$, with a random and fixed $\mathbf{x}$, from an oracle returning uniform samples. It was shown that this version is equivalent to the *search* version of the LPN problem, where, given oracle access to $\Lambda_{\tau,\ell}(\mathbf{x})$, one needs to find $\mathbf{x}$.

3.2 The SLPN Problem

In the LPN Subspace problem (SLPN, for short), the opponent can request products of the type $A\mathbf{x} + \mathbf{b}$, where A is a matrix that has a sufficiently high rank. Given a minimum size $d \leq \ell$, a secret $\mathbf{x} \in \mathbb{Z}_2^{\ell}$, any matrix $A \in \mathbb{Z}_2^{\ell \times \ell}$ and $\mathbf{b} \in \mathbb{Z}_2^{\ell}$, we define the following distribution:

$$\Gamma_{\tau,\ell,d}(\mathbf{x}, A, \mathbf{b}) = \Lambda_{\tau,\ell}(A\mathbf{x} + \mathbf{b}) \text{ if } \mathrm{rank}(A) \geq d, \text{ error otherwise.}$$

Definition 3. *The $SLPN_{\tau,\ell,d}$ decision problem is $(t,Q,\epsilon)-hard$ if, for each distinguisher D of time t making at most Q queries,*

$$|Pr[D^{\Gamma_{\tau,\ell,d}(\boldsymbol{x},\cdot,\cdot)} = 1] - Pr[D^{U_{\ell+1}(\cdot,\cdot)} = 1]| \leq \epsilon$$

where $U_{\ell+1}(\cdot,\cdot)$, on input A and $\boldsymbol{b}$, outputs uniform samples only if $rank(A) \geq d$, and an error otherwise.

The SLPN problem is as difficult as the LPN problem if $d = \ell$. For our construction, however, we need only a weaker version of the $SLPN_{\tau,\ell,d}$ problem, called the LPN subset problem (SLPN*, for short).

3.3   The SLPN* Problem

The opponent does not request products with A and $\mathbf{b}$ as input, but only with subsets of $\mathbf{x}$ with size $\geq d$. Precisely, given $\mathbf{v} \in \mathbb{Z}_2^\ell$, let $diag(\mathbf{v}) \in \mathbb{Z}^{\ell\times\ell}$ be a matrix with all zero except for the diagonal which is the vector $\mathbf{v}$. Then, given $\mathbf{x}, \mathbf{v} \in \mathbb{Z}_2^\ell$ and $diag(\mathbf{v}) \in \mathbb{Z}^{\ell\times\ell}$, we define:

$$\Gamma_{\tau,\ell,d}^*(\mathbf{x},\mathbf{v}) = \Gamma_{\tau,\ell,d}(\mathbf{x},diag(\mathbf{v}),0^\ell) = \Lambda_{\tau,\ell}(\mathbf{x}\wedge\mathbf{v}) \text{ if } wt(\mathbf{v}) \geq d, \text{ error otherwise.}$$

Definition 4. *Given $\ell,d \in \mathbb{Z}$ where $d \leq \ell$, the $SLPN_{\tau,\ell,d}^*$ decision problem is $(t,Q,\epsilon)-hard$ if, for each distinguisher D of time t making at most Q queries,*

$$|Pr[D^{\Gamma_{\tau,\ell,d}^*(\boldsymbol{x},\cdot)} = 1] - Pr[D^{U_{\ell+1}(\cdot)} = 1]| \leq \epsilon$$

where $U_{\ell+1}(\cdot)$, on input $\boldsymbol{v}$, outputs uniform samples only if $wt(\boldsymbol{v}) \geq d$, and an error otherwise.

3.4   Previous Works

Several authentication protocols based on the LPN problem have been proposed over the last twenty years. We refer the reader to [8] for full references and a detailed discussion of previous proposals. We briefly discuss the main ones. Hopper and Blum [5] introduced the approach and gave the first protocol, named HB. Starting from their work, the most relevant protocols proposed were HB$^+$ [6] and HB# [2]. The main difference between HB and HB$^+$ is that the first protocol is secure against passive attacks, while HB$^+$ is secure against active attacks but succumbs to MIM attacks [3]. HB# was designed to deal with MIM attacks. Unfortunately, no long after its presentation, it was shown to be vulnerable to a general MIM attack [9].

Our work is based on the work by Kiltz et al. [8] and on the work by Halevi et al. [4]. The first work introduces a new two-round authentication protocol with active security. Its main characteristics are that the Prover generates the matrix R by itself, and the Verifier chooses which bits of the secret s to use in each authentication session. We focused on the modified version of the protocol given in [8], where some checks are removed to simplify the initial protocol.

The second work presents tree-based HB protocols, for privacy-preserving authentication of RFID Tags. We employ the tree-based approach of [4], proposing a new instance of a tree-based HB protocol, which uses the findings of [8].

3.5 Practical Settings

Authentication protocols based on the LPN problem have been designed primarily for devices with reduced computational capabilities, such as RFID tags. The acronym RFID (Radio-Frequency IDentification) refers to an automatic identification technology, based on the propagation of electromagnetic waves in the air, to detect objects, animals or people which are equipped with electronic Tags. An RFID system is characterised by three main elements: a Reader, used both for reading and writing, one or more Tags, and an information system for data management.

An RFID system can operate in low frequency, medium frequency, high frequency or very high frequency. It is often necessary to find a cryptographic trade-off between efficiency and security to use authentication protocols on such devices. An often suggested solution is the use of cryptographic systems that base their security on the LPN problem and its SLPN or SLPN* sub-problems.

4 Our New Instance of the Authentication Protocol

In a practical scenario a Reader has to authenticate a population of one million or one billion Tags. Therefore, a first phase of identification of the right Tag to authenticate is necessary to make the authentication phase efficient. Using the approach from [4], we divide the cycle of interactions between Tags and Readers into three distinct phases: the registration phase, the identification phase, and the authentication phase. Before the execution of these three phases, it is necessary to perform a system setup. We define: a parameter N, that represents the upper bound to the number of Tags that the system can actually support; the parameter r, which denotes the number of parallel executions; the parameter d, which denotes the height of the tree stored by the Reader, and the parameter β, which denotes the branching factor of the tree (Table 1).

Table 1. Public parameters.

Public parameters	
$\ell \in \mathbb{N}$	length of the secret key $s \in \mathbb{Z}_2^{2\ell}$
$\tau \in]0, 1/2[$	Bernoulli distribution parameter
$\tau' = 1/4 + \tau/2$	acceptance threshold
$r \in \mathbb{N}$	number of parallel executions
$N \in \mathbb{N}$	supported Tags upper bound
d	height of the tree stored
β	branching factor of the tree

- **Registration Phase.** Both the Prover (the Tag) and the Verifier (the Reader) are involved. The Reader stores a tree structure, in which Tags are associated to the leaves (see Fig. 1). Every node has a key. The keys stored in the nodes on the path, from the root to a leaf node, are provided to corresponding Tag. Precisely, let $n_j^0, n_j^1, ..., n_j^d$ define the path inside the tree, starting from the root n_0^0 down to the leaf n_j^d, associated with the Tag. For each node n_j^i, where $j = 1, ..., \beta$ and $i = 1, ..., d$, the Tag receives a secret key $\mathbf{y}_{n_j^i}$, associated with that node. In addition, the Tag receives a key $\mathbf{s}$, the shared secret, and the two vectors $\mathbf{b}^v, \mathbf{b}^z$ (see Fig. 2). The Tag must store all this information to be used in the identification and authentication phases.

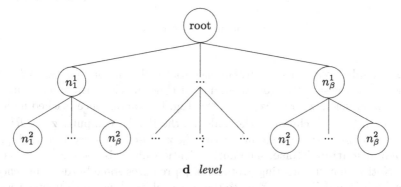

d *level*

Fig. 1. Tree stored by the Reader.

- **Identification Phase.** In this phase the Tag tries to identify itself to the Reader. More precisely, for each $\mathbf{y}_{n_j^i}$ key, stored in setup phase, the Tag computes $\mathbf{z}_i = R^T \cdot \mathbf{y}_{n_j^i} \oplus \mathbf{e}_i$, where $R \leftarrow_\$ \mathbb{Z}_2^{2\ell \times r}$ and $\mathbf{e}_i \leftarrow_\$ Ber_\tau^r$, for $i = 0, ..., d$. The Tag will then send $(R, \mathbf{z}_i\text{'s})$ to V so that it can actually verify its identity. Indeed, given R and the $\mathbf{z}_i$'s, the Reader computes $\mathbf{z}_c$, for each level of the tree, and matches $\mathbf{z}_i$ with the proper $\mathbf{z}_c$, selecting the node with the value $\mathbf{z}_c$ closer to $\mathbf{z}_i$. V computes these operations and repeats them until it reaches the last level of the tree (the leaves) and obtains the Tag identifier, i.e., the path from the root to the leaf.

Prover	Verifier
	$\mathbf{s} \leftarrow_\$ \mathbb{Z}_2^{2\ell}$
	$\{\mathbf{y}_{n_j^1}, \mathbf{y}_{n_j^2} ... \mathbf{y}_{n_j^d}\} \leftarrow_\$ \mathbb{Z}_2^{2\ell}$
	$\mathbf{b}^v \leftarrow_\$ \mathbb{Z}_2^{2\ell}$
	$\mathbf{b}^z \leftarrow_\$ \mathbb{Z}_2^r$

$$\xleftarrow{\quad y_{n_i}\text{'s}, \mathbf{s}, \mathbf{b}^v, \mathbf{b}^z \quad}$$

The tag stores the keys.

Fig. 2. Registration phase.

Prover	Verifier

$R \leftarrow_\$ \mathbb{Z}_2^{2\ell \times r}$

$\mathbf{e}_i \leftarrow_\$ Ber_\tau^r$, for $i = 0, ..., d$

$\mathbf{z}_i = R^T \cdot \mathbf{y}_{n_j^i} \oplus \mathbf{e}_i$, for $i = 0, ..., d$

$$(R, \mathbf{z}_i's)$$

$\longrightarrow$

Checks, for all levels,

$\mathbf{z}_c = R^T \cdot \mathbf{y}_c$

until gets the Tag ID.

Fig. 3. Identification phase.

For example, let us consider $\mathbf{z}_1$. For each root-child c it computes $\mathbf{z}_c = R^T \cdot \mathbf{y}_c$, where $\mathbf{y}_c$ is the secret vector stored in that child. It selects the child c with the value $\mathbf{z}_c$ closer to $\mathbf{z}_1$, received from the Tag. In general, once reached node n_j^i at i level, for each child c of the node n_j^i, the Reader computes $\mathbf{z}_c = R^T \cdot \mathbf{y}_c$ and, as before, it selects the child c with the $\mathbf{z}_c$ closer to the received $\mathbf{z}_i$ (Fig. 3).

- **Authentication Phase.** The authentication phase is the one described in [8]. Notice that the starting protocol of [8] requires some burdensome checks (for both P and V). According to the proposal in [8], we use a lighter version in which the checks are removed and are replaced in the protocol by two random vectors $\mathbf{b}^v$ and $\mathbf{b}^z$, and larger parameters. The two random vectors $\mathbf{b}^v \in \mathbb{Z}_2^{2\ell}$ and $\mathbf{b}^z \in \mathbb{Z}_2^r$ are used to hide the messages exchanged during the authentication phase. Details are given in Fig. 4

  The Verifier chooses a random vector $\mathbf{v} \leftarrow_\$ \mathbb{Z}_2^{2\ell}$ and sends it to the Prover. The Prover picks a random matrix $R \leftarrow_\$ \mathbb{Z}_2^{2\ell \times r}$ and a vector $\mathbf{e} \leftarrow_\$ Ber_\tau^r$ to compute $\mathbf{z} = R^T \cdot (\mathbf{s} \wedge (\mathbf{v} \oplus \mathbf{b}^v)) \oplus \mathbf{b}^z \oplus \mathbf{e}$, using the secret $\mathbf{s}$, the vector $\mathbf{v}$, and the two vectors $\mathbf{b}^v$ and $\mathbf{b}^z$. The random vectors $\mathbf{b}^v$ and $\mathbf{b}^z$ are used to blind $\mathbf{v}$ and $\mathbf{z}$. The Verifier checks if $wt((\mathbf{z} \oplus (R^T \cdot \mathbf{y} \oplus \mathbf{b}^z))) \geq r \cdot \tau'$ and authenticates the Prover only if the number of errors is less than $r \cdot \tau'$

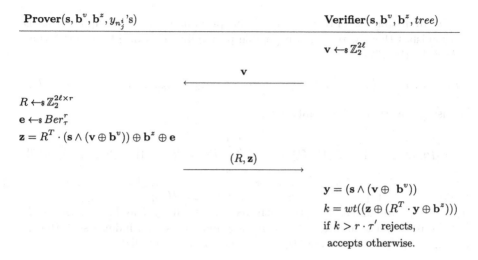

Fig. 4. Authentication phase.

5   Security Analysis

We start by showing that, regarding the identification phase, Tag sessions are indistinguishable. Hence, the privacy of the Tag is preserved. Loosely speaking, we recall that a function $F(\cdot,\cdot)$ is a PRF if, for any efficient time-t distinguisher D,

$$|Pr[D^{F_y(\cdot)} = 1] - Pr[D^{U(\cdot)} = 1]| \le \epsilon$$

where y is chosen uniformly at random, $U(\cdot)$ is a function chosen uniformly at random with same domain and codomain of $F_y(\cdot)$, $D^{F_y(\cdot)}$ and $D^{U(\cdot)}$ denote oracle access to the function values by D through queries, and ϵ is a negligible probability.

Claim. If $F_{\mathbf{y}}(R) = R^T \cdot \mathbf{y} \oplus noise$, for $\mathbf{y}$ chosen uniformly at random, is a PRF $F(\cdot,\cdot)$, then Tag sessions are indistinguishable.

Proof. (Sketch.) A standard hybrid argument is used. At the end of an identification phase we have as *output*:

$$Z = (z_1, z_2, ..., z_d) \in \mathbb{Z}_2^{d \cdot r}$$

where each $\mathbf{z}_i = R^T \cdot \mathbf{y}_{n_i} \oplus \mathbf{e}$, the value d is equal to the number of keys $\mathbf{y}_{n_j^i}$, and the value r is the number of parallel executions. Let $U = (u_1, u_2, ..., u_d) \in \mathbb{Z}_2^{d \cdot r}$, where each u_i is uniformly and randomly sampled. We want to show that, for each time-t distinguisher D:

$$|Pr[D(Z) = 1] - Pr[D(U) = 1]| \le \epsilon$$

i.e. D can distinguish only with a negligible probability ϵ. Let us suppose that D distinguishes them with a non-negligible probability ϵ'. Consider the following *hybrid* distributions:

$$H_0 = Z, \ H_1 = (z_1, z_2, ..., z_{d-1}, u_d), \ H_2 = (z_1, z_2, ..., z_{d-2}, u_{d-1}, u_d) \ ... \ H_d = U$$

By using the triangle inequality, we have:

$$\epsilon' = |Pr[D(Z) = 1] - Pr[D(U) = 1]| \leq \sum_{i=0}^{d-1} |Pr[D(H_i) = 1] - Pr[D(H_{i+1}) = 1]|$$

where $H_i = (z_1, z_2, ..., z_{d-i}, u_{d-i+1}, ..., u_d)$ and $H_{i+1} = (z_1, z_2, ..., z_{d-i-1}, u_{d-i}, ..., u_d)$ are different in the i-th vector, i.e. in z_{d-i} and u_{d-i}. But if D distinguishes between Z and U, then there must exists an index i such that it distinguishes between H_i and H_{i+1}. For such an i we get that

$$|Pr[D(H_i) = 1] - Pr[D(H_{i+1}) = 1]| \geq \epsilon'/d$$

which is still non-negligible. Therefore, D could be used to distinguish between samples from the PRF and samples from the uniform distribution. However, this is not possible because it would contradict our assumption. Hence, D cannot exist, and the two distributions are indistinguishable. It follows that *any* two Tag identification sessions are indistinguishable.

5.1   Active Security of the Authentication Phase

Assuming that the subset LPN problem is hard, we show that the authentication phase of our protocol is secure.

The security reduction we present shows that, if there exists an efficient active adversary A which breaks the authentication phase with non-negligible probability then, there exists an efficient distinguisher which succeeds with non-negligible probability in distinguishing a subset LPN oracle from a uniform oracle.

The security reduction is similar to the one given in [8]. Therefore, we introduce some terms therein defined that will be used next. Precisely:

- The value d: for a constant $\gamma > 0$, define $d = \ell/(2 + \gamma)$
- The probability $\alpha^*_{\ell,d}$: the probability that an ℓ-size random vector has an Hamming weight $\leq d$. In [8] it was shown that $\alpha^*_{\ell,d} \leq 2^{-c_\gamma \cdot \ell}$.
- The probability $\alpha''_{\tau',r}$: the probability that a random vector $y \in \mathbb{Z}_2^r$ has Hamming weight $\leq r \cdot \tau'$. In [8] it was shown that $\alpha''_{\tau',r} \leq 2^{-c_\tau \cdot r}$.

Let O be either a subset LPN oracle $\Gamma^*_{\tau,2\ell,d}(\mathbf{x}, \cdot)$ or $U_{2\ell+1}$, and let A be an efficient adversary who breaks the protocol with non-negligible probability ϵ'. We define an efficient adversary B^O, which uses A as a black-box, in such a way that:

$$Pr[B^{\Gamma^*_{\tau,2\ell,d}(\mathbf{x},\cdot)} = 1] \geq \epsilon'$$

and

$$Pr[B^{U_{2\ell+1}(\cdot)} = 1] \le \alpha''_{\tau',r} + Q \cdot \alpha^*_{\ell,d}$$

Thus, B^O distinguishes between $\Gamma^*_{\tau,2\ell,d}(\mathbf{x}, \cdot)$ from $U_{2\ell+1}$ with probability at least $\epsilon = \epsilon' - Q \cdot \alpha^*_{\ell,d} - \alpha''_{\tau',r}$.

The reduction is a bit technical and uses some tricks. At the beginning B^O samples:

$$\mathbf{x}^* \in \mathbb{Z}_2^{2\ell} \ , \ \mathbf{v}^* \leftarrow_\$ \{\mathbf{y} \in \mathbb{Z}_2^{2\ell}\} \ , \ \mathbf{b}^v \in \mathbb{Z}_2^{2\ell} \ \text{and,} \ \mathbf{b}^z \in \mathbb{Z}_2^r$$

The intuition is the following: assume that the oracle O is the subset LPN oracle, with a secret key $\mathbf{x}$. In the first phase of the simulation, B^O has to provide outputs $(R, \mathbf{z})$ to the queries $\mathbf{v}$ from A, which must have the same distribution they would have if generated by a legitimate Prover. To this aim, B^O simulates a Prover whose secret key $\mathbf{s}$ is equal to:

$$\mathbf{s} = (\mathbf{x}^* \wedge \mathbf{v}^*) \oplus (\mathbf{x} \wedge \overline{\mathbf{v}^*})$$

Notice that half of the simulated key $\mathbf{s}$ depends on $\mathbf{x}^*$, known to B^O, while half depends on $\mathbf{x}$, which is the Oracle secret and is unknown to B^O. However, by using such an $\mathbf{s}$, we will see that B^O is able to forge replies to A's queries with the correct distribution and, later on, in the second phase, to give the challenge $\mathbf{v}^*$ to A and check whether it outputs a valid forgery.

On the other hand, if O is the uniform oracle $U_{2\ell+1}$, then B^O cannot use the same *trick* and A outputs a valid forgery only with an exponentially small probability.

Let us move to the details. In the first phase, B^O invokes A, which considers B^O as its legitimate Prover. A sends to B^O a query $\mathbf{v}$, and B^O answers with $(R, \mathbf{z})$ constructed as follows:

1. Sets $\mathbf{u}^* = (\mathbf{v} \oplus \mathbf{b}^v) \wedge \mathbf{v}^*$ and $\mathbf{u} = (\mathbf{v} \oplus \mathbf{b}^v) \wedge \overline{\mathbf{v}^*}$.
2. Makes r queries to its oracle by giving it $\mathbf{u}$ as input. If the oracle outputs an error, then B^O outputs 0 and stops. Otherwise, let $(R_1, \mathbf{z}_1)$, where $R_1 \in \mathbb{Z}_2^{2\ell \times r}$ and $\mathbf{z}_1 \in \mathbb{Z}_2^r$, be the r oracle outputs;
3. Samples R_0 and sets $\mathbf{z}_0 = R_0^T \cdot (\mathbf{x}^* \wedge \mathbf{u}^*)$;
4. Returns $(R, \mathbf{z})$ where $\mathbf{z} = \mathbf{z}_0 \oplus \mathbf{z}_1 \in \mathbb{Z}_2^r$ and $R \in \mathbb{Z}_2^{2\ell \times r}$ is uniquely determined by $R_{\downarrow\mathbf{v}^*} = R_0$ and $R_{\downarrow\overline{\mathbf{v}}^*} = R_1$.

Notice that, since $\mathbf{z}_0$ is computed with the part of $\mathbf{s}$ that contains only bits from $\mathbf{x}^*$, that $\mathbf{z}_1$ is computed with the part of $\mathbf{s}$ that contains only bits from $\mathbf{x}$, and due to the equality $(\mathbf{v} \oplus \mathbf{b}^v) = (\mathbf{u}^* \oplus \mathbf{u})$, the value $\mathbf{z}$ is equal to:

$$\begin{aligned} \mathbf{z} = \mathbf{z}_0 \oplus \mathbf{z}_1 &= ((R_0^T \cdot (\mathbf{x}^* \wedge \mathbf{u}^*)) \oplus (R_1^T \cdot (\mathbf{x} \wedge \mathbf{u}) \oplus \mathbf{e})) \oplus \mathbf{b}^z \\ &= (R^T \cdot (\mathbf{s} \wedge (\mathbf{v} \oplus \mathbf{b}^v)) \oplus \mathbf{e}) \oplus \mathbf{b}^z \end{aligned}$$

In the second phase, B^O works as follows:

1. B^O sends the challenge $\mathbf{v}^* \oplus \mathbf{b}^v$ to A;
2. A answers to B^O with $(R^*, \mathbf{z}^*)$;
3. B^O checks if:

$$wt((\mathbf{z}^* \oplus R^{*T} \cdot (\mathbf{x}^* \wedge \mathbf{v}^*)) \oplus \mathbf{b}^z) \leq r \cdot \tau'$$

B^O outputs 1 if the check is valid, 0 otherwise.

Notice that, the choice of $\mathbf{v}^* \oplus \mathbf{b}^v$ implies that, when A computes $\mathbf{z}^*$, it computes $\mathbf{v}^* \oplus \mathbf{b}^v \oplus \mathbf{b}^v = \mathbf{v}^*$;

Remark. B^O can check the validity of the forgery by using only $\mathbf{x}^*$ because $(\mathbf{s} \wedge \mathbf{v}^*) = (\mathbf{x}^* \wedge \mathbf{v}^*)$. Indeed:

$$(\mathbf{s} \wedge \mathbf{v}^*) = ((\mathbf{x}^* \wedge \mathbf{v}^*) \oplus (\mathbf{x} \wedge \overline{\mathbf{v}^*})) \wedge \mathbf{v}^* = (\mathbf{x}^* \wedge \mathbf{v}^* \wedge \mathbf{v}^*) \oplus (\mathbf{x} \wedge \overline{\mathbf{v}^*} \wedge \mathbf{v}^*)$$
$$= (\mathbf{x}^* \wedge \mathbf{v}^*)$$

The second equality can be checked by computing the truth tables.

Claim 1. It holds that:

$$Pr[B^{U_{2\ell+1}(\cdot)} = 1] \leq \alpha''_{\tau',r} + Q \cdot \alpha^*_{\ell,d}$$

We notice that $U_{2\ell+1}(\cdot)$ outputs an error if the query generated by using $\mathbf{u} = (\mathbf{v} \oplus \mathbf{b}^v) \wedge \overline{\mathbf{v}^*}$ has $wt(\mathbf{u}) < d$. Given $\mathbf{v}^*$ and $\mathbf{b}^v$ uniformly random, for each $\mathbf{v}$, the probability that $wt((\mathbf{v} \oplus \mathbf{b}^v) \wedge \overline{\mathbf{v}^*}) < d$ is, as defined above, $\alpha^*_{\ell,d}$. If we upper bound this probability for each Q query, we get the total probability $Q \cdot \alpha^*_{\ell,d}$.

In the second phase, since the vector $\mathbf{x}^*$ is uniformly random, $(\mathbf{v} \oplus \mathbf{b}^v)$ is uniformly random (it is the result from the XOR between two uniformly random vectors) and $\mathbf{b}^z$ is uniformly random, then:

$$\mathbf{y} = \mathbf{z}^* \oplus R^{*T} \cdot (\mathbf{x}^* \wedge (\mathbf{v}^* \oplus \mathbf{b}^v)) \oplus \mathbf{b}^z$$

is itself uniformly random. Because of this, the probability that $Pr[wt(\mathbf{y}) \leq r \cdot \tau']$ is $\alpha''_{\tau',r}$.

Claim 2. It holds that:

$$Pr[B^{\Gamma^*_{\tau,2\ell,d}(\mathbf{x},\cdot)} = 1] \geq \epsilon'$$

The proof is split in two parts. First we show that B outputs 1 with a probability $\geq \epsilon'$ if the oracle SLPN accepts subsets of ordinary size, i.e.:

$$Pr[B^{\Gamma^*_{\tau,2\ell,0}(\mathbf{x},\cdot)} = 1] \geq \epsilon'$$

Then, we notice that:

$$Pr[B^{\Gamma^*_{\tau,2\ell,d}(\mathbf{x},\cdot)} = 1] \geq Pr[B^{\Gamma^*_{\tau,2\ell,0}(\mathbf{x},\cdot)} = 1]$$

This it true because $\Gamma^*_{\tau,2\ell,()}(\mathbf{x}, \cdot)$ behaves exactly like $\Gamma^*_{\tau,2\ell,d}(\mathbf{x}, \cdot)$ until queries $\mathbf{v}$, where $wt((\mathbf{v} \oplus \mathbf{b}^v) \wedge \overline{\mathbf{v}^*}) < d$, are made. The result holds because:

1. The replies given to A by $B^{\Gamma^*_{\tau,2\ell,()}(\mathbf{x},\cdot)}$ in the first phase, have the same distribution they would have if A interacts with a legitimate Prover with secret key $\mathbf{s}$. Thus, $\mathbf{z} = \mathbf{z}_0 \oplus \mathbf{z}_1$ is uniformly random because both $\mathbf{z}_0$ and $\mathbf{z}_1$ are uniformly random.
2. The challenge $\mathbf{v}^*$ sent to A in the second phase is uniformly random and has the same distribution it would have in a regular active attack.
3. Since $B^{\Gamma^*_{\tau,2\ell,()}(\mathbf{x},\cdot)}$ returns 1 if the Hamming weight check is valid (only when A's reply to the challenge is valid), this probability is ϵ'.

Thus, from the above two claims, it follows that the probability that B^O distinguishes between the two oracles is at least $\epsilon = \epsilon' - Q \cdot \alpha^*_{\ell,d} - \alpha''_{\tau',r}$.

6 Implementation: A Trade-Off

We suggest to use a pseudo-random generator (PRG) for the tree structure stored by the Reader. This technique involves the use of a secret seed $\mathbf{k} \in Z_2^{2\ell}$ both during the registration and the identification phases. The pseudo-random generator has an expansion factor β:

$$G : \{0,1\}^{2\ell} \longrightarrow \{0,1\}^{2\ell \cdot \beta}$$

When the Reader needs to register a Tag, it makes the first call to the generator, using the vector $\mathbf{k}$ as the seed. He obtains a string $G(k) = y_1^1, y_2^1, ..., y_\beta^1$ whose length is $2\ell \cdot \beta$. It is possible to divide this string into β sub-strings of length 2ℓ, and use one of them (chosen randomly or according to an order) to generate the next level. The same process is repeated d times, until the last level of the tree is reached and the Tags identifying key is obtained. In the identification phase, the same computation is repeated.

7 Evaluating Practical Applicability

Parameters usually recommended for protocols similar to HB and based on the LPN problem are $\ell = 768$ and $\tau = 0.05$, which offer a security level $\epsilon \approx 2^{-80}$. This value is high enough to guarantee active security in protocols HB-like (based on the LPN problem). Since the protocol proposed in this paper is based on the $SLPN^*$ problem, according to [8], the length of ℓ should be $\approx \ell + 80$. The recommended number of repetitions, instead, is about 360. Talking about the tree stored by the Reader, d and β should be chosen depending on N, the upper bound to the number of Tags supported by the system, so that $\beta^d \geq N$. Assuming that on average a system should be able to handle at least 1.000.000 Tags, the tree stored by the Reader can have an height equal to 2 or 3. In the first case, the tree will have a branching factor $\beta = 1000$ while, in the second case, will have a branching factor $\beta = 100$. Given the values:

$$l = 850, r = 360, N = 1.000.000, d = 3, \beta = 100, \tau = 1/8, \tau' = 5/16$$

we have approximately the complexity reported in Table 2.

Table 2. Summary table for the complexity of the protocol.

Memory		Communication	
Tag	*Reader*	*Tag*	*Reader*
0,7 KB	21 GB	153 KB	1,4 KB

We have performed an analysis of some products on the market, considering the most significant producers such as: Alien Technology, Caen RFID, Fujitsu, Intermec, Smartrac and Xerafy. We have analysed only Tags because Readers should be powerful enough to be able to make even burdensome computations and to store a large amount of data. We have divided products into three categories: low frequency, high frequency and ultrahigh frequency Tags. We show in the following table the features of the chosen Tags. The selected Tags can normally be purchased on online stores. In Table 3 is reported for each: the name, the size, the amount of user memory available and the frequency at which they operate.

Table 3. Some commercial Tags on the market.

Name	Size	Memory	Frequency
Low frequency tags			
ShopNFC RFID Card	85 x 54 x 0,84 mm	64 bit	125 kHz
IN Tag HITAG S	50 x 50 x 3 mm	0,256 KB	125 kHz
GAO RFID Card	85.6 x 53.98 x 1.8 mm	0,125 KB	125 ± 6 kHz
Omnia Key Fob	53 x 33 x 4.75 mm	128 bit	125 or 134.2 kHz
TheTagFactory M-Prince	90 x 34 x 7 mm	256 bit	125 kHz
High frequency tags			
Smartrac Block Lite	50 x 50 x 1.97 mm	0,316 KB	13.56 MHz
Smartrac Idisc-tag	50 x 3 mm	2 KB	13.56 MHz
Invengo NTOUCH	32 x 15 mm	0,888 KB	13.56 MHz
GAO RP Tag	82 x 49 mm	1,25 KB	13.56 MHz
Core RFID Card	86 x 54 x 0.8 mm	1 KB	13.56 MHz
Ultra-high frequency Tags			
Xerafy Sky-ID	35.3 x 20 x 4.2 mm	8 KB	860–960 MHz
Fujitsu FRAM Tag	50.8 x 25.4 x 6.22 mm	64 KB	860–960 MHz
IronTag Flex	55 x 25 x 4 mm	10 KB	902–928 MHz or 915–921 MHz
Intermec Low Profile tag	111 x 21 x 5 mm	512 bit	860–960 MHz
RFcamp Titan	150 x 30 mm	4 KB	865–868 or 902–928 MHz

Normally, the memory of a Tag consists of four types of memory:

- **Reserved Memory.** This memory stores the kill password and the access password (usually each are 32 bits). The kill password permanently disables the Tag and the access password is set to lock and unlock the write capabilities.
- **EPC Memory.** This memory stores the EPC code (Electronic Product Code) and it has usually 96 bits of writable memory.
- **TID Memory.** This memory is used to store the unique ID number by the manufacturer.
- **User Memory.** It is the memory that can be used by users if the EPC is not sufficient. The dimensions may vary depending on the type and the manufacturer.

What we have reported in Table 3 refers to the user memory since it is the most significant and useful for the purposes of our study. Assuming that the memory expected on the Readers should not be a problem despite the 21 GB, we focus only on the evaluation of Tags. Comparing the values with those required by the selected commercial products, we have the results showed in Table 4.

As shown in Table 4, the applicability on low frequency Tags is limited by the memory required to store all the necessary keys and parameters. On Tags

Table 4. Applicabilty on some commercial Tags.

Name	Applicability
Low frequency tags	
ShopNFC RFID Card	x
IN Tag HITAG S	x
GAO RFID Tag	x
Omia Key Fob	x
TheTagFactory M-Prince	x
High frequency tags	
Smartrac Block Lite	x
Smartrac Idisc-tag	✓
Invengo NTOUCH	✓
GAO RP Tag	✓
Core RFID Card	✓
Ultra-high frequency tags	
Xerafy Sky-ID	✓
Fujitsu FRAM Tag	✓
IronTag Flex	✓
Intermec Low Profile Tag	✓
RFcamp Titan	✓

of this type that normally do not have a memory greater than 2048 bits, any type of protocol is quite difficult to implement, including this one. Obviously, for a more accurate analysis it would be necessary to perform an evaluation on the real computational capabilities, as the Tag needs to generate vectors and matrices at run-time.

8   Conclusions

Our findings point out that the applicability of the protocol to low frequency Tags is difficult. Ignoring evaluations of the computational capabilities, the requested memory is too much. From the market analysis we have performed, and briefly reported in the above tables, it seems difficult to find low frequency Tags with more then 2048 bits user memory. This aspect makes the applicability of any type of secure and private protocol quite challenging.

References

1. D'Arco, P.: Ultralightweight cryptography. In: Lanet, J.-L., Toma, C. (eds.) SECITC 2018. LNCS, vol. 11359, pp. 1–16. Springer, Cham (2019). https://doi.org/10.1007/978-3-030-12942-2_1

2. Gilbert, H., Robshaw, M.J.B., Seurin, Y.: HB#: Increasing the Security and Efficiency of HB+. In: Smart, N. (ed.) EUROCRYPT 2008. LNCS, vol. 4965, pp. 361–378. Springer, Heidelberg (2008). https://doi.org/10.1007/978-3-540-78967-3_21

3. Gilbert, H., Robshaw, M., Sibert, H.: An active attack against HB+ - a provably secure lightweight authentication protocol, Cryptology ePrint Archive, Report 2005/237 (2005)

4. Halevi, T., Saxena, N., Halevi, S.: Tree-based HB protocols for privacy-preserving authentication of RFID tags. In: Radio Frequency Identification: Security and Privacy Issues. Springer (2010)

5. Hopper, N.J., Blum, M.: Secure human identification protocols. In: Boyd, C. (ed.) ASIACRYPT 2001. LNCS, vol. 2248, pp. 52–66. Springer, Heidelberg (2001). https://doi.org/10.1007/3-540-45682-1_4

6. Juels, A., Weis, S.A.: Authenticating pervasive devices with human protocols. In: Shoup, V. (ed.) CRYPTO 2005. LNCS, vol. 3621, pp. 293–308. Springer, Heidelberg (2005). https://doi.org/10.1007/11535218_18

7. Katz, J., Shin, J.S., Smith, A.: Parallel and concurrent security of the HB and HB+ protocols. J. Cryptol. **23**, 402–421 (2010)

8. Kiltz, E., Pietrzak, K., Cash, D., Jain, A., Venturi, D.: Efficient authentication from hard learning problems. In: Paterson, K.G. (ed.) EUROCRYPT 2011. LNCS, vol. 6632, pp. 7–26. Springer, Heidelberg (2011). https://doi.org/10.1007/978-3-642-20465-4_3

9. Ouafi, K., Overbeck, R., Vaudenay, S.: On the security of HB# against a man-in-the-middle attack. In: Pieprzyk, J. (ed.) ASIACRYPT 2008. LNCS, vol. 5350, pp. 108–124. Springer, Heidelberg (2008). https://doi.org/10.1007/978-3-540-89255-7_8

Effective Ransomware Detection Using Entropy Estimation of Files for Cloud Services

Kyungroul Lee⬡, Sun-Young Lee⬡, and Kangbin Yim$^{(\boxtimes)}$⬡

Soonchunhyang University, Asan 31538, South Korea
{carpedm, sunlee, yim}@sch.ac.kr

Abstract. A variety of data-based services such as cloud services and big data-based services have emerged. These services store data and derive the value of the data, and the reliability and integrity of the data must be ensured. Attackers have taken valuable data hostage for money in attacks called ransomware, and systems infected by ransomware, it is difficult to recover original data from files because they are encrypted and cannot be accessed without keys. To solve this problem, there are cloud services to back up data; however, encrypted files are synchronized to the cloud service, so that when victim systems are infected, which means that the original file cannot restored even from the cloud. Therefore, in this paper, we propose a method to effectively detect ransomware for cloud services by estimating entropy. As experiment results, we detected 100% of the infected files in target files. We demonstrated that our proposed ransomware detection method was very effective compared with other existing methods.

Keywords: Cloud service · Malicious code detection · Ransomware · Entropy

1 Introduction

Due to the fourth industrial revolution, data-based services such as cloud computing and big data have emerged. Cloud computing is a technology that processes and stores information in computing environments that provide high-level resources at low cost [1]. Big data refers to extremely large amounts of unstructured data that have value based on their characteristics and that require analysis technique that can process vast amount of data [2]. The basis of cloud services is data, and these services cannot operate successfully, if the reliability and integrity of the data are not guaranteed. Meanwhile, the valuable data stored in the cloud are attractive targets; attacks can cause serious damage in attacks called ransomware that threaten to manipulate data unless money is paid [3].

Ransomware restricts access by holding computer systems hostage and demanding ransom in exchange for releasing the restrictions. Specifically, ransomware encrypts sensitive information stored in victim system and then requires money in exchange for providing the decryption keys [4, 5]; most ransomware target systems are PCs. Investigators have tested a variety of methods for detecting ransomware and preventing system infections [6–9].

© Springer Nature Switzerland AG 2019
C. Esposito et al. (Eds.): I-SPAN 2019, CCIS 1080, pp. 133–139, 2019.
https://doi.org/10.1007/978-3-030-30143-9_11

Existing ransomware detection methods cannot detect infected files that are transmitted to cloud services. When a ransomware attack happens, victims are not able to restore or overwrite their in-house files with their cloud backups because the cloud files are locked as well. Therefore, in this paper, we study a method for effectively detecting ransomware in cloud storage files to solve this problem.

2   The Proposed Method

The proposed detection method utilizes a feature that appears in ransomware-infected files that is not a feature of clean files. Ransomware generally encrypts to prevent access to files containing sensitive information. In terms of the characteristics of cryptography, cipher text generated by the cryptography is statistically uniform; for example, if the value of the cipher result is from 0x00 to 0xFF, the probability of each generated cipher value should be the same [10]. If a bias is applied to cipher text such as a specific value or a specific range of values, the problem is that it is possible to decrypt based on the probabilities of values that are generated more or less frequently [11]. In order to solve this problem, the cryptography technique we propose is designed so that the probability of occurrence of each value generated by the cipher text is substantially the same. Therefore, the data in files infected with ransomware are statistically uniform because ransomware encrypts the file and the cipher text itself is uniform. Moreover, when we can detect ransomware-infected files by measuring the numbers represented by these features. Therefore, if the encrypted data are uniform, the entropy is high. In other words, the data in a file encrypted with ransomware are uniform, and the entropy of the encrypted file is higher than that of the original clean file. In this paper, we detect ransomware based on uniformity in infected files.

The ransomware detection module proposed in this paper detects files infected by ransomware by measuring the entropy of files transferred to the cloud server, and the module is located between the client software that provides the cloud service and the cloud server. This module needs file path information to read the file data to measure the entropy of each file. In particular, the entropy changes according to the file format, so the module has to obtain the file format, which comprises a file that contains sensitive user information and operation files, that is system, document, image, source code, and executable files. Namely, the list of files to be delivered to the cloud server is obtained, and then the paths of the files included in the list are extracted; finally, the file formats are obtained. Afterward, the entropy of the file is measured, and the infected file is detected by comparing it with the threshold according to the file format. Through this process, it is possible to detect whether the victim system is infected with ransomware and also to detect infected files. Furthermore, if the module detects that a file transferred to the cloud server is infected by ransomware, the file will not synchronize with the uploaded file for file recovery. For this reason, the original file can be restored by downloading the uploaded file from the server.

To establish the effectiveness of the detection method proposed in this paper, we experimented with Dropbox, a commercial cloud service, and verified its concept. First, the information from the file to be transferred must be extracted in order to obtain the file path. The detection module used hooking technique for the CreateFileW function to obtain the list of files to be synchronized to the Dropbox server. As a result, the path of the synchronized file is obtained from the detection module that embeds to the Dropbox software using hooking technique, and the experimental result is shown in Fig. 1. In this process, some paths are duplicated or assumed to be Dropbox files or folders. For example, there are "config.dbx-journal" file and "Dropbox" folders, and "Confidential data.txt" file is duplicated. In this way, unnecessary and duplicate files are removed to obtain optimized synchronized file paths and lists.

Fig. 1. Synchronized file paths extracted from the detection module

By extracting the file list and file path, the detection module can read the data of the files being synchronized with Dropbox server, and then detect the infected files by measuring the entropy based on the read data. For measuring entropy, NIST provides both statistics-based and predictor-based methods but, predictor-based measurement has the disadvantage that it takes a comparatively long time, and thus it is difficult to use in measuring entropy in real time. Therefore, we utilize faster, statistic-based measurement in this paper. Figure 2 shows the result of measuring the entropy of a file uploaded to the Dropbox server.

On left of the figure, the Injector injects the implemented detection module into the Dropbox software, and the injected detection module measures the entropy of the synchronized file. On the right side is the detection module, which outputs a list of files to be synchronized and an entropy estimate result of the files included in the list. In the

Fig. 2. Entropy estimation results for a single file synchronized to Dropbox

experiment, "Confidential File" is synchronized to the Dropbox server. Respectively, the resulting most common value estimate, collision test estimate, Markov test estimate, and compression test estimate were 0.654851, 0.553649, 0.025006, and 0.426463. Hence, the min-entropy was 0.426463.

3   Experiment Results

Based on the methodology proposed in Sect. 2, we verify the detection of ransomware by measuring the entropy of the files uploaded to the Dropbox cloud server. The specific target files are a system file, a document file, an image file, a source code file, and an executable file, which are files related to sensitive user information and to system operations. For the experiment, we assumed that 10 file formats were infected with 100 files in each format. That is, we analyzed the entropy measurement results and entropy change trends to effectively detect ransomware when 10, 20, ..., 100 files were infected. Through this process, the module determined a threshold for effectively detecting infection by comparing and analyzing the entropy measurement results for the ransomware infection and encryption processes.

First, because measuring entropy requires reference values for each format of clean files, our module measured the entropy of 100 files in each format; the result is shown in Fig. 3. As the figure shows, the entropy results change for some but not all formats of clean files; specifically, there were 4, 7, 10, 3, and 4 high peaks corresponding, respectively, to system, document, image, source code, and executable files. That is, some but not all clean files showed high entropy. By amount, respectively, fewer than 6, 8, 8, 4, and 6, system, document, image, source code, and executable files showed entropy. By averages fewer than 3, 5, 4, 3, and 3, system, document, image, source code, and executable files, respectively, showed entropy. Therefore, we derived the threshold for detecting ransomware-infected files based on average and peak entropy, which occurs as a high peak in clean files.

The entropy increases as the number of infected files increases. Therefore, reference values are required for detecting specific minimum numbers of ransomware-infected files. To determine these reference values, we compared and analyzed the changes in

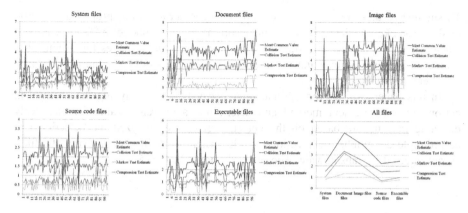

Fig. 3. Entropy estimation results for 100 clean files per file format

entropy according to the number of infections. For this paper, we assumed that 100 files were infected with ransomware per 10 files and derived the entropy changes by number of infections. The result is shown in Fig. 4.

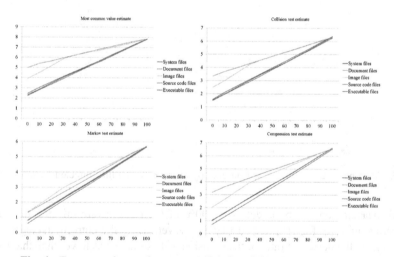

Fig. 4. Entropy estimate changes per 10 infected files by estimate method

Respectively, the results showed that the file formats with the highest entropy according to most common value estimation, collision test estimation, Markov test estimation, and compression test estimation were document, document, image, and document files, and source code files had the lowest entropy. According to the change trend, the measurement method with the sharpest change by number of infected files was the most common value estimate, and the method with the slightest change was the collision test estimation. The file formats with sharp changes were system, source code, and executable files, and the document files showed the slightest changes.

To summarize these results, when entropy changes abruptly, our proposed detection module was likely to detect ransomware according to the number of infections. That is, when entropy was measured using the most common value estimates for system files, source code files, and executable files, we could effectively detect ransomware in a cloud environment.

In this paper, we derived optimal reference values by analyzing the changes in entropy by measurement method and determined a reference value for effectively detecting ransomware based on the detection rate. We analyzed the detection rate according to the number of infections by file format, assuming that in every 100 files, 10 are infected by ransomware. The result is shown in Fig. 5.

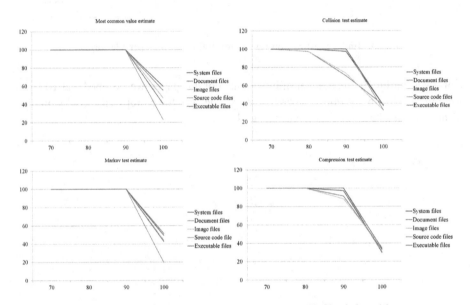

Fig. 5. Average detection rate based on entropy average per 10 files infected by ransomware

All measurement methods detected 100% of the ransomware-infected files using the average entropy for 70 infected files. However, using the entropy average for 80 infected files, the detection rate for the collision test estimate was lower than that for the other measurement methods. Moreover, the detection rate dropped sharply for all measurement methods using the average entropy of 100 infected files. In particular, the compression test estimate had the lowest detection rate, whereas the most common value estimate had the highest rate.

By file format, using the entropy average of 80 infected document and image files, we identified several ransomware-infected files that could not be detected, but our proposed method detected all ransomware-infected source code and executable files using the average entropy of 90 infected files.

4   Conclusions

In this paper, we proposed a method to effectively detect ransomware by measuring entropy of files stored on a cloud server. The idea of the proposed detection method is uniformity, one of the characteristics of ransomware-infected encrypted files; that is, the probability that each value included in the data range for the encrypted files is almost the same. Therefore, we measured the uniformity of files synchronized to the cloud server based on entropy. For the experiment, we collected system, document, image, source code, and executable files which are the files necessary for system operation and which include sensitive user information, and we estimated the entropy by comparing the entropy of ransomware-infected encrypted files with that of clean files. To derive the baseline entropy for infected files, we compared and analyzed the entropy by file format and number of ransomware infections; based on these results, we derived the optimal baseline values for detecting ransomware-infected files. The baseline value we derived detected 100% of all ransomware-infected files. In short, our proposed ransomware detection method completely and effectively detected ransomware-infected files.

Acknowledgement. This work was supported by the National Research Foundation of Korea (NRF) grant funded by the Korea government (MSIT) (No. 2018R1A4A1025632).

References

1. Wikipedia, Cloud computing. https://en.wikipedia.org/wiki/Cloud_computing. Accessed 5 Apr 2019
2. Wikipedia, Big data. https://en.wikipedia.org/wiki/Big_data. Accessed 5 Apr 2019
3. Gazet, A.: Comparative analysis of various ransomware virii. J. Comput. Virol. **6**(1), 77–90 (2010)
4. Wikipedia, Ransomware. https://en.wikipedia.org/wiki/Ransomware. Accessed 5 Apr 2019
5. Everett, C.: Ransomware: to pay or not to pay? J. Comput. Fraud. Secur. **2016**(4), 8–12 (2016)
6. Cabaj, K., Gregorczyk, M., Mazurczyk, W.: Software-defined networking-based crypto ransomware detection using HTTP traffic characteristics. J. Comput. Electr. Eng. **66**, 353–368 (2018)
7. Paik, J., Choi, J., Jin, R., Wang, J., Cho, E.: A storage-level detection mechanism against crypto-ransomware. In: 25th ACM SIGSAC Conference on Computer and Communications Security, Toronto, Canada, pp. 2258–2260. ACM (2018)
8. Chen, J., Wang, C., Zhao, Z., Chen, K., Du, R., Ahn, G.: Uncovering the face of android ransomware: characterization and real-time detection. J. IEEE Trans. Inf. Forensics Secur. **13** (5), 1286–1300 (2017)
9. Akbanov, M., Vassilakis, V., Logothetis, M.: Ransomware detection and mitigation using software-defined networking: the case of WannaCry. J. Comput. Electr. Eng. **76**, 111–121 (2019)
10. Li, Z., Xiang, C., Wang, C.: Oblivious transfer via lossy encryption from lattice-based cryptography. J. Wirel. Commun. Mob. Comput. **2018**(5973285), 11 (2018)
11. Boura, C., Canteaut, A.: On the boomerang uniformity of cryptographic Sboxes. J. IACR Trans. Symmetric Cryptol. **2018**(3), 290–310 (2018)

Modeling and Formal Verification of the Ticket-Based Handoff Authentication Protocol for Wireless Mesh Networks

Zahra Ebadi Ansaroudi[1(✉)] and Saeid Pashazadeh[2(✉)]

[1] Department of Computer Science,
University of Salerno, Salerno - Fisciano, Italy
zebadiansaroudi@unisa.it
[2] Department of Information Technology, Faculty of Electrical and Computer
Engineering, University of Tabriz, Tabriz, Iran
pashazadeh@tabrizu.ac.ir

Abstract. As Wireless Mesh Networks (WMNs) are growing day-by-day, a seamless and secure handoff is gaining significant importance for supporting multi-hop WMNs. On this point, various authentication protocols, such as the ticket-based handoff authentication, for wireless mesh networks have been proposed. Modeling and formal verification of the aforementioned protocol using CPN Tools and ASK-CTL statement are the purposes of this paper. To this aim, the resistance of the protocol against attacks, such as the man in the middle attack is investigated and then, it is concluded that it is secure.

Keywords: Colored Petri Nets · ASK-CTL · WMNs · Handoff ·
Authentication protocol · Man-in-the-middle attack

1 Introduction and Related Works

The usage of Internet has quickly increased in our daily lives and upon that, Wireless Mesh Networks (WMNs) are widely considered as a very promising technology. A WMN consist of a wireless infrastructure of mesh routers and clients. The mesh routers connect to the Internet through mesh gateways. In addition, Mesh clients connect to these mesh routers to use the connectivity and services provided by a WMN. Therefore, to ensure continuous connectivity in WMNs, the mesh clients must be able to securely handoff from one mesh router to the next. Recently, various authentication protocol for handoff have been proposed. In 2014, Xu et al. proposed a Ticket-based Hand-off Authentication Protocol for WMNs to support fast and secure handoff [1]. By pre-distributing the tickets to a mesh client, the mesh client and its appropriate neighboring mesh router for handoff are able to authenticate each other. Xu et al. have proved the security of protocol against attacks as man in the middle using AVISPA. In this paper it is tried to use the Colored Petri Nets (CPNs) and CPN Tools as formal method tools for security analysis.

Here, there are two questions to be considered: first, why use formal methods? Second, why CPNs have been chosen?

© Springer Nature Switzerland AG 2019
C. Esposito et al. (Eds.): I-SPAN 2019, CCIS 1080, pp. 140–154, 2019.
https://doi.org/10.1007/978-3-030-30143-9_12

In order to design an authentication protocol, it is crucial to consider all the possible behaviors of hypothetical attackers. In the other words, an attacker is able to behave in many ways at each protocol step to eavesdrop, fabricate and so on. Hence, despite the existence of the best recommendations [2], the manual design of a new authentication protocol can be a challenging task. Integrating clear security properties, adversary models, and formal methods into the design process can improve protocol security [3]. Since formal verification of authentication protocols can detect design flaws that lead to protocol failure, it is considered as an essential method for analysis of security protocols [4].

Formal methods, as mathematics of software and hardware systems, include modeling languages and tools. These methods model and analyze systems by means of specific mathematical techniques for the specification and verification of model properties. The act of constructing a model and analyzing its behavior is a way to gain greater confidence in the proposed designs and to help reveal inconsistencies, ambiguities, and incompleteness that might otherwise go undetected [5, 6]. There are different formal model checking tools such as Athena [7], AVISPA [8], SATMC [9], OFMC [10] and CPN Tools [11].

CPN Tools is a tool editing, simulating and analyzing untimed and timed, hierarchical Colored Petri nets. It has a graphical representation and an elaborated mathematical syntax which provide a clear simulation and analysis [11–13]. There has been considerable interest in using CPNs as a formal technique for analysis of security protocols in recent years [14–17].

The structure of the present paper is as follows: Sect. 2 includes preliminaries. Section 3 describes details of the TbHA protocol and its modeling using CPN tools. Section 4 presents the simulations and verifies the security of the TbHA protocol against a special man-in-the-middle attack using ASK-CTL statement. Finally, Sect. 5 presents the conclusion and a guideline for further investigation.

2 Preliminaries

2.1 Man-in-the-Middle Attack

In the Ticket-based Hand-off Authentication Protocol for WMNs (in short TbHA), a man-in-the-middle is a third party who controls all the communication that take place between the protocol parties (the MCs, the MRs, and the AS). It has capability to read, modify, delete messages or even worse, start and finish a session without involving destination parties (bypass the parties). Therefore, it has capability to violate the authentication property of the protocol. To verify these violation criteria, a special intruder model is considered. The intruder model is described in Sect. 3.2.

The authentication property violation can be defined in details as follows:

The authentication property of the TbHA protocol is violated if the intruder in network channels intercepts the messages during exchanges between communication parties and modifies the messages and forwards or even does not forward them to the destination party; instead, the intruder sends its own responses by using the intercepted messages.

2.2 CPN Modelling

CPNs are graphs that are made up of two types of nodes, places (circles or ellipses) and transitions (rectangular boxes) connected by arcs. The places from which an arc leads to a transition are called the input places of the transition; the places to which arcs lead from a transition are called the output places of the transition. Each place may contain tokens which assign to place by marking. Moreover, these tokens have a type called colorset. Colorset determines the set of tokens colors, data values like an integer, attached to them. Additionally, these tokens may move from input places of transition to its output places by firing transition. A transition is fired (enabled) if each variable that appears in any of the input arc expressions can be bound to a token color that is present on the corresponding input place, while satisfying the guard of the transition. Figure 1, shows an abstract CPN model.

In particular, with the CPN hierarchical models, a model can have submodules. A module exchanges tokens with other modules by means of port places. In a model port places can be indicated by blue rectangular port tags ("In", "Out" or "I/O") positioned closed to them specifying whether the port place is an input, output, or input/output port. The reader is referred to [12, 13] for more information about CPNs.

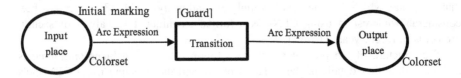

Fig. 1. An abstract model of CPN

2.3 The CPN Tools ASK-CTL

ASK-CTL logic is an extension of Computational Temporal Logic (CTL) [18], a CTL-like temporal logic, which is a branching time logic. CTL is able to reason about certain facts based on a model state space (also called the occurrence graph or reachability graph/tree) and provides a model of time using a tree structure. In this structure, the future is not determined and different paths can occur. Any of the branches might be an actual path that is realized [19]. That is to say, in ASK-CTL, CTL is extended in order to take into account state information coupled with transition information. Addition-ally, the ASK-CTL also contains a model checker. It takes an ASK-CTL formula as an argument, checks the formula against the current state space to decide whether the authentication property is met. The ASK-CTL logic and model checker are imple-mented in SML (a general-purpose functional programming language), and queries are formulated directly in SML syntax. For a detailed review on SML see [20].

3   Modeling the TbHA Protocol Using CPN

3.1   The TbHA Protocol Details

The TbHA protocol consists of two phases, each phase is described briefly, and the full description of the protocol is presented in [1].

Ticket Issuing

As Fig. 2, after full successful authentication of the Mesh Client (MC) while re-authenticating, step by step, the home mesh router (HMR) sends the identities of its one-hop neighbors, and the identity of MC to the authentication server (AS). The AS uses identities to generate handoff tickets for the authentication between the MC and its next foreign mesh router (FMR) as in Eqs. (1), (2) and (3) afterward sends them to the MC. The MC decrypts tickets and saves them for the next usages, as Eq. (4).

$$TAK_i = H_{MK_{FMR_i}}(ID_{HMR}|ID_{FMR_i}|ID_{MC}|n|t) \tag{1}$$

$$T_i = \{TAK_i, ID_{HMR}, ID_{FMR_i}, ID_{MC}, n, t\} \tag{2}$$

$$CT = ENC_{H_{(MK_{MC})}}(T1|T2|T3|\ldots) \tag{3}$$

$$T1|T2|T3|\ldots = DEC_{H_{(MK_{MC})}} \tag{4}$$

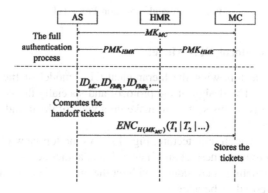

Fig. 2. Ticket Issuing Phase [1]

Re-authentication

As Fig. 3, the MC chooses a FMR and performs a three-way-handshaking with the chosen FMR to authenticate each other as Eqs. (5), (6), (7), (8), (9). Eventually, the MC and the FMR establish security keys as Eq. (10).

$$m_{FMR} = ID_{FMR_i} | g^{r_{MC}} | g^{r_{FMR_i}} \tag{5}$$

$$MAC_{TAK_i}(m_{FMR}) = H_{TAK_i}(m_{FMR}) \tag{6}$$

$$TSK_i = (g^{r_{FMR_i}})^{r_{MC}} \tag{7}$$

$$mMC = IDMC | g^{r_{MC}} | g^{r_{FMR_i}} \tag{8}$$

$$MAC_{TAK_i}(m_{MC}) = H_{TAK_i}(m_{MC}) \tag{9}$$

$$TSK_i = (g^{r_{MC}})^{r_{FMR_i}} \tag{10}$$

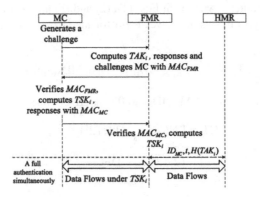

Fig. 3. Re-authentication Phase [1]

3.2   The TbHA Protocol CPN Model

It is described in the following the hierarchical CPN model of the protocol and its various components. The design of the protocol and specially the network design has been described briefly in this section to make up a view of the intruder model that will be displayed on the Sect. 3.3.

Considering the overall architecture, Fig. 4 shows the top view of this CPN model that includes mesh routers, mesh clients, network and authentication server substitution transitions. First modeling is considered without the presence of an intruder, afterward, the intruder is supposed to be added.

In order to design a comprehensive model and make it easier to understand, two MCs and three MRs are considered. The 'Current position' place with the color of Pos, denotes the current position of MCs, and assign each MC to its related MR for future steps. Different places with their special colorset has been used to transfer the messages between the identities (MRs, MCs, AS) through network. to give you an example of what it means, the place with colorset of MRM1 is used to exchange the message of HMR to AS, include the identities of its one-hop neighbors and the identity of MC (the green line). The list of colorsets, variables, and functions used in the CPN model of the TbHA protocol are shown in Appendix A.

Figure 5 shows the MR subpage which include various transitions. For example, when the 'sending message' substitution transition gets token it creates a message with the identities of the FMRs and the MC to pass to the AS through the 'Network substitution transition'.

Figure 6 shows the 'Network subpage' of the CPN model. As can be seen, it has six different channels for exchanging different messages between the identities. When there is no intruder, the network channels just forward messages (see the 'Network channel1' design in Fig. 7). It is important to mention that in the design of the Network channels, it has been assumed some places to store data and allocate them to the related identity. For instance, the 'Network channel2' stores its received message in a place

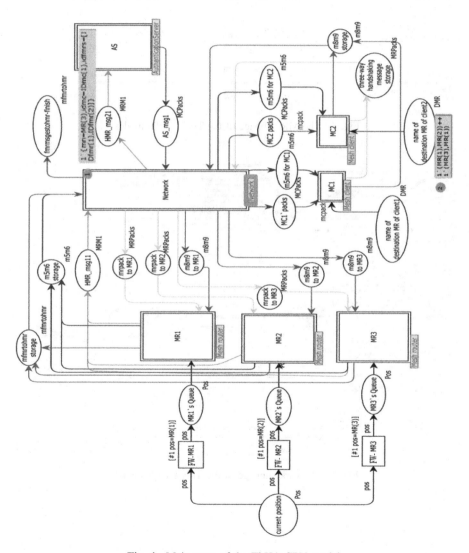

Fig. 4. Main page of the TbHA CPN model

with the name of 'AS_msg2' coupled with color of 'MCPacks' and then based on the following two transition guards of '#mci(mcpack) = MC1' and '#mci(mcpack) = MC2' forwards it to destination MC. At that time the MC decrypts it using the 'decrypting message 1' transition as Eq. (4) and stores it in 'ticket list' place for later three-way handshaking as Fig. 8.

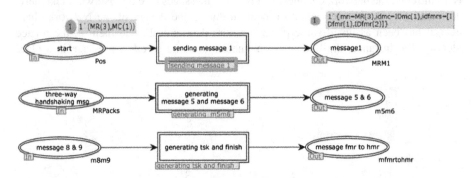

Fig. 5. The MR subpage of the TbHA CPN model

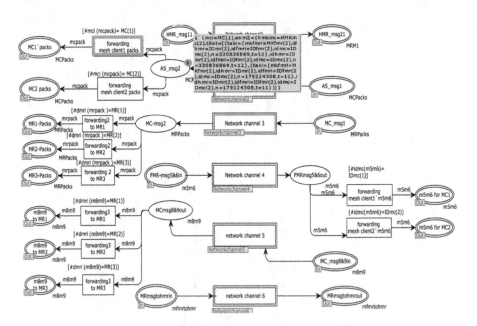

Fig. 6. Network subpage of the TbHA CPN model

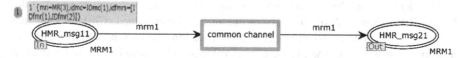

Fig. 7. Network channel1 of the TbHA CPN model

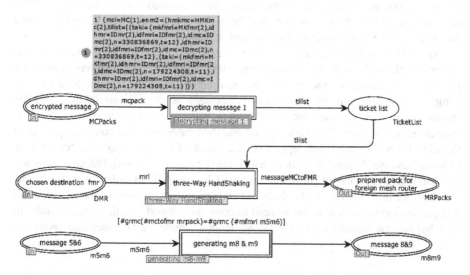

Fig. 8. The MC subpage of the TbHA CPN model

3.3 TbHA Intruder Model

With the aim of verifying the TbHA protocol, the intruder model is considered based on the Dolev-Yao approach [21]. In this method, the intruder acts as a man in the middle who controls all the communications that take place between the protocol parties (the MCs, the MRs, and the AS) and it can modify messages, create a new message, or bypass the receiver of messages. The intruder interaction with communication parties follows the model of Fig. 9.

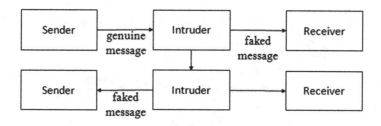

Fig. 9. Intruder interaction model

In order to model the intruder behavior, the design of the 'Network subpage' of the TbHA CPN model is developed. By means of a colorset named 'Chstate' with two values of {common, intruder}, in case it is common, there is no intruder and the network works as usual. And in case it takes value intruder, there is an intruder that can forward a message, creates a new message or bypasses receiver. And also Places with the blue label of 'Fusion1' are add to access the intruder database. The intruder database is considered to store the messages content coupled with the name or identity of their owner or receiver to be exploited later. As an instance, Figs. 10 and 11 shows the intruder behaviors model in the 'network channel1'.

As shown in Fig. 10, there are five transitions, the considered guard for the 'common channel' and the 'temporarily store message 1' transitions which are [#1state = common], [#1state = intruder] are used to enable the transitions, if the first component of the state token (#1state) is common so there is no intruder and the transition just forwards message but if it takes value intruder, it stores message temporarily in the 'intruder DB' fusion place and then based on the second component of the state token (#2state) and depend on the guard of the 'fwdmsg', the 'create new message' and the 'bypass' transitions which are [#2state = forward], [#2state = create], [#2state = bypass], one of the transitions will be enabled. In order to create a new message, the intruder uses its database and extracts the components of the message and merges them to create a new one to send through the network. Furthermore, in order to do a bypass, the intruder uses its database again to create the fake message instead of

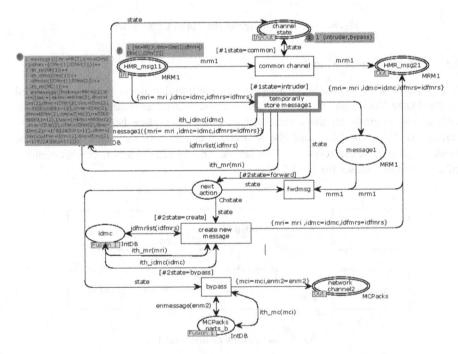

Fig. 10. Network channel1 in the presence of the intruder – 'temporarily store message 1' step

the AS. The bypass of AS is shown in Fig. 11, if the next action place gets token with the state value of bypass it will enable bypass transition to create a fake message. The intruder uses its database to extract the message with the encryption of ticket list also the name of MC that should be send to it.

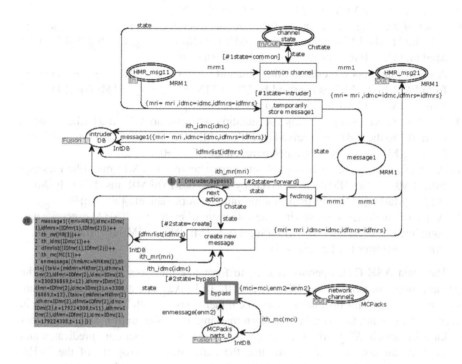

Fig. 11. Network channel1 in the presence of the intruder – 'bypass' step

4   Verification of the TbHA Protocol

The violation of the authentication property of the TbHA protocol could be formalized using the ASK-CTL statement. A special ASK-CTL formula is required to formalize authentication property. In the other word, verify not only if a session has ended successfully, but also if communication parties are not involved in the protocol exchanges. To this end, the following notations and predicates are defined:

1. Let M be the set of all reachable marking of the TbHA CPN model,
2. The initial marking of the TbHA CPN model is M0,
3. The set of all reachable markings from M0 is [M0⟩,
4. PHMR_msg21Networkchannel1: A CPN place with the name of HMR_msg21 on the CPN page called Networkchannel1
5. Marking (Mi, PHMR_msg21Networkchannel2): The set of tokens at the CPN place PHMR_msg21Networkchannel2 at a marking Mi where Mi ∈ M0⟩

6. A set of markings representing the situation whereby no HMR_msg (the message from MR to the AS) is received by AS is MNoHMR_msg = {Mi |Mi ∈ [M0⟩∧ | Marking(Mi, PHMR_msg21Networkchannel1)| ==0};

7. A set of markings representing the situation whereby no AS_msg (the message from the AS to MC) is received by MC is MNoAS_msg = {Mi |Mi ∈ [M0⟩∧ | Marking(Mi, : PAS_msg2 Networkchannel2)| ==0};

8. A set of markings representing the situation whereby no MC_msg (the message from MC to the FMR) is received by FMR is MNoMC_msg = {Mi |Mi ∈ [M0⟩∧ | Marking(Mi, : PMC_msg2 Networkchannel3)| ==0};

9. A set of markings representing the situation whereby no FMR_msg (the message from FMR to the MC) is received by MC is MNoFMR_msg = {Mi |Mi ∈ [M0⟩∧ | Marking(Mi, : PFMRmsg56outNetworkchannel4)| ==0};

10. A set of markings representing the situation whereby no MC_msg1 (the message from MC to the FMR) is received by FMR is MNoMC_msg1 = {Mi |Mi ∈ [M0⟩∧ | Marking(Mi, : PMCmsg89_outNetworkchannel5)| ==0};

11. A set of markings representing the situation whereby no FMR_msg (the message from FMR to the HMR) is received by HMR is MNoFMR_msg1 = {Mi |Mi ∈ [M0⟩∧ |Marking(Mi, : PMRmsgtohmr_out Networkchannel6)| ==0}q;

12. A set of markings representing the situation whereby the TbHA executio was completed successfully is MEndSuccess = {Mi |Mi ∈ [M0⟩∧ |Marking(Mi, : Pfmrmsgestohmr twoPhase)| > 0};

The main ASK-CTL operator is used to formalize the violation condition of the authentication property is the EXIST_UNTIL (A1, A2) operator. A1 and A2 are Boolean formulae. This operator returns true if there exists a path by which A1 holds in every marking along the path from a given marking (e.g., M0) until it reaches another marking by which A2 holds. Having described the above notations, predicates and operator, it can now formally prove that the authentication property of the TbHA protocol is violated if, from M0, the ASK-CTL statement as Eq. (11) returns true.

$$\text{EXIT\_UNTIL (MNoHMR\_msg} \wedge \text{MNoAS\_msg} \wedge \text{MNoMC\_msg} \wedge$$
$$\text{MNoFMR\_msg} \wedge \text{MNoMC\_msg1} \wedge \text{MNoFMR\_msg1, MEndSuccess)} \qquad (11)$$

To verify the authentication property, different scenarios (with or without the presence of an intruder) are considered and the state spaces for them are generated. The written SML code for the ASK-CTL formula and its result without or with the presence of the intruder in Network Channel1 is demonstrated in Figs. 12 and 13. As it can be seen it shows that the ASK-CTL statement result in both cases is false which means that the authentication property of the protocol is held and protocol is resistant to the man in the middle attack.

```
fun Mnomsg n=(Mark.Networkchannel1'HMR_msg21 1 n = [] andalso
Mark.Networkchannel2'AS_msg2  1 n = [] andalso Mark.Networkchannel3'MC_msg2 1 n = [] andalso
Mark.Networkchannel4'FMRmsg56out  1 n = [] andalso Mark.Networkchannel5'MCmsg89_out  1 n = [] andalso
Mark.Networkchannel6'MRmsgtohmr_out  1 n = [] );
fun MEndSuccess n=(Mark.twoPhase'fmrmsgestohmr  1 n <> []);
val Send=NF("messages  has been sent",Mnomsg);
val End=NF("protocol has been sucssefuly run",MEndSuccess);
val myASKCTLformula=EXIST_UNTIL(Send,End);
eval_node myASKCTLformula InitNode;
```
```
val Mnomsg = fn : Node -> bool
val MEndSuccess = fn : Node -> bool
val Send = NF ("messages  has been sent",fn) : A
val End = NF ("protocol has been sucssefuly run",fn) : A
val myASKCTLformula =
  EXIST_UNTIL
    (NF ("messages  has been sent",fn),
     NF ("protocol has been sucssefuly run",fn)) : A
val it = false : bool
```

Fig. 12. The result of ASK-CTL formula without the presence of the intruder

```
fun Mnomsg n=(Mark.Networkchannel1'HMR_msg21 1 n = [] andalso
Mark.Networkchannel2'AS_msg2  1 n = [] andalso Mark.Networkchannel3'MC_msg2 1 n = [] andalso
Mark.Networkchannel4'FMRmsg56out  1 n = [] andalso Mark.Networkchannel5'MCmsg89_out  1 n = [] andalso
Mark.Networkchannel6'MRmsgtohmr_out  1 n = [] );
fun MEndSuccess n=(Mark.twoPhase'fmrmsgestohmr  1 n <> []);
val Send=NF("messages  has been sent",Mnomsg);
val End=NF("protocol has been sucssefuly run",MEndSuccess);
val myASKCTLformula=EXIST_UNTIL(Send,End);
eval_node myASKCTLformula InitNode;
```
```
val Mnomsg = fn : Node -> bool
val MEndSuccess = fn : Node -> bool
val Send = NF ("messages  has been sent",fn) : A
val End = NF ("protocol has been sucssefuly run",fn) : A
val myASKCTLformula =
  EXIST_UNTIL
    (NF ("messages has been sent",fn),
     NF ("protocol has been sucssefuly run",fn)) : A
val it = false : bool
```

Fig. 13. The result of ASK-CTL formula with the presence of the intruder in Network channel 1

5   Conclusion and Future Works

As stated in the Introduction, the research carried out in order to verify the security of the recent handoff authentication protocol, Ticket-based Handoff Authentication Protocol for WMNs. It was proposed a formal model-based approach to analysis authentication property of the protocol on the basis of CPN model state spaces and ASK-CTL statement. A hierarchical Colored Petri Net model for the protocol has been presented. Later, a Dolev-Yao-based intruder model is developed and integrated into the protocol model. ASK-CTL verifies the violation condition of the authentication property and it is demonstrated through the results of its model checking that it satisfies the specified authentication property. The authentication property is satisfied and the protocol is resistant against the man-in-the-middle attack. we'd like to point out that the main purpose of the TbHA protocol was to reduce the latency in the handoff authentication and this is the main advantage of the protocol over other protocols in this field. Future studies on the current topic are therefore suggested in order to check the handoff latency using Timed CPNs.

Acknowledgements. We would like to express our deep gratitude to Professor Paolo D'Arco for his patient guidance, support and valuable suggestions for this research work.

Appendix A: The TbHA CPN Model Colorsets, Variables and Functions

The colorsets, variables, and functions used in the TbHA protocol CPN model are detailed in Figs. 14 and 15.

```
var messageMCtoFMR :MmcTofmri;
var en:Enable;
var m5m6:m5m6;
var mcd:MCdata;
var taki:TAKi;
var ti:Ticket;
var tlist,tilist:TicketList;
var enm2:CT;
var gvalue:Generator;
var rvalue:randNO;
var mfmri:mFMR;
var mcpack:MCPacks;
var mrpack:MRPacks;
var nb:MRdata;
var mac:MACtakimfmr;
var m8:m8;
var m9:m9;
var m8m9:m8m9;
var mfmrtohmr:mfmrtohmr;
fun rand()=discrete(100,999999999):int;
fun Expirationtime()=discrete(1,250):int;
fun Ticketselection(tilist:TicketList,idfmrn:IDfmr) : Ticket=
if (idfmrn= #idfmri(List.hd tilist)) then List.hd tilist
 else List.hd (List.drop(tilist,1))
fun MRChoosen (nb:MRdata , mrpack:MRPacks): MR ms =
if ((#idhmr(#mctofmr (mrpack)))=(#2 nb)) then 1`(#1 nb)
else empty
fun MKfmrChoosen (mri:MR , mri1:MR , fmri:FMR) :HMKfmr ms  =
let
val z=
if (mri=(#1 fmri) andalso mri1=(#2 fmri)) then 1`(#4 fmri)
else empty
in
(z)
end;
fun takGenerator(hmkfmri:HMKfmr, idhmr:IDmr,idfmri:IDfmr,idmc:IDmc,n:Nonce,t:INT) :TAKi =
let val z= {hmkfmri=hmkfmri,idhmr=idhmr,idfmri=idfmri,idmc=idmc,n=n,t=t}
in
(z)
end;
```

Fig. 14. List of variables and functions of the TbHA protocol CPN model

```
val mc=2;
val mr=3;
colset MR=index MR with 1..mr;
colset MC= index MC with 1..mc;
colset IDmc=index IDmc with 1..mc;
colset IDmr=index IDmr with 1..mr;
colset HMKmc=index HMKmc with 1..mc;
colset HMKfmr= index HMKfmr with 1..mr-1;
colset HMKfmrlist=list HMKfmr;
colset IDfmr =index IDfmr with 1..mr-1;
colset IDfmrlist= list IDfmr ;
colset MRdata=product MR*IDmr*IDfmrlist*HMKfmrlist;
colset DMR=product MR*MR;
colset randNO = with rmc1|rmc2|rfmr1|rfmr2;
colset Generator=with grmc1|grmc2|grfmr1|grfmr2|grfm1rmc1|grfmr2rmc1|grfmr1rmc2|grfmr2rmc2|grmc
colset FMR = product MR*MR*IDfmr*HMKfmr*randNO*Generator;
colset MCdata=product MC*IDmc*HMKmc*randNO*Generator;
colset Enable=with enable|disable;
colset Nonce =int;
colset Pos = product MR*MC;
colset Membership=list Pos;
colset MRM1 = record mri:MR*idmc:IDmc*idfmrs:IDfmrlist;
colset mFMR =record idfmri:IDfmr*grmc:Generator*grfmri:Generator;
colset INT = int;
colset INTINF = intinf;
colset TAKi= record hmkfmri:HMKfmr*idhmr:IDmr*idfmri:IDfmr
*idmc:IDmc*n:Nonce*t:INT;
colset Ticket=record taki:TAKi*idhmr:IDmr*idfmri:IDfmr
*idmc:IDmc*n:Nonce*t:INT;
colset TicketList= list Ticket;
colset CT=record hmkmc:HMKmc*tilist:TicketList;
colset MACtakimfmr = record mfmri:mFMR *taki:TAKi ;
colset MmcTofmri=record grmc:Generator*idhmr:IDmr*idfmri:IDfmr*idmc:IDmc*n:Nonce*t:INT;
colset MRPacks=record dmri:MR*mctofmr:MmcTofmri;
colset MCPacks=record mci:MC*enm2:CT;
colset m5m6=record mac:MACtakimfmr*mfmri:mFMR*idmc:IDmc;
colset m8= record idmc:IDmc*grmc:Generator*grfmri:Generator;
colset m9= record m8:m8 * taki:TAKi;
colset m8m9=record m8:m8 * m9:m9 *dmri:MR;
colset TSK=record gvalue:Generator * rvalue:randNO;
colset mfmrtohmr= record idmc:IDmc* t:INT * taki:TAKi ;
```

Fig. 15. List of colorsets of the TbHA protocol CPN model

References

1. Xu, L., et al.: Ticket-based handoff authentication for wireless mesh networks. Comput. Netw. **73**, 185–194 (2014)
2. Abadi, M., Needham, R.: Prudent engineering practice for cryptographic protocols. IEEE Trans. Softw. Eng. **1**, 6–15 (1996)
3. Basin, D., et al.: Improving the security of cryptographic protocol standards. IEEE Secur. Priv. **13**(3), 24–31 (2015)
4. Avalle, M., Pironti, A., Sisto, R.: Formal verification of security protocol implementations: a survey. Formal Aspects Comput. **26**(1), 99–123 (2014)
5. Saffarian Eidgahi, Z., Rafe, V.: Security analysis of network protocols through model checking: a case study on mobile IPv6. Secur. Commun. Netw. **9**(10), 1072–1084 (2016)
6. Wing, J.M.: A specifier's introduction to formal methods. Computer **23**(9), 8–22 (1990)
7. Song, D.X.: Athena: a new efficient automatic checker for security protocol analysis. In: Proceedings of the 12th IEEE Computer Security Foundations Workshop, IEEE (1999)

8. Armando, A., et al.: The AVISPA tool for the automated validation of internet security protocols and applications. In: Etessami, K., Rajamani, S.K. (eds.) CAV 2005. LNCS, vol. 3576, pp. 281–285. Springer, Heidelberg (2005). https://doi.org/10.1007/11513988_27

9. Armando, A., Carbone, R., Compagna, L.: SATMC: a sat-based model checker for security-critical systems. In: Ábrahám, E., Havelund, K. (eds.) TACAS 2014. LNCS, vol. 8413, pp. 31–45. Springer, Heidelberg (2014). https://doi.org/10.1007/978-3-642-54862-8_3

10. Basin, D., Mödersheim, S., Vigano, L.: OFMC: A symbolic model checker for security protocols. Int. J. Inf. Secur. **4**(3), 181–208 (2005)

11. Jensen, K., Kristensen, L.M., Wells, L.: Coloured petri nets and CPN tools for modelling and validation of concurrent systems. Int. J. Softw. Tools Technol. Transf. **9**(3–4), 213–254 (2007)

12. Jensen, K.: Coloured Petri Nets: Basic Concepts, Analysis Methods and Practical Use, vol. 1. Springer Science & Business Media, Berlin (2013). https://doi.org/10.1007/978-3-662-03241-1

13. Jensen, K., Kristensen, L.M.: Coloured Petri Nets: Modelling and Validation of Concurrent Systems. Springer Science & Business Media, Berlin (2009). https://doi.org/10.1007/978-3-662-03241-1

14. Al-Azzoni, I.: The verification of cryptographic protocols using coloured petri nets (2004)

15. Aly, S., Mustafa, K.: Protocol Verification and Analysis using Colored Petri Nets. Depaul University, Chicago (2003)

16. Seifi, Y., et al.: Analysis of two authorization protocols using Colored Petri Nets. Int. J. Inf. Secur. **14**(3), 221–247 (2015)

17. Xu, Y., Xie, X.: Modeling and analysis of security protocols using colored petri nets. JCP **6**(1), 19–27 (2011)

18. Christensen, S., Mortensen, K.H.: Design/cpn ask-ctl manual. University of Aarhus (1996)

19. Cheng, A., Christensen, S., Mortensen, K.H.: Model checking coloured petri nets-exploiting strongly connected components. DAIMI Report Ser. **26**(519), 169–177 (1997)

20. Clarke, E.M., Emerson, E.A., Sistla, A.P.: Automatic verification of finite-state concurrent systems using temporal logic specifications. ACM Trans. Program. Lang. Syst. (TOPLAS) **8**(2), 244–263 (1986)

21. Dolev, D., Yao, A.: On the security of public key protocols. IEEE Trans. Inf. Theor. **29**(2), 198–208 (1983)

TRUST: TRust Unguarded Service Terminals

Daniele Casola[1], Giuseppe Cattaneo[1], Luigi Catuogno[1(✉)],
Umberto Ferraro Petrillo[2], Clemente Galdi[3], and Gianluca Roscigno[1]

[1] Dip. di Informatica, Università di Salerno, Fisciano (SA), Italy
lcatuogno@unisa.it
[2] Dip. di Scienze Statistiche, Università degli Studi di Roma "La Sapienza",
Rome, Italy
[3] Dip. di Studi Politici e Sociali, Università di Salerno, Fisciano (SA), Italy

Abstract. Nowadays, plenty of digital services are provided to citizens
by means of terminals located in public unguarded places. In order to
access the desired service, users, authenticate themselves by providing
their credentials through such terminals. This approach opens up to the
problem of fraudulent devices that could be installed in place of regular terminals to capture users' confidential information. Indeed, despite
the development of increasingly secure systems aiming at guaranteeing
an acceptable security level, users are frequently unable to distinguish
between terminals on which security measures are enforced (*trusted* terminals) and malicious terminals that *pretend to be trusted*.

We deal with this problem by presenting a human-compatible authentication protocol, leveraging *Graphical Passwords*, helps user to authenticate a terminal before using it. We also present a prototype implementation of this protocol, called **TRUST** (*TRust Unguarded Service Terminals*).
The usability of our solution has been analyzed by means of a preliminary
experimentation.

Keywords: Authentication · Graphical password · Human-computer
interaction · Kiosk security · ATM security

1 Introduction

Nowadays, according to a worldwide trend, an increasing number of essential
public services, such as e-Health and tax-paying, are made accessible through
the deployment of service terminals installed in public places and connected to
the Internet. In this scenario, users interact with a remote service provider by
means of a front-end application running on the terminal. This straightforward
and consolidated architecture actually raises several security issues. Consider, for
example, the case of unguarded terminals like ATMs located in dimly lit streets
or electronic kiosks deployed in rural underdeveloped areas [1]. In these cases
users often are not provided with any tool or other means to establish whether
the system they are providing their credentials is trusted or fake. Even if, for

© Springer Nature Switzerland AG 2019
C. Esposito et al. (Eds.): I-SPAN 2019, CCIS 1080, pp. 155–169, 2019.
https://doi.org/10.1007/978-3-030-30143-9_13

example, (a) sophisticated security measures leveraging Trusted Computing are used, (b) the applications interact with the user only through a tamper resistant Trusted I/O path and (c) the integrity of the local terminal is assured by means of a remote attestation protocol, the user has no means to realize if she is using a "trusted terminal" rather than a terminal which *pretends* to be trusted.

This problem, on one hand, is the basis of the success of many insidious attack techniques, including "phishing". On the other hand, it makes the users mistrustful and hostile with respect to the system and the provider itself, undermining the possibility of improving the spread and the effectiveness of services of major importance.

Our Contribution. In this paper we present a scheme allowing users to establish a trust relationship with a terminal running a front-end application for accessing a service implemented by a remote provider. More precisely, the user is enabled to "assess" the terminal integrity, prior to provide her credential in order to be, in turn, authenticated by the service provider.

To this end, the user starts a "challenge-response" authentication protocol with the server through the terminal. Having received the correct response, the user is assured that the terminal is trusted and thus she can go on with the usual operation. This protocol relies on three assumptions:

1. Only the legitimate server can win the challenge.
2. The challenge-response cycle can be completed only if the terminal is trusted, as the server does not forward any response through untrusted terminals.
3. Fake terminals can not compute correct responses on their own.

We highlight that, in our protocol, it is the user that plays the roles of challenger and verifier with respect to the server. This requires the user to have the capability to efficiently (a) generate "good" challenges and (b) to be able to correctly verify the server's responses. This might raise some usability concerns as the user could be required of a noticeable effort. At first glance, the problem could be solved by providing the user with a personal *ad hoc* device or an application running on her smartphone, involved in the authentication protocol. However, this kind of solutions poses other problems such as: the use of a personal device/application might not be affordable in terms of costs and skills by certain categories of users, or the need of establishing a trust relationship would be raised, in turn, by the smartphone application.

To overcome these problems, we propose a human computable challenge-response protocol based on a *reversed Graphical Password* scheme. In our protocol, the role of the user and of the service provider are exchanged with respect to traditional schemes. In facts, here, it is the user who composes the "graphical challenge" and submits it to the service provider through the terminal whereas the service provider is required to compute and send back the correct response. Eventually, the user is asked to verify that the response is correct with respect to the challenge.

As far as we know, our system is the first one which allows human users to authenticate a terminal without the aid of any additional computing device.

In order to validate our approach, we present a prototype implementation, called **TRUST** (*TRust Unguarded Service Terminals*), and discuss the results of our early experiments aiming at investigating usability and user acceptance aspects of our proposal.

2 Related Work

Understanding the mechanisms laying behind the establishment of trust between humans and information systems has turned out increasingly important for ICT operators. Therefore, the quest for a model for human-machine trust relationships, mainly focusing on networking systems, has required growing efforts in the last decades.

In [2], the authors propose a model of trust in e-banking services considering how do perceived security and perceived privacy influence the customer's trust, whereas Lee *et al.* [3] empirically evaluate whether the customer's trust to traditional "off-line" bank services can be transferred to on-line services provided by the same institute.

Costante *et al.* [4] provide a general trust perception model, which allows to assess the trustworthiness of a web site.

Due to the sensitiveness of the application scenarios, establishing a correct and *conscious* trust relationship between human and systems is crucial. Indeed, both low level of trust as well as operators' overtrust severely threaten the reliability and effectiveness of on-line services [5].

Studies aiming at evaluating the effects that users' knowledge on the employed technologies have on the trust in the services produced conflicting results [6,7], whereas usability is amongst the main ingredients of trust [8].

Guaranteeing secure and reliable transaction over untrusted channels is a classical branch of research in security. Traditional approaches to establish trust between front-end terminals and remote servers leverage (i) challenge-based proof-of-identity schemes (such as Bank of America's SiteKey [9,10]); (ii) additional personal devices (including mobile phones) [11–13] possibly enriched with (iii) biometric measurements [14].

Again, the tradeoff between usability and security is still a matter of major concerns [15–17]. Unskilled people may not be able to deal with such devices, while in certain application scenarios (*e.g.*, rural areas), personal devices might be not available.

Graphical Passwords are possible solution to these drawbacks. In a Graphical Password scheme [18,19], a remote system authenticates a user by means of a challenge/response protocol in which the system challenges the user by "showing something" on the terminal screen. This challenge can be correctly understood and won by those legitimate users who know a certain secret. The user replies to the challenger with the output of a *cognitive function* that takes as inputs the secret and what she sees on the screen. Typically, the system pseudo-randomly generates the challenges that are sent to the user. On the other hand, the user, given a challenge, uses a deterministic and human-affordable algorithm to compute the response.

Existing schemes essentially vary according to the cognitive process they are based on, such as the human capability to recognize objects, to remember and reproduce behaviors [20–24].

The main security threat a Graphical Password is known as *shoulder surfing attack* [25] and is related to the adversary's capability to observe whatever happens during users' authentication and possibly collect any kind of leaked information that could be useful to guess/extract the secret [26, 27]. In order to cope with this problem (safeguarding usability) several schemes have been proposed, aiming at limiting the capability of the adversary to gather or understand [28] the information released during the authentication session.

In this paper, we use a graphical password scheme in which it is the human user who challenges the system, in order to verify its integrity. As far as we know, this is one of the earliest proposals following this approach.

3   The Scenario

The scenario we consider in this paper is the following. A *service provider* deploys a number of *dedicated terminals* in certain public places over a geographical area, in order to allow *subscribers* to access its services in a wide variety of locations.

Subscribers access services on an occasional basis, therefore they cannot make any assumption about the state, security and integrity of the device that is going to be used. In other words, a user is neither able to establish a trust relationship with the terminal nor to rely on a trust relationship established *a priori*, as in the case of her own devices.

Moreover, in our scenario we make two important assumptions:

- In order to establish a trust relationship with the terminal, users can not use any computing support, *i.e.*, they do not hold any secure token, OTP generator or other similar devices. However, the only thing users are assumed to be able to is playing a "challenge-response" cognitive game with the system, on the basis of a pre-determined shared knowledge and using the interaction means provided by the terminal itself. We will clarify this point later.
- Dedicated terminals are used exclusively for the sake of the services they provide, so that their hardware and software layouts are tailored accordingly. Moreover, we assume that every *untampered* terminal recognizes and communicate exclusively with an *untampered* service provider and vice versa. The untampered terminals and the untampered service provider can, thus, mutually authenticate and exchange data securely. We stress that, consequently, a tampered device can only "pretend" to be connected to a remote service provider.

3.1   Threat Model

In this paper we consider a model in which the service provider is trusted by the user. We assume that the service provider is able to identify an untampered terminal. Similarly, an untampered terminal is able to correctly identify the proper service provider. In case one of the untampered actors recognizes a tampered counterpart, it stops the session immediately. The communication between the untampered terminal and the service provider are encrypted and mutually authenticated.

Given the above operational scenario, an adversary is unable to tamper a public terminal or impersonate the service provider without being detected by an untampered counterpart. We consider a non-adaptive adversary that operates in two phases.

– Collect Phase: In a first phase the adversary observes a number authentication sessions executed by a given user. We assume the adversary has access to the whole interaction between the user and the terminal, *e.g.*, by means of a high resolution camera capturing the terminal touchscreen, but she is not able to interfere with the authentication process.
– Attack Phase: The adversary analyzes by means of some software the collected data. Given the output of the software, the adversary interacts with the user trying to impersonate a legitimate service provider.

The attack is successful if, at the end of the second phase, the user trusts the terminal.

4   Our Proposal

In this section we describe a protocol that can be used to authenticate a terminal equipped with a graphical touchscreen before providing it with some confidential data (*e.g.*, a password). We also discuss about a reference implementation of our protocol, called *TRust Unguarded Service Terminals* (TRUST).

Our protocol is based on a *recognition-based* scheme. The user, willing to use a certain terminal, draws on its touchscreen a graphical challenge. Then, the terminal responds by showing to the user an image that is generated on-the-fly by a remote third-party (*i.e.*, service provider server) according both to the graphical challenge and to some confidential information provided by that user in a preliminary phase. The interaction with the service provider requires the terminal to pass a registration phase where it has to prove to the third-party to not have been tampered. If it fails to pass this phase, the terminal will be unable to answer to the user's challenge, thus revealing its tampered state.

4.1   The Protocol

Our protocol requires the existence of three entities. *Terminal* is a graphical touchscreen device allowing registered users to access some services offered by a service provider. *User* is a person interested in accessing these services using terminal, provided that it has not been tampered. *Service provider* is a trusted remote server storing, along the credentials of all registered users, some additional confidential information used to assess the integrity of terminal.

At startup, terminal runs a *remote attestation* protocol (see, *e.g.*, [29]) to prove its integrity to service provider before being allowed to establish a working connection.

Fig. 1. Examples of markers usable in our prototype implementation TRUST to anchor the sketches of a doodle.

Enrollment Phase. The user interacts with a client application in a secure environment where she is presented with a palette of several graphical markers (see Fig. 1). After choosing from 2 to 4 of them (Fig. 2a), the user has to place these markers in an arbitrary position on a white empty canvas. Then, for each pair of markers, she has to draw an arbitrary sketch starting from the first marker and ending in the second marker. When finished, the content of the canvas (*i.e.*, the *doodle*) is sent to the service provider for being processed (Fig. 2b). In turns, the service provider extracts a set of features from it (*e.g.*, which markers have been used, their relative position, the shape of the sketches) and save them along with the profile of that user. Additional doodles for a same user can be generated by repeating this process.

Verification Phase. Initially, the user needs to provide her username and interact with the terminal.

The service provider extracts at random a set of photos from an internal database. Each image is modified with the addition of a variable number of markers (from 2 to 4), chosen and positioned at random. Then, the service provider extracts at random one more photo that is modified with the introduction of the markers selected by the user for one of the doodles she created in the Enrollment phase. In this last case, markers are placed in their original positions. The resulting images will be sent to terminal that will proceed by showing them to user (Fig. 2c).

User selects the image that she recognizes to contain the markers existing in one of her doodles. At this point, she can move these markers and submit the modified image to the service provider through terminal (Fig. 2d). If service provider recognizes the received image to contain the markers existing in one of the doodles of that user, it proceeds by adding to this image the sketches available in the original doodle, distorted according to the actual position of the markers. If not, it replies by returning a doodle generated at random.

In the first case, the modified image is sent back to user through terminal for a final verification. At this point, if user recognizes the sketches existing in the received image as belonging to one of her doodles, she has the proof that terminal is trusted (Fig. 2e).

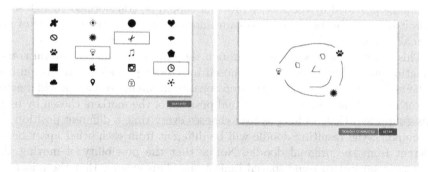

Enrollment. Selection of the markers.   *Enrollment.* Drawing of the doodle.

Verification. Selection of the image Verification. Challenge generation (*i.e.*, containing the correct markers.   the markers are moved by the user).

Verification. Decision about the integrity of the terminal.

Fig. 2. Screenshots of our prototype implementation TRUST when used to establish the integrity of a terminal.

Doodle Generation. The security of our protocols hinges on the ability of the service provider to submit to user a modified doodle that is recognized by the user herself as a derivative of one of her initial doodles. At the same time, the doodle provided by the service provider should be transformed enough so to make it difficult for an attacker to gain information about the structure of the original doodle.

This problem has been solved through the implementation of several transformation steps. Let $\mathcal{D}$ the doodle chosen by service provider at the beginning of the verification phase. The first step consists in having service provider scale and/or rotate $\mathcal{D}$ according to the actual position of the markers chosen by user. This guarantees that, as long as user chooses every time a different position for the markers, the resulting doodle will be different from each other apart being different from the original doodle. Notice that the possibility of moving the markers is subject to some spatial limitations. This ensures that the relocated markers follow the same clockwise order of the original doodle. As a result, the transformed doodle will be easier for user to be recognized as a derivative of $\mathcal{D}$. The second step consists of adding some noise to the doodle via the introduction of other sketches not existing in $\mathcal{D}$. To prevent the attacker from easily guessing which sketches have been added for making the doodle noisy, these sketches are not generated completely at random but follow a vectorial structure similar to that of the original sketches. The last step consists of embedding the transformed and noisy doodle in a single image file to be transferred to the terminal.

4.2 Security Considerations

Although a fake terminal cannot establish a connection with the service provider server, it can still collect everything that is provided to the user on the screen and monitor the interaction between the user and the terminal. In fact, the choice to drop a *recall-based* scheme of graphical password was motivated by the need to minimize the provided information and to avoid *replay attacks*.

We first notice that the mild assumptions on *untampered* endpoints has the great advantage to dramatically reduce the computational abilities required to the user. We require the user to authenticate the terminal by simply using her ability to recognize images. We stress that the usage of TRUST ends right *before* the start of the user identification protocol. The user needs to provide her username and interact with the terminal. If the user understands the terminal is fake, she can stop immediately the interaction, not providing any sensitive information to the adversary.

The challenge provided by user consists in the appropriate arrangement of the markers on the background image. This random input guarantees the user from replay attacks in which the adversary might simply reuse all the information that were displayed in a previous session.

The usage of a background image is twofold. On one hand it is a further help for the user to identify reply attacks. Indeed a terminal showing a background image that the user remembers, under the guarantee that such images are drawn from huge set, indicates the high probability of an attack. On the other hand, the presence of random images makes harder the extraction of the doodle from the image that contains the background *and* the doodle.

To the best of our knowledge, TRUST is the first system that allows terminal authentication by means of a human user without the need of computing support using graphical password. Our protocol proposal is mainly aimed to explore the feasibility of such kind of authentication, in a minimal set of prerequisites, while guaranteeing high usability and acceptance.

A number of modifications to the system might increase its security. We here list some of them as remarks. Currently the markers are placed on the background image in the same order in which the user placed them during the registration phase. A first possible modification is the random placement of markers in the challenge. This modification further reduces the possibility of reply attacks.

Currently the doodles are drawn by means of black lines. At the verification time, TRUST adds noise to the doodle and, *independently* from the background image, overlaps it to the image. A possible extension of this scheme considers a doodle pre-processing phase. Here we can modify doodle so that it is dependent on the background image, for example, changing sketches' colors or adding noise according the contents of the background image. This idea makes harder the automatic extraction of the doodle from the challenge.

The TRUST prototype *adds* random segments to the image. If we consider two subsequent authentications, this might reveal most of the doodle designed by the user. A possible extension of the current scheme consists in adding random segments and *removing* some of the segments in the original doodle. Clearly, for this approach requires an extensive experimental evaluation of the recognisability of the doodle as a function of the percentage of added and removed segments.

4.3   Implementation Details

We developed a reference implementation for the protocol described in Sect. 4.1 we called TRUST. It consists of a client-server system modelled after the *Model View Controller* (MVC) pattern. The client (*i.e.*, the terminal) is written in HTML and JavaScript, while the server (*i.e.*, the service provider) is based on a web service written in Scala and Java. Client and server communicate with each other by exchanging JSON messages via the HTTPS protocol.

The main component of this implementation is the *controller* layer, which actually handles the logic of *business* (server side). The *presentation* (or view) layer has both a client and a server component.

Doodles are maintained in a vectorial graphical format (svg). This allows, on a side, to simplify the application of distortions to the sketches; on the other side, it makes it possible to keep unaltered the quality of the sketches, even after the distortions.

5   Usability and Acceptance

In this section we present the results of an experimental analysis we conducted to assess the performance of TRUST. This has been done by performing a user-experience study about the reference implementation of our protocol, whose performance have been measured according to the three standard *Key Performance Indicators* (KPIs) dictated by the ISO 9241-11 standard in [30]:

Efficiency. It is the speed with which a user accomplishes a task. In our case, we considered the time required to a registered user to run the verification phase of TRUST, starting from the instant where a portfolio of images is shown to the user to the moment where a decision is taken (*i.e.*, the user accepts or rejects the proposed doodle). We define this time as *verification time*.

Effectiveness. It is the level of completeness and accuracy of the system to get the user's goals. In our case, we considered the number of times a registered was able to correctly discern among untampered and tampered terminals after running the verification phase of TRUST by accepting or rejecting the doodle being presented by the terminal. Along this line, we also considered the following KPIs:

– **True Positives:** number of times that a terminal has been correctly identified as untampered;
– **True Negatives:** number of times that a terminal has been correctly identified as tampered;
– **False Positives:** number of times that a tampered terminal has been wrongly identified as untampered;
– **False Negatives:** number of times that a untampered terminal has been wrongly identified as tampered;

In addition we also collected the number of *markers selection errors* that describes the scenario in which an user in a verification process did not remember her own markers and she has chosen an image containing other markers. This case does not fit into the above four categories.

Satisfaction. It reports the simplicity and intuitiveness of a system. In our case, this has measured by a set of multiple choice questions aiming at assessing if the system is pleasant and easy to use.

5.1   Participants

The experiment was conducted on 40 volunteers. 18 of them were computer science university students, the remaining ones were members of a sports club.

5.2   Conditions

The experiment took place in two sessions. At the beginning of *Session I*, each participant registered to the service provider following to the enrollment phase described in Sect. 4.1. Then, she was asked to perform three times the verification phase of our protocol. Multiple trials were chosen to make the results more consistent. *Session II* took place one week after *Session I*. Even in this case, each participant was asked to perform three runs of the verification phase of our protocol. At the end of this session, each participant filled a survey about the usability of TRUST.

From the technical viewpoint, the experiment has been conducted using, as terminal, a touchscreen-based personal computer running the Windows 10 operating system. Moreover, in order to focus on the performance of the users attending the experiment and leave out the possible latencies due to network congestions, we installed the service provider component on the same device running the terminal interface. This makes almost instantaneous the communication between these two entities.

5.3   Tasks

In *Session I*, each participant was instructed about the purpose of the experiment as well as about the basic notions required to use TRUST. In particular, they were asked to pay particular attention to the doodle generation phase as the security of the considered system would rely on her ability to remember that drawing. Then, they were requested to undergo the enrollment procedure described in Sect. 4.1. Finally, they were asked to perform 3 runs of the verification phase of our protocol.

Session II was identical to *Session I*, except for the absence of the enrollment phase.

5.4   Results

In this section we review the results of our experiments according to the three KPIs introduced in Sect. 5.

Efficiency. The boxplots drawn in Fig. 3 compare the efficiency exhibited by the participants to the experiments in the two sessions. Interestingly, this efficiency remains approximately the same (in the average) a week after the enrollment phase. This seems to indicate that the memorability of the type of information provided during enrollment persists (at least) a week after this phase. However, we notice that this has not been true for all participants. There were some of them that required about 40 seconds to perform verification during *Session I*. In general, almost all of them required even more time during *Session II*, thus revealing a sort of inability to deal with this form of verification.

Effectiveness. Table 1 compares the effectiveness exhibited by the participants to the experiments in correctly discerning among untampered and tampered terminals during the two sessions. We notice, first of all, that almost all participants were able to successfully accomplish this task during *Session I* (*i.e.*, about the 96% of correct answers, that is the true positive and negative rate).

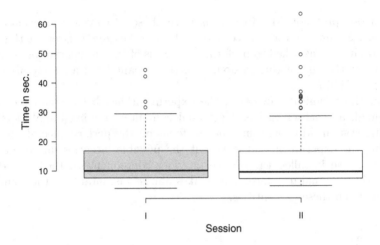

Fig. 3. *Boxplot of the efficiency* of **TRUST** exhibited by the participants to the experiment in the two sessions (120 trials per session), in terms of *verification time*. All times are reported in seconds.

Table 1. *Effectiveness*. Results of verification runs executed by users in two sessions.

	Session I	Session II
Verification runs	120	120
True positive	85	73
True negative	30	34
False positive	3	2
False negative	1	7
Markers selection errors	1	4

This is expectable as this session includes a run of the enrollment phase and so participants have fresh in their minds the doodles provided at registration time. Switching to *Session II*, we notice that the effectiveness gets slightly worse, but is still high (*i.e.*, about the 89% of correct answers). Another phenomenon worth to be observed is about the relatively high number of false negatives in *Session II*. We focused on these cases by taking into account also the answers provided by the corresponding users to the questionnaires at the end of the experiment. The results seem to suggest that false negatives were mostly due to participants having trouble remembering the doodles provided during the enrollment phase. This led them to adopt a sort of conservative approach when assessing the integrity of terminal. In addition, in *Session II* there are 4 runs where an user did not remember her own markers and she has chosen an image containing other markers (*i.e.*, Markers Selection Errors).

Satisfaction. The overall satisfaction of the participants about the usefulness and the usability of TRUST has been high. For example, approximately 87.5% of the participants found TRUST to be easy to use, while over the 95% of them found the system to be pleasant to use. In a similar way, most of the participants perceived TRUST as useful for allowing to assess the integrity of a terminal thus leading to an improvement of the perceived safety of a target system.

6 Conclusion

The scope of this paper is to investigate the feasibility of a human-computable protocol aiming at "convincing" users that the terminal they are using to access a remote service is safe, provided it has already been successfully attested by the remote service provider. The assumption at the basis of this work is that users trust the remote server and rely on its capability to verify the integrity of the local terminals. The way through which the server proves that such a verification succeeded, is winning the challenge posed by the user through the terminal. The technique the service provider uses to verify the terminals' integrity is out of the scope of this paper. We suggest that both parties support a remote attestation protocol built on top of cryptographic tamper-resistant hardware.

One of main goals of our investigation is evaluating the grade of user confidence in a graphical password scheme as mechanism to establish a trust relationship with the terminal. To this end, we designed and implemented a prototype scheme which features some of components we identified as essential to the communication between the user and the remote server: the background, the markers, the doodle and the transformations. Hence, our first concern has been the acceptance, by users, of a human-machine interaction based on such components. To have an idea on how users could interact with such components, our prototype keeps them well distinct and evident. The results outcoming from our experiments are encouraging both in terms of effectiveness and usability. In particular, we observed that most part of the participants to our experiment were not only able to correctly assess the integrity of the terminal but were able to do this in a relatively short amount of time. The results suggest also that the memorability of the doodles provided during enrollment phase persists (at least) a week after this phase. We also investigated about the usability of our prototype implementation and about 90% of the participants found TRUST to be easy and pleasant to use.

In graphical password schemes, the tradeoff between security and usability is a struggling point, as increasing the former leads to worsening the latter and vice versa. From a "human computability" point of view, our scheme looks even simpler than other recall-based schemes. However, inverting the roles of challenger and prover has a considerable impact on usability. In facts, in our protocol, both challenge generation and response verification are now up to the user. Strengthening the security e.g., by furtherly increasing the size of the secret, might result in an unaffordable workload to the user of ours. There is space for further research on this aspect.

Man in the middle attacks are still possible. The adversary could steal a legitimate terminal and replace it with a fake one. Having induced a user to interact with the fake terminal, the adversary captures her actions and relays the protocol messages back and forth between the fake terminal and the remote server through the stolen terminal. This threat is common to plenty of similar application scenarios. For this purpose, measures to measure the terminal physical integrity are on the shelf, but are out of the scope of this work.

References

1. Guo, S., et al.: Design and implementation of the KiosKnet system. Comput. Netw. **55**(1), 264–281 (2011)
2. Yousafzai, S.Y., Pallister, J.G., Foxall, G.R.: A proposed model of e-trust for electronic banking. Technovation **23**(11), 847–860 (2003)
3. Lee, K.C., Kang, I., McKnight, D.H.: Transfer from offline trust to key online perceptions: an empirical study. IEEE Trans. Eng. Manag. **54**(4), 729–741 (2007)
4. Costante, E., Den Hartog, J., Petkovic, M.: On-line trust perception: What really matters. In: 2011 1st Workshop on Socio-Technical Aspects in Security and Trust (STAST), pp. 52–59. IEEE (2011)
5. Atoyan, H., Duquet, J.R., Robert, J.M.: Trust in new decision aid systems. In: Proceedings of the 18th Conference on l'Interaction Homme-Machine, pp. 115–122. ACM (2006)
6. Hoffman, D.L., Novak, T.P., Peralta, M.: Building consumer trust online. Commun. ACM **42**(4), 80–85 (1999)
7. Jiang, J.C., Chen, C.A., Wang, C.C.: Knowledge and trust in e-consumers' online shopping behavior. In: 2008 International Symposium on Electronic Commerce and Security, pp. 652–656. IEEE (2008)
8. Hoffman, L.J., Lawson-Jenkins, K., Blum, J.: Trust beyond security: an expanded trust model. Commun. ACM **49**(7), 94–101 (2006)
9. Youll, J.: Fraud vulnerabilities in SiteKey security at bank of America (2006). www.cr-labs.com/publications/SiteKey-20060718.pdf
10. Karlof, C., Tygar, J.D., Wagner, D.: A user study design for comparing the security of registration protocols. UPSEC **8**, 1–14 (2008)
11. Garriss, S., Berger, S., Sailer, R., van Doorn, L., Zhang, X., et al.: Towards trustworthy kiosk computing. In: Eighth IEEE Workshop on Mobile Computing Systems and Applications, HotMobile 2007, pp. 41–45. IEEE (2007)
12. Surie, A., Perrig, A., Satyanarayanan, M., Farber, D.J.: Rapid trust establishment for pervasive personal computing. IEEE Pervasive Comput. **6**(4), 24–30 (2007)
13. Weigold, T., Kramp, T., Hermann, R., Höring, F., Buhler, P., Baentsch, M.: The Zurich trusted information channel – an efficient defence against man-in-the-middle and malicious software attacks. In: Lipp, P., Sadeghi, A.-R., Koch, K.-M. (eds.) Trust 2008. LNCS, vol. 4968, pp. 75–91. Springer, Heidelberg (2008). https://doi.org/10.1007/978-3-540-68979-9_6
14. Masdari, M., Ahmadzadeh, S.: A survey and taxonomy of the authentication schemes in telecare medicine information systems. J. Netw. Comput. Appl. **87**, 1–19 (2017)
15. Schechter, S.E., Dhamija, R., Ozment, A., Fischer, I.: The emperor's new security indicators. In: IEEE Symposium on Security and Privacy, SP 2007, pp. 51–65. IEEE (2007)

16. Gunson, N., Marshall, D., Morton, H., Jack, M.: User perceptions of security and usability of single-factor and two-factor authentication in automated telephone banking. Comput. Secur. **30**(4), 208–220 (2011)

17. Weir, C.S., Douglas, G., Carruthers, M., Jack, M.: User perceptions of security, convenience and usability for ebanking authentication tokens. Comput. Secur. **28**(1–2), 47–62 (2009)

18. Biddle, R., Chiasson, S., Van Oorschot, P.C.: Graphical passwords: learning from the first twelve years. ACM Comput. Surv. (CSUR) **44**(4), 19 (2012)

19. Suo, X., Zhu, Y., Owen, G.S.: Graphical passwords: a survey. In: 21st Annual Computer Security Applications Conference (ACSAC 2005), p. 10. IEEE (2005)

20. Jermyn, I., Mayer, A., Monrose, F., Reiter, M.K., Rubin, A.D.: The design and analysis of graphical passwords. In: Proceedings of the 8th USENIX Security Symposium, Washington D.C., USA, pp. 1–15, 23–26 August 1999

21. Weinshall, D.: Cognitive authentication schemes safe against spyware. In: 2006 IEEE Symposium on Security and Privacy (S&P 2006), p. 6. IEEE (2006)

22. Catuogno, L., Galdi, C.: On the security of a two-factor authentication scheme. In: Samarati, P., Tunstall, M., Posegga, J., Markantonakis, K., Sauveron, D. (eds.) WISTP 2010. LNCS, vol. 6033, pp. 245–252. Springer, Heidelberg (2010). https://doi.org/10.1007/978-3-642-12368-9_19

23. Catuogno, L., Galdi, C.: Analysis of a two-factor graphical password scheme. Int. J. Inf. Secur. **13**(5), 421–437 (2014)

24. Martinez-Diaz, M., Fierrez, J., Galbally, J.: Graphical password-based user authentication with free-form doodles. IEEE Trans. Hum. Mach. Syst. **46**(4), 607–614 (2016). Cited By 0

25. Tari, F., Ozok, A., Holden, S.H.: A comparison of perceived and real shoulder-surfing risks between alphanumeric and graphical passwords. In: Proceedings of the Second Symposium on Usable Privacy and Security, pp. 56–66. ACM (2006)

26. Asghar, H.J., Steinfeld, R., Li, S., Kaafar, M.A., Pieprzyk, J.: On the linearization of human identification protocols: attacks based on linear algebra, coding theory, and lattices. IEEE Trans. Inf. Forensics Secur. **10**(8), 1643–1655 (2015)

27. Golle, P., Wagner, D.: Cryptanalysis of a cognitive authentication scheme (extended abstract). In: IEEE Symposium on Security and Privacy, pp. 66–70 (2007)

28. Catuogno, L., Galdi, C.: On user authentication by means of video events recognition. J. Ambient. Intell. Hum. Comput. **5**(6), 909–918 (2014)

29. Jain, L., Vyas, J.: Security analysis of remote attestation. Technical report, CS259 Project Report (2008)

30. DIS, I.: 9241–210: 2010. ergonomics of human system interaction-part 210: Human-centred design for interactive systems. International Standardization Organization (ISO), Switzerland (2009)

Cloud Fog and Edge Computing

Nature-Inspired Protocols for Cloud Computing and Security Systems

Marek R. Ogiela[1(✉)] and Lidia Ogiela[2]

[1] Cryptography and Cognitive Informatics Research Group,
AGH University of Science and Technology, 30 Mickiewicza Ave,
30-059 Kraków, Poland
mogiela@agh.edu.pl
[2] Department of Cryptography and Cognitive Informatics,
Pedagogical University of Krakow, Podchorążych 2 St., 30-084 Kraków, Poland
lidia.ogiela@gmail.com

Abstract. This paper describes new nature-inspired security solutions and protocols, oriented for secure authentication and strategic data management in Cloud Computing. In particular will be presented the ways of using advanced cognitive approaches and personal characteristics for creation of secure management protocols, oriented on user authentication, and efficient data management in Big Data infrastructures. Advanced computing procedures connected with cognitive cryptography will be introduced.

Keywords: Cognitive protocols · Security systems · Cryptographic authentication procedures

1 Introduction

Development of computer systems in recent years is also associated with the need to propose the more and more advanced techniques for data security and user authentication. This is particularly important in distributed systems and Cloud Computing, where access to resources or services is associated with the need of confirmation the access rights. In this context, the methods of data management and authentication procedures, which are based on biologically inspired algorithms, are of particular importance. They are part of the wider research associated with the development of modern cryptography, in which biologically inspired methods can also be used, and which create a new area of cognitive cryptography [1, 2].

In the further part of this paper, new solutions will be discussed, which enrich the methods of cognitive cryptography, which will be oriented towards creating the so-called perceptual keys, which allow to authenticate users in computer systems and Cloud Computing services. These methods will be related to the use of human perceptual properties that, based on individual recognition thresholds, will allow the reconstruction of the authentication codes at various levels related to the access rights to services or data [3, 4].

© Springer Nature Switzerland AG 2019
C. Esposito et al. (Eds.): I-SPAN 2019, CCIS 1080, pp. 173–177, 2019.
https://doi.org/10.1007/978-3-030-30143-9_14

2 Perception Features in Security Protocols

Nature-inspired security protocols can be proposed thanks to the application of perception abilities and cognitive features. In previous research authors proposed several classes of cognitive vision systems [5–7], which allow to evaluate personal characteristics or perceptual features. Also the image evaluation systems were proposed, which allow describe personal perception abilities, which can be used for security purposes. In case of personal feature evaluation, such systems allow to extract very specific personal characteristics, behavioral patterns, and also perception thresholds at which users can properly understand visual patterns. This type of individual thresholds can be applied in creation of new authentication procedures that take the form of visual verification codes. Authentication using such codes requires special perception abilities, which are necessary for proper semantic evaluation of analyzed visual patterns. Such codes allow to perform very selective authentication, especially for users representing different groups and having particular perception abilities.

Visual perception codes allow to develop of secure protocols for data division and services management in distributed systems and Cloud Computing [8]. Authorization procedures allow to consider different accessing grants for participants of the protocol at different levels in cloud infrastructure, as well as consider individual personal cognitive thresholds while evaluating visual authentication code.

3 Perception-Based Hierarchical Access to Cloud Services

Cloud Computing infrastructure and hierarchical distributed systems are characterized by the occurrence of many different levels of information processing, as well as data acquisition. Such structures can distinguish different levels of data flow, on which the same information can be stored and processed [9]. In practice, this means that we can enter different levels of access to the data being analyzed, and establish different access rights to users, who have access only to the infrastructure at a given level. The access rights will then depend on the level, at which the user works, as well as on the number of authorized users who have access to services at a given level. Thus, it can be seen that in such structures, data sharing methods can be used as authentication keys necessary to obtain access rights to given resources. Such keys may take the form of visual patterns, which can be split in a threshold manner between all participants of the protocol, and require a specific number of shares to restore visual key that gives access to data or services at a given level [10].

The perceptual approach may additionally be related to the reconstruction of visual keys in the form of blurred or softened images, on which all elements are not visible and thus they can be interpreted in various ways by different participants. In such protocols, it becomes possible to determine individual perception thresholds, at which a given user will be able to properly interpret the content of a visual key, and other users will not have such a possibility. The individual thresholds of perception will then depend on the personal characteristics of perception by a given user, but they can also depend on some content or semantic meaning of visual key [11].

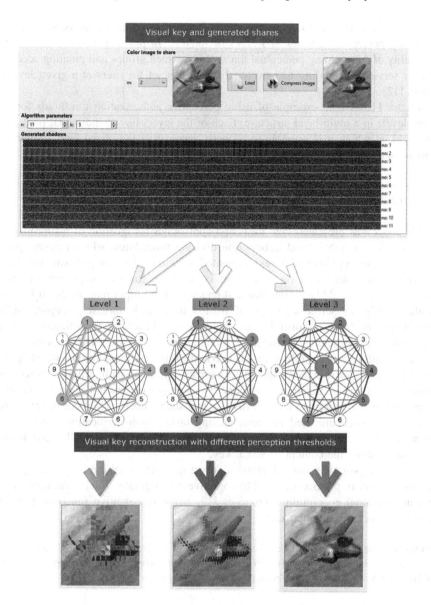

Fig. 1. User authentication using perception keys with multiple thresholds, depending on the layer and access permissions. Visual key image was divided into 11 parts distributed among users at different levels. Key image was reconstructed on different levels with different perception thresholds

Visual patterns used as visual keys may present content previously known to users, or be completely new. They may also be related to the selected topic area or user's interests. They can also present topics related to previous experience or user's expectations, which will significantly facilitate its analysis and recognition.

An important feature of this type of codes is the ability to authenticate people grouped according perceptual abilities and areas of interest. In practice, this also means the possibility of determining perceptual thresholds for such groups and granting access to data or services, according to perceptual thresholds set for users at a given level of access [12].

Figure 1 shows an example of using perceptive authorization thresholds for different levels in a multi-layer structure. Each of the layers has an individual perceptual threshold, at which it is possible to properly reconstruct the visual key, allowing to authenticate users at a given level.

4 Conclusions

In this paper was presented new ideas and approaches for creation of nature-inspired authentication protocols, and information division procedures, which require special perception and cognitive abilities. Presented solution allow to perform distributed authentication tasks based on perception keys in the form of sequences of visual patterns, which should be recognized and understand in proper manner. Such keys are available only for selected groups of trusted users with special perceptual skills. Described approaches perform division and authentication tasks for different levels in hierarchical data structures, considering different numbers of users and accessing grants to secured information. Authentication is based on proper recognition and interpretation of visual codes, which can be recognized by users with different perception thresholds. During verification it is necessary to proper understand semantic meaning of divided visual pattern so the security features such authentication codes are similar to threshold procedure used in secret sharing tasks. Such verification approach are oriented for special groups of users with particular perception skills, and having expectation about the content of visual key.

Presented protocols extend classical cryptographic procedures by adding new classes of security protocols related to cognitive cryptography. Such techniques allow to join traditional encryption approaches [13, 14] with cognitive functions and perceptual abilities of particular users.

Acknowledgments. This work has been supported by the National Science Centre, Poland, under project number DEC-2016/23/B/HS4/00616. This work has been supported by the AGHUniversity of Science and Technology research Grant No 16.16.120.773.

References

1. Ogiela, M.R., Ogiela, L.: On using cognitive models in cryptography. In: IEEE AINA 2016 - The IEEE 30th International Conference on Advanced Information Networking and Applications, Crans-Montana, Switzerland, 23–25 March, pp. 1055–1058 (2016)
2. Ogiela, M.R., Ogiela, L.: Cognitive keys in personalized cryptography. In: IEEE AINA 2017 The 31st IEEE International Conference on Advanced Information Networking and Applications, Taipei, Taiwan, 27–29 March, pp. 1050–1054 (2017)

3. Meiappane, A., Premanand, V.: CAPTCHA as Graphical Passwords - A New Security Primitive: Based on Hard AI Problems. Scholars' Press (2015)
4. Osadchy, M., Hernandez-Castro, J., Gibson, S., Dunkelman, O., Perez-Cabo, D.: No bot expects the DeepCAPTCHA! Introducing immutable adversarial examples, with applications to CAPTCHA generation. IEEE Trans. Inf. Forensics Secur. **12**(11), 2640–2653 (2017)
5. Ogiela, M.R., Ogiela, U., Ogiela, L.: Secure information sharing using personal biometric characteristics. In: Kim, T.-h., Kang, J.-J., Grosky, W.I., Arslan, T., Pissinou, N. (eds.) FGIT 2012. CCIS, vol. 353, pp. 369–373. Springer, Heidelberg (2012). https://doi.org/10.1007/978-3-642-35521-9_54
6. Ogiela, M.R., Ogiela, L., Ogiela, U.: Biometric methods for advanced strategic data sharing protocols. In: The Ninth International Conference on Innovative Mobile and Internet Services in Ubiquitous Computing (IMIS-2015), Blumenau, Brazil, 8–10 July, pp. 179–183 (2015). https://doi.org/10.1109/imis.2015.29
7. Ogiela, L., Ogiela, M.R.: Bio-inspired cryptographic techniques in information management applications. In: IEEE AINA 2016 - The IEEE 30th International Conference on Advanced Information Networking and Applications, Crans-Montana, Switzerland, 23–25 March, pp. 1059–1063 (2016)
8. Ogiela, U., Ogiela, L.: Linguistic techniques for cryptographic data sharing algorithms. Concurr. Comput. Pract. E. **30**(3), e4275 (2018). https://doi.org/10.1002/cpe.4275
9. Ogiela, L., Ogiela, M.R.: Insider threats and cryptographic techniques in secure information management. IEEE Syst. J. **11**, 405–414 (2017)
10. Ogiela, M.R., Ogiela, U.: Secure information management in hierarchical structures. In: Kim, T.-h., Adeli, H., Robles, R.J., Balitanas, M. (eds.) AST 2011. CCIS, vol. 195, pp. 31–35. Springer, Heidelberg (2011). https://doi.org/10.1007/978-3-642-24267-0_5
11. Ogiela, L., Ogiela, M.R., Ogiela, U.: Efficiency of strategic data sharing and management protocols. In: The 10th International Conference on Innovative Mobile and Internet Services in Ubiquitous Computing (IMIS-2016), 6–8 July, Fukuoka, Japan, pp. 198–201 (2016). https://doi.org/10.1109/imis.2016.119
12. Ogiela, L.: Advanced techniques for knowledge management and access to strategic information. Int. J. Inf. Manag. **35**(2), 154–159 (2015)
13. Easttom, Ch.: Modern Cryptography: Applied Mathematics for Encryption and Information Security. McGraw-Hill Education, New York (2015)
14. Schneier, B.: Applied Cryptography. Wiley, Indianapolis (2015)

Containers Scheduling Consolidation Approach for Cloud Computing

Tarek Menouer$^{(\boxtimes)}$ and Patrice Darmon

UMANIS, 7 Rue Paul Vaillant Couturier, 92300 Levallois-Perret, France
{tmenouer,pdarmon}@umanis.com

Abstract. Containers are increasingly gaining popularity and are going to be a major deployment model in cloud computing. However, consolidation technique is also used extensively in the cloud context to optimize resources utilization and reduce the power consumption. In this paper, we present a new containers scheduling consolidation approach for cloud computing environment based on a machine learning technique. Our approach is proposed to address the problem of a company that aims to adapt dynamically the number of active nodes to reduce the power consumption when several containers are submitted online each day by their users. In our context, the frequency of containers submission varies within one hour. However, for each hour, the submission frequency is essentially the same each day. The principle of our approach consists into applying a machine learning technique to detect, from a previous containers submission historical, three submission periods (high, medium and low). Each submission period represents a time slot of one day. For instance, the high submission period represents the slot time where the number of submitted containers is the highest compared to other periods. Then, according to the submission periods slot time, our approach dynamically adapts the number of active nodes that must be used to execute each new submitted container. Our proposed consolidation approach is implemented inside Docker Swarmkit which is a well-known container scheduler framework developed by Docker. Experiments demonstrate the potential of our approach under different scenarios.

Keywords: Container technology · Cloud computing · Resource management · Scheduling

1 Introduction

Cloud computing is experiencing rapid growth both in research and industry. Currently, different forms of cloud computational resources exist such as virtual machines (VMs), containers, or bare-metal resources, having each their own characteristics. A container is a lightweight OS-level virtualization technique that allows running an application and its dependencies in a resource-isolated process. According to [13], among the cloud computing advantages we cite: cost effectiveness, on-demand scalability, and ease of management. Theses advantages

© Springer Nature Switzerland AG 2019
C. Esposito et al. (Eds.): I-SPAN 2019, CCIS 1080, pp. 178–192, 2019.
https://doi.org/10.1007/978-3-030-30143-9_15

encourage service providers to adopt them and offer solutions via cloud models. It in turn encourages platform providers to increase the underlying capacity of their data centers to accommodate the increasing demand of new customers. Nevertheless, one of the main drawbacks of the growth in capacity of cloud data centers is the need for more energy to power these large-scale infrastructures. With ever-increasing popularity of cloud computing, data centers power consumption is anticipated to double [16].

In this paper, we present a new consolidation approach based on machine learning in cloud computing environment. The goal is to dynamically adapt the number of active cloud nodes to reduce the global power consumption of the cloud infrastructure. Our approach addresses the problem of a company that aims to reduce the power consumption of its private cloud infrastructure when it executes several containers submitted online each day by their users.

In our context, containers are submitted with different frequencies, which means that the number of submitted containers varies from one hour to another. However, for each hour, every day containers are submitted almost with the same frequency. For instance, in the downloading music context, download music frequency tends to be high in the evening, medium in the afternoon and low in the morning. The music download can be seen as a request encapsulated in a container. The novelty of our approach consists into minimizing the power consumption of the cloud infrastructure by dynamically adapting the number of active nodes based on containers submission historical. The containers submission historical represent the number of containers submitted each hour during one day. It can also be averaged across several historicals of several days. To adapt the number of active nodes, we firstly propose to determine the different submission periods, then we decide for each submission period which node must be active or stopped.

To detect the different submission periods, we propose to apply the k-means algorithm [8] on a containers submission historical. K-means is an unsupervised machine learning algorithm which regroups objects on k clusters according to their similarity. In our context, each object represents the number of containers submitted by users in a period of one hour. For the sake of the simplicity of presentation, we propose to detect three submission periods (high, medium and low). These submission periods represent the most popular periods in the day. It is also possible to use in our approach more than three periods easily. Each submission period detected by the K-means algorithm corresponds to a time slot of one day. For example, the high submission period stands for the slot time with the highest number of submitted containers compared to the other periods. After the definition of the users submission periods, our approach applies a mathematical function to decide the number of nodes which must be active or stopped. When our approach decides to stop a $node_x$, it must to migrate all the running containers of $node_x$ to the different active nodes of the cloud infrastructure. For example, with cloud infrastructure that has 3 nodes ($node_1$, $node_2$ and $node_3$), if the high submission period is between 15 h until 22 h, the active nodes are $node_1$, $node_2$ and $node_3$ (the total number of nodes that form the cloud). However, if the low period is between 5 h until 14 h, only $node_1$ is active (one third of the total number of nodes that form the cloud). In this situation, all containers running on $node_2$ and $node_3$ are migrated to $node_1$. Our approach can also be used to have a dynamic allocation of nodes to reduce the price of using nodes. For instance, if the low period is between 5 h until 14 h, the company can reserve from the cloud provider only one node from 5 h until 14 h. Then, when the submission period changes, the company can change its nodes reservation.

In order to validate our strategy, we made an implementation in the Go language[1] inside Docker Swarmkit [18], with minimum change in the Docker Swarmkit code. Docker swarmkit is a well-known container scheduler framework developed by Docker and used by several companies. Indeed, our approach is tested in a real cloud infrastructure.

The paper is organized as follows. Section 2 presents some related works. Section 3 describes our container consolidation approach. Section 4 introduces exhaustive experiences that validates our approach. Finally, a conclusion and some future works are given in Sect. 5.

2   Related Work

In this section, we will start by presenting briefly some studies related to containers' scheduling in the cloud computing (Subsect. 2.1). Then, giving a short overview of some consolidation studies proposed in the literature (Subsect. 2.2). Finally, we will conclude by a positioning in Subsect. 2.3.

2.1   Cloud Computing Containers Scheduling Studies

Several frameworks and studies are proposed to schedule containers in the literature [11,15,17–19]. From an industrial point of view, we document, as examples of concrete projects, the schedulers inside Google Kubernetes [19], Docker Swarmkit [18] and Apache Mesos [17].

Google Kubernetes [19] is a scheduler framework which represents an orchestration system for Docker containers based on pods concept. Pods are a group of one or more containers. They are always co-located, co-scheduled and run in a shared context. Moreover, they will be run on the same physical or virtual machine. In the Google Kubernetes the scheduling can be summarized in two steps. The first step consists of filtering all nodes to remove the one that do not meet certain requirements of the pod. The second step consists of classifying the remaining nodes using priorities to find the best fit to execute a pod. A priority is a key/value representing the name of the priority from the list of existing ones and its weight. For each remaining node, a priority function gives a score which scales from 0 to 10. Each priority function is weighted by a positive number and the final score of each node is calculated by adding up all the weighted scores.

---

[1] https://golang.org.

When all scores of all nodes are calculated, Google Kubernetes chooses the node with the highest score to run the container.

Docker Swarmkit [18] is an important container scheduler framework developed by Docker. The Swarm manager is in charge of scheduling on nodes. It also has two steps to finally choose which node will execute the container. First, it uses filters to select suitable nodes to execute the container. Then, it uses the most suitable one according to the used ranking strategy. The current version of Docker Swarmkit (v1.12), uses the Spread scheduling strategy. It allows to execute each new container on the node having the least number of executed containers.

2.2 Short Overview of Consolidation Studies

In the cloud consolidation context, several studies are proposed in [1,2,4,6,9,13].

Piraghaj et al. [13] proposes to improve the energy efficiency of servers by proposing a framework that consolidates containers on virtual machines. The principle firstly allows to formalize the container consolidation problem. Then, compare a number of algorithms and evaluate their performance against metrics such as energy consumption, Service Level Agreement violations (SLA), average container migrations rate, and the average number of created virtual machines. In this work, authors confirm that their framework can be used in a private cloud to reduce the energy consumption, or in a public cloud to reduce the total number of hours the virtual machines leased.

Beloglazov et al. [2] propose an approach consisting in consolidation of virtual machines (VMs) and switching idle nodes off. The goal of the authors is to optimize resource usage and to minimize the energy consumption. Their idea is to propose a dynamic consolidation approach of VMs based on adaptive utilization thresholds, which ensures a high level of meeting the Service Level Agreements (SLA). The authors' work validates the high efficiency of the proposed consolidation approach across different kinds of workloads using workload traces from more than a thousand PlanetLab servers.

Hirofuchi et al. [9] proposes a reactive post-copy enabled server consolidation framework. The goal is to optimize VM placement during random load changes. The proposed framework consists of three modules: load monitor, relocation planner, and VM controller. The load monitor collects system resource statistics such as CPUs usage, disk I/O usage, network I/O, etc. The relocation planner decides whether the shared server is overloaded or under-loaded based on resource usage statistics analysis (via the load monitor) prior to calculating the relocation plans. The VM controller is responsible for executing migration and suspending/resuming servers based on the relocation planner's command.

Ben Maaouia et al. [3] proposes a study in order to planning services that improve the use of data center resources in a dynamic environment to reduce the energy consumption. The idea consist to use a new heuristic which predicts the allocation of dynamic and independent services. The new heuristic allows to respect several criteria as the availability, capacity of machines and the number of applications duplications.

Catuogno et al. [4] proposes an approach for simplifying the measurements of resources used by a software service. The authors approach is based on the isolation properties of a containerized virtualization system to properly measure all the resources used by a specific service. At the same time, using the resource limitation functionalities provided by the virtualization system, authors propose also an approach that can be used to limit the effects of malware by limiting the amount of resources that can be accessed on a system. To validate this study, authors consider the specific case of attacks targeting the overuse of power consumption.

2.3   Positioning

In contrast to studies presented previously, we present in this paper a new containers scheduling consolidation approach which consists to adapt dynamically the number of active nodes basing on a learning technique. Our approach is implemented inside the current Docker Swarmkit version (v1.12) and it is validated by performing experiments in a real cloud infrastructure.

3   Containers Scheduling Consolidation Approach Based on Machine Learning Technique

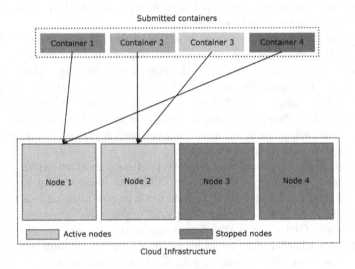

Fig. 1. How to reduce the power consumption of the cloud infrastructure by adapting dynamically the number of active nodes?

As shown in Fig. 1, the purpose of our paper is to address the problem stated as follows. For a company which receives each day several containers submitted online by their users to be executed in a private cloud infrastructure, how to satisfy all containers while reducing the power consumption of the cloud infrastructure?

To answer the previous question, we present in this paper a new container scheduling consolidation approach based on a machine learning technique for cloud computing environment. The main goal of our approach is to dynamically adapt the number of active cloud nodes. Our approach is based on two steps: (i) Detection of submission periods from the history of previous containers submission; and (ii) Dynamic adaptation of the number of active nodes according to the different submission periods. In the following we present in detail these two steps.

```
1 - 200 submitted containers between 00:00 until 01:00
2 - 210 submitted containers between 01:00 until 02:00
                    ......
23 - 100 submitted containers between 22:00 until 23:00
24 - 105 submitted containers between 23:00 until 00:00
```

Fig. 2. Example of 24-h containers submission history

3.1 Detection of the Submission Periods

The goal of this step is to detect the submission periods based on a previous history of containers submission for 24 h (one day). As shown in Fig. 2, the history of the submission is composed of 24 lines. Each line represents the number of containers submitted in one hour. For example, the first line represents the number of containers submitted from 00h:00 until 01h:00. We consider that the history of containers submission can represent the history of one day or an average of histories across several days. As discussed previously in Sect. 1, we propose to detect three submission periods: (i) High; (ii) Medium; and (iii) Low. Each time a new container is submitted, its submission time is included in one period of the day where the submission frequency is high, medium or low compared to the other periods of the day. To automatically detect the different submission periods, we propose to use a machine leaning technique.

Machine learning algorithms are classified in three categories [14]: (i) Supervised and semi-supervised learning; (ii) Unsupervised learning; and (iii) Reinforcement learning. The unsupervised learning (clustering) analysis is applied to automatically detect different classes. In the literature, several unsupervised learning algorithms are proposed [10]. As in our context we already defined three submission periods classes, a clustering algorithm that determines the three classes at once is the most suitable for our work. The popular k-means clustering algorithm [8] is selected for this proposed. The goal of this algorithm is to defined clusters in the data, with the number of clusters represented by the variable K. The algorithm works iteratively to assign each data object to one of K clusters. In our context, each object represent the number of containers submitted by users and saved in the containers submission history during one hour. Using K-means algorithm, data objects are clustered based on feature similarity.

Algorithm 1. K-means Algorithm

Require: k, number of clusters.

1: Randomly choose k objects as center objects.
2: Calculate the distance between each object and each center object.
3: Assign each object to the cluster which has the nearest center object.
4: Recalculate the new center object of each cluster.
5: Repeat step 2, 3 and 4 until you achieve a cluster stability.

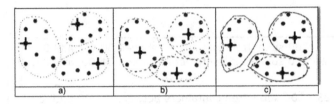

Fig. 3. Partitioning based on K-means [8]

The similarity is defined as the distance between objects. Let's suppose that we have three objects (o_1, o_2, o_3). We say that object o_1 is similar to object o_2 if the distance between o_1 and o_2 is smaller than the distance between o_1 and o_3.

The principle of the K-means algorithm is described in Algorithm 1.

Example of How the K-Means Algorithm Works. Let us consider a set of objects, as depicted in Fig. 3 which is presented in [8]. Let us also suppose that the number of clusters we want to have is equal to 3 (k = 3). We firstly arbitrarily choose three objects, each object represents an initial cluster center. In Fig. 3(a), each initial center is marked by the symbol (+). Then, each object from the set of objects is assigned to a cluster based on the cluster center to which it is the nearest. Next, the cluster centres are updated. That means, each cluster recalculated its center based on the current objects in the cluster. Then, using the new cluster centres, the objects are redistributed to the clusters based on which cluster center is the nearest (Fig. 3(b)). The process of iteratively reassigning objects to clusters to improve the partitioning is referred to as iterative relocation (Fig. 3(c)). Eventually, no reassignment of the objects in any cluster occurs and so the process terminates.

In our context, K-means take the history of the containers submission for 24 h. Then, it return as output three submission periods (high, medium and low) as presented in Figs. 4 and 5.

Example of How the Detection of the Submission Periods Step Works.
Figure 4 (resp. Fig. 5) shows the submission periods obtained by applying K-means algorithm in a history of submission of 317478 requests (resp. 332772 requests) during one day on 04-03-2013 (resp. 05-03-2013). The submission history is obtained from the real-world trace files of an international company called

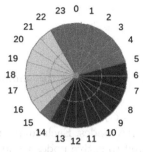

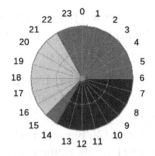

Fig. 4. Submission periods on 04/03/ 2013

Fig. 5. Submission periods on 05/03/ 2013

Prezi[2]. Prezi company offers a presentation editing service which is available on multiple platforms. Therefore they have to convert some of their created media files to other formats before they can display them on all devices.

From Fig. 4, we note that K-means algorithm return three submission periods:

- High submission period is between 15h00 and 22h00;
- Medium submission period is between 22h00 and 5h00 and between 14h00 and 15h00;
- Low submission period is between 5h00 and 14h00.

We also note from Figs. 4 and 5 that the two days containers submission histories have almost similar submission periods.

3.2 Dynamic Adaptation of the Number of Active Nodes

After the determination of the submission periods, we propose in this step to adapt the number of active cloud nodes for each submission period. Firstly we set the following variables according to the containers submission historical:

- $ANSC_{high}$: Average Number of Submitted Containers in one hour during all *high* submission periods;
- $ANSC_{medium}$: Average Number of Submitted Containers in one hour during all *medium* submission periods;
- $ANSC_{low}$: Average Number of Submitted Containers in one hour during all *low* submission periods.

Let's suppose that the cloud infrastructure is composed of n nodes. In this case, the number of *Actives Nodes* (AN) is computed for each submission period as following:

---

[2] http://prezi.com/scale/ and now available at https://lipn.univ-paris13.fr/ ~menouer/Jobs_Prezi.txt.

1. High submission period: $AN = |\frac{ANSC_{high} \times n}{ANSC_{high}}|$;
2. Medium submission period: $AN = |\frac{ANSC_{medium} \times n}{ANSC_{high}}|$;
3. Low submission period: $AN = |\frac{ANSC_{low} \times n}{ANSC_{high}}|$.

After the computing of AN, three possibilities appear following the number of the Current Active Nodes (CAN):

- If $AN > CAN$: our approach must activate $AN - CAN$ nodes;
- If $AN < CAN$: our approach must stop $CAN - AN$ nodes. Each time a node is stopped, all its running containers are migrated to active nodes to be sure that all containers are executed;
- If $AN = CAN$: our approach does nothing.

How to Choose Which Node Must Be Active or Stopped. In our approach, we propose to always activate nodes that have high numbers of resources to be able to satisfy the maximum number of submitted containers. We also propose to always stop nodes which have small numbers of resources. The goal is to keep nodes with high numbers of resources active in order to execute the maximum number of containers. However, before stopping each node, we must migrate its running containers to other active nodes.

Example of How Our Adaptation of the Number of Active Nodes Works. Let's suppose that we have a cloud infrastructure composed of 24 nodes. Let's also suppose that: (i) $ANSC_{high} = 19965$; (ii) $ANSC_{medium} = 14025$; and (iii) $ANSC_{low} = 7279$. In that case, the number of Active Nodes (AN) is computed for each submission period as presented in Fig. 6 following the next steps:

1. High submission period: $AN = |\frac{19965 \times 24}{19965}| = 24$;
2. Medium submission period: $AN = |\frac{14025 \times 24}{19965}| = 16$;
3. Low submission period: $AN = |\frac{7279 \times 24}{19965}| = 8$.

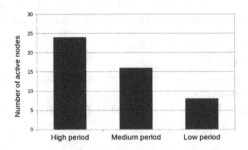

Fig. 6. Number of active nodes

Figure 6 shows that all nodes are active in the high submission period. However, the number of active nodes is smaller than the high submission period in the medium and low periods. This is in line with the goal of our approach which aims to reduce the amount of cloud nodes in the medium and low submission periods to reduce the global power consumption of the cloud infrastructure.

4   Experimental Evaluation

To validate our approach we propose to implement it (with Go language (see Footnote 1)) inside the current Docker Swarmkit version (v1.12) [18] and to perform experiments in a real cloud infrastructure. The used platform is Grid5000 [7]. It is an experimental large-scale testbed for distributed computing in France. For the following experiences, we booked an infrastructure of 96 computing cores, distributed over 3 nodes each node contains 32 cores and 64 GB of memory. To compute the power consumption, we use the Kwapi [5] framework include in the Grid5000 nodes and which give during a time interval (defined by start time and end time) the average power consumption by second in each node. Kwapi is a framework designed in the context of the Grid'5000 testbed, that unifies measurements for both power consumption and network traffic.

In the following, the containers submission history is the same as the Prezi requests submission traces on 04-03-2013. To validate our approach, we do experiences by submitting 76176 containers according to the Prezi submission traces on 05-03-2013 (see Footnote 2). The 76176 containers represent 22.89% from the total number of submitted requests of the Prezi traces on 05-03-2013. We note that all containers are submitted, in each hour, with the same submission frequency as the original Prezi traces. Each submitted container is executed using 1 CPU during a raw value set to 10 s.

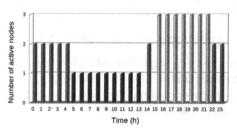

Fig. 7. Variation of the number of active nodes during one day according to the three submission periods

Figure 7 shows the variation of the number of active cloud nodes according to the submission period. The result obtained in Fig. 7 confirms our expectation. That means that the higher the submission period is, the bigger the number of active cloud node is.

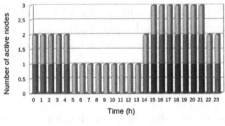

Fig. 8. Repartition of actives nodes during one day

Table 1. Comparison between nodes usage time

Comparison	Each node usage time			All nodes usage time
	$Node_1$	$Node_2$	$Node_3$	
Docker swarmkit with consolidation	24 h	15 h	7 h	**46 h**
Docker swarmkit without consolidation	24 h	24 h	24 h	**72 h**

Figure 8 shows how nodes are used for a day. We note that: (i) $node_1$ is used all the day (high, medium and low submission periods); (ii) $node_2$ is used from 22:00 until 5:00 and from 14:00 until 15:00 (medium and low submission periods); (iii) $node_3$ is used from 15:00 until 22:00 (low submission period).

4.1 Comparison Between the Performance Obtained with Our Consolidation Approach Inside Docker Swarmkit and the Basic Docker Swarmkit Approach

In this section, we propose to compare two approaches:

– Our consolidation approach implemented inside the Docker Swarmkit which adapt dynamically the number of active nodes;
– The basic Docker Swarmkit without consolidation approach which always use all nodes that form the cloud infrastructure.

Comparison Between Nodes Usage Time. Table 1 shows a comparison between nodes usage time using our consolidation approach inside Docker Swarmkit and the basic Docker swarmkit without consolidation approach. As expected, nodes are less used in Docker Swarmkit using our consolidation approach.

Comparison Between the Average Number of Containers Executed in Each Node. Figure 9 (resp. Fig. 10) shows the average number of containers executed in each node using docker swarmkit with consolidation approach (resp. without consolidation approach). The average number of containers is computed

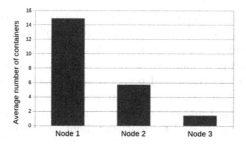

Fig. 9. Average number of containers executed in each node using docker swarmkit with consolidation

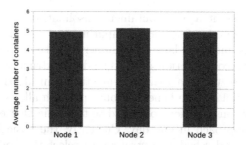

Fig. 10. Average number of containers executed in each node using docker swarmkit without consolidation

during one day. We note from Figs. 9 and 10 that without consolidation approach the average number of containers is practically the same in all nodes. However, using consolidation approach, the node which works most execute more containers than others. In our experiences, and as presented in Table 1, the $node_1$ is the most used node.

Comparison Between the Power Consumption. To study the power consumption, our experiment is perfomed thanks to the wattmeter installed inside the Grid5000 testbed for distributed computing in France [5].

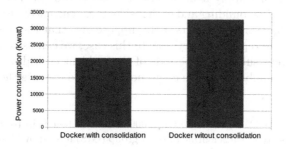

Fig. 11. Comparison between the global power consumption

Figure 11 shows the difference between the global power consumption using our consolidation approach inside Docker Swarmkit and the basic Docker swarmkit without consolidation approach. The Fig. 11 confirms that our approach reduces the power consumption. We note in this experience that our approach reduces 35.98% of the global power consumption compared to the basic Docker swarmkit without consolidation approach in one day. In terms of computing time, we note in these experiments, that containers are executed during one day with consolidation and without consolidation approach.

5   Conclusion

In this paper we present a new container consolidation approach based on a machine learning technique for cloud computing environment. The goal of our approach is to dynamically adapt the number of active cloud nodes in order to reduce the power consumption of the cloud infrastructure. To validate our approach, we propose to do a real implementation inside the current Docker Swarmkit version (v1.12). The benefit of our approach allows to reduce 35.98% of the global power consumption compared to the basic Docker Swarmkit without consolidation approach in one day. Currently, the basic Docker Swarmkit version uses the Spread scheduling strategy to select the node that must execute a container. In [12], a new scheduling strategy is proposed which allows to reduce the computing time of executing a set of containers. In [12] the number of active nodes is always fixed and equal to all the nodes that form the cloud infrastructure. As a first perspective, we propose to combine our consolidation approach with the work proposed in [12] to improve the performance when executing containers in a cloud infrastructure in term of computing time and power consumption.

In our approach, we suppose that each time a container is assigned to a node it will be executed without problems. As a second perspective, we propose to work on the problem of fault tolerance in case that a node breaks down in the cloud infrastructure. In this situation, we propose to use a smart replica approach of containers.

As another perspective, we propose to use our consolidation approach inside Docker Swarmkit and apply it in the smart building context. For example, let's consider residents in a building and each resident, concurrently, starts or requests services encapsulated in containers. Lets suppose also that the requests submitted by residents are repeated every day. In this case, we can use our approach to detect the different submission periods of the resident each day, then to adapt dynamically the number of active cloud nodes used to execute the resident containers.

Acknowledgments. We thank the Grid5000 team for their help to use the testbed. Grid'5000 is supported by a scientific interest group (GIS) hosted by Inria and including CNRS, RENATER and several universities as well as other organizations.

References

1. Ahmad, R.W., Gani, A., Hamid, S.H.A., Shiraz, M., Yousafzai, A., Xia, F.: A survey on virtual machine migration and server consolidation frameworks for cloud data centers. J. Netw. Comput. Appl. **52**, 11–25 (2015). http://www.sciencedirect.com/science/article/pii/S1084804515000284
2. Beloglazov, A., Buyya, R.: Adaptive threshold-based approach for energy-efficient consolidation of virtual machines in cloud data centers. In: Proceedings of the 8th International Workshop on Middleware for Grids, Clouds and e-Science, MGC 2010, pp. 4:1–4:6. ACM, New York (2010). http://doi.acm.org/10.1145/1890799.1890803
3. Ben Maaouia, O., Fkaier, H., Cerin, C., Jemni, M., Ngoko, Y.: On optimization of energy consumption in a volunteer cloud. In: Vaidya, J., Li, J. (eds.) ICA3PP 2018, Part II. LNCS, vol. 11335, pp. 388–398. Springer, Cham (2018). https://doi.org/10.1007/978-3-030-05054-2_31
4. Catuogno, L., Galdi, C., Pasquino, N.: An effective methodology for measuring software resource usage. IEEE Trans. Instrum. Measur. **67**(10), 2487–2494 (2018)
5. Clouet, F., et al.: A unified monitoring framework for energy consumption and network traffic. In: TRIDENTCOM - International Conference on Testbeds and Research Infrastructures for the Development of Networks and Communities, Vancouver, Canada, p. 10, June 2015. https://hal.inria.fr/hal-01167915
6. Dong, Z., Zhuang, W., Rojas-Cessa, R.: Energy-aware scheduling schemes for cloud data centers on Google trace data. In: 2014 IEEE Online Conference on Green Communications (OnlineGreenComm), pp. 1–6, November 2014
7. Grid5000. https://www.grid5000.fr/. Accessed 25 Jan 2019
8. Han, J., Kamber, M., Pei, J.: Data Mining: Concepts and Techniques, 3rd edn. Elsevier, New York (2011)
9. Hirofuchi, T., Nakada, H., Itoh, S., Sekiguchi, S.: Reactive consolidation of virtual machines enabled by postcopy live migration. In: Proceedings of the 5th International Workshop on Virtualization Technologies in Distributed Computing, VTDC 2011, pp. 11–18. ACM, New York (2011). http://doi.acm.org/10.1145/1996121.1996125
10. Le, Q.V., et al.: Building high-level features using large scale unsupervised learning. In: Proceedings of the 29th International Coference on International Conference on Machine Learning, ICML 2012, USA, pp. 507–514. Omnipress (2012). http://dl.acm.org/citation.cfm?id=3042573.3042641
11. Medel, V., Tolón, C., Arronategui, U., Tolosana-Calasanz, R., Bañares, J.Á., Rana, O.F.: Client-side scheduling based on application characterization on kubernetes. In: Pham, C., Altmann, J., Bañares, J.Á. (eds.) GECON 2017. LNCS, vol. 10537, pp. 162–176. Springer, Cham (2017). https://doi.org/10.1007/978-3-319-68066-8_13
12. Menouer, T., Darmon, P.: New scheduling strategy based on multi-criteria decision algorithm. In: 2019 27th Euromicro International Conference on Parallel, Distributed and Network-Based Processing (PDP), pp. 101–107, February 2019
13. Piraghaj, S.F., Dastjerdi, A.V., Calheiros, R.N., Buyya, R.: A framework and algorithm for energy efficient container consolidation in cloud data centers. In: 2015 IEEE International Conference on Data Science and Data Intensive Systems, pp. 368–375, December 2015
14. Silver, D.L., Yang, Q., Li, L.: Lifelong machine learning systems: beyond learning algorithms. In: AAAI Spring Symposium: Lifelong Machine Learning, vol. 13, p. 05 (2013)

15. Menouer, T., Cérin, C., Saad, W., Shi, X.: A resource allocation framework with qualitative and quantitative SLA classes. In: Mencagli, G., et al. (eds.) Euro-Par 2018. LNCS, vol. 11339, pp. 69–81. Springer, Cham (2019). https://doi.org/10.1007/978-3-030-10549-5_6
16. Zheng, K., Wang, X., Li, L., Wang, X.: Joint power optimization of data center network and servers with correlation analysis. In: IEEE INFOCOM 2014 - IEEE Conference on Computer Communications, pp. 2598–2606, April 2014
17. The apache software foundation. Mesos, apache. http://mesos.apache.org/. Accessed 25 Jan 2019
18. Docker swarmkit. https://github.com/docker/swarmkit/. Accessed 25 Jan 2019
19. Kubernetes scheduler. https://kubernetes.io/. Accessed 25 Jan 2019

Power Efficiency Containers Scheduling Approach Based on Machine Learning Technique for Cloud Computing Environment

Tarek Menouer[1(✉)], Otman Manad[1], Christophe Cérin[2], and Patrice Darmon[1]

[1] UMANIS, 7 Rue Paul Vaillant Couturier, 92300 Levallois-Perret, France
{tmenouer,omanad,pdarmon}@umanis.com
[2] UMR 7030, University of Paris 13,LIPN/CNRS, 93430 Villetaneuse, France
christophe.cerin@lipn.univ-paris13.fr

Abstract. Recently, containers have been used extensively in the cloud computing field, and several frameworks have been proposed to schedule containers using a scheduling strategy. The main idea of the different scheduling strategies consist to select the most suitable node, from a set of nodes that forms the cloud platform, to execute each new submitted container. The Spread scheduling strategy, used as the default strategy in the Docker Swarmkit container scheduling framework, consists to select, for each new container, the node with the least number of running containers. In this paper, we propose to improve the Spread strategy by presenting a new container scheduling strategy based on the power consumption of heterogeneous cloud nodes. The novelty of our approach consists to make the best compromise that allows to reduce the global power consumption of an heterogeneous cloud infrastructure. The principle of our strategy is based on learning and scheduling steps which are applied each time a new container is submitted by a user. Our proposed strategy is implemented in Go language inside Docker Swarmkit. Experiments demonstrate the potential of our strategy under different scenarios.

Keywords: Container technology · Cloud computing · Power Consumption · Scheduling strategy

1 Introduction

In recent years, cloud computing industry has grown quickly and a variety of virtualization technologies have emerged such as virtual machines (VMs), containers, or bare-metal resources, having each their own characteristics. A container is a lightweight OS-level virtualization technique that allows running an application and its dependencies in a resource-isolated process. The advantage of the container is that the application process runs directly in the host's kernel, that means that the container does not have its own kernel and there is no hardware virtualization [4]. Therefore, containers are much lighter than traditional virtual machines.

The big jump of containers history, from a massive adoption in production systems point of view, started in 2013 with the Docker project [3]. During this time, Docker

ⓒ Springer Nature Switzerland AG 2019
C. Esposito et al. (Eds.): I-SPAN 2019, CCIS 1080, pp. 193–206, 2019.
https://doi.org/10.1007/978-3-030-30143-9_16

containers became a lightweight [14] container technology that can be easily deployed on a variety of Infrastructure as a Service (IaaS) or Platform as a Service (PaaS).

In the literature, several frameworks have been proposed to schedule containers on cloud computing such as Kubernetes [21], Swarmkit [20] and Mesos [19]. However, each framework uses its particular scheduling strategy to assign a container to a node, from a set of nodes that form the cloud infrastructure. The difference between strategies depend on their scheduling goal. As example, the Swarmkit [20] (version 1.12) uses the Spread strategy as a default scheduling strategy. Its principle consists to execute a container on the node having the least number of running containers. The benefit of the Spread strategy is balancing the containers' load between nodes. However, one drawback is that it selects a node without any consideration of the total amount of power consumed by the cloud infrastructure.

To improve the Docker Swarmkit Spread strategy, we propose in this paper a new power efficiency scheduling strategy based on the power consumption of nodes. The goal of our strategy is to answer the problem stated as follows. For a company that receives online containers submitted by their users in a private heterogeneous cloud infrastructure, how will they select, for each container, the best node which allows to reduce the global power consumption of the heterogeneous cloud infrastructure.

The principle of our strategy goes through learning and scheduling steps. Since we assume that, in our context, we have an heterogeneous cloud composed of nodes with multiple architecture types, the learning step is applied to estimate the power consumption of each node. Then, it groups the nodes that form the heterogeneous cloud infrastructure into clusters according to their power consumption and by applying the k-means algorithm [15]. K-means is an unsupervised machine learning algorithm which regroups objects on k clusters according to their similarity. The second step is the scheduling step which is applied to select the nodes cluster which has the lowest power consumption compared to the others nodes clusters. Then, a Spread strategy is applied for the nodes inside the selected cluster to elect the most suitable node that will execute the new submitted container and also to balance the containers' load between nodes.

One key motivation for this decomposition is to better adapt the decision of placement with continuing 'fresh' information regarding the state of the cloud platform in terms of power consumption. Another motivation is to accelerate the decision process. Instead of managing and deciding on a pool of N nodes, we decide on a pool of N/K nodes if our clustering technique builds K clusters of even size. The intelligence of the algorithm is with the scoring and the ranking process, followed by a Spread step. At last, our overall approach is a moderate platform-aware approach. It's only the learning step that makes the approach 'platform aware'.

To validate our strategy, we made an implementation of our proposal in Go language[1] inside Docker Swarmkit[2]. The main contributions of this work are summarized as follows:

– Improve the default Docker Swarmkit Spread strategy by proposing a new container scheduling strategy based on power consumption;

---

[1] https://golang.org.

[2] https://github.com/docker/swarmkit.

- Reduce the global power consumption of an heterogeneous cloud infrastructure by choosing, for each container, the node that consumes the least in terms of power;
- Implement our strategy inside the Docker Swarmkit with minimum change in the Docker Swarmkit code;
- Prove that our strategy reduces the power consumption compared to the default Spread strategy implemented in the Docker Swarmkit (version 1.12).

The paper is organized as follows. Section 2 presents some related works. Section 3 shows the impact of the power consumption according to clouds nodes. Section 4 describes our container scheduling strategy. Section 5 shows an example of how our container scheduling strategy works. Section 6 introduces exhaustive experiments that validate our strategy. Finally, a conclusion and some future works are given in Sect. 7.

2   Related Work

In this section, we will start by briefly presenting some studies related to containers' scheduling in the cloud computing (Subsect. 2.1). Then, we provide an overview about some works proposed in the scheduling context (Subsect. 2.2). Finally, we contribute with a positioning in Subsect. 2.3.

2.1   Container Scheduling Systems

In the literature, all problems of resource allocation or resource management refer to the same class of scheduling problems. They consist generally in associating a user's container to one or several computing cores. Most of these problems are *NP*-hard [18]. From an industrial point of view, we document, as examples of concrete projects, the schedulers inside Kubernetes [21], Swarmkit [20] and Mesos [19].

Kubernetes [21] is a scheduler framework which represents an orchestration system for Docker containers based on pods concept. Pods are a group of one or more containers. They are always co-located, co-scheduled and run in a shared context. Moreover, they will be run on the same physical or virtual machine. In the Google Kubernetes the scheduling can be summarized in two steps. The first step consists of filtering all nodes to remove the one that do not meet certain requirements of the pod. The second step consists of classifying the remaining nodes using priorities to find the best fit to execute a pod. A priority is a key/value representing the name of the priority from the list of existing ones and its weight. For each remaining node, a priority function gives a score on a scale of 0 to 10. Each priority function is weighted by a positive number and the final score of each node is calculated by adding up all the weighted scores. Once all scores of all nodes are calculated, Google Kubernetes chooses the node with the highest score to run the container to.

Swarmkit [20] is an important container scheduler framework developed by Docker. The Swarm manager is in-charge of scheduling on nodes. The Docker Swarmkit also has two steps to finally choose which node will execute the container. First, it uses filters to select a set of nodes to execute the container according to some criteria. Then, it selects the most suitable one according to the used scheduling strategy. The Docker

Swarmkit (version 1.12), uses the Spread strategy as the default scheduling strategy. It consists to select for each new container the node having the least number of executed containers.

Mesos [7] is an Apache project. It is a thin resource sharing layer that enables fine-grained sharing across diverse cluster computing frameworks, by giving frameworks a common interface for accessing cluster resources. Marathon [3], runs on top of Mesos, and it is a production-grade container orchestration platform.

2.2 Overview About Scheduling Strategies

In this sub-section we present some studies proposed in the scheduling context. In the past few years, many studies have been proposed [9–12, 17]. In the following, we present some examples.

In [11], authors present a new scheduling algorithm named Multipot. The Multipot algorithm allows to select for each container a node by taking into consideration five criteria: (i) CPUs usage of every node, (ii) memory usage of every node, (iii) the time consumed transmitting images on the network, (iv) the association between containers and nodes, (v) the clustering of containers, which affect the performance of applications in containers. The novelty of the authors is that the Multipot algorithm selects a node to deploy a container by defining a metric method for every key factor and establishes a scoring function for each one and then combines them into a composite function.

In [13], authors propose to define each node, from the set of nodes that form the cloud computing, through several criteria as the number of running containers, the availability of CPUs and memory in each node. Then, to find the most suitable node, authors propose to use a multi-criteria algorithm. The multi-criteria algorithm used in this study is Technique for the Order of Prioritization by Similarity to Ideal Solution (TOPSIS) algorithm.

In [8], authors propose a container scheduling algorithm based on ant colony optimization algorithm. The purpose of which is to balance the use of resources so that applications in container cluster will have a better performance.

In [17], authors propose a Docker container scheduling algorithm based on load balancing. The principle is that the algorithm dynamically controls the load of each container within a threshold in the cluster, so that the load of each container is not too high nor too low. When the container's load is too high, a new container will be opened to load balance. When the container's load is too low, the container will be closed to save energy.

In [16], authors introduce a Cloud VM scheduling algorithm that took into account already running VM resource usage over time by analyzing past VM utilization levels. Authors also introduce a synthesis of approaches for cloud platform scheduling, energy efficiency, resources provisioning and VM placement regarding the most used method found in the literature.

We note also that there are in the literature some studies proposed in the context of power consumption, as studies proposed in [1, 2].

---

[3] https://mesosphere.github.io/marathon/.

2.3 Positioning

In this paper, we present a new power efficiency container scheduling strategy based on power consumption of nodes. Our strategy is implemented in Go language[4] inside Docker Swarmkit. The difference between our strategy and other proposed scheduling strategies, especially the default Docker Swarmkit strategy (Spread), is that the goal of our strategy consists to execute containers in a set of nodes which have the low power consumption to reduce the global power consumption of the considered heterogeneous cloud infrastructure. Our strategy allows also to balance the containers' load between nodes that have low power consumption.

3 Impact of the Power Consumption According to the Cloud Nodes Architecture

In this section we quickly present the impact of the power consumption according to the number of running containers in each node and according to the cloud nodes architecture.

Figures 1 and 2 show the result of an experiment obtained by varying the number of executed containers on two different nodes belonging to Docker Swarmkit [20] infrastructure deployed on Grid5000 platform [6]. Grid5000 platform is an experimental large-scale testbed for distributed computing in France. In this experiment, we start by executing one container in one node, then we measure the average power consumption by second (during a time interval defined by start and end time) using the Kwapi [5] framework included in the Grid5000 nodes. Then, we repeat this operation each time the number of running container increases. Kwapi is a framework designed in the context of the Grid'5000 testbed, that unifies measurements for both power consumption and network traffic.

Figure 1 shows the variation of the average power consumption according to the number of running containers in a cloud node (Intel Xeon E5-2620 v4) with the following configuration: Broadwell, 2.10GHz, 2 CPUs/node, 8 cores/CPU. We note that each time the number of containers increases, the cloud node consumes more power until it reaches its maximum consumption.

Figure 2 shows the variation of the average power consumption according to the number of running containers in a cloud node (Intel Xeon E5-2630) with the following configuration: Sandy Bridge, 2.30GHz, 2 CPUs/node, 6 cores/CPU. We note the same behavior related to the power consumption as it has been presented previously in Fig. 1.

We deduce from Figs. 1 and 2 that, the power consumption varies according to the architecture of the node and its charge.

Moreover, there exists in the literature other methods that can be used to compute the power consumption of nodes. For instance, in the concrete work done by the VIFIB/NEXEDI[5] team related to the SlapOS cloud[6], authors consider a discrete model

---

[4] https://golang.org.

[5] http://www.vifib.com/press/news-CO2.

[6] https://www.slapos.org.

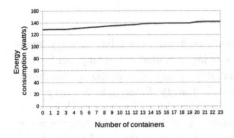

Fig. 1. Average energy consumption according to the number of running containers in Intel Xeon E5-2620 node

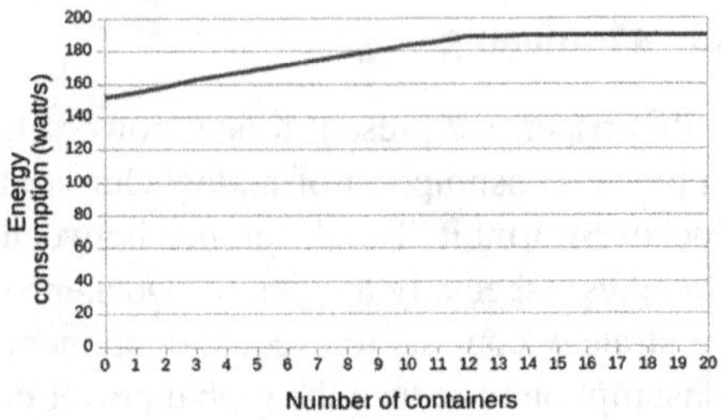

Fig. 2. Average energy consumption according to the number of running containers in Intel Xeon E5-2630 node

that, for a given CPU load, gives the power (Watt) that the processor card consumes. The discrete models representing the power consumed by 3 processors cards and reported by VIFIB is as follows:

- Shuttle Computer;
- Intel NUC[7] – A powerful but small and compact computer;
- Rikomagic Linux device[8]

The corresponding discrete power models $\mathcal{E}(x)$ is defined as following:

- the Shuttle Computer model:

$$\mathcal{E}(x) = \begin{cases} 21.5 + 1.06 * x \text{ when } x \leq 25\% \\ 48 + 0.29 * x \text{ otherwise} \end{cases}$$

- the Intel NUC model:

$$\mathcal{E}(x) = \begin{cases} 8.5 + 0.46 * x \text{ when } x \leq 25\% \\ 20 + 0.08 * x \text{ otherwise} \end{cases}$$

- Rikomagic Linux device model:

$$\mathcal{E}(x) = \begin{cases} 2.2 + 0.04 * x \text{ when } x \leq 25\% \\ 3.2 + 0.008 * x \text{ otherwise} \end{cases}$$

In our experiences (Sect. 6), we do not use this mode to compute the power consumption because our experiences are performed inside Grid5000 testbed which include the Kwapi [5] framework which returns the power consumed on the Grid5000 nodes.

---

[7] http://www.intel.com/content/www/us/en/motherboards/desktop-motherboards/nuc.html.
[8] http://www.cloudsto.com/mk802iii-le-mini-linux-pc.html.

4 Container Scheduling Strategy Based on Power Consumption of Nodes

The main purpose of our container scheduling strategy consists to reduce the global power consumption of heterogeneous cloud infrastructure when executing containers submitted by users. Each time a new container is submitted, our strategy selects from all nodes of the cloud infrastructure the node which has the lowest power consumption.

Algorithm 1. Main loop of our strategy

1: **while** new container C_x is submitted by a user **do**
2:    Apply the learning step
3:    Apply the scheduling step to select the most suitable node ($Node_x$)
4:    Execute the container C_x on $Node_x$
5: **end while**

As presented in Algorithm 1, the principle of our strategy has two steps: (i) learning; and (ii) scheduling. The two steps are defined in the following sub-sections.

4.1 Learning Step

Algorithm 2. Learning step

Require: n, number of nodes that form the cloud infrastructure
1: **for** i=0;i< n;i++ **do**
2:    Computes the average power consumption by $node_i$
3: **end for**
4: Classify the n nodes into k clusters according to their power consumption profiles by applying the k-means algorithm
5: **for** i=0;i< k;i++ **do**
6:    Score of $cluster_i$ = average power consumed between all nodes of the $cluster_i$
7: **end for**

As previously presented in Sect. 3, the power consumption varied according to: (i) the architecture of the cloud node; and (ii) the number of running containers in each node. For this reason, we propose to apply, each time a new container is submitted, the learning step. This step adds an overhead to our strategy, but allow also to give a good global vision about the power consumed by the heterogeneous cloud infrastructure. As introduced in the Algorithm 0, the learning step consists firstly to compute the power consumption of each node. Then, we classify nodes according to their power consumption into a set of clusters by applying a clustering algorithm. The popular k-means clustering algorithm [15] is selected for this proposed. The goal of this algorithm is to define nodes clusters, with the number of clusters represented by the variable K. The algorithm works iteratively to assign each node to one of K clusters. Nodes are clustered based on feature similarity in term of power consumption. In our context, we propose to set k as the number of different architectures of the heterogeneous cloud infrastructure. The principle of the K-means algorithm is described in algorithm 3.

Algorithm 3. K-means Algorithm

Require: k, number of clusters.
 1: Randomly choose k nodes as center nodes
 2: Calculate the distance between each node and the k center nodes in term of power consumption
 3: Assign each node to the cluster which has the nearest distance in terms of power consumption
 4: Recalculate the new center nodes of each cluster
 5: Repeat step 2, 3 and 4 until you achieve a cluster stability

---

In the learning step, each cluster is defined by a set of nodes and also by a score. In our approach, the score of each cluster represents the average power consumption between all nodes of the cluster. We could also, as example, take the power consumption of the node which is the centroid of the cluster.

4.2   Scheduling Step

Algorithm 4. Scheduling step

Require: $container_x$, new container
 1: **if** $container_x$ is submitted by a user **then**
 2:     $cluster_x$ = the cluster with the lowest score among c clusters found in the learning step and which has at last one node that can execute $container_x$
 3:     $node_x$ = the node selected by Spread strategy among the set of nodes of the $cluster_x$
 4: **end if**

The scheduling step is applied to select for each container the best node that allows to reduce the power consumption and also to balance the containers' load between nodes that consume the least, in term of power, comparing to all nodes of the cloud infrastructure.

As presented in Algorithm 4, the scheduling step consists firstly to select from the set of cluster nodes defined in the learning step (see Subsect. 4.1), the nodes cluster with the low score, i.e, the nodes cluster which has the lowest power consumption. The selected cluster must have at last one node that can execute the new container submitted by the user. Then, when the nodes cluster is selected, the Spread strategy is applied to choose the most suitable node that can execute the container submitted by a user. As presented previously in Sect. 1, the principle of the Spread strategy consists to select the node that has the least number of running containers and which allows to have a good load balancing between nodes in terms of containers. The Spread strategy is also used to answer to the problem of fault tolerance, if one node shuts down, we are sure that we don't lose all running containers.

5   Example to Explain How Our Strategy Works

To better illustrate the principle of our container scheduling strategy, we introduce an example in order to schedule 4 containers submitted at the same time on 4 nodes. In this example we suppose that each container is executed using 1 CPU during 600 s.

The first step of our strategy consists to apply the learning step which starts by computing the power consumption of each node. Let's suppose in this example that nodes have different architectures: (i) $node_1$ and $node_2$ have the same architecture; and (ii) $node_3$ and $node_4$ have the same architecture. Lets also suppose, that the average power consumed by each node and by each container is as follows:

- $Node_1$: Average power consumption without any running container = 125 W/s and each time a new container is executed in $node_1$, it consumes on average 1.5 W/s;
- $Node_2$: Average power consumption without any running container = 127 W/s and each time a new container is executed in $node_2$, it consumes on average 1.5 W/s;
- $Node_3$: Average power consumption without any running container = 151 W/s and each time a new container is executed in $node_3$, it consumes on average 3 W/s;
- $Node_4$: Average power consumption without any running container = 153 W/s and each time a new container is executed in $node_4$, it consumes on average 3 W/s.

After computing the power consumed by each node, our strategy classifies nodes in two clusters by applying the k-means algorithm and computes for each cluster a score as follows:

1. $Cluster_1$:
   - Nodes: $node_1$ and $node_2$
   - Score = $\frac{125+127}{2}=126$
2. $Cluster_2$:
   - Nodes: $node_3$ and $node_4$
   - Score = $\frac{151+153}{2}=152$

To select the node that executes the first container ($container_1$), our strategy applies the scheduling step. Firstly, $cluster_1$ is selected because it has the lowest score (126). Then, by applying the Spread strategy, $node_1$ will be selected as the node that must execute $container_1$. In the same way, Fig. 3(a) shows how containers are scheduled in nodes.

In this example, we suppose that all containers are executed at the same time and the total execution time is equal to 600 s. With this information, the power consumed by the infrastructure can be calculated as follows:

- $node_1$: As it has 2 running containers, the average power consumption = 125 W/s + 1.5 W/s + 1.5 W/s = 128 W/s $\Rightarrow$ It consume 128 * 600 = 76800 Watt.
- $node_2$: As it has 2 running containers, the average power consumption = 127 W/s + 1.5 W/s + 1.5 W/s = 130 W/s $\Rightarrow$ It consume 130 * 600 = 78000 Watt.
- $node_3$: As it does not have any running containers, the average power consumption = 151 W/s $\Rightarrow$ It consume 151 * 600 = 90600 Watt.
- $node_4$: As it does not have any running containers, the average power consumption = 153 W/s $\Rightarrow$ It consume 153 * 600 = 91800 Watt.
- Total power consumed by the infrastructure ($node_1 + node_2 + node_3 + node_4$) = 76800+78000+90600+91800 = 337200 Watt.

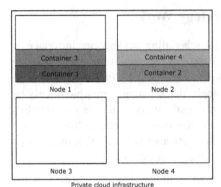
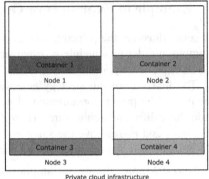

(a) Scheduling using our strategy.   (b) Scheduling using Spread strategy.

Fig. 3. Scheduling of containers

5.1 Comparison Between the Performance Obtained Using Our Strategy and the Spread Strategy

Let's suppose that we have the same infrastructure (4 nodes) and the same number of containers (4 containers) as the previous example presented in Sect. 5. Figure 3(b) shows how containers are scheduled by using the default Docker Swarmkit Spread strategy.

To compute the total power consumption, let's suppose also that all containers are executed at the same time as in the previous example (Sect. 5) and the execution time of each container is also equal to 600 s. With this information, the power consumed by the infrastructure can be calculated as follows:

- $node_1$: As it has 1 running container, the average power consumption = 125 W/s + 1.5 W/s = 126.5 W/s $\Rightarrow$ It consumes 126.5 * 600 = 75900 Watt.
- $node_2$: As it has 1 running container, the average power consumption = 127 W/s + 1.5 W/s = 128.5 W/s $\Rightarrow$ It consumes 128.5 * 600 = 77100 Watt.
- $node_3$: As it has 1 running container, the average power consumption = 151 W/s + 3 W/s = 154 W/s $\Rightarrow$ It consumes 154 * 600 = 92400 Watt.
- $node_4$: As it has 1 running container, the average power consumption = 153 W/s + 3 W/s = 156 W/s $\Rightarrow$ It consumes 156 * 600 = 93600 Watt.
- Total power consumed by the infrastructure $(node_1+node_2+node_3+node_4)$ = 75900+77100+92400+93600 = 339000 Watt.

As a result, we note that using the Spread strategy, the infrastructure consumes 339000 Watt. However, using our strategy, the infrastructure consumes 337200 Watt. This demonstrates the potential of our approach in reducing the power consumption.

6   Experimental Evaluation

In this section, we introduce some experimentations with our new scheduling strategy to check if it meets our expectations. For these experimentations, we use the Grid5000 platform [6], an experimental large-scale testbed for distributed computing in France. For our experimental evaluation, we booked an infrastructure of 128 computing cores, distributed over 4 nodes: (i) 2 nodes are Intel Xeon E5-2620 v4; and (ii) 2 nodes are Intel Xeon E5-2630. To validate our strategy, we used, in the learning step, the information returned by Kwapi [5] framework included in the Grid5000 nodes and which give during a time interval (defined by start time and end time) the average power consumption by second in each node. As previously said in Sect. 3, Kwapi is a framework designed in the context of the Grid'5000 testbed, that unifies measurements for both power consumption and network traffic.

The performance of our strategy is based on containers submitted online with two different constant frequencies: (i) a constant frequency equal to 2 s, i.e. every 2 s, 3 containers are submitted by 3 different users; and (ii) a constant frequency equal to 5 s, i.e. every 5 s, 3 containers are submitted by 3 different users. The first submission type with a constant frequency equal to 2 s stresses the scheduling system. However, the submission with a constant frequency equal to 5 s represent a normal operating mode. In our experiences, each container is executed during 15 mins. The execution time of containers does not depend on the node architecture, it is always fixed to 15 min.

In the following section, we propose a comparison between the performance obtained using our container scheduling strategy and the Docker Swarmkit Spread scheduling strategy.

6.1 Comparison Between the Number of Used Nodes and the Running Containers

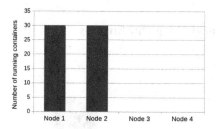
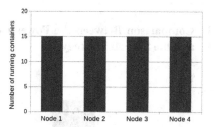

Fig. 4. Number of running containers using our scheduling strategy for containers submitted online with a constant frequency equal to 1 and 3 s

Fig. 5. Number of running containers using Spread scheduling strategy for containers submitted online with a constant frequency equal to 1 and 3 s

Figure 4 (resp. Fig. 5) shows the number of running containers in each node using our container scheduling strategy (resp. Docker Swarmkit Spread strategy) for containers submitted online with a constant frequency equal to 2 and 5 s. We note that the number of running containers is partitioned between $node_1$ and $node_2$ (30 running containers for each node) using our scheduling strategy. However, using the Spread scheduling strategy the number of containers is partitioned between all nodes: $node_1$, $node_2$, $node_3$ and $node_4$ with 15 running containers in each node.

We note also from Figs. 4 and 5 that using our strategy only 2 nodes are used. This can be explained by the fact that our strategy privileges nodes which have the lowest power consumption. However, with Spread strategy all nodes that form the infrastructure are used.

6.2 Comparison Between the Computing Time Using Our Strategy and the Spread Strategy

Table 1. Comparison of computing time

Scheduling	Computing time (s)	
strategies	Constant frequency equal to 2 s	Constant frequency equal to 5 s
Our strategy	1062.54	1210.99
Spread strategy	1036.9	1216.64

To study the cost (complexity) of our strategy, we present in Table 1 the computing time obtained using our strategy and the Spread strategy. We note that with a containers submission type that stresses the scheduling (submission frequency equal to 2 s), our scheduling strategy adds an overhead in term of computing time compared to Spread strategy. However, with a containers submission type that represents a normal operation mode (submission frequency equal to 5 s), our strategy has practically the same computing time as the Spread strategy.

6.3 Comparison Between the Power Consumed Using Our Strategy and the Spread Strategy

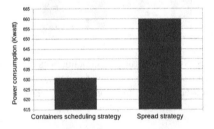

Fig. 6. Comparison between the power consumed between our strategy and Spread strategy for containers submitted online with a constant frequency equal to 2 s

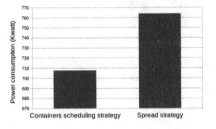

Fig. 7. Comparison between the power consumed between our strategy and Spread strategy for containers submitted online with a constant frequency equal to 5 s

Figure 6 (resp. Fig. 7) shows a comparison between the power consumed by our container scheduling strategy and the Docker Swarmkit Spread strategy for containers submitted online with a constant frequency equal to 2 s (resp. 5 s). It is clear that our container scheduling strategy reduces the power consumption compared to the Spread strategy. This result can be explained by the fact that our strategy chooses the nodes with the lowest power consumption as it is presented in the previous sub-section (Subsect. 6.1).

7   Conclusion

In this paper we presented an algorithm for scheduling containers on heterogeneous cloud nodes with the goal to improve power consumption. The approach consists of three steps: node grouping in clusters, choosing cluster with the lowest power consumption and Spread strategy for executing container in the selected cluster. A learning step guides the approach by updating the power consumption of the infrastructure. Our approach is implemented in the Docker Swarmkit and compared for real scenario to the default Spread strategy.

In our approach we suppose that each time a container is assigned to a node it will be executed without any fault. As a perspective, we propose to work on the problem of fault tolerance. In this situation, we propose to use a smart replica approach of containers. The scientific question is in mastering the power consumption, to keep it for instance, below a global threshold.

From an energy efficient perspective, it would be better to fill the used nodes and switch off nodes that are not in use to reduce the consumed energy.

We would like also to apply our approach in a smart bulding context. For example, let's consider residents in a building. Each resident, concurrently, starts or requests at some time some services encapsulated in containers. In this case, we can propose a new approach to adapt dynamically the number of active cloud nodes used to execute the resident containers.

Acknowledgment. We thank the Grid5000 team for their help to use the testbed. Grid5000 is supported by a scientific interest group (GIS) hosted by Inria and including CNRS, RENATER and several universities as well as other organizations.

References

1. Catuogno, L., Galdi, C., Pasquino, N.: Measuring the effectiveness of containerization to prevent power draining attacks. In: 2017 IEEE International Workshop on Measurement and Networking (M&N), pp. 1–6 (2017)
2. Catuogno, L., Galdi, C., Pasquino, N.: An effective methodology for measuring software resource usage. IEEE Trans. Instrum. Meas. **67**(10), 2487–2494 (2018)
3. Choi, S., Myung, R., Choi, H., Chung, K., Gil, J., Yu, H.: Gpsf: general-purpose scheduling framework for container based on cloud environment. In: IEEE International Conference on Internet of Things and IEEE Green Computing and Communications and IEEE Cyber, Physical and Social Computing and IEEE Smart Data, pp. 769–772, Dec (2016)
4. Chung, M.T., Quang-Hung, N., Nguyen, M., Thoai, N.: Using docker in high performance computing applications. In: 2016 IEEE Sixth International Conference on Communications and Electronics (ICCE), pp. 52–57, (July 2016)

5. Clouet, F., et al.: A unified monitoring framework for energy consumption and network traffic. In: TRIDENTCOM - International Conference on Testbeds and Research Infrastructures for the Development of Networks & Communities, p. 10. Vancouver, Canada (June 2015)
6. Grid5000: https://www.grid5000.fr/. Accesssed 25 Mar 2019
7. Hindman, B., et al.: Mesos: a platform for fine-grained resource sharing in the data center. In: NSDI, pp. 22–22 (2011)
8. Kaewkasi, C., Chuenmuneewong, K.: Improvement of container scheduling for docker using ant colony optimization. In: 2017 9th International Conference on Knowledge and Smart Technology (KST), pp. 254–259 (Feb 2017)
9. Lin, W., Xu, S., Li, J., Xu, L., Peng, Z.: Design and theoretical analysis of virtual machine placement algorithm based on peak workload characteristics. Soft Comput. **21**(5), 1301–1314 (2017)
10. Lin, W., Zhu, C., Li, J., Liu, B., Lian, H.: Novel algorithms and equivalence optimisation for resource allocation in cloud computing. Int. J. Web Grid Serv. **11**, 193 (2015)
11. Liu, B., Li, P., Lin, W., Shu, N., Li, Y., Chang, V.: A new container scheduling algorithm based on multi-objective optimization. Soft Comput. **22**, 1–12 (2018)
12. Maaouia, O., Fkaier, H., Cérin, C., Jemni, M., Ngoko, Y.: On optimization of energy consumption in a volunteer cloud. In: 18th International Conference, ICA3PP 2018, Guangzhou, China, November 15–17, 2018, Proceedings, Part II, pp. 388–398. (Nov 2018)
13. Menouer, T., Darmon, P.: A new container scheduling algorithm based on multi-objective optimization. In: 27th Euromicro International Conference on Parallel, Distributed and Network-based Processing, Pavia, Italy, (Feb 2019)
14. Merkel, D.: Docker: lightweight linux containers for consistent development and deployment. Linux J. **2014**(239), 2 (2014)
15. Pei, J.H.M.K.J.: Data Mining: Concepts and Techniques, 3rd edn. Elsevier, Amsterdam (2011)
16. Sotiriadis, S., Bessis, N., Buyya, R.: Self managed virtual machine scheduling in cloud systems. Inf. Sci. **433–434**, 381–400 (2018)
17. Sureshkumar, M., Rajesh, P.: Optimizing the docker container usage based on load scheduling. In: 2017 2nd International Conference on Computing and Communications Technologies (ICCCT), pp. 165–168. (Feb 2017)
18. Ullman, J.: Np-complete scheduling problems. J. Comput. Syst. Sci. **10**(3), 384–393 (1975)
19. The apache software foundation. mesos, apache: http://mesos.apache.org/. Accessed 25 Mar 2019
20. Docker swarmkit: https://github.com/docker/swarmkit/. Accessed 25 Mar 2019
21. Kubernetes scheduler: https://kubernetes.io/. Accessed 25 Mar 2019

A Clustering-Based Approach to Efficient Resource Allocation in Fog Computing

Leila Shooshtarian[1], Dapeng Lan[2], and Amir Taherkordi[2(✉)]

[1] Shahid Beheshti University, Tehran, Iran
l.shooshtarian@sbu.ac.ir
[2] University of Oslo, Oslo, Norway
{dapengl,amirhost}@ifi.uio.no

Abstract. Fog computing, which provides low-latency computing services at the network edge, is an enabler for the next generation Internet of Things (IoT) systems. In scenarios such as *smart cities*, multiple applications are simultaneously deployed and distributed across the Cloud and fog nodes, offering various IoT-based services. Moreover, each application has its own quality of service (QoS) and resource requirements that must be met. Appropriate resource allocation mechanisms are needed to determine which fog node or group of nodes can host the services of a given application. A critical challenge is how to select fog nodes for resource allocation in order to maximize fog resources utilization and minimize service latency, while satisfying QoS requirements of the application. This paper is aimed to address this challenge through a two-phase QoS-aware resource allocation scheme. Firstly, in the *layering* phase, we assume a hierarchical architecture for fog nodes—organizing heterogeneous nodes into a multi-layered hierarchy based on node resources capacity and network characteristics. Layering facilitates finding fog node(s) based on application requirements, and improves resource management. In the second phase, the fog nodes are *grouped* to facilitate resource pooling and reducing delay in service provisioning. We use the Agglomerative Hierarchical Clustering algorithm for classifying fog nodes. This helps selecting those fog node(s) in a fog layer with which the latency will be minimized. We evaluate the proposed approach through simulation. The evaluation results show that the proposed approach promises high application acceptance rate (80% on average), and reduces considerably the application placement time.

Keywords: Fog computing · Hierarchical fog architecture · Resource allocation · Agglomerative Hierarchical Clustering

1 Introduction

Internet of Things (IoT) aims to connect every device (*e.g.*, smart cameras, wearable, environmental sensors, home appliances, and vehicles) to the Internet, hence generating massive volume of data that can overwhelm storage systems and data analytics applications [4]. IoT applications are proliferating into

© Springer Nature Switzerland AG 2019
C. Esposito et al. (Eds.): I-SPAN 2019, CCIS 1080, pp. 207–224, 2019.
https://doi.org/10.1007/978-3-030-30143-9_17

a massive scale, thereby, IoT data, services and applications are being pressed to move to the Cloud, enabling powerful processing and sharing of IoT data beyond the capability of individual things. However, there are many safety-critical applications such as health monitoring and emergency response systems that require low latency IoT data processing and transmission [7]. The delay caused by transferring data to the Cloud and then back to the application can seriously impact its performance. To overcome this limitation, Fog computing paradigm has been proposed, where cloud services are extended to the edge of the network to decrease latency and network congestion, as well as to support better mobility of users and devices, and location-aware services [14]. Fog Computing is a highly virtualized platform that provides compute, storage, and networking services between end devices and cloud platforms [3].

To realize the full potential of Fog and IoT paradigms for real-time analytics, several challenges need to be addressed, such as multi-tenancy, fog federation, and fog services distribution. One critical problem is designing *resource management* techniques that determine which modules of analytics applications are pushed to which edge devices in order to maximize fog resources utilization and minimize service latency while satisfying QoS requirements of the application. Generally, resource management deals with allocation and deallocation of computation, storage, communication resources, and power/energy resources. Besides this, the important aspect of fog resources management is finding a node or a group of nodes as the best candidate for allocating resources [9]. The recent applications on fog platforms like smart city systems, are often deployed simultaneously on shared fog platforms [15]. Therefore, the optimization of resource allocation becomes more crucial in such cases, in addition to the fact that the latency in service provisioning should be minimized.

The aforementioned application types introduce divers constraints in the deployment and execution of services over fog platforms. They also demand different resources and QoS requirements, privacy and security restrictions, on premise requirements of application data and services, etc. On the other hand, fog nodes in the network are often highly heterogeneous with varying resource configurations, network access latency and bandwidth characteristics, mobility, ownership, etc., which are often identified by their physical location. This implies that, in the allocation fog resources to application services, heterogeneity of fog nodes should be carefully taken into account.

While the theoretical foundations of fog computing are established quite well by the research community and industry, there is still a lack of concrete solutions on resource allocation and management. Existing work on fog resources allocation is mainly focused on resource virtulization and prediction [1,2,17], while a limited body of work is carried out on distribution algorithms [13]. Apart from the question of how to virtualize the resources offered by fog nodes, another major issue for adoption of fog computing is the challenge of how to efficiently allocate fog resources, and at the same time minimize the latency in service provisioning, which is the focus of this paper.

In this paper, we propose a QoS-aware resource allocation model for fog computing environments which is aimed for resource allocation between different application classes considering the sensitivity towards their QoS requirements and service latency. The contributions of this paper are summarized as follows:

- A classification model for hierarchical fog architectures, which reduces the time needed in finding the fog node(s) with required resource capacity for resource allocation or application placement. Agglomerative Hierarchical Clustering algorithm is adopted as a basis for classification. We assume a logically multi-layered hierarchical computing architecture of heterogeneous fog nodes for improving resource utilization. Furthermore, we show that the hierarchical Fog Computing architecture is suitable for fog resource allocation.
- A clustering method for finding the optimal fog node(s) belonging to a specific layer in the fog hierarchy using Agglomerative Average Linkage Hierarchical clustering method. Layering phase is applied to meet the QoS demanded by application. Then, clustering phase is used to minimize the latency.
- A simulation-based evaluation, within MATLAB Simulink to show the efficiency of the proposed model in the fog environment. The experimental results show significant improvement in the total time required for application placement, application acceptance rate, and resource utilization compared to the QoS-aware placement policy presented in [13].

The rest of this paper is organized as follows. In Sect. 2 the hierarchical fog architecture is presented, while an overview of clustering is provided in Sect. 3. Our resource allocation model is presented in Sect. 4, and the evaluation results are reported in Sect. 5. A discussion on related work, and the concluding remarks are provided in Sects. 6 and 7, respectively.

2   Hierarchical Fog Architecture

In fog environments, there are different node types. Sets of nodes with similar type are often connected over the network with similar network characteristics (e.g., bandwidth and latency) [12]. Heterogeneity in fog nodes is attributed to a number of factors as listed in Table 1. A combination of these parameters will define a fog category. With the fact that each category of nodes has different resource characteristics, associating a category of fog nodes to a layer in fog hierarchy helps in quick identification of fog nodes based on required resources. Therefore, resource characteristics of a given fog node can be approximately known from the layer it is assigned to.

Table 1. Factors defining hierarchy in Fog [12]

Factor	High fog layer	Low fog layer
Node resource capacity	High	Low
Network latency	High	Low
Network bandwidth	Low	High
Geographic dispersion	Co-located	Dispersed
Security/privacy control	Low	High

2.1 Layering

Figure 1 shows an overview of the hierarchical topology of fog nodes. The hierarchical Fog computing architecture can offer high performance computing and communication to address the challenges of big data analysis and provide quick response in cloud environments (*e.g.*, in smart cities). This is achieved by parallelizing the workloads of data analysis on massive edge devices and computing nodes. Each edge device or intermediate fog node only performs light-weight computing tasks; thus, their massive use in parallel offers high-performance computing power for extensive data analysis. More importantly, such parallel computing mechanisms can balance the throughput and load among edge devices and fog nodes, preventing potential computing bottlenecks. While the massive parallelization of Fog Computing offers high-performance computing, its hierarchical architecture also reduces burdens on communication bandwidth. A massive amount of data is generated from widely distributed sensors at the IoT device layer. Instead of transmitting the raw data to the Cloud directly, the hierarchical distributed edge devices and intermediate computing fog nodes at fog layers execute computing tasks and upload only high-level data representation to the Cloud, reducing considerably the data volume transmitted to the Cloud.

As shown in Fig. 1, the communication within the same layer is also allowed, which enables IoT nodes or computing nodes to exchange the data with their neighbors. The communication between two adjacent layers and within the same layer could be wireless and/or wired, depending on specific applications. While wireless networks have many important applications in remote and mobile monitoring, wired networks can provide robust and reliable communication among different devices. At the top layer, the Cloud resides to perform high level computing tasks and data storage.

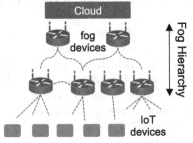

Fig. 1. An overview of the hierarchical architecture of fog nodes

2.2   A Prototype of Smart City: Resource Allocation View

To illustrate better the usage of the hierarchical fog architecture with respect to resource allocation, in this subsection we present the implementation of a 4-layer Fog computing architecture for smart cities and discuss its design details. The pictorial representation of 4-layer Fog computing nodes with varied resource configurations is shown in Fig. 2.

IoT Device Layer: At the edge of the network, end devices are the sensing devices which are equipped with numerous sensors. Those sensors are highly reliable, and low cost; thus, they can be widely distributed at public infrastructures. Multiple applications can be serviced using these end devices. It should be noted that massive sensing data streams are generated from these end devices that are geospatially distributed, which have to be processed as a coherent whole.

Fog Layer 1: The end devices forward the raw data to the next layer, Layer 1, which is composed of a large number of low-power, and low latency computing nodes or edge devices, located close to data sources and users. Each edge device at Layer 1 is connected to and in charge of a group of local IoT devices that cover a neighborhood or a small community, performing data analysis in a timely manner. At this level, the output of these edge devices has two parts: (i) the results of processing heavy tasks sent to an intermediate computing node at its next upper layer, (ii) short, simple and quick feedback to the local infrastructure to respond to isolated and light computation tasks of the infrastructure components. In addition, the nodes in this layer perform data transfer as they cannot rely upon their own limited storage resources. These nodes have average compute resources, and low storage and network resources. Nevertheless, they have very low access latency as compared to the higher layers.

Fog Layer 2: Layer 2 is composed of medium resource configurations, each of which is connected to a group of fog nodes at Layer 1. The nodes in this layer can deal with medium-scale processing of data and simple computation, however they cannot be used to store data for long durations.

Fog Layer 3: Layer 3 consists of a number of intermediate computing nodes with high resource configurations and these nodes can be leveraged to perform basic analytics. Execution of large scale analytics is not possible due to lack of historical data, as the data cannot be stored for long time on these nodes due to limited resources.

Fog Layer 4: These fog nodes have sufficient resource capacity to support local analytics and store data for short time period.

Cloud: The top layer is a cloud computing data center, which collects data and information from each intermediate computing node at lower layers. This layer is composed of ample resources. The high performance distributed computing and storage capacity of the Cloud allows us to perform complex, long-term, and city-wide behavior analysis at this layer, such as large-scale event detection, long-term pattern recognition, and relationship modeling, to support dynamic decision making. Servers in the Cloud layer have higher latency as compared to fog nodes in lower layers.

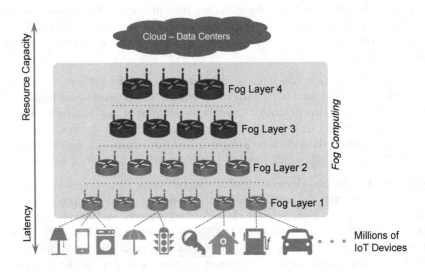

Fig. 2. An overview of the hierarchical Fog architecture for smart city scenarios

In the proposed architecture, we assume that the fog nodes are layered according to their *resources*. Fog nodes with similar resource characteristics are placed at the same fog layer. On the other hand, on each IoT device, various applications can be running, while fog nodes in the hierarchy are in charge of providing services to the deployed applications. The required resources for each application will be determined by the application vendor. We assume that, the resource requests for each application are sent to the fog layer that can satisfy the requirements of that application. In this way, the fog layer that can respond to a request will be found. In summary, the four-layer Fog computing architecture supports quick response at different levels, providing high computing performance and it is efficient for resource allocation in future smart cities. It should also be noted that considering four layers in the proposed architecture is essentially to demonstrate that it is a minimum, yet efficient number of layers for fog-level data processing and resource allocation. Therefore, the architecture can be extended with more layers based on the target application domain and resource allocation constraints.

In the next section, we provide an overview of clustering as a basis for the clustering method that we propose in Sect. 4.

3   Clustering

In this section, we provide a brief overview of hierarchical clustering for grouping data. Hierarchical clustering has the potential to be used for grouping nodes of a fog layer for resource allocation in the presented architecture. Thus, the technique for grouping fog nodes is very important for efficient resource allocation.

Clustering is considered as a machine learning technique for data mining which is grouping of similar data for analysis purposes. For a given set of data points and a similarity measure, we regroup the data such that data points in the same group are similar and data points in different groups are dissimilar. Such groups are called as *clusters*, comprised of several similar data items or objects with respect to a referral point.

Hierarchical clustering has significant importance in data analytics especially because of the exponential growth of real-world data. Often the data is unlabeled and there is little prior knowledge available. A hierarchical clustering is a nested sequence of partitions. This method works on both bottom-up and top-down approaches. The hierarchical clustering approach is further sub-divided into agglomerative and divisive approaches [11]:

- **Agglomerative:** This is a "bottom up" approach. It starts with the points as individual clusters and, at each step, merges the most similar or closest pair of clusters. This requires a definition of cluster similarity or distance.
- **Divisive:** This is a "top down" approach. It starts with one, all-inclusive cluster and, at each step, splits a cluster until only singleton clusters of individual points remain. In other words, all observations start in one cluster, and splits are performed recursively as one moves down the hierarchy. In this case, we need to decide, at each step, which cluster to split and how to perform the split.

Both approaches come with their own advantages and disadvantages, depending on different situations. Agglomerative techniques are more common. Generally, the hierarchical clustering has significant advantages, including *(i)* Embedded flexibility concerning the extent of granularity; *(ii)* Ease of handling of any types of similarity or distance; *(iii)* Consequently, applicability to any attribute varieties; *(iv)* In contradiction, K-Means algorithm needs the number of clusters to be specified first and for that we need to have a strong assumption; *(v)* it does not need assumptions and parameter setting for making good clusters; *(vi)* The constructed clusters are not dependent on assumptions as much as other clustering algorithms.

3.1   Agglomerative Hierarchical Clustering

The Agglomerative hierarchical technique [16] follows the bottom-up approach. Hierarchical clustering uses different metrics which measures the (dis)similarity between two tuples and the linkage criteria, which specifies the (dis)similarity in the sets as a function of the pair-wise distances of observations in that sets. The linkage criteria could be of three types: single linkage, average linkage and complete linkage. Several different algorithms can be used in hierarchical cluster analysis to determine how the *linkages* are created. In cluster analysis, a large number of measures are available for classifying objects on the basis of their (dis)similarities.

Similarity Measure. An important step in any clustering technique is to select a (dis)similarity measure. Distance and similarity play an important role in cluster analysis. In the literature of data clustering, similarity measure, similarity coefficient, dissimilarity measures, or distance are used to describe quantitatively the similarity or dissimilarity of two data points or two clusters. Often, similarity measures and similarity coefficient are used to describe quantitatively how similar the two data points are or how similar two clusters are: the greater the similarity coefficient, the more similar are the two data points. Dissimilarity measure and distance are the other way around: the greater the dissimilarity measure or distance, the more dissimilar are the two data points or two clusters. In order to decide which clusters should be combined (for agglomerative), or where a cluster should be split (for divisive), a measure of (dis)similarity between sets of observations is required. This will influence the shape of the clusters, as some elements may be close to one another according to one distance and further away according to another. For clustering in the numeric field, there are many well-known methods such as Euclidean distance, Minkowski distance, Manhattan (City-Block), Mahalanobis distance, etc.

Linkage Criteria. The distances between each pair of clusters are computed to choose two clusters that have more opportunity to merge. Methods for measuring association between clusters are called linkage methods. There are several ways to calculate the distances between the two clusters, including Single Linkage, Complete Linkage, Average Linkage, weighted and unweighted average linkage clustering, Centroid linkage clustering, etc. Different methods of hierarchical agglomerative cluster analysis have different rules for how to decide which two clusters are most similar. For instance, in the single linkage (*i.e.*, nearest neighbor) method the similarity between two clusters is given by the (dis)similarity of the two subjects, one from each of those two clusters that are most similar. What method of cluster analysis is most appropriate of course depends on the specific situation.

3.2   Simple Agglomerative Clustering Algorithm

For n samples, agglomerative algorithms begin with n clusters and each cluster contains a single sample or a point. Then, two clusters will merge so that the similarity between them is the closest until the number of clusters becomes 1 or as specified by the user. We summarize the traditional agglomerative hierarchical clustering procedure as follows:

1. Start with n clusters, and a single sample indicates one cluster.
2. Compute the similarity between all pairs of clusters, *i.e.*, calculate a similarity matrix whose ij^{th} entry gives the similarity between the ith and j^{th} clusters.
3. Merge the most similar (closest) two clusters.
4. Update the similarity matrix to reflect the pairwise similarity between the new cluster and the original clusters.
5. Repeat steps 2 and 3 until only a single cluster remains.

In iteration 1, the two most similar subjects are joined to form one cluster giving in all $n-1$ clusters. In iteration 2, the two most similar clusters are joined to form one cluster, giving in all $n-2$ clusters. The process is repeated until every subject is in one and the same cluster that occurs at step $n-1$.

4   Proposed Approach

The overall idea behind our approach is that in a hierarchical fog architecture, after the desired layer has been determined, we use a clustering method among all fog nodes belonging to the selected fog layer to find the appropriate node(s) for resource provisioning to given IoT device(s). All the nodes placed on the selected layer and the layers above that layer can answer a request from the resources point of view. Since the fog layers are ordered in terms of resource capacity and that higher layers have higher resource capacity, when a layer is able to meet the needs of a request, the layers above can also satisfy those resource requests. Below, we demonstrate an approach to group the fog nodes into clusters using the Agglomerative Average Linkage Hierarchical Clustering technique.

4.1   Clustering

An important step in any clustering technique is to select a distance measure, which will determine how the similarity of two elements is calculated. To minimize the latency, we select those fog nodes of the selected fog layer that are nearest to the given IoT device(s). As nodes belonging to a given fog layer are connected over networks of similar characteristics, link latency between any two nodes can be approximated by the distance between them. Thus, the clustering objective is to minimize the average inter-node distance between any two nodes within a cluster, which means minimizing average inter-node latency (assuming that physical distance is the main cause of latency). To measure similarity, the Euclidean Distance and Average Linkage criteria are chosen in this paper.

Euclidean Distance: It is the most commonly chosen type of distance. It simply is the geometric distance in a multidimensional space [6]. The Euclidean distance between points $P = (p_1, p_2, ..., p_n)$ and $Q = (q_1, q_2, ..., q_n)$, in Euclidean n-space, is calculated using:

$$d(P, Q) = \sqrt{\sum_{i=1}^{n}(p_i - q_i)} \tag{1}$$

Where for two-dimensional space, p_i is the data point in x-axis and q_i is the data point in y-axis.

Average Linkage: The linkage criterion determines the distance between sets of observations as a function of the pairwise distances between observations.

We have grouped fog nodes into clusters using the Agglomerative Average Linkage Hierarchical clustering technique. This method involves looking at the distances between all pairs and averages all of these distances [16]. Mathematically, the linkage function—the distance $d(C_i, C_j)$ between clusters C_i and C_j—is described by the following function:

$$d(C_i, C_j) = \frac{l}{kl} \sum_{i=1}^{k} \sum_{i=1}^{l} d(X_i, Y_i) \tag{2}$$

Where,
$X_1, X_2, ..., X_k$ = Observations from cluster C_i
$Y_1, Y_2, ..., Y_l$ = Observations from cluster C_j
$d(x, y)$ = distance between a subject with observation vector x and a subject with observation vector y.

Modified Agglomerative Hierarchical Clustering. If an IoT device issues a resource request and an specific fog layer is selected with n fog nodes according to the requested resources, the modified agglomerative hierarchical clustering procedure is summarized as follows:

1. Start with $n + 1$ clusters. The IoT device and each fog node indicate one cluster.
2. Compute the distance between the IoT device and the fog node in each individual cluster $1, ..., n$ (cf. step 1).
3. Find the most similar (closest) fog node (*i.e.*, a cluster) to the cluster of the IoT device, then add that fog node to a cluster.
4. Update the distance matrix to reflect the pairwise distance between the new cluster and the original clusters.

The objective function of clustering is to form a final cluster of fog node(s) such that the average distance between fog node(s) belonging to the final cluster and the IoT device is minimal, which means minimizing the average inter-node latency.

4.2 Modeling

In order to determine QoS-aware resource allocation policy, we need a suitable representation of the involved entities. For that, we provide a model of an IoT application which comprises the related set of QoS requirements of the application, the fog node model, and task requests. Then, the resource allocation algorithm is proposed. These models are briefly described below.

Application Model. Let $\bigcup_{i=1}^{k} app_i$ be the set of applications to be placed in the fog environment. An application $app_i \in APP$ is characterized by its demands for computational resources $app_i = (AppRes_i^{req})$, in which $AppRes_i^{req}$ is a set of its demands for computational resources (*i.e.*, CPU), RAM, storage, bandwidth, etc. In the proposed policy, we assume that four different IoT applications are deployed for execution in the fog environment. Each application has its own Service Level Agreement (SLA) and needs satisfying its QoS requirements for being able to run. Without loss of generality, we consider two types of resources (*i.e.*, CPU and RAM) for each application. An application app_i is characterized by a user-defined deadline D_{app_i} which defines the maximum amount of time allowed for the application execution. The minimum QoS requirements of the applications is shown in Table 2.

Table 2. Minimum QoS requirements of applications.

Services	CPU demand (MIPS)	RAM demand (MB)	Deadline (sec)
App_1	200	120	300
App_2	40	30	240
App_3	120	50	360
App_4	80	30	360

Fog Node Model. Our proposed model has four fog layers $FL = (FL_1, FL_2, ..., FL_{|FL_N|})$ $1 \leq N \leq 4$, and each layer consists of a set of fog nodes. Each fog node $FN_i = (FNRes_i^{avail}, loc_i)$ is characterized by its available resources and its location. Like applications for fog nodes, we also consider two resource types (*i.e.*, CPU and RAM). Contrary to traditional cloud servers, fog nodes can be identified by their physical locations, *i.e.*, loc_i for FN_i. In our model, this physical position helps find the nearest fog node in the clustering algorithm.

Task Request Model. We use the notion of task requests for computational duties, which need to be accomplished using cloud or fog resources. Let $REQ = \bigcup_{i=1}^{n} req_i$ be the set of task requests to be placed in the fog environment. A request is described as $req_q = (IoTDevice_q, app_q)$ and it is characterized by its issuer IoT device $IoTDevice_q$ and its application or requested service (*i.e.*, app_q).

4.3 Proposed Algorithm

The proposed resource allocation policy aims to determine an optimal mapping between IoT applications and computational resources of fog nodes with the objective of optimizing the fog environment utilization while satisfying QoS requirements of applications.

As described in the layering phase, the fog nodes are layered according to their resource(s) (Algorithm 1 step 3). The classification methods can be used for fog nodes layering. Multicriteria classification methods can also be applied if fog nodes have several resource types. Each layer has a numerical range for each computational resource. The fog nodes whose amount of available resource falls within this range are placed in this layer. For each request, a specific fog layer is selected based on the requested resources by the given application (Algorithm 1 step 4). In other words, a task is sent to a fog layer where requested resources of task are less than or equal to the available resources of the fog nodes belonging to that layer. It is noteworthy that at the end of the algorithm (Algorithm 1 step 20), after mapping the fog node to the request, the amount of the remaining resource of the assigned fog node(s) is calculated and updated. If another request is issued while this node is busy, layering is again performed based on the new value of the available resource of this fog node. In this case, busy fog node(s) may be placed in the lower fog layer according to their available resources.

After selecting the right fog layer (Algorithm 1 step 4), the nearest fog node of that layer to the IoT device is placed in the final cluster in the first iteration of the clustering algorithm (Algorithm 2 step 5). Then, available resources of the selected fog node will be evaluated (Algorithm 1 step 10). The selected fog node will be assigned to the request if its available resource meets the application requirements and then the request is accepted, the amount of new available resources of fog nod is calculated and updated, and the algorithm ends.

Algorithm 1. Resource Allocation Algorithm

Input: $req_q = (IoTDevice_q, app_q)$
Output: success or fail

1: $FinalCluster \leftarrow \{\}$;
2: $ClusterRes^{avail} \leftarrow 0$;
3: $FL \leftarrow$ layering all fog nodes base on their available resource(s)
4: $L \leftarrow$ find fog layer number that has resource corresponding to $AppRes_q^{req}$ in layering phase;
5: $C_d \leftarrow$ assume $IoTDevice_q$ as a cluster;
6: Each $FN_i \in FL_L$ indicates one cluster. start with $|FL_L| + 1$ clusters.
7: **do**
8:     $(FinalCluster, ClusterRes^{avail}) \leftarrow$ AGGLOMERATIVECLUSTER-ING$(L, C_d, FinalCluster)$
9: **while** $(AppRes_i^{req} > ClusterRes^{avail})$ && (there is unmarked $FN_i \in FL_L$)
10: **if** $AppRes_i^{req} > ClusterRes^{avail}$ **then**
11:     $L \leftarrow L + 1$;
12:     **if** $L > 4$ **then**
13:         reject req_q
14:         return fail
15:     **end if**
16:     got to line 6
17: **else**
18:     accept request req_q
19:     assign $FinalCluster$ node to req_q
20:     compute residual resource FN_i and update FL_L
21:     return success
22: **end if**

However, if the available resources of the selected fog node could not satisfy the requested resource, the next nearest fog node of that layer to the IoT device will be added to the final cluster in the next iteration (Algorithm 2 step 5). The total available resources of the fog node(s) within the final cluster is evaluated in each iteration (Algorithm 2 step 7). As long as the available resources of fog node(s) within the final cluster are less than the application requirements, the clustering algorithm is repeated and the next closest fog node to the IoT device is added to the final cluster (Algorithm 1 step 7 to 9). If the total available resources of fog nodes in the selected layer are less than the application requirements, the clustering algorithm will run on higher-level nodes (Algorithm 1 step 11). Afterwards, the nearest fog node of the higher layer to the IoT device is added to the final cluster. Then, the total available resources for the fog nodes within the final cluster are calculated and compared to the requested resource and so on. After selecting the fog node(s), fog node(s) resources are assigned and their remaining available resources are calculated and updated. After the service is completed, resources of the fog node(s) are released.

Algorithm 2. Agglomerative Clustering

Input: $(L, C_d, FinalCluster)$
Output: $ClusterRes^{avail}$ and $FinalCluster$
 1: $C_{FN} \leftarrow$ find the closest and unmarked clusters $FN_i \in FL_L$ to the C_d according to Equation (2) that has nonzero $FNRes_i^{avail}$
 2: **if** $C_{FN} == \{\}$ **then**
 3:     return $ClusterRes^{avail}$ and $FinalCluster$
 4: **else**
 5:     $FinalCluster = \{C_{FN}\} \bigcup FinalCluster$
 6:     marked FN_i
 7:     $ClusterRes^{avail} \leftarrow ClusterRes^{avail} + FNRes_i^{avail}$
 8:     return $ClusterRes^{avail}$ and $FinalCluster$
 9: **end if**

---

5   Evaluation

The proposed Qos-aware resource allocation policy is compared with different QoS and QoE-aware policies. The QoS-aware application placement policy in [13] meets execution deadline of applications. However, while comparing the proposed policy with the aforementioned policy, application placement time, application acceptance rate, and fog resource utilization are considered as performance metrics. For this, we use simulation.

5.1   Evaluation Environment

To evaluate the proposed policy, a Fog environment is simulated using MATLAB Simulink. In our experiment, we build a prototype of a smart city. We assume that it is a snapshot of a 4-layer fog architecture. There are 355 fog nodes in total spread over an area of 1000×1000 sq. units with 200 nodes in Fog Layer 1, 100 nodes in Fog Layer 2, 50 nodes in Fog Layer 3, and 5 nodes in Fog Layer-4. Each fog node's location was generated randomly by uniform distribution over the coordinate space of $(0,0)...(999,999)$. The x and y coordinates represent latitude and longitude (from GPS) of fog nodes in a real-world deployment, respectively. Uniform random distribution of fog nodes is assumed to reflect the layout of nodes in a city center which is likely to have uniform population density and hence the need for IoT resources. The first resource values include non-negative integer numbers distributed with a uniform distribution (*e.g.*, CPU) in the range of 20 to 49 for fog nodes in Layer 1, 50 to 99 for fog nodes in Layer 2, 100 to 149 for fog nodes in Layer 3, and 150 to 300 for fog nodes in Layer 4. A summary of the fog layer information is provided in Table 3.

Table 3. Number of nodes and their resource settings at each Fog layer.

Layer	No. of fog nodes	CPU capacity (MIPS)	RAM capacity (MB)
1	200	20–49	30–49
2	100	50–99	50–79
3	50	100–149	80–100
4	5	150–300	100–200

According to the layering phase of the proposed policy and the above assumptions, requests belonging to app_1 are assigned to Fog Layer 4. In the same way, fog nodes in Layer 1, Layer 3, and Layer 2 can host requests belonging to the app_2, app_3, and app_4, respectively. This layering technique yields a rapid mapping of devices into the fog nodes that can satisfy their demanded QoS. This fast mapping, in addition to reducing response time, reduces application placement time, network load, congestion, and thus reducing delay.

5.2 Experiments and Discussions

Figure 3 represents the average application placement time for the proposed policy and the QoS-aware policy in [13]. The amount of application request affects the amount of workload, and the number of model variables and constraints, thereby it influences the computational time. In Fig. 3, the average distribution of the average application placement time

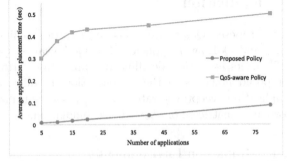

Fig. 3. Application placement time vs number of applications

is shown according to the number of incoming applications. With the increasing number of applications, placement time increases accordingly. The measurements of average application placement time show that proposed policy is solved in less than a second even in the case of submitted applications with large number of services. This reduction in the placement time is due to the layering phase in the proposed algorithm. Each task at the layering phase in the beginning of the algorithm is assigned to the fog layer whose nodes' available resources are greater than or equal to the resources requested by the task. Directing requests to layers that meet their requested resources will prevent blind search and congestion in the network. In this way, it reduces the response time and the placement time.

We use acceptance rates to determine the percentage of accepted requests to the total incoming requests. In Fig. 4, the average application acceptance rate is shown according to the number of incoming applications. In the proposed model, the acceptance rate is reduced by increasing the number of inputs. At first, requests are accepted when fog resources are free and available. As

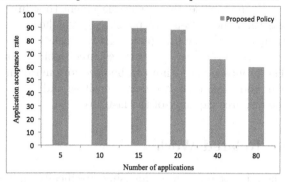

Fig. 4. Application acceptance rate vs number of applications

time goes on and more requests with bigger requested resources are coming, a number of requests are re-registered.

The utilization of the fog environment in the proposed approach and the QoS-aware policy [13] is shown in Fig. 5. Applications in fog environments should be able to run both on fog nodes and the Cloud. Tasks are propagated to the Cloud in the case that cloud resources are necessary for the fulfillment of task requests. If fog resources are not sufficient, cloud-based computational resources are used to

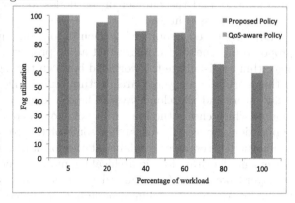

Fig. 5. Fog utilization with respect to the percentage of the workload

fulfill the task requests. As can be seen in Fig. 5, at the beginning of the simulation, when the fog resources are free, services are placed only on fog resources. As time goes and fog resources are occupied, the tasks that need high resources will be sent to the Cloud. If we compare the two policies at the busiest time (when 100% of the workload is loaded) we obtain the following results.

With the exception of the initial simulation time, at other stages, the proposed policy sends more tasks to the Cloud than the QoS-aware algorithm [13]. In the same way, in the busy time and when 100% of the workload is loaded, in the QoS-aware policy 30% of all services are propagated to the Cloud, but the proposed policy sends 40% of the task requests to the Cloud in the same condition. These 40% are selected among heavy tasks and those tasks that require more resources. Heavy tasks in the proposed policy are tasks that are assigned to the last layer in the layering phase or they request more resources than resources of nodes belonging to the last layer.

To summarize, the service placement time in the proposed approach is much less than the QoS-aware policy [13] and heavy tasks are sent to the Cloud in comparison to the first policy. Heavy tasks are not delay-sensitive or cannot be executed in the Fog, *e.g.*, very resource-intensive Big Data analysis task requests. The proposed algorithm can be used for environments where time factor is critical, and most tasks are delay-sensitive and do not require more resources than the resource capacity of the last layer.

6 Related Work

There is not much work focusing specifically on resource allocation in Fog computing systems. However, resource allocation has been an extensively researched area in distributed systems, such as cloud computing [8] and mobile cloud computing [5,10]. The works in these domains cannot be easily adopted for fog computing scenarios since fog landscapes are basically more volatile than cloud environments and the number of fog nodes for service provisioning is usually larger, as discussed in Sect. 2.

Layering based resource allocation in fog computing environments has been proposed in some works. Agarwal et al. [2] propose an architecture as well as an algorithm to distribute the workload between the fog layers and the Cloud. The authors propose a layered architecture, consisting of an IoT/end-users layer, a fog layer, and the cloud layer. The fog layer involves a fog server manager module which checks the availability of enough computational resources to host application services. It dispatches some of the components to the cloud layer if not enough resources available at the fog layer. Taneja et al. [17] propose a placement algorithm for hierarchical fog models. The algorithm iterates from the fog layer towards the Cloud in order to place computation tasks first on the free fog nodes. In this algorithm, a node is represented as a set of three attributes: computation, memory, and network bandwidth. The above works are different from the model proposed in this paper, which is focused on efficient utilization of fog resources and minimizing latency.

Skarlat et al., in [13], present a Fog service placement approach that targets QoS-aware application placement on virtualized Fog resources. The authors consider deadline satisfaction of applications as the QoS parameter and adopt the earliest deadline prioritization while executing the applications. The proposed resource allocation policy runs through a colony-based orchestration among the

Fog nodes and handles resource requirements of the applications with available fog resources. Each colony connects the Cloud through a middleware for additional resources. We have compared our approach with [13], reported in the previous section.

Wang et al. [18] propose a solution to solve dynamic placement of computation tasks for mobile environments with variable available resources. The authors cosigner a set of parameters including the location and preference of a user, database location, and the load on the system. A method is proposed to predict the values of the parameters when service instances of a user are placed in a certain configuration. The predicted values result in an expected cost and optimal placement configuration with lowest cost. Aazam and Huh present a sophisticated resource provisioning mechanism based on the prediction of resource demands [1]. This work is focused on dynamic allocation of resources in advance during the design time of the system. The proposed mechanism is based on cost optimization, and the resource allocation depends on the probability fluctuations of the demand of the users, types of services, and pricing models. As indicated, the above category of works are rather focused on resource prediction in fog environments.

7   Conclusions and Future Work

One key challenge in Fog computing is the allocation of fog resources to IoT applications. To address the concern of maximizing utilization of fog resources and minimizing latency in fog resources allocation, this article proposed a two-phase QoS-aware resource allocation scheme. Layering of fog nodes in the first phase and then clustering them in the second phase are accomplished. In the layering phase, fog nodes are layered based on their available resources. Application requests are assigned to the correct fog layer according to their requested resources. Then, we use a clustering method to find the optimal fog node from the selected layer. Grouping of fog nodes belonging to a specific layer is performed by Agglomerative Average Linkage Hierarchical clustering method. The goals of clustering are resource pooling, local control, and finding the nearest fog node to the IoT device in order to minimize delay. In summary, QoS limitations of applications are taken into account by layering, and minimizing delay is achieved by clustering. Further research needs to be conducted regarding identification of layering criteria. Moreover, in cloud environments, heterogeneous networks and resources are often shared between different applications with different QoS requirements. Therefore, the joint edge-network resource scheduling problem is another challenge that must be studied.

References

1. Aazam, M., Huh, E.: Dynamic resource provisioning through fog micro datacenter. In: PerCom Workshops, March 2015

2. Agarwal, S., Yadav, S., Kumar Yadav, A.: An efficient architecture and algorithm for resource provisioning in fog computing (2016)
3. Bonomi, F., Milito, R., Zhu, J., Addepalli, S.: Fog computing and its role in the internet of things. In: MCC Workshop on Mobile Cloud Computing, MCC 2012 (2012)
4. Cai, H., Xu, B., Jiang, L., Vasilakos, A.V.: IoT-based big data storage systems in cloud computing: perspectives and challenges. IEEE Internet Things J. 4(1), 75–87 (2017)
5. Chen, X., Li, W., Lu, S., Zhou, Z., Fu, X.: Efficient resource allocation for on-demand mobile-edge cloud computing. IEEE Trans. Veh. Technol. 67(9), 8769–8780 (2018)
6. Euclidean distance. http://en.wikipedia.org/wiki/Euclidean_distance. Accessed 2018
7. Gupta, H., et al.: iFogSim: a toolkit for modeling and simulation of resource management techniques in the internet of things, edge and fog computing environments. Softw. Pract. Exp. 47(9), 1275–1296 (2017)
8. Hameed, A., et al.: A survey and taxonomy on energy efficient resource allocation techniques for cloud computing systems. Computing 98(7), 751–774 (2016)
9. Hong, C., Varghese, B.: Resource management in fog/edge computing: a survey. CoRR, abs/1810.00305 (2018)
10. Kwak, J., et al.: DREAM: dynamic resource and task allocation for energy minimization in mobile cloud systems. IEEE J. Sel. Areas Commun. 33(12), 2510–2523 (2015)
11. Rokach, L., Maimon, O.: Clustering methods. In: Maimon, O., Rokach, L. (eds.) Data Mining and Knowledge Discovery Handbook. Springer, Boston (2005). https://doi.org/10.1007/0-387-25465-X_15
12. Shaik, S., Baskiyar, S.: Hierarchical and autonomous fog architecture. In: Proceedings of the 47th International Conference on Parallel Processing Companion, ICPP (2018)
13. Skarlat, O., Nardelli, M., Schulte, S., Dustdar, S.: Towards QoS-aware fog service placement. In: 2017 IEEE 1st International Conference on Fog and Edge Computing (ICFEC) (2017)
14. Taherkordi, A., Eliassen, F.: Poster abstract: data-centric IoT services provisioning in fog-cloud computing systems. In: 2017 IEEE/ACM IoTDI (2017)
15. Taherkordi, A., Eliassen, F., Mcdonald, M., Horn, G.: Context-driven and real-time provisioning of data-centric IoT services in the cloud. ACM Trans. Internet Technol. 19(1), 7 (2018)
16. Tan, P.-N., Steinbach, M., Kumar, V.: Introduction to Data Mining, 1st edn. Addison-Wesley Longman Publishing Co., Inc., Boston (2005)
17. Taneja, M., Davy, A.: Resource aware placement of IoT application modules in fog-cloud computing paradigm. In: 2017 IFIP/IEEE Symposium on Integrated Network and Service Management (IM), pp. 1222–1228 (2017)
18. Wang, S., Urgaonkar, R., He, T., Chan, K., Zafer, M., Leung, K.K.: Dynamic service placement for mobile micro-clouds with predicted future costs. IEEE Trans. Parallel Distrib. Syst. 28(4), 1002–1016 (2017)

Communication Solutions

Enhanced Probability-Based Grant-Free Uplink Data Transmission in 5G mMTC

Dongyao Wang[1], Sung hwan Kim[2($\boxtimes$)], and Xiaoqiang Zhu[1]

[1] Jiangsu Automation Research Institute Shanghai Branch, Shanghai, China
wdyrobot@gmail.com
[2] Department of SW Convergence Education Institute,
Chosun University, Gwangju, South Korea
shkimtop@chosun.ac.kr

Abstract. Massive Machine-Type-Communication (mMTC) is expected to play a crucial role in 5G networks to enable Internet of Things (IoT). But with deployment of lots of mMTC devices, mobile cellular network will suffer from problems of congestion and large system overhead in both the Radio Access Network (RAN) and Core Network (CN). Currently multiple proposals, such as extended access barring (EAB) and access class barring (ACB), have been broadly discussed in Third Generation Partnership Project (3GPP) to combat the problem of Random Access Channel (RACH) congestion. However, less effort has been put on the efficiency issue of uplink transmission for mMTC traffics featured with small data packets and infrequent transmissions. To address this problem, we present an enahnced grant-free access scheme for mMTC uplink transmissions based on the probability concept, where a type of specific resource called Probability-Based Access (PBA) channel is allocated with congestion probability indicated. Thus the mMTC device can initiate the uplink transmission based on the probability, i.e. data can be transferred directly on the PBA channel, or fall back to the legacy procedure by using contention-based random access scheme. The performance of the proposed scheme is evaluated by numerical simulations and its effectiveness and advantages are validated.

Keywords: mMTC · 5G · RACH congestion · Random access control · Infrequent transmission · PBA

1 Introduction

The fast advances of communication and networking technologies have highlighted a bright future which would embrace the vision of IoT. By definition, IoT, or mMTC in 3GPP, usually refers to systems whereby a machine

This research was supported by the MIST (MInistry of Science & ICT), Korea, under the National Program for Excellence in SW supervised by the IITP (Institute for Information & communications Technology Promotion) (2017-0-00137).

© Springer Nature Switzerland AG 2019
C. Esposito et al. (Eds.): I-SPAN 2019, CCIS 1080, pp. 227–239, 2019.
https://doi.org/10.1007/978-3-030-30143-9_18

communicates with another machine without any human intervention [1,2]. Nowadays, a vast number of mMTC applications comprising a large number of fields, have already been deployed, such as Smart City, Smart Grid, Intelligent Transport System (ITS) and Healthcare [1,4]. In the future, we may see Machine-to-Machine (M2M) technology in nearly every aspect of our daily life. Because of the vast diversity of M2M applications, a massive number of mMTC devices are envisioned by 2020 [5–7].

Due to the significant increase in demand for mMTC applications, several associations including the Third Generation Partnership Project (3GPP) and the Institute of Electrical and Electronics Engineers (IEEE) have started the standardization in this area [1]. Up to now, the wide-deployed cellular mobile network, e.g. Long Term Evolution (LTE) networks, is considered as the best candidate for enabling mMTC connections [1,2], since it can serve mMTC User Equipments (UEs) in most urban and rural areas, and provide communication bridges between mMTC UEs and mMTC application servers [8].

However, the current cellular mobile networks are initially designed and optimized for Human-to-Human (H2H) communication, and deploying a massive number of mMTC UEs in the cellular mobile networks would face many challenges [7,10,11], one of which is the congestion problem. With the traditional scheme utilized in H2H communications, to request an uplink connection, an mMTC device randomly chooses and transmits a preamble on a RACH channel. Therefore, massive concurrent access requests generated by mMTC UEs may congest the RACH channels of the cellular networks and thus, result in intolerable delay, packet loss or even service unavailability for all the terminals in the network [7]. Intolerable delay means that it would take mMTC UEs a long time to access the network. While waiting, mMTC UEs have to stay in the active state and thus result in higher consumption of the power and shorter battery life [6,7]. To avoid or alleviate the aforementioned congestion problem of random access, multiple solutions have been proposed in 3GPP, such as separating the RACH resources, dynamic allocation of RACH resources, ACB and EAB etc [1,2,6].

Another fundamental problem for the transmission of mMTC traffic is the low efficiency [8,10]. Compared with H2H communications that have high data rates, mMTC traffics usually feature low data rates and infrequent transmissions. The size of signaling overhead spent to synchronize the mMTC UEs and resolve contentions can be much larger than the size of user data packets for mMTC applications. The problem of low efficiency is even worse for battery powered mMTC UEs since most of their limited power is used to transmit signaling packets [8]. Grant-free data transmission with no dedicated resource for mMTC UEs has been proposed with the challenge on reliability [9]. In this paper we present an enhanced grant-free access scheme to address both the efficiency and reliability problems. With the proposed scheme, a type of specific resource associated with estimated congestion probability is allocated by eNodeB for mMTC uplink transmission, and the mMTC UEs can initiate the uplink transmission based on this probability, i.e. to perform data transfer directly on the specific resource, or to follow the legacy procedure by using contention-based random access scheme.

The remainder of this paper is organized as follows. In Sect. 2, we briefly summarize the related work on this topic. The proposed scheme with detailed implementations is described in Sect. 3. In Sect. 4, the performance of our scheme is evaluated by numerical results, followed by conclusion in Sect. 5.

2 Related Work

2.1 LTE-A Random-Access Procedure

According to 3GPP specification, a terminal in LTE and LTE-Advanced (LTE-A) triggers a random access procedure when it needs to establish or re-establish a data connection with an eNodeB [5]. There are two forms of RACH procedure: contention-based and contention-free RACH procedures [6]. The former is generally used when the connection request is triggered from the terminal side, e.g. to restore the uplink synchronization. On the other hand, the contention-free RACH procedure is often used for network-initiated connection request to cope with delayed-constrained access requests with high success requirements, e.g. when there is handover or downlink data arrival [6,7]. Obviously the mMTC traffic has limited impacts on the contention-free RACH procedure.

For both contention-based and contention-free RACH specified in LTE/LTE-A standards, eNodeB will reserve a number of subchannels in some subframes for random access requests. The procedure of contention-based RACH can be divided into four steps [2,5,6]. The first step, known as Msg1, consists of the transmission of a randomly chosen preamble from UE side. This step allows eNodeB to estimate the transmission timing of the terminal that would be later used for adjusting the Timing Advance (TA) for uplink synchronization and the power transmission of the terminal to guarantee the power efficiency. As the preamble is randomly chosen, more than one terminal may use the same preamble to perform random access requests on the same RACH channel, which results in collision. In this case, all the collision terminals will back off and retry this step. On the second step, the terminal monitors the Physical Downlink Control Channel (PDCCH) to receive the Random Access Response (RAR) message, i.e. Msg2, during the RAR window. This response message contains a set of parameters, such as TA, the terminal's identifier Temporary Cell-Radio network temporary identifier (TC-RNTI), and uplink resource to be used by the terminal in the next step. After the successful reception of RAR message, the terminal adjusts the uplink synchronization and sends the message Msg3 containing its ID and RRC (Radio Resource Control) Connection Request to the network. In the last step, the network responses with the message Msg4 to complete the setup of RRC connection with contention resolved [6]. In the case the terminal cannot receive the message Msg4, it regards the preamble transmission as a collision and retries the RACH procedure after a random backoff. Subsequently the success terminals will exchange their messages with eNodeB through dedicated channels and hybrid automatic repeat request (HARQ) is used to protect the message transmission [3].

From the descriptions above, in order to launch the transmission of one data packet, at least 4 signaling messages are required for uplink channel access in RAN. Assuming that the processing time of the radio signal on eNodeB and UE is 3 ms, the latency for this uplink channel access is 16 ms in the best case [11]. If RACH collision occurs, the signaling cost and latency will be increased further.

2.2 RACH Overload Control Schemes

Overload control is considered as one of the most important features to protect the system from excessive connectivity of massive devices. In other words, massive devices would generate a huge number of signaling flows and congest RAN and CN. Various methods have been proposed to alleviate the RACH congestion problem due to massive mMTC UEs deployment. These schemes can be categorized as push-based and pull-based solutions based on which entity initiates the RACH procedure, i.e. mMTC UEs or networks [6].

Push-Based Solutions. In the push-based solutions, RACH procedures are triggered by autonomous requests from mMTC UEs. Separation of RACH resources, dynamic allocation of RACH resource, ACB methods are popular candidate solutions [4,6–8]. Separation of RACH resources involves distinguishing the available resources into two groups: one for mMTC traffic and one for non-mMTC traffic. While this scheme limits the impact of mMTC traffic on non-mMTC traffic, it introduces a new problem, i.e. load balancing between two groups. Dynamic allocation of RACH resources can be viewed as an improvement of the precedent one [7]. The eNodeB dynamically allocates PRACH resources based on the prevailing network load and the PRACH load condition. Although this scheme better handles the congestion problem, it can be applied only when the network is aware of the traffic arriving time. Regarding the ACB method, the network accesses of different mMTC UEs are differentiated by introducing separate access classes for mMTC UEs [7]. The ACB scheme classifies access classes according to a predefined criterion. For each class, eNodeB holds its access probability and barring time, and periodically informs the UEs of these values. The mMTC UEs refer to these values to determine whether or not they should initiate their random-access procedures. ACB mechanisms are quite effective in preventing PRACH overload, but at the cost of longer access delay for mMTC UEs. Furthermore, ACB does not solve the access contention problem when many delay-constrained mMTC UEs need to access the channel in a short time interval. Last but not least, EAB, which allows the network to selectively control access attempts from the UEs, can tolerate longer access delays or higher failure probability [3].

Pull-Based Solutions. Pull-based random-access triggering allows eNodeB to directly trigger initiation of a random-access procedure [4,6,7]. This category is known as centralized control solutions. In this scheme, eNodeB directly designates target mMTC UEs through the paging channel and only the paged devices will initiate their random-access procedures. This method is appropriate when applied to a system with low number of devices [6]. However, the method becomes infeasible when there are a large number of mMTC UEs since in this case additional significant paging loads can be an issue. One solution of this problem is to use Group Paging (GP) method, whereby all the members of the group are paged by just one paging message [6,7].

3 Probability-Based Access Scheme

mMTC traffics are typically characterized by small and infrequent data transmissions/receptions with a higher level of delay-tolerance compared to devices supporting H2H communications [10]. In LTE/LTE-A conventional procedure, in order to complete the delivery of one small data packet of mMTC traffic, the mMTC UE has to perform the RACH procedure firstly to move from RRC_IDLE to RRC_CONNECTED. According to the analysis in Sect. 2, the signaling overhead is much larger than the data load which will result in low data throughput and intolerable delay. This motives us to design a new uplink channel access method to improve the efficiency and reduce the latency.

3.1 Basic Proposal

In this study, we assume an eNodeB is deployed in the cell with a number of mMTC UEs served. These mMTC UEs have previously registered with the eNodeB which means that the eNodeB is aware of the total number of mMTC UEs within its coverage. Also all these mMTC UEs are assumed with fixed locations (e.g. smart meters), and no mobility will be considered in this paper. Since the mMTC UEs are static, the fixed uplink TA between the mMTC UEs and the eNodeB can be determined in the first network access.

We assume that the data arrives at mMTC UE follows certain distribution, e.g., Poisson distribution. According to LTE/LTE-A conventional mechanism, the mMTC UE will be activated to RRC_CONNECTED state when the traffic of small data packets arrives, and deactivated to RRC_IDLE state after finishing the uplink transmission of these small data packets. In order to reduce the signaling overhead and support our proposed probability-based access scheme, here a modification is made on the management of RRC connection. Initially when the mMTC UE firstly enters the network, one RRC connection is established through RACH procedure, just as the conventional 3GPP RAN. However later this RRC connection and its context will not be released, but maintained on both eNodeB side and mMTC UE side. In other words, for our proposal, it is possible for the mMTC UE to transmit data packets immediately without need to re-setup RRC connection.

Furthermore, a type of resource block called PBA channel is defined to be only used by mMTC UEs to initiate the first packet transmission for the traffic burst. It should be noted that the PBA channel is separated from the conventional RACH channel. As this PBA channel is not UE specific but rather allocated for all or a group of mMTC UEs, collisions may happen when multiple mMTC UEs select the same PBA channel. The congestion probability of the PBA channel is designed to alleviate this congestion. On network side, the eNodeB can estimate this probability based on the historical traffic experiences and inform individual mMTC UEs of this probability. More specifically, the eNodeB can configure this separated PBA channel by using the same scheme as PRACH channel to inform mMTC UEs about the allocations of the PBA channel. The difference is that on the subframe where the PBA channel is allocated, the value of its congestion probability will be broadcasted in certain UCI (Uplink Control Information) within the PDCCH. Also the Modulation Coding Scheme (MCS) used for uplink transmission on this PBA channel can be indicated in the same UCI if necessary.

3.2 Detailed Implementation

In the running time, mMTC UEs are dynamically classified into two groups on eNodeB side, i.e. (1) Group A: these mMTC UEs are in the process of uplink data transmission, and all these transmissions including BSR (Buffer Status Report) and traffic data are allocated with dedicated resources by eNodeB. Thus here no contention-based process is involved. (2) Group B: these mMTC UEs has no uplink data for transmission at the moment, which means that eNodeB will not allocate any dedicated resource for these mMTC UEs. If new uplink data arrives on an mMTC UE, it will use the following proposed scheme to launch the uplink data transmission.

Initially all the mMTC UEs belong to the Group B. When an mMTC UE of Group B launched the uplink data transmission, it will be migrated from Group B to Group A. On the other hand, if the mMTC UE finished the transmission of all the buffered data, it will be migrated back from Group A to Group B.

At first, the eNodeB configures the allocation of PBA channels and broadcasts this configuration within the cell via SIB information. This configuration of PBA channels, e.g. the density of PBA channels, can be determined based on mMTC traffic load and certain algorithm may be required for optimization which is out of the scope of this paper. On every subframe where there is a PBA channel, the eNodeB will determine the value of congestion probability p_0. Assuming that at this moment, the number of mMTC UEs within Group B is M, the traffic bursts of mMTC UE $i(i = 1, \cdots, M)$ arrive following a random process and in a finite interval t the number of such arrives, i.e. $N(t)$, obeys a probability distribution $P_i\{N(t) = K\}$, the congestion probability of this PBA channel can be calculated as Eq. (1)

$$p_0 = 1 - \prod_{i=1}^{M} P_i\{N(t) = 0\} - \sum_{i=1}^{M} \left(P_i\{N(t) > 0\} \prod_{j=1, j \neq i}^{M} P_j\{N(t) = 0\} \right) \quad (1)$$

where the second item denotes the probability of no traffic bursts arriving on all the mMTC UEs during the interval, and the third item describes the probability that only one mMTC UE has traffic bursts arriving within the interval.

At the mMTC Group B UE side, if a new data burst arrives, the mMTC UE will first detect the allocation of PBA channels from SIB information. On the nearest subframe where a PBA channel is allocated, the mMTC UE decodes the congestion probability and MCS (if existed) of the PBA channel from PDCCH. After that it will generate a random number p within the range of $[0, 1]$, and compare the number with the congestion probability. If the number is larger than the congestion probability, the mMTC UE activates the direct data transmission on the PBA channel. Otherwise, the mMTC UE falls back to the legacy procedure, i.e. it first tries the contention-based random access on RACH channel and then data transmission on dedicated resources. In detail, the subsequent procedure can be divided into three cases.

Case I:

If $p < p_0$, this mMTC UE will launch the RACH process to initialize the transmission of uplink data, as shown in Fig. 1. The procedure is very similar to the conventional procedure defined in 3GPP RAN with the following two modifications: (1) since the RRC connection is always maintained for mMTC UEs, here the RACH procedure does not need to re-setup a RRC connection. (2) after succeded RACH process, the eNodeB will update the set of Group A and B by migrating this mMTC UE from Group B to Group A, which means later this mMTC UE is assigned with dedicated resources for uplink data transmission, and will not involve in the competition of PBA channels. It should be noted that all the solutions discussed in 3GPP to alleviate or avoid the RACH congestion can be applied here, such as ACB scheme and separation of RACH resources, etc.

Since there is an extra signaling message required in this case, i.e. congestion probability in PDCCH, both the signaling cost and latency for uplink channel access are a little higher than those of the conventional RACH procedure, i.e. 5 signaling messages and 20 ms latency in the best case.

Case II:

If $p \geq p_0$, this mMTC UE will try to launch the uplink data transmission by transmitting the first packet directly on this PBA channel, as shown in Fig. 2. Here the mMTC UE will package the data in units of MAC PDU based on the MCS and size of the PBA channel. If there is still uplink data left in the buffer, the mMTC UE should schedule a piggybacked BSR on this PBA channel. On the eNodeB side, if no collision occurs on this PBA channel, the eNodeB can receive and decode the data packet and BSR correctly. Then it should reply an Acknowledge (ACK) message to mMTC UE and allocate new uplink grants (if BSR received) for the subsequent uplink data transmission as the conventional scheme. At the same time, the eNodeB will update the set of Group A and B by migrating this mMTC UE from Group B to Group A.

In this case, the data is successfully delivered on the PBA channel. The required signaling message is just the notification of congestion probability from eNodeB to mMTC UEs, and the latency is only 4 ms.

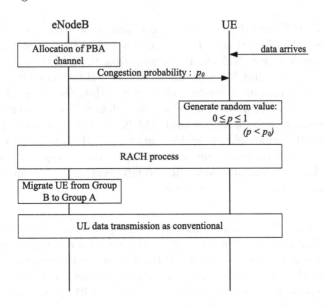

Fig. 1. Case pf $p < p_0$

Case III:

As mentioned before, this PBA channel is not UE specific but rather allocated for all mMTC UEs of Group B. Collision occurs when multiple mMTC UEs transmit data packets on the same PBA channel. In this case, the eNodeB cannot decode the data packet correctly and will not reply any message. On mMTC UE side, a timer will be initiated when it completes the transmission of data packets on the PBA channel. The timer will be cancelled if the ACK message is received from the eNodeB. In case of no ACK message received before the timer expires, the mMTC UE will launch the RACH procedure to initialize the transmission of uplink data as shown in Fig. 3. Similar to case 1, RRC connection setup is not required in this RACH procedure. After a successful RACH procedure, the eNodeB will update the set of Group A and B by migrating this mMTC UE from Group B to Group A.

Obviously, this case is the same with Case I in term of signaling cost. Since the mMTC UE needs to wait the expiry of the timer, the latency for uplink channel access includes the RACH procedure and should be at least 24 ms under the assumption that the timer is set to be 4 ms.

For each of the three cases, all the buffered data will be finally delivered from this mMTC UE to network. If no further data transmission, the eNodeB will migrate this mMTC UE from Group A back to Group B. Thus, when new data arrives in future, the mMTC UE can participate in the competition of PBA channels again.

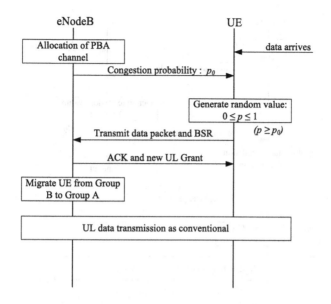

Fig. 2. Case pf $p \geq p_0$ and successful transmission

4 Numerical Results

In this section, the proposed probability-based access scheme is evaluated by comparing to the conventional uplink transmission based on the RACH procedure. We consider a scenario in which a fixed number of mMTC UEs are deployed in a cell. The eNodeB of the cell allocates the PBA channel with a fixed interval. For all the mMTC UEs, the corresponding traffic arrivals follow a Poisson process, and the duration of a session is assumed to be very short comparing to the interval of PBA channels. In addition, except for the PBA channels, the system allocates separated RACH channels for the legacy RACH procedure of mMTC UEs.

In the evaluation, it is assumed that the traffic bursts of mMTC UE $i(i = 1, \cdots, M)$ arrive following a Poisson process with rate $\lambda_i(i = 1, \cdots, M)$. If a PBA channel is allocated on subframe n with M mMTC UEs within Group B at that moment, and the elapsed time slots since the last allocation of the PBA channel is T, then the probability distribution $P_i\{N(T) = K\}$ is expresssed as Eq. (2)

$$P_i\{N(T) = K\} = \frac{(\lambda_i T)^K}{K!} e^{-\lambda_i T} \tag{2}$$

Therefore, according to Eqs. (1) and (2), the calculation of congestion probability p_0 for this PBA channel is denoted as Eq. (3) and its value will be encoded in the corresponding PDCCH of subframe $(n - 4)$.

$$p_0 = 1 - \left(1 - M + \sum_{i=1}^{M} e^{\lambda_i T}\right) \prod_{i=1}^{M} e^{-\lambda_i T} \tag{3}$$

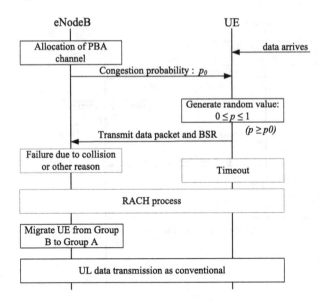

Fig. 3. Case pf $p \geq p_0$ and fail transmission

As summary, the system parameter values used in this evaluation are provided in Table 1. For simplicity, the arrival rates of the Poisson processes are assumed to be identical for all mMTC UEs. Fixed MCS, e.g. QPSK 1/2, is configured for the transmission on PBA channels.

Table 1. Parameter setting

Parameter	Value
M	$10, 50, 100, 200, 500, 800, 1000, 5000$
T	$0.1, 1.0, 10.0, 20.0, 50.0, 100.0$ [s]
$\lambda \, (\lambda_i = \lambda_j)$	$1/180, 1/600, 1/1800, 1/10800, 1/18000, 1/36000$ [1/s]

Figure 4 presents the results by comparing our proposal with the conventional RACH-based uplink access. Here the PBA channel is scheduled to be allocated with 1000 ms interval, and the arriving rate of Poisson process is set as 1/1800. The results in terms of relative signaling cost ratio (RSCR) and relative access latency ratio (RALR) show that both the signaling cost and access latency can be drastically reduced by using the proposed probability-based access scheme, especially when the number of mMTC UEs is small, e.g. about 50% reduction in the case of 500 mMTC UEs. However, as the increase of mMTC UE number, the advantage of the proposal will vanish gradually. This is due to the fact that the congestion of PBA channel will become more severe for the large scale of mMTC UEs. One feasible solution is to categorize the mMTC UEs into different

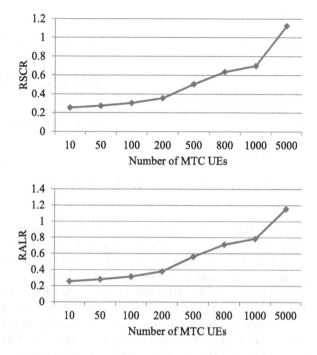

Fig. 4. Performance vs. Number of mMTC UEs

classes based on the metrics such as traffic characteristic and/or geometry information, etc. Our proposed scheme can be applied to each class independently. Thus the expected advantage of the proposal can be guaranteed by limiting the number of mMTC UEs within each class. Figure 5 illustrates the impact of the density of PBA channels. Here the number of mMTC UEs is fixed to 200. It is observed that with the decrease of the PBA channel density, the average congestion probability of the PBA channels is increased. It is reasonable because fewer PBA channels mean that more mMTC UEs will compete on the same PBA channel, thus results in higher collision possibility. Since not all the PBA channels are used by mMTC UEs, these PBA channels can be classified into two groups: (1) Busy PBA channels where uplink transmissions from mMTC UEs is either successful in case there is only one uplink transmission or failure due to collision from multiple uplink transmissions. (2) Free PBA channels where no uplink transmission occurs. From Fig. 5, we can see that the ratio of successful PBA channels within busy PBA channels is firstly decreased due to fewer PBA channels and higher collision possibility. After the point where the interval of PBA channel is 20s, this ratio is increased again because the access tries on PBA channels from mMTC UEs are automatically blocked by the congestion probabilities of the PBA channels. Obviously, with large PBA interval and high congestion probability, there are more wasted PBA channels as illustrated by the two curves of the Ratio of free PBA channels and the Ratio of successful

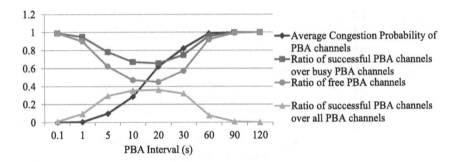

Fig. 5. Performance vs. Interval of PBA channels

PBA channels over all PBA channels. Therefore from the viewpoint of the whole system, certain tradeoff should be considered when configuring the allocation of PBA channels. Additionally, as shown in Fig. 6, decreasing the arriving rate of mMTC bursts, which means increasing the average interval between two continuous traffic bursts of an mMTC UE, will result in the decrease of average congestion probability of the PBA channel due to the fact that the collision probability will be much lower in case of fewer mMTC sessions. With lower congestion probability, fewer mMTC UEs will compete on the same PBA channel, which results in higher successful contention ratio over the busy PBA channels. On the other hand, low congestion probability with low session density means that there are lots of PBA channels on which no uplink transmission occurs, thus to be wasted. These results are validated by the ratios of successful PBA channels and free PBA channels in Fig. 6.

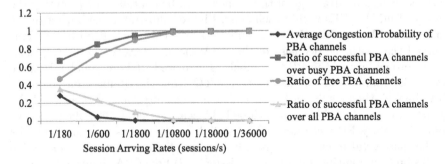

Fig. 6. Performance vs. mMTC session arriving rates

5   Conclusion

In this paper, to accommodate an mMTC scenario in the future, we presented an enhanced grant-free access scheme for mMTC uplink transmission by introducing the PBA channel. With the proposed scheme, the PBA channel associated with estimated congestion probability is allocated by the eNodeB. And based on this probability, the mMTC UEs can either perform the uplink data transmission directly on the PBA channel to reduce the access delay and signaling overhead, or fall back to the legacy procedure by using contention-based random access scheme to guarantee the availability of network access.

In this study, the PBA channel is allocated with a static density. However, on eNodeB side, according to the statistics of uplink transmissions, including RACH processes and collisions, the eNodeB can dynamically adjust the allocation of the PBA channels, especially the density of the PBA channels. The objective of such kind of adjustment can be for the further improvement of resource efficiency and reduction of collision, which will be our future research work.

References

1. Tavana, M., Shah-Mansouri, V., Wong, V.W.S.: Congestion control for bursty M2M traffic in LTE networks. In: IEEE International Conference on Communications (ICC), pp. 5815–5820, London UK (8–12 June, 2015)
2. Ilori, A., Tang, Z., He, J., Blow, K., Chen, H.-H.: A random channel access scheme for massive machine devices in LTE cellular networks. In: IEEE International Conference on Communications (ICC), pp. 2985–2990. London UK, (8–12 June 2015)
3. Cheng, R.-G., Chen, J., Chen, D.-W., Wei, C.-H.: Modeling and analysis of an extended access barring algorithm for machine-type communications in LTE-A networks. IEEE Trans. Wireless Commun. **14**(6), 1956–2968 (2015)
4. Kim, J.S., Lee, S., Chung, M.Y.: Efficient random-access scheme for massive connectivity in 3GPP low-cost machine-type communications. In: IEEE Transactions on Vehicular Technology, vol. 99, pp. 1–10. (IEEE Early Access Articles) (2016)
5. Ali, K.T., Rejeb, S.B., Choukair, Z.: An enhanced random access scheme and performance evaluation for M2M communications in 5G/HetNets. In: International Symposium on Networks, Computers and Communications (ISNCC), Yasmine Hammamet, Tunisia, pp. 1–6 (11–13 May, 2016)
6. Arouk, O., Ksentini, A., Taleb, T.: Group paging-based energy saving for massive MTC accesses in LTE and beyond networks. IEEE J. Selected Areas Commun. **34**(5), 1086–1102 (2016)
7. Arouk, O., Ksentini, A., Taleb, T.: Performance analysis of RACH procedure with beta traffic-activated machine-type-communication. In: IEEE Global Communications Conference (GLOBECOM), pp. 1–6. San Diego, CA, USA (6–10 December, 2015)
8. Duan, S., Shah-Mansouri, V., Wang, Z., Wong, V.W.S.: D-ACB: adaptive congestion control algorithm for bursty M2M traffic in LTE networks. In: IEEE Transactions on Vehicular Technology, vol. 65, No. 12, pp. 9847–9861 (2016)
9. Yang, X., Wang, X., Zhang, J.: Compressed sensing based ACK feedback for grant-free uplink data transmission in 5G mMTC. In: IEEE International Conference on Personal, Indoor, and Mobile Radio Communications (PIMRC), pp. 1–5. Valencia, Spain (4–8 Sept 2016)
10. Andreev, S., et al.: Efficient small data access for machine-type communications in LTE. In: IEEE International Conference on Communications (ICC), Budapest, Hungary, pp. 3569–3574 (9–13 June, 2013)
11. Zhou, K., Nikaein, N., Knopp, R., Bonnet, C.: Contention based access for machine-type communications over LTE. In: IEEE 75th Vehicular Technology Conference (VTC Spring), pp. 1–5. Yokohama, Japan (6–9 May, 2012)

The Registration-Based Collision Avoidance Mechanism for IEEE 802.11ah

Chung-Ming Huang[1]($\boxtimes$), Rung-Shiang Cheng[2], and Yin-Ming Li[1]

[1] Department of Computer Science and Information Engineering,
National Cheng Kung University, Tainan, Taiwan
{huangcm, liym}@locust.csie.ncku.edu.edu.tw
[2] Department of Information Technology,
Overseas Chinese University, Tainan, Taiwan
rscheng@ocu.edu.tw

Abstract. IEEE 802.11ah, which is also called WiFi HaLow, is considered to be a promising protocol for Internet of Things (IoT). The legacy 802.11ah proposes a number of grouping mechanisms, which are based on the hierarchical organization, to relieve channel access's collision in the IoT's communication environment. However, the legacy 802.11ah still cannot effectively avoid collisions in a crowded environment. This work proposed the Registration-based Collision Avoidance (RCA) mechanism to avoid collisions and furthermore reduce the waiting time of backoff. The RCA mechanism lets the AP know the network situation in advance and then schedule stations to avoid collision. Comparing with the legacy 802.11ah, experimental results shown that the proposed RCA mechanism has the lower collision rate and better throughput when the number of stations in a time slot is high.

Keywords: IOT · IEEE 802.11ah · WiFi HaLow · Collision avoidance · Backoff

1 Introduction

One of the most important development trends of the future network is to integrate existed network systems, such as Internet of Things (IoT), cloud computing, smartphone networks, social networks, and industrial networks [1]. In order to manage the system effectively, an appropriate low-power wireless network technology is needed to achieve Machine-to-Machine (M2M) communication in the IOT networking environment [2].

To tackle the networking characteristics and requirement of IoT, IEEE proposed 802.11ah [3], which was also known as Wi-Fi HaLow, to deal with related issues. 802.11ah provides the transmission range of up to 1 km while keeping the data rate of 150 kbps and its PHY layer is inherited from 802.11ac. The channels that 802.11ah uses are 1, 2, 4, 8 and 16 MHz. Only 1 and 2 MHz bands are mandatory.

Due to the considered domain of using IEEE 802.11ah [4, 5], i.e., it allows up to 8192 stations, which can be scattered in 1 km, to connect to an 802.11ah AP, it needs to design mechanisms of power saving, scheduling, etc., to have the smooth operation. Thus, the IEEE 802.11ah MAC layer introduces several mechanisms to tackle related

© Springer Nature Switzerland AG 2019
C. Esposito et al. (Eds.): I-SPAN 2019, CCIS 1080, pp. 240–255, 2019.
https://doi.org/10.1007/978-3-030-30143-9_19

problems. To have the smooth scheduling, IEEE 802.11ah adopts the hierarchical organization based on Association Identifiers (AIDs). That is, all of the existed wireless stations connected to an IEEE 802.11ah AP are partitioned into several groups. Each wireless station can have data downlinking and uplinking during its group's assigned time slot and then keep sleep in the other time. Fast association and authentication and Restricted access window (RAW) are used to prevent collisions to improve throughput. Traffic indication map (TIM) segmentation is used to save power to extend the life of devices.

However, the aforementioned mechanisms of IEEE 802.11ah are not able to prevent collisions in a dense network environment, i.e., many active stations contend for the channel at the same time. If there are too many stations contending for the channel at the same time, it may cause many collisions and decrease the performance.

A novel mechanism called the Registration-based Collision Avoidance (RCA) mechanism was proposed in this work to improve the performance of 802.11ah in a dense network environment, which is used to avoid collisions, and furthermore reduce the waiting time of backoff. The RCA mechanism utilizes mechanisms of legacy 802.11ah to let the AP know the backoff time of each station in advance and defines two types of stations to facilitate the AP to schedule stations. In this way, the AP can schedule stations before stations contend for the channel and avoid collisions. If there are two or more stations that are assigned to the same period having the same backoff value, the AP can adjust the backoff values of the corresponding stations to avoid collisions.

The remaining part of this paper is organized as follows. Section 2 provides an overview of the IEEE 802.11ah. Section 3 presents relative work. The proposed RCA mechanism is given in Sect. 4. Section 5 presents the performance analysis. Finally, conclusion remarks are given in Sect. 6.

2 Overview of IEEE 802.11ah

This Section has a brief overview of IEEE 802.11ah.

2.1 TIM Segmentation

Each station is assigned an Association Identifier (AID), which is a unique value, by the IEEE 802.11ah AP in the association procedure. IEEE 802.11ah introduces the Traffic Indication Map (TIM) segmentation to tackle the power consuming problem. The TIM segmentation is a mechanism that divides stations into several TIM groups using their AIDs and then the AP schedules the period of channel access based on the grouping to achieve the power saving purpose. In this way, a station only wakes up on specific time and listens to the corresponding TIM beacon; the station can sleep on the rest of the time.

Two kinds of beacons in 802.11ah are (1) Delivery Traffic Indication Map (DTIM) beacon and (2) TIM beacon. DTIM beacon is a group-based presentation, for which each bit indicates a TIM group and means whether there are one or more stations in the corresponding TIM group having some downlink data or not. When the AP receives downlink data for a station in a specific TIM group, it buffers the data and modifies the DTIM's bit denoting the corresponding TIM group to which the station belongs. TIM beacon is a station-based presentation, for which each bit indicates a station and denotes whether the station in the corresponding TIM group has downlink data or not. When the AP receives downlink data for station x, it buffers the data and sets (1) the DTIM's bit of the corresponding group to which station x belongs and (2) the TIM's bit denoting station x to 1.

2.2 Restricted Access Window (RAW)

To alleviate the serious collision, IEEE 802.11ah introduces a mechanism called Restricted Access Window (RAW), which aims to reduce collisions and improve throughput. The RAW mechanism splits stations into groups and allows stations to access the channel only at the specific time that belong to their group. The AIDs of stations are used to determine to which RAW group each station belongs. Each RAW group is delimited by the highest AID and the lowest AID.

Each TIM interval can have one or more RAW groups, which is determined by the number of *RAW Assignment subfields* in a RAW Parameter Set (RPS) information element. RPS information elements are contained in the TIM beacon. A *RAW Assignment subfield* in a RPS information element specifies the stations that belong to the RAW group, channel indication, RAW type, slot attribute, and the interval's starting time. Moreover, there are one or more slots in the RAW. There are two slot assignment methods for stations. Stations use implicit assignment, which means that the RAW slot is not allocated by the AP directly, but is calculated by the station itself according to their AIDs and TIM bitmap. The formula is as follows:

$$i_{slot} = (x + N_{offset}) \bmod N_{RAW}. \tag{1}$$

where i_{slot} represents the index of the slot, N_{RAW} is the number of slots in the RAW; N_{offset} is a parameter for improving the fairness among stations in the RAW and equals the two least significant bytes of the frame check sequence (FCS) of the beacon; x is determined by the setting, for which x is the AID of the station when the RAW is not restricted to stations whose AID bits in the TIM element are equal to 1 (AID-based assignment); otherwise, x is the position index of the station among others (Index-assignment). Figure 1 is an example of using these two slot assignment methods.

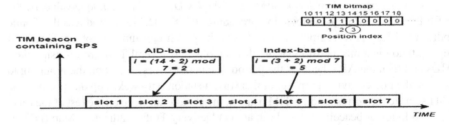

Fig. 1. An example of using these two slot assignment methods.

Let the AID of the station be 14 and N_{offset} be 2. When the AID-based assignment is used, x would be AID 14; thus, the station is assigned to slot 2. If the index-based assignment is used, x would be the index in the TIM bitmap, which is 3; thus, the station is assigned to slot 5. Stations use Enhanced Distributed Channel Access (EDCA) to contend for the channel inside its assigned slot.

3 Related Work

To reduce the chance of collisions using the IEEE 802.11ah, two main directions that can be used to improve the network performance are (1) optimized grouping [6–8] and (2) modifying the channel access protocol [9–11].

The first direction is to optimize the number of groups. However, the 802.11ah standard does not describe how to group stations. In [6, 7], the authors did some experiments and proved that the grouping strategy affects the system performance, and the optimized RAW grouping changes with many different factors. Therefore, it needs to have a method that can dynamically adjust grouping when the network environment changes. Seo et al. [8] also introduced the problem of extreme grouping. A small number of groups caused many retransmissions; a large number of groups causes unnecessary overheads. Thus, they proposed a simple guideline for the number of grouping. The simple guideline is as follows: (i) the number of the groups is proportional to the number of stations and (ii) the traffic arrival rate and the beacon interval are inversely proportional to the number of active stations.

The second direction is to modify the channel access protocol, which means changing the channel access behavior of stations and improving the performance. In [9], authors proposed a novel assignment scheme, which divides a RAW into two parts: downlink slot and uplink slot. For the downlink slot, the slot assignment is the same as the standard, which assigns a downlink slot to each station based on the position index of the station. For the uplink slot, stations that have uplink data can pick an uplink slot randomly and then perform a contention-base channel access in that slot. The proportion between downlink and uplink RAW size is equal to the proportion of downlink and uplink traffic. The defined access order is multicast, downlink slots, and uplink slots. However, the proposed method cannot divide the RAW into downlink and uplink segment depending on real-time traffic, which may result in performance degradation in unstable environments. Ahmed and Hussain [10] also proposed a similar assignment scheme, for which the defined access order is uplink slots and then downlink slots. In [11], the authors proposed a mechanism to solve the priority of the event-driven traffic. Two types of RAWs are Critical RAW (CRAW) for event-driven traffic and Periodic RAW (PRAW) for periodic traffic. The event-driven traffic has higher priority to be processed, i.e., when the event-driven traffic and periodic traffic happen at the same time, the event-driven traffic should be processed before the periodic traffic.

4 The Proposed Registration-Based Collision Avoidance (RCA) Mechanism

In this paper, the RCA mechanism is proposed. Using the proposed RCA mechanism, a station can generate a backoff value it desires at the stage of association or during data exchange. Then the station piggybacks the backoff value on the request association message or frames and sends it to the AP. The AP records the backoff value of the station. With the backoff values of all stations, the AP is able to schedule the data transmission of the corresponding stations to avoid collision. Finally, the AP notifies each station by broadcasting the TIM beacon or a response ACK.

The RCA mechanism is divided into three phases: (i) association phase, (ii) registration phase and (iii) communication phase.

The Association Phase

In the association phase, each station that wants to associate with the AP (1) generates a backoff value b from the contention window and (2) piggybacks the backoff value b on the association request message, and then sends the association request message to the AP. Then the AP (3) assigns an AID to the station and stores the AID in a list of AIDs, which is associated with backoff value b in the RCA bit vector. After that, the AP (4) piggybacks the AID on the association response (ACK) message and sends it back to the station. Finally, the station (5) gets its assigned AID.

Two types of stations are defined as follows.

(1) *Known station:* the AP knows that these stations have data to send/receive, e.g., stations that have downlink data and stations that transmit uplink data with the more Data bit of 1 during the communication phase.

(2) *Unknown station:* the AP does not know whether these stations have data to send/receive or not, e.g., (i) stations that have neither uplink data nor downlink data after the association phase and (ii) stations that have transmitted uplink data with the more Data bit of 0 during the communication phase.

Note that these two kinds of stations generate backoff values for registration, but the AP only schedules known stations. In other words, when two unknown stations have the same backoff value, the AP dose not schedule them to avoid collision because there may not be a collision, and thus just stores these two backoff values.

The Registration Phase

In the registration phase, the AP calculates to which group a station should belong and registers the station's registered backoff value regardless of whether the station has data to transmit or not. That is, even if the station has neither uplink data nor downlink data, the station still generates a backoff value to the AP (i) during the association phase or (ii) having data transmission during the communication phase, and the AP still records the backoff value into the RCA bit vector. In this way, the AP can know all of the registration information of all stations and schedule them when it is needed.

In this work, a RCA bit vector is used to record each station's registered backoff value. RCA bit vectors are stored in the AP side. Each slot is associated with a RCA bit vector and each RCA bit vector indicates the backoff values' status in a time slot, for which bit i in a RCA bit vector denotes the registration status of backoff value i. In a RCA bit vector, the ith bit is associated with a list of AIDs, for which the corresponding stations registered backoff value i. Bit i is set to 1 when there is a known station registered backoff value i; in other words, bit i is set to 0 when there is no station registered backoff value i or only unknown stations registered backoff value i.

An example of using the RCA bit vector is depicted in Fig. 2. Let there be six stations, whose AIDs are 1, 3, 5, 7, 9, and 11 and these six stations be assigned to the same slot. Let these six stations' registered backoff values be 7, 10, 14, 2, 10 and 7 respectively. After the association process, the registered backoff values of all stations, which have no data to send/receive during the association phase, are stored in the RCA bit vector, which is depicted in Fig. 2(a). Then, there are downlink data for stations 1 and 5, i.e., these two stations turn from unknown stations to known stations. Thus, bits 7 and 14 are set to 1, which is depicted in Fig. 2(b). Bit 2 and Bit 10 are set to 0 because only unknown stations registered them. Other bits with an empty list of AIDs are set to 0 because no station registered them. Note that each bit can only be registered for up to one known station to avoid collision; but each bit can be registered by unlimited number of unknown stations. Therefore, when there are downlink data for station 11 and station 11 turns from an unknown station to a known station, two known stations registered the same backoff value, which means that there will be a collision. At this time, the AP should modify the backoff value of known station 11 by counting down its backoff value from 7, i.e., 6, to avoid collision, which is depicted in Fig. 2(c). If bit 0 to bit 6 are equal to 1, the AP should modify the backoff value of known station 11 by counting up its backoff value from 7, i.e., 8.

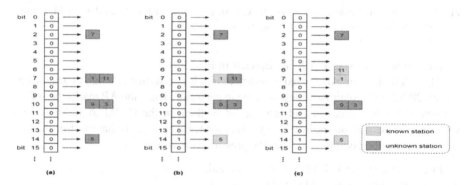

Fig. 2. An illustrated example of the RCA bit vector.

The Communication Phase

In the communication phase, the AP checks RCA bit vectors of the upcoming TIM group, marks the known station that has the minimum backoff value in each slot as the first accessor. The AP generates a bitmap called Channel Access Indication Map (CAIM), which indicates the first accessor in each slot, and sets the bits of the corresponding stations that are marked as the first accessor to 1. The AP associates the CAIM with the TIM beacon, for which those stations that belong to this TIM can wake up to receive it. Each station that belongs to the TIM receives CAIM and checks its corresponding bit. If the bit is 1, it changes its backoff value to 0 because it has been assigned at the first user to access the channel on the corresponding slot; at the same time, those unknown stations whose backoff values are 0 and belongs to the same time slot should change their backoff values to avoid colliding with the first accessor of this time slot. When a station transmits a frame, it should generate a new backoff value for reserving its next data transmission and piggyback it on the frame sent to the AP.

After the first accessor finishes the data transmission, the AP marks the known station with the minimum backoff value in the group as the next accessor. The AP indicates the next accessor through the ACK, which shows the AID and the backoff value of the next accessor.

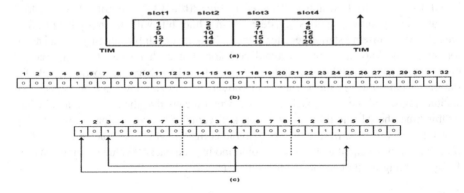

Fig. 3. An illustrated example of using the CAIM. (a) slot assignment, (b) the CAIM without compression and (c) the CAIM with compression.

An example of using CAIM is depicted in Fig. 3(a).

The RAW uses the AID-based assignment and it is assumed that known stations 5, 18, 19, 20 have the minimum backoff value in each slot. Thus, the AP marks these four stations as the first accessor and sets the bit of them in the CAIM to 1. The corresponding CAIM is depicted in Fig. 3(b). However, it is observed that most of the bits are 0, so it can be compressed. The compression rule is as follows:

- Integrated 8 bits into 1 bit, i.e., 8 bits organize a group.
- The first 8 bits of the CAIM indicates 8 groups.
- When the bit of a group is 1, it indicates that one or more bits are set to 1 in that group, then adds the corresponding group details behind the bitmap.
- Otherwise, the group details can be ignored.

Thus, the CAIM of the aforementioned example can be compressed as that depicted in Fig. 3(c).

Figure 4 depicts an example of the communication phase. Referring to Fig. 4, stations 5, 9 and 13 are assigned to the same slot. Let station 5 have a frame to send, station 9 and 13 have two frames to send, and their initial backoff values be 3, 5 and 0 respectively. Station 13 is an unknown station. At first, the AP (1) picks a known station with the minimum backoff value as the first accessor. So station 5 is picked, and thus (2) the AP sets the corresponding bit of the picked station in the CAIM to 1. Next, the AP (3) piggybacks the CAIM on the TIM beacon and broadcasts the TIM beacon. When stations receive the TIM beacon, they (a) check their bits of the CAIM. The CAIM shows that station 5 is the first accessor because it has the minimum backoff value. Therefore, station 5 (b) changes its backoff value to 0, which means station 5 can access the channel immediately when its slot time is coming. Unknown station 13 has a backoff value of 0, but it is not the first accessor. So, it should (c) generate a new backoff value when it receives the TIM beacon, which indicates that it is not the first accessor, to avoid colliding with station 5 because station 5 can transmit data immediately using the same backoff value. Before station 5 transmits, it should (d) generate a new backoff value and piggyback the backoff value on the data frame for registration. After station 5 completes the transmission, it (e) enters into the sleeping mode because the more Data bit is 0, which means that there is no data to send, and station 5 turns from a known station to an unknown station. Next, the AP (4) finds the station with the minimum backoff value from known stations as the next accessor and thus station 9 is picked. The AP (5) piggybacks the information, which includes the AID and the backoff value of the next accessor, on the ACK message. Station 9 (f) receives the ACK and can have its transmission. After station 9 transmits its first frame, the AP indicates that the next accessor is still station 9 because station 9 is the known station with the minimum backoff value. However, since the backoff value 3 of unknown station 13 is smaller than the backoff value of known station 9, unknown station 13 can transmit data when its backoff time is due. That is, unknown stations can only transmit data spontaneously. If the remaining time of the slot is not enough for a frame transmission, the AP (6) will not piggyback any information on the ACK. If stations receive an ACK that does not contain any information about the next accessor, stations can enter into the sleep mode.

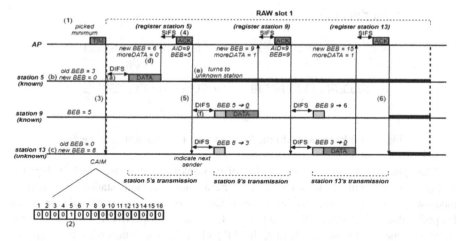

Fig. 4. An illustrated example of the execution procedure in the communication phase.

For the proposed RCA architecture, the type of the station plays an important role in the registration phase and the communication phase. Three ways that a station can be changed from the unknown one to the known one by the AP are as follows: (i) When there are some downlink data for unknown station x: the AP knows that unknown station x has data to send through downlink buffer. (ii) When station x is associating with the AP and station x sets the bit of uplink data petition to 1: the AP knows that station x has data to send through the uplink request. (iii) When the AP receives data from unknown station x and the more Data bit piggybacked on the data frame equals 1: the AP knows that unknown station x has data to send through uplink traffic. One way that the AP can change a station from the known one to the unknown one is as follows: (a) After known station y completes the uplink transmission and the more Data bit piggybacked on the data frame equals 0 and (b) known station y has no downlink data, i.e., known station y has no downlink traffic or uplink traffic. The AP changes station y to the unknown one because the AP has no idea when station y will have data to send or receive. In the following part, some examples of collisions are used to illustrate the collision situation of the proposed method.

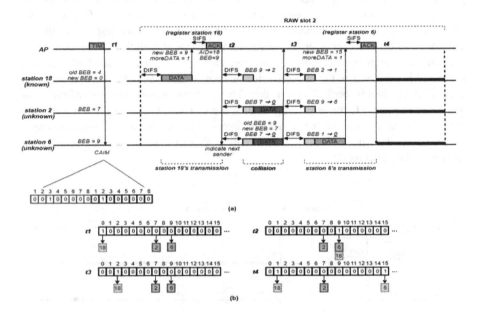

Fig. 5. (a) Example 1; (b) the RCA bit vector on different time points.

Example 1 demonstrates the collision of two unknown stations, which is depicted in Fig. 5. In example 1, let (i) station 18 be a known station, stations 2 and 6 be unknown stations; (ii) stations 18, 2 and 6 have two frames to send; (iii) the initial backoff values of stations 18, 2 and 6 be 4, 7 and 9, respectively; (iv) these three stations be assigned to slot 2. At first, the AP picks a known station with the minimum backoff value, and sets the corresponding bit of the picked station in the CAIM to 1. Thus, known station 18 is picked. Next, the AP piggybacks the CAIM on the TIM beacon and broadcasts the TIM beacon. When stations receive the TIM beacon, they check their corresponding bits of the CAIM. The CAIM shows that known station 18 is the first accessor because it has the minimum backoff value. Therefore, known station 18 changes its backoff value to 0. Before known station 18 transmits, it generates the new backoff value 9, sets the moreData bit to 1, and then transmits the data frame. After known station 18 completes the data transmission, the AP sends back an ACK frame, which indicates that the next accessor is known station 18 and its backoff value is 9.

However, unknown station 6 also has the backoff value 9, thus it should generate a new backoff value randomly to avoid collision. Unfortunately, the backoff value generated by unknown station 6 is 7, unknown station 2 also has backoff value 7. It means that a collision will happen. After the collision, both unknown stations 2 and 6 generate a new backoff value. Note that they have received the ACK frame before and knew the backoff value of known station 18, so they would avoid choosing the same backoff value, i.e., 9 − 7 = 2, as that of known station 18.

A known station and an unknown station may also collide. The situation that should be considered is when the uplink data is generated. The situation can be divided into four cases:

(1) Uplink data is generated before an ACK is received, and both stations have different backoff values during contention.
(2) Uplink data is generated before an ACK is received, and both stations have the same backoff value during contention.
(3) Uplink data is generated after an ACK is received, and both stations have different backoff values during contention.
(4) Uplink data is generated after an ACK is received, and both stations have the same backoff value during contention.

Case 1 and case 3 will not collide because both stations have different backoff values. Case 2 will not collide because the AP changes the backoff value of the unknown station. Case 4 will collide because the unknown station wakes up after an ACK has passed.

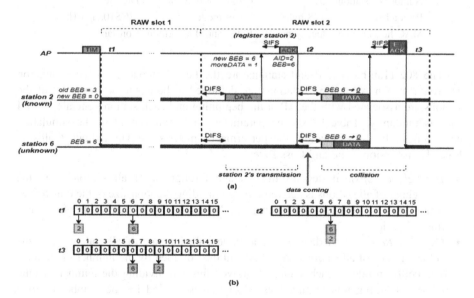

Fig. 6. (a) Example 2; (b) the RCA bit vector on different time points.

An example of case 4 is depicted in Fig. 6. Let (i) a RAW have two slots, (ii) known station 2 have two frames to send, (iii) the initial backoff values of known stations 2 and 6 are 3 and 6 respectively and (iv) both be assigned to slot 2. Since unknown station 6 wakes up after an ACK has passed, it cannot know the information about known station 2. Both stations have the same backoff value 6, which causes a collision. After the collision, the AP does not know backoff values of both of them because the AP cannot decode the frame piggybacked their new backoff value. Thus, both stations change from known stations to unknown stations.

5   Performance Analysis

This Section presents the performance analysis of the proposed method. The proposed RCA mechanism is compared with the legacy IEEE 802.11ah. The simulation is based on a WiFi simulator that adopts the IEEE 802.11ah infrastructure-based network model, which implements RAW grouping and TIM segmentation mechanisms using the C++ programming language. In this Section, how the simulation environment was built and the comparison results are presented.

Table 1. Parameters and their setting in the simulation environment.

Parameter	Value	Parameter	Value
CWmin	16	DTIM interval	2.56 s
CWmax	1024	Number of slots	4
Number of stations	512	Cross slot boundary	Disable
Payload size	128 bytes	Wi-Fi mode	MCS10, 1 MHz
MAC header type	legacy header	Rate control algorithm	Constant

The 802.11ah-based AP and stations are the key components in the simulation environment. An AP and 512 stations are deployed to build the network. All of the stations are associated with the AP at the beginning and each station generates 0 to 4 packets randomly. Table 1 lists the parameters and their setting in the simulation environment. In the evaluation, the performance metrics are Throughput, Collision Rate, Transmission Time and Loss Rate:

- *Throughput (bps):* It denotes the average throughput of all stations, i.e., the throughput of all stations is derived through dividing the total size of the transmitted data frames by the transmission time, i.e., the time length of transmitting these data frames' period.
- *Collision Rate (%):* It denotes the average collision rate of all stations, i.e., the collision rates of all stations are added and then divided by the number of stations. The collision rate of each station is derived through dividing the number of total collisions during transmitting these data frames' period by the number of total channel accesses.

- *Transmission Time (secs):* It denotes the average transmission time of all stations. The transmission time is the time period from the time point station x wakes up due to the first frame's exchange to the time point station x's all frames' exchange are finished.

- *Loss Rate (bps):* It denotes the average loss rate of all stations. Collisions result in the increase of the loss rate. The loss rate of each station is derived through dividing the total size of the lost data frames due to the transmission error (akas. bit error or collision) by the transmission time, i.e., the time length of transmitting these data frames' period.

Hereafter, "Legacy" means using the legacy IEEE 802.11ah protocol and "RCA" means using the RCA mechanism. In the following Figures, the x-axis denotes the number of groups, which also indicates the number of RAWs, e.g., if there are 3 TIM groups and each of which has 2 RAW groups, the number of groups are 6.

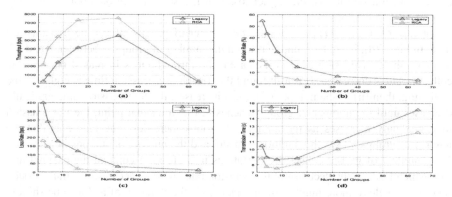

Fig. 7. Results of the experiments with 4 time slots: (a) throughput, (b) collision rate, (c) loss rate and (d) transmission time.

Figure 7 depicts the simulation results of using these three schemes. In the case of fewer/more groups, the number of stations allocated to each time slot is bigger/smaller, which causes the number of active stations, i.e., the number of known stations and unknown stations having uplink data, in each slot to be bigger/smaller and the environment is more dense/sparse. Figure 7(a) depicts that the legacy IEEE 802.11ah has low throughput because the collision rate is very high, which is shown in Fig. 7(b). When the number of groups increases, the collision rate decreases, which is depicted in Fig. 7(b), and the throughput is getting better when the number of groups is equal to or smaller than 32, which is depicted in Fig. 7(a). The reason is that when the number of groups increases, the number of stations in each slot decreases and thus the collision rate decreases and more time can be used. The RCA mechanism has higher throughput and lower collision rate than that of the legacy IEEE 802.11ah. The reason is that the RCA scheme can relieve collisions, especially in the dense environment, which has a large number of stations in a group. However, there are still collisions using this scheme because unknown stations are unpredictable and thus collisions cannot be completely eliminated. It is also found that when the number of groups is between32 and 64, the throughput decreases severely. The reason is that the duration of the slot is only 10 ms when the number of groups is 64, for which environment, it takes about 6.8 ms to transmit a data frame, i.e., the slot can transmit at most one packet. As a result, the actions of stations will be postponed to the next DTIM interval continuously and thus the transmission time is increased.

Referring to Fig. 7(a) and (b), in the denser network environment (2 groups), the experimental result shows that (i) the throughput of the RCA mechanism is 765.85% (2130-246/246*100%) better than that of the legacy one and (ii) the collision rate is 34.29% (54.56%-20.27%) lower than that of the legacy one. In the more sparse network environment (32 groups), (i) the throughput of the RCA mechanism is still 36.35% (7540-5530/5530*100%) better than that of the legacy one and (ii) the collision rate is 4.85% (6.63%-1.78%) lower than that of the legacy one. Referring to Fig. 7 (c), the average loss rate is roughly proportional to the collision rate. Obviously, the higher collision rate it has, the higher loss rate it results; the throughput is inversely proportional to the loss rate.

In case of a fixed DTIM interval, the number of groups affects the transmission time. In Fig. 7(d), it can be found that when the number of groups is between 8 and 32, although the transmission time is increased, the throughput is increased because the collision rate is decreased. It is also found that (i) the transmission time is higher at the beginning, then (ii) as the number of groups increases, the transmission time gradually decreases until the number of groups reaches 8; (iii) after that point, the transmission time gradually increases as the number of groups increases. The reason is that the number of groups affects the duration of a slot and the number of stations in each slot. More number of groups causes fewer stations in a group to contend the channel in a slot, which leads to the decrease of the collision rate and thus decrease the transmission time; nevertheless, more number of groups causes the duration of a slot to be shorter, which causes the packet transmission to be more easily postponed to the next DTIM interval. As a result, when the number of groups is equal to or smaller than 8, the transmission time is decreasing when the number of groups is increasing; on the contrary, when the number of groups is greater than 8, the transmission time is increasing when the number of groups is increasing.

The experiments of having different numbers of stations and a fixed number of groups were executed, for which the experiments were divide into two parts: (i) the lower-number-group network environment (4 groups) and (ii) the high-number-group network environment (16 groups). The more the number of stations it has, the more dense network environment it is, which means that the number of active stations is increased. Figure 8 depicts the simulation result with 4 groups. Referring to Fig. 9(a), when the number of stations is increased, the collision rate and transmission time are increased and the throughput is decreased. The reason is that the number of stations in a slot is increased and thus cause the collision rate to be increased and the transmission time to be increased.

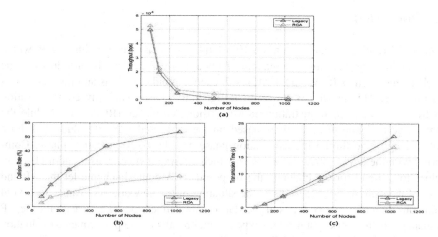

Fig. 8. Results of the experiments with 4 groups: (a) throughput, (b) collision rate and (c) transmission time.

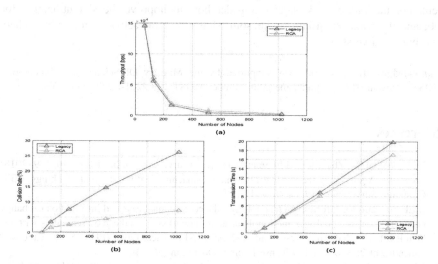

Fig. 9. Results of the environment with 16 groups: (a) throughput, (b) collision rate and (c) transmission time.

Figure 9 depicts the simulation result with 16 groups. Referring to Fig. 9, it is found that the trends of throughput, collision rate, transmission time are similar to the results of the-4-group situation. In addition, it is also found that the throughput of the-16-group's situation is higher than that of the-4-group situation. The reason is that the bigger number of groups there are, the fewer stations there is in a slot; as a result, the collision rate and the transmission time become lower, and the throughput become higher.

6 Conclusion

Legacy IEEE 802.11ah allows up to 8192 stations to be associated with an AP, which causes a high probability of collision. Although IEEE 802.11ah introduces some mechanisms, such as RAW and TIM, it still cannot avoid collisions and thus can affect performance. This paper has proposed a registration-based two-way communication control scheme called Registration-base Collision Avoidance (RCA) to schedule the channel access time of all stations based on the registered backoff values that those stations registered during the association phase and the communication phase. Comparing with the legacy 802.11ah scheme, which allows all stations use random backoff values to contend for the channel, the proposed RCA control scheme let the AP and most of the stations be able to know the situation of the network in advance and avoid collisions. In addition, two types of the stations are defined to make it easier for the AP to manage the network system. The experimental results of the performance evaluation have shown that the proposed RCA scheme outperforms the legacy scheme. The more stations a slot has, the better the improvement it can have, i.e., the proposed RCA mechanism improves the networking performance more in a dense network environment. For the future work, it can consider how to improve the slot utilization for imbalanced-payload environment, i.e. some slots have more active stations while others have fewer active stations.

Acknowledgment. This work was supported by the Ministry Of Science and Technology (MOST), Taiwan (R.O.C.) under the grant number MOST 108-2221-E-006-056-MY3.

References

1. Li, S., Da Xu, L., Zhao, S.: 5G Internet of Things: a survey. J. Ind. Inf. Integr. **10**, 1–9 (2018)
2. Gazis, V.: A survey of standards for machine-to-machine and the Internet of Things. IEEE Commun. Surv. Tutor. **19**(1), 482–511 (2017)
3. IEEE Standard for Information technology—Telecommunications and information exchange between systems Local and metropolitan area networks—Specific requirements—Part 11: Wireless LAN Medium Access Control (MAC) and Physical Layer (PHY) Specifications— Amendment 2: Sub 1 GHz License Exempt Operation (2016)
4. Khorov, E., Lyakhov, A., Krotov, A., Guschin, A.: A survey on IEEE 802.11ah: an enabling networking technology for smart cities. Comput. Commun. **58**, 53–69 (2015)
5. Qiao, L., Zheng, Z., Cui, W., Wang, L.: A survey on Wi-Fi HaLow technology for Internet of Things. In: Proceeding of 2018 2nd IEEE Conference on Energy Internet and Energy System Integration (EI2), pp. 1–59 (2018)
6. Tian, L., Deronne, S., Latré, S., Famaey, J.: Implementation and validation of an IEEE 802.11ah module for ns-3. In: Proceedings of the Workshop on ns-3, pp. 49–56 (2016)
7. Tian, L., Famaey, J., Latré, S.: Evaluation of the IEEE 802.11ah restricted access window mechanism for dense IoT networks. In: Proceeding of 2016 IEEE 17th International Symposium on a World of Wireless, Mobile and Multimedia Networks (WoWMoM), pp. 1–9 (2016)

8. Seo, J.O., Nam, C., Yoon, S.G., Bahk, S.: Group-based contention in IEEE 802.11ah networks. In: Proceeding of 2014 International Conference on Information and Communication Technology Convergence (ICTC), pp. 709–710 (2014)
9. Bel, A., Adame, T., Bellalta, B., Barcelo, J., Gonzalez, J., Oliver, M.: CAS-based channel access protocol for IEEE 802.11ah WLANs. In: European Wireless 2014; Proceeding of 20th European Wireless Conference, pp. 1–6 (2014)
10. Ahmed, N., Hussain, M.I.: Relay-based IEEE 802.11ah network: a smart city solution. In: 2016 Cloudification of the Internet of Things (CIoT), pp. 1–6 (2016)
11. Ahmed, N., De, D., Hussain, M.I.: A QoS-aware MAC protocol for IEEE 802.11ah-based Internet of Things. In: Proceeding of 2018 Fifteenth International Conference on Wireless and Optical Communications Networks (WOCN), pp. 1–5 (2018)

Accurate and Lightweight Range-Free Localization for Wireless Sensor Networks

Flavio Frattini[1]([⊠]), Marcello Cinque[2], and Christian Esposito[2]

[1] Research and Innovation for Security Laboratory, Naples, Italy
flavio.frattini@rislab.it
[2] Department of Electrical Engineering and Information Technology,
University of Naples Federico II, Naples, Italy
macinque@unina.it, christian.esposito@unina.it

Abstract. Wireless sensor networks demands proper means in order to obtain an accurate location of their nodes for a twofold reason: on the one hand, the exchanged data must be spatially meaningful since their content may be unusual if the location of where they have been produced is not associated to them, on the other hand, such networks need efficient routing algorithms where optimal routing decisions must be based on location information. Accuracy is not the only demands for positioning of sensors, but also simplicity and infrastructure independence in order to avoid excessive energy consumption and deployment costs. For these reasons, GPS is not used but the RF technologies are mainly preferred. Based on those technologies, most of the solutions tailored for sensors are designed so as to determine a location based on simple measurements of the signal intensity of the received messages. Despite being able to satisfy the peculiar requirements for localization in sensor networks, those methods have been proved to be particularly inaccurate, due to the unreliability of the adopted measurements upon which location is inferred. This article proposes a novel approach for range-free localization by obtaining intensity measurements at different Power of Transmission levels, using them as inputs for multiple location estimators, and aggregating the outputs of those estimators in order to achieve a more accurate determination of a sensor position. We have implemented our solution on real sensor platforms and performed some experiments in order to show how this simple solution allows halving the localization error and reducing the energy consumption of about 18% with respect to the state-of-the-art algorithms.

1 Introduction

A wireless sensor network consists of a massive number of interconnected low-cost, low-power and multi-functional tiny sensors that are capable of communicating in short distances. WSNs are facing an increasing interest in several application scenarios, such as environment monitoring, military surveillance, disaster recovery, home automation or user tracking (e.g., in a hospital). These application scenarios are characterized by the need of localizing sensors so as to

© Springer Nature Switzerland AG 2019
C. Esposito et al. (Eds.): I-SPAN 2019, CCIS 1080, pp. 256–272, 2019.
https://doi.org/10.1007/978-3-030-30143-9_20

exchange geographically meaningful data. Let us consider the case of a WSN used for environmental monitoring, e.g., controlling the occurrence of fire within a forest. The mere information of the presence of fire is not useful if it is not correlated with the information on where such fire is present. This is made by attaching to the exchanged messages the location of the sender, e.g., the sensor that detected the fire. Moreover, the location information of sensors can be used in certain routing algorithms relying on a geographic approach to perform proper optimizations [1]: such algorithms consider position information to forward the data towards certain regions rather than the whole network so as to lower the generated network load.

A localization algorithms can be effective within the context of WSN if it satisfied two key design requirements: the battery use (which should be keep as low as possible in order to extend the availability of the sensors) and the use of extra hardware, dedicated to positioning purposes (which should be avoided so to keep low the costs to deploy a WSN). The solutions able to jointly verify such requirements are the ones proposed in the literature that are based on the Received Signal Strength Indicator (RSSI), since all the available wireless communication technologies allows to measure the intensity of the received RF signals [19]. The RSSI values depend on the output gain of the signal emitters and the distance between emitter and receiver, therefore it is possible to use them for location estimation by means of multilateral triangulation. In particular, Ring Overlapping based on Comparison of RSSI (ROCRSSI) [3] is a simple positioning method based on RSSI for WSNs, which computes the device location by comparing the RSSI values obtained from the messages exchanged between the node to be localized (unknown node) and a set of nodes with known location (anchor or beacon nodes).

Despite satisfying all the requirements imposed by WSN on the adopted positioning method, RSSI-based solutions are not optimal due to their poor accuracy. In fact, the degradation of the intensity of a RF signal does not depend on the distance covered by the signal from its emitter, but also on attenuation caused by traversed obstacles, multi-path fading, environment electromagnetic pollution and shadowing phenomena [11], which represent a noise for the input of the localization method and cause the location error to increase. We have empirically investigated such a problem by implementing the mentioned solution on real sensor platforms and conducting some experiments, which have highlighted a mean error of about 40% in indoor environments, with four anchors in a medium size workspace, which is unsuitable according to the requirements of typical sensing applications in those environments. Moreover, not all the parameters of such algorithms are controllable, so it is possible to adjust the controllable parameters until a certain accuracy is reached, but beyond this it is not possible to have further improvements by only playing with the controllable parameters. To achieve a better accuracy, a winning solution can be to adopt a multi-modal localization, i.e., the position is estimated by combining the outputs from several location estimators working on different inputs but applying the same localization approach, or fusing the outputs from multiple localization solutions working on the same inputs. However, having multiple localization solutions and/or obtaining multiple different inputs may imply the need of equipping the sensors with some extra hardware, which is strongly discouraged in WSN to not increase costs.

In this paper, we propose a novel localization algorithm named *Power-Based ROCRSSI* (PB-ROCRSSI), which combines several RSSI estimations at different Power of Transmission (PoT) levels of beacon nodes. The intuition is to use different PoT levels to achieve a progressive finer-grained partitioning of the workspace. This allows correcting the location estimation and reducing the energy consumption as well. PB-ROCRSSI has been already described in our previous work [5]. The present work extends the previous contribution with a more detailed comparison of them in terms of accuracy, battery exhaustion, and localization time. We have implemented some prototypes of the described algorithms and conducted experiments on real sensor devices, which demonstrated that the proposed solution, although adopting RSSI as the main metric, is able to reduce by about 50% the localization error to a value of about 20%, with four beacons and to reduce the energy consumption of about 18%.

2   Range-Free Localization Algorithms Based on RSSI

In this section, we describe in details the main localization algorithms that use RSSI to compute relative distances and, hence, the estimated positions of unknown nodes. RSSI-based localization algorithms exploit the trend of the RSSI depending on the geographical distance. Theoretically, the measured RSSI of the exchanged RF signals reduces as the distance of the emitter from the receiver increases. In fact, the antenna used by sensors to exchange RF signals is characterized by a *Emitter Signal Strength* (ESS), *i.e.*, the output gain of the signals radiated by the antenna of the sensor. Along their path from the emitter to the receiver, signals lowers their intensity by experiencing the so-called *Path Loss* (PL), which depends on the distance covered by the signals to reach their receiver and the number and type of the traversed obstacles and floors. The intensity of the signal at the receiver antenna, namely *Receiver Signal Strength* (RSS), is typically computed as the difference of the ESS and PL. RSSI values are different than RSS ones, since they represent an indicator, while RSS is the real intensity value. RSS values are, mostly negative, real number measured in dBm, while RSSI values are always positive real number obtained from RSS through scaling. While RSS is a precise value, RSSI is more vague since how to obtain it from RSS has not been standardized and each vendors and chipset makers implement their own solution, by offering own accuracy, granularity, and range for the RSSI values (from 0 to $RSSI\_Max$). This is the cause of the low accuracy of the methods based on RSSI and their use for coarse-grained location estimation. However, thanks to the possibility of acquiring those values in any possible sensor methods by using the API of the communication component, RSSI is a simple method to determine distances among sensors in a WSN. For instance, let us consider that a sensor A receives signals from sensor B and C, from which it computes their mean RSSI values, indicated respectively as

$RSSI_{AB}$ and $RSSI_{AC}$. It is reasonable to suppose that B is closer to A than C if and only if $RSSI_{AC} > RSSI_{AB}$. Each of the following algorithm takes advantage of this relation between sensor proximity and the measured RSSI values in its own manner to locate the unknown sensors by using the available beacons.

2.1   APIT

As previously mentioned APIT is one of the first range-free anchor-based localization algorithms based on the RSSI, where device location is computed by partitioning the workspace into triangular regions whose vertices are occupied by beacons. Considering the possible triangular regions built by using the available beacons in the workspace, it is possible to estimate the presence of an unknown node inside or outside such triangular regions and to restrict the area in which it can potentially reside within the workspace. The location estimation is performed by exploiting the known location of beacons, RSSI values among them, and RSSI measures between the unknown sensor and the beacons. The APIT states: *If no neighbor of an unknown node M is further from/closer to all three beacon nodes vertices of a triangle A, B and C simultaneously, M assumes that it is inside the triangle ABC. Otherwise, M assumes it resides outside this triangle* [18].

The algorithm underlying APIT, described in [18], behaves as follows. Each unknown node has a number of beacon nodes close enough to establish a communication channel, *near-by beacons*. The required input parameters are the RSSI between the unknown node and the near-by beacons ($BeaUnkRSSI$), the RSSI values for each couple of beacons ($BeaRSSI$), and the position of each beacon ($BeaPosition$), which is also used in order to obtain the distances among beacons. Actually, $BeaRSSI$ and $BeaUknRSSI$ are matrices that have to be filled during the first phase of the algorithm, when it is configured. Such a phase consists in the exchange of messages among the beacon nodes so as to evaluate the RSSI among them. RSSI vales between the unknown node and each of the three beacon nodes of a triangular region in which the workspace is partitioned are used to perform the APIT, i.e., to estimate if it is inside the given triangular region. Such an estimation is repeated as many times as the overall number of triangular regions available in the workspace ($\binom{N}{3}$ if there are N near-by beacon nodes) or until the required accuracy has been achieved. The algorithm determine the intersection of all the identified triangles, whose center of gravity is returned as the location of the unknown node.

2.2   Grid Scan Algorithm

In [18], it is also introduced a Grid Scan Algorithm that simplifies the computation of the intersection areas and discretizes the set of possible positions in which an unknown sensor can be located. Such an algorithm considers a WSN as deployed on a grid considered as a Cartesian coordinate plane. Each node of the network is assumed to be positioned in the center of a cell. A counter is

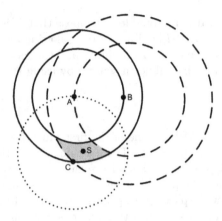

Fig. 1. Localization using ROCRSSI.

associated to each cell. Its value is updated at every iteration of the localization algorithm. In the case of APIT algorithm, when the APIT determines the node is inside a particular region, the counters of the cells in such a triangular region are incremented. On the contrary, when the APIT determines the node is outside a region, the counters of the corresponding cells are decremented. Once all computations are done (i.e., when the termination condition of algorithm is satisfied), the intersection area is identified as the set I of cells whose counter is the maximum. The coordinates (x, y) of the center of gravity of the intersection area can be simply computed as follows:

$$x = \frac{1}{n} \sum_{i=1}^{n} x_i \quad y = \frac{1}{n} \sum_{i=1}^{n} y_i \tag{1}$$

where x_i and y_i are the coordinates of a generic cell in the set I, and n is the cardinality of I.

All the algorithms discussed in the following use the Grid Scan to simplify the computation of the unknown node location.

2.3 ROCRSSI

ROCRSSI is another range-free, RSSI-based localization algorithm proposed in [3] to improve accuracy and reduce the communication overhead with respect to the APIT algorithm. The algorithm can be explained with the example shown in Fig. 1. A, B and C are three beacon nodes, while S is an unknown node. Let us indicate with $d_{A,B}$, $d_{B,C}$ and with $d_{A,C}$, the distances between the sensors indicated in the eq:eq3. To estimate the RSSI for each couple of nodes, sensors exchange messages among themselves so as to estimate the mean RSSI vales for the exchanged signals. Then, let us consider that the following inequalities are verified:

$$RSSI_{AC} < RSSI_{SA} < RSSI_{AB}, \quad RSSI_{BC} < RSSI_{SB} < RSSI_{AB}, \\ RSSI_{AC} < RSSI_{SC} \tag{2}$$

We can suppose that S is in the annulus centered at A and bounded by two concentric circles, whose respective radiuses are $d_{A,B}$ and $d_{A,C}$ (drawn with unbroken line in Fig. 1). Similarly, Eq. 2 suggests that the unknown node S is within the annulus whose center is placed at B, with radiuses equal to $d_{A,B}$ and $d_{A,B}$ (drawn with a dashed line in the figure). Finally, S may be localized in a circle centered at C and with $d_{A,B}$ as radius (drawn with dotted line in the figure). The estimated location of the unknown node S is the center of gravity of the intersection area of the identified rings and the circle.

The algorithm underlying ROCRSSI is very similar to the one of APIT and with same inputs, i.e., the *BeaRSSI* and *BeaUknRSSI* matrices determined at the first phase of the algorithm. For each beacon node A to be farer to the unknown node S, the algorithm compares the RSSI value between S and A with the RSSI values between A and other beacon nodes close to S. S_{A1} contains all the beacons whose distance from A is estimated to be less than the distance from A to S. S_{A2}, instead, contains the beacons that are considered to be more far from A than how A is far from S. As a consequence, S is estimated to be in the circle with outer radius the distance from A of the node in S_{A2} with the largest RSSI towards A, and outer radius the distance from A of the node in S_{A1} with the smallest RSSI towards A. This is repeated for all the beacons reachable by S. In such a way an intersection of rings, and possibly circles (if S_{A1} is empty), is achieved. The center of gravity of such an intersection is the estimated position of the unknown node.

2.4   ROCRSSI+

The ROCRSSI algorithm assumes unknown nodes being located in the areas delimited by beacon nodes, as illustrated in Fig. 1. This does not always occur, as in the case shown in Fig. 2, where A, B, and C are beacon nodes and S is an unknown node, and we have inequalities like the following one:

$$RSSI_{AC} > RSSI_{SC} \tag{3}$$

which are not considered by the ROCRSSI algorithm. If the ROCRSSI is applied to this case, the estimated location will be affected by a considerable localization error. Let us considering the example in Fig. 2, ROCRSSI will assign to S the position of sensor C. In fact, information obtained by sensors whose range does not contain sensor S, such as A and B, are not considered during the location estimation.

The ROCRSSI+ algorithm [15] removes the above-mentioned assumption of unknown nodes being surrounded by beacon nodes, and considers also the RSSI values assigned to sensors whose range does not contain the unknown sensor. Specifically, ROCRSSI+ computes the center of gravity of the intersection among rings and circles of sensors whose range contains the node S, and the areas outside the range of nodes whose range does not contain S. With such a correction, in the above-mentioned example, the location estimated by ROCRSSI+ for the sensor S is the center of gravity, indicated as S', that is closer to the real location of the sensor S than the position of sensor C.

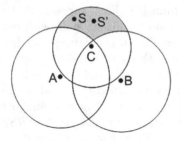

Fig. 2. A, B, and C are beacon nodes; S is an unknown node, not surrounded by beacon nodes.

Indeed, the ROCRSSI+ algorithm tries to locate a node also if the set S_{A2} is empty, namely if the unknown node is estimated to be outside a circle.

2.5 ROCRSSI++

In our previous work presented in [9], we have shown that ROCRSSI and ROCRSSI+ have some problems:

– *Inconsistency.* The estimated location of the unknown node depends on the order in which RSSI values are considered. When there are couples of beacon nodes with the same RSSI values but different distances, it is possible that ROCRSSI and ROCRSSI+ may return different results since the unknown node can be considered to be in a circle whose radius length depends on the order in which RSSI values are compared.
– *Variability of RSSI.* The obtainable RSSI varies over the time due to several physical phenomena, such as reflection, refraction and interferences, and changes in the electromagnetic pollution of the workspace.
– *Asymmetry of communication channels.* The communications channels between nodes are not symmetric, therefore the measured RSSI at a node diverges from the one obtained by the other nodes despite their distance does not change.
– *Storing RSSI values.* To store the RSSI values between a sensor and other neighboring nodes, each node needs a NxN matrix, where the element $a(i,j)$ represents the RSSI value estimated by i-th node along the channel to the j-th node. Similar observations can be made for distance values. In a typical WSN deployment, N may assume a high value, implying the need of storing a large amount of data.

In [9], we have proposed a novel approach, named ROCRSSI++, so as to resolve those problems, as follows. To treat the first problem, we have proposed to consider the longest distance when the same RSSI values correspond to different distances, since it is surely to be more dependent on distance and less on possible met obstacles. For the second problem, we consider a mean value for multiple RSSI values. To avoid that different RSSI values are assigned to the same channel, the two sensors are to agree on the RSSI value representing their distance and this is obtained by deciding on the greatest value. For the last problem we can notice that we consider the channels as being symmetric (or made like it for construction), so that element $a(i,j)$ is equal to $a(j,i)$. As a consequence, the RSSI and distance matrices are *strictly triangular*; hence, we have proposed to use *packed storage matrices*, so as to save $50 \cdot (1 + \frac{1}{N}) \cdot 100\ \%$ of memory but also to limit the amount of data to be exchanged among nodes.

ROCRSSI++ is structured in two phases. During *Phase 1*, as illustrated by the pseudocode in Algorithm ??, each node N sends and receives $RSSIMsg$ messages to evaluate the average strength of the received signal and fill $BeaRSSI$ and $BeaUknRSSI$ matrices. The OR in square brackets is due to the fact that the message sender X can be a beacon node or an unknown node. Function $BeaRSSI.set()$ is to be implemented for a $getRSSI$ function provides the strength with whom the message has been received. Once a beacon knows the RSSI from all other beacons or from the unknown node, it broadcasts its $BeaRSSI$ and $BeaUknRSSI$ matrices. On receiving such matrices a node updates the local ones in order to simulate channels symmetry and solve the consensus problem. During *Phase 2*, as illustrated by the pseudocode in Algorithm ??, by using $BeaRSSI$ and $BeaUknRSSI$ returned by the first phase, the estimated location of the unknown node is computed. To solve the inconsistency problem, the case of equal RSSI values is explicitly considered and treated as previously mentioned. Besides, ROCRSSI++ selects beacon nodes from sets S_{A1} and S_{A2} considering the elements with maximum distance. If S_{A2} is empty, d_2 is equal to 0 and the exterior of circumference with center A and radius d_1 is considered. If S_{A1} is empty and d_1 is equal to 0, or the maximum distances in S_{A1} and S_{A2} are equals, circle with center A and radius d_2 is considered. The inaccuracy of RSSI values may led to cases in which farer nodes have RSSI values greater than the ones of closer nodes. Hence, if $d_1 > d_2$ the values are swapped. The default behavior of the algorithm is to build the ring with center A, inner radius d_1, and outer radius d_2.

3   Power-Based ROCRSSI

Despite of the improvements presented in Sect. 2.5 with respect to ROCRSSI and ROCRSSI+, the location estimation provided by ROCRSSI++ still presents an error of about 18% with 6 beacons, which is about 1.5 m in a 31 square meters environment (see Sect. 4). It is possible to adopt various expedients in order to optimize the achievable precision and accuracy of a given localization algorithm; however, there is a theoretical limit beyond which it is not possible to further improve these algorithms. In fact, the Cramer-Rao bound (CRB) provides a lower bound on the variance achievable by any unbiased location estimator [12], and represents a benchmark for location estimation algorithms [13]. In the case of RSSI-based algorithms, CRB depends on the algorithm parameters that users can control and optimize [16], such as the beacons density and their placement, RSSI quantization level or network size. However, such a bound also depends on uncontrollable parameters, such as all the phenomena that imply a variability in the path loss experienced by the signals (such as reflection, refraction and interferences). Due to this uncontrollable parameters, it is possible to tune the controllable ones (by increasing or decreasing their values) until the localization algorithm reaches a certain accuracy value, but the tuning increases the complexity of the solution and it has to be repeated periodically. For this reason, in the cases where the error has to be kept as low as possible (by going beyond the theoretical limit represented by the CRB), a commonly-accepted solution is to make use of multi-modal localization algorithms where more than one technology is adopted to estimate location. Despite its unquestionable success in improving localization accuracy, such a solution is not feasible within the context of WSN. We propose a different solution by further reducing the localization error without using extra hardware, as suggested by multi-technology localization algorithms.

Our idea is instead to exploit the possibility of using different levels of Power of Transmission (PoT), so as to have smaller RSSI ranges with lower PoT levels and to achieve a finer-grained partitioning of the workspace. The estimations obtained with the different used PoT levels can be combined so as to have a more precise sensor location determination. This does not only improves accuracy (by lowering the localization error in average), but also have positive effects on the precision (by reducing the standard deviation of the error). In fact, ROCRSSI algorithms suffer from the variability of the measured RSSI values. However, we achieved empirical evidence that when transmitting signals with reduced PoT levels, the variance of RSSI values results smaller. Figure 3a shows an example of the trend of the RSSI values at two different PoT levels measured on an Iris Mote sensors by Crossbow [6]. For such sensors, $PoT = 0$ indicates the highest power of transmission; $PoT = 15$ indicates the lowest power of transmission. It is possible to observe that the RSSI estimation with $PoT = 0$ exhibits less fluctuations than the one achieved with $PoT = 15$. In general, we observed that when using a reduced power of transmission, RSSI values are more stable and can be considered more reliable. As a consequence, the localization is more precise, as confirmed in Sect. 4. Localization achieved with a reduced power of transmission only uses closest beacon nodes, which have shown to be more indicative of the actual location of the unknown node. However, when decreasing the used PoT level, the number of reachable nodes decreases as well, as clearly illustrated in Fig. 3b in this case an Iris Mote sensors are used. As expected, when the PoT is equal to 0, RSSI assumes its maximum value. Instead, when the PoT is equal to 15 RSSI assumes its minimum value. In such a case, the unknown node is within the reachability area of less than 3 beacons, then its position can not be determined.

Based on this rationale, we have defined a novel algorithm, *Power-Based ROCRSSI* (PB-ROCRSSI), presented in Algorithm ??, which executes

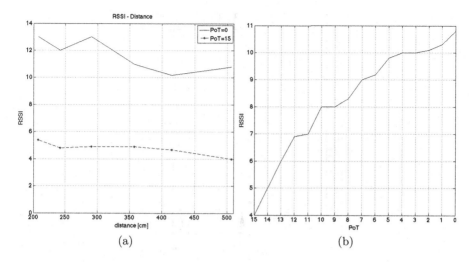

Fig. 3. RSSI trend between two Iris Mote sensors (a) when varying the distance at different PoT levels, and (b) when 5 meters apart and incrementing the power of the transmitted signal.

ROCRSSI++ by varying the applied PoT level thrice, whose values are indicated as *low*, *medium*, and *high*, and in combining the three estimated locations so as to compute the position of the unknown node. The combination of the estimated positions is made by computing the center of gravity of the triangle whose vertexes are the three estimated positions. This algorithm does not require additional hardware, since, as for RSSI estimation, changing the PoT is allowed by almost all radio boards (see, for instance [2]).

As an example, consider the case shown in Fig. 4. Six beacon nodes, namely 1, 2, 3, 4, 5, and 6, are placed in the cells $(2; 2)$, $(9; 2)$, $(2; 7)$, $(9; 7)$, $(2; 12)$, $(9; 12)$, respectively, of a Cartesian coordinate system; sensor 7 is an unknown node placed in the cell $(5; 12)$. When using ROCRSSI++ with signals transmitted with the minimum power of transmission (PoT_{low}), the unknown sensor 7 is estimated to be located in point L, with coordinates $(4.50; 10.50)$; localization error is equals to 70.70 cm. When running the same algorithm with signals transmitted with the maximum power (PoT_{high}), the unknown node is estimated to be located in the point H $(0.67; 12.83)$, obtaining an error equal to 197.14 cm. Finally, the localization estimated when executing the algorithm with signals transmitted with a medium power of transmission (in the specific case $PoT_{medium} = 7$), the unknown node is estimated to be located in the point M in Fig. 4 with coordinates equal to $(9.29; 13.43)$, obtaining an error equals to 202.20 cm. The point P represents the centre of gravity of the triangle LMH and is returned as the estimated location, causing an error of 1.73%, which corresponds to 12.75 cm in absolute.

While the choice of the high and of the medium PoT levels are rather easy (for the former, the maximum PoT level provided by the radio chip can be used;

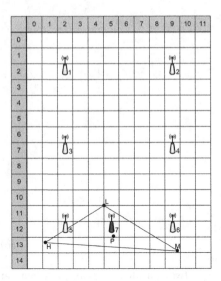

Fig. 4. A rectangular environment with six beacon nodes $(1-6)$ and an unknown node (7). To simplify the localization, the environment is organized like the first quadrant of a Cartesian coordinate system.

for the latter, the average between the high and the low can be used), the choice of the low PoT level is critical. In fact, using the lowest PoT level provided by the radio board may imply that no beacon, or few of them, can be reached and the localization can not be performed. On the contrary, using as low PoT level a too high value implies to loose the advantages of the proposed algorithm. Hence, a tuning of this parameter has to be performed based on the considered environment.

In some cases, the workspace of the algorithm can be accessed (e.g., in the case of patient monitoring in hospitals); hence, it is possible to test various values of the PoT in order to decide which one is to be used. If the environment can not be accessed (e.g., in the case of blazes or landslides when environment monitoring is conducted), beacon nodes can evaluate the minimum PoT level to be used. To this aim, a node may use dummy messages sent with PoT levels, namely p, equal to the lowest power of transmission and test how many nodes are reachable. If at least three nodes are reachable, p can be used as PoT_{low}; otherwise, p is incremented by 1 and the test is repeated. All the nodes have to agree on the same value by executing a distributed agreement protocol.

Another parameter to be tuned is the number of messages necessary to compute the RSSI values. Since the execution of the PB-ROCRSSI algorithm requires the ROCRSSI++ algorithm to be executed three times, we decided to make only one third of the RSSI measures required by a typical run of ROCRSSI++ per each given PoT level. In such a way, we avoid to increase the cost of the algorithm in terms of the number of exchanged messages. As a consequence, PB-ROCRSSI does not introduce extra costs and it allows to reduce the power consumption (which is lower when low PoT levels are used) and the time required for the localization (see next section).

4   Comparison of the Algorithms

Hence, just the localization error is not enough to evaluate the overall quality of such algorithms.

To compare the described algorithms in terms of localization error, we have implemented several prototypes and conducted on-field experiments on real sensors in an indoor environment. The used sensors consists in the Iris Motes by Crossbow Technology equipped with a ZigBee RF Transceiver and TinyOS 2.0 operating system [6]. We have also used other devices and software provided by the same manufacturer, such as MIB520 programming board to flash the ROM of the sensors, a Base Station and a software, XSniffer, to capture all the radio traffic on a specified ZigBee channel. Sniffed traffic helped to control messages and information exchanged among sensors in order to verify the correctness of the implementation and execution of the algorithms, whereas the latter ones also perform the computation of the estimated position.

The rectangular environment where experiments have been performed is a computer laboratory that is 497 cm long and 622 cm wide with a consequent area of about 31 square meters. Such a test area is free of physical obstacles, and the beacon nodes have been deployed as shown in Fig. 4. In our experiments we have varies the location of the unknown node (for a total of 20 different locations within the laboratory) and repeated each test 10 times.

In each experiment, we have computed the absolute error as the distance of the real position from the estimated one, and compared it with respect to the maximum distance detectable in the environment (i.e., the diagonal of the rectangular experimental environment), so as to obtain the percentage error. Considering that the diagonal of our test area is 796.17 cm, if we obtain an absolute error of 238.77 cm, the percentage error is equal to $\frac{238.77\,cm}{796.17\,cm} \cdot 100 = 29.99\%$. Preliminary tests on the environments allowed us to tune the values for the high, medium and low PoT levels as 0, 7, and 11, respectively.

4.1   Localization Error

Table 1 shows the results of the experimental campaign. It contains the estimated average error of the localization (both in centimeters and in percentage) and the standard deviation of the percentage errors when varying the number of beacons from 3 to 6.

Results show that PB-ROCRSSI outperforms the other algorithms when using at least 4 beacons and, in particular, the error is halved with 5 and 6 beacon nodes with respect to APIT, ROCRSSI and ROCRSSI+, and significanty improved with respect to ROCRSSI++. It is also worth noting that results of APIT when using 3 beacon nodes are meaningless. Indeed with three beacon

Table 1. Comparison of the localization error of the described algorithms.

# beacons			APIT	ROCRSSI	ROCRSSI+	ROCRSSI++	PB-ROCRSSI
3	error	cm	238.77	349.60	260.90	269.26	269.42
		%	29.99	43.91	32.77	33.82	33.84
	st.dev		0	35.97	8.99	7.54	7.68
4	error	cm	244.26	342.91	337.89	204.14	153.98
		%	30.68	43.07	42.44	25.64	19.34
	st.dev		7.50	28.16	11.11	8.34	11.81
5	error	cm	241.48	269.42	298.09	207.00	125.24
		%	30.33	33.84	37.44	26.00	15.73
	st.dev		10.34	19.53	23.03	6.60	12.07
6	error	cm	248.96	262.90	245.38	145.38	126.83
		%	31.27	33.02	30.82	18.26	15.93
	st.dev		10.64	21.11	21.75	11.60	10.99

nodes, the point in triangulation test can be performed with just one combination of nodes (considering one triangle with the three beacons as vertices), the estimated location is the center of gravity of such a triangle, and each run of the same experiment returns the same result. As a consequence, the standard deviation is null. The variance of the PB-ROCRSSI algorithm is similar to the one achieved with the APIT algorithm, but in the former case the error is lower.

Finally, the last column in the Table 1 shows that the localization error is reduced when augmenting the number of beacon nodes, so as to demonstrate that the achievable localization accuracy is a function of the amount of beacons deployed within the workspace. In fact, having more beacons allows to APIT to identifying more triangles, while to ROCRSSI to have more rings and circles so that the intersection area for both algorithms result smaller. However, the curve error-number of beacons has an asymptotic behavior. In our experimental settings, after using 5 beacon nodes there is no improvement of the localization. This means that the RSSI/Range-based algorithms have an intrinsic error that also depends on the environment and can not be overcame increasing the number of beacon nodes in the network. Furthermore, when increasing the number of beacon nodes, also the number of messages to be exchanged among nodes increases, with a resultant increase of battery consumption and time to localize (for further details see Sect. 4.2). Hence, there is a trade-off among localization error, battery consumption and time to localize.

4.2   Energy Consumption

Because of the reduced dimensions of the used devices, which prohibit using large batteries, and the difficulty in accessing them in several applications, it is important that localization algorithms have reduced energy consumption. We can assume the consumption being mainly affected by the number of sent and received messages (*I/O bound*). Indeed, the consumption due to information processing (*CPU bound*) is negligible if compared to the one induced by the radio chip [17]. For the implementations of APIT, ROCRSSI, ROCRSSI+, and ROCRSSI++, 15 messages are used to evaluate an average value for the RSSI, in order to face signal fluctuation issues, as stated in [9]. In the case of ROCRAP, instead, 5 messages are used to evaluate RSSI values for each of the three PoT levels.

The energy estimate is optimistic especially for state-of-art algorithms, such as APIT and ROCRSSI, since we do not consider the fragmentation of messages (more probable in ROCRSSI and ROCRSSI+ than in the proposed algorithm, since they do not use packed storage matrixes) and collisions (more probable when transmitting with the maximum power [10]).

Let m be the number of exchanged messages to evaluate RSSI, n the number of beacon nodes in the network, B a generic beacon node, and consider the case of a single unknown node X that is to be localized. Power consumption is different for beacon and unknown nodes.

Assuming $m = 15$ and $n = 6$, as in our experiments, the number of transmitted byes is 591 in the case of APIT, ROCRSSI, and ROCRSSI+, and 570 for ROCRSSI++ and PB-ROCRSSI. The number of received bytes is 547 for all the algorithms. Taking values from [14] we assume $T_{tx} = T_{rx} = 416 \times 10^{-6}$ s. For the voltage, instead, we assume $V = 3$ V. Current consumption is from [2]. $A_{tx} = 16.5$ mA at the maximum PoT. Considering for the PB-ROCRSSI algorithm the three levels 0, 7, and 11 for the PoT (+3.0 dBm, −1.2 dBm, and −5.2 dBm, respectively), $A_{tx_{PoT1}} = A_{tx} = 16.5$ mA, $A_{tx_{PoT2}} = 13.0$ mA, and $A_{tx_{PoT3}} = 11.5$ mA. The current supplied in the receive state is $A_{rx} = 15.5$ mA. We have indicated in Table 2 the energy consumption for all the presented algorithms.

4.3 Time for Localization

Another important characteristic of localization algorithms is the time required for the identification of the location of the unknown nodes. As seen in Sect. 1, WSNs are often used for patient monitoring in hospitals or in the case of fires or landslides. In such cases, localization is to be performed quickly to allow a timely intervention.

We define the *time for localization* (T_{loc}) of a localization algorithm as the time required by the algorithm for the localization of an unknown node in a network that has just been initialized.

The time required by CPU for data processing is negligible (tens of milliseconds). In fact, in our experiments we noticed that after receiving data from beacon nodes, the unknown node was able to communicate its estimated position in a very short time. As a consequence, the time required for the localization of an unknown node mainly depends on the time required for the message exchange for evaluating RSSI values and for communicating such values as well as the positions of beacon nodes. In turn, the time for transmitting or receiving a message depends on its length in number of bytes. We consider the time for transmitting a byte (T_{tx}) and the one for receiving a byte (T_{rx}) being the same and equals to 416×10^{-6} s (see also Sect. 4.2). Another factor influencing the time for localization is the time between the transmission of consecutive messages. For instance, when sending $RSSIMsgs$, after a message has been sent, a beacon nodes has to wait for a certain time before sending another message. The lasting of such a time interval may depend on design choices as well as on hardware characteristics. We denote it with T_{bm}.

Previously, we showed that the number of exchanged messages is the same for all the algorithms, hence we can assume that all the algorithms have the same T_{loc}.

We consider that after the network initialization (instant t_0) all the nodes start sending and receiving messages for the localization. For instance, assuming $T_{bm} = 0.25$ s (which is allowed by most of the commercially available sensors), in the case of APIT, ROCRSSI and ROCRSSI+ $T_{loc} = 4.623136$ s, while for ROCRSSI++ and PB-ROCRSSI $T_{loc} = 4.605664$. The value of T_{bm} can be changed and adapted for exploiting the capabilities of the radio module of the sensors to significantly reduce the time necessary for localizing a node. In Table 2 a definition of the localization time is represented.

Table 2. Comparison of the described algorithms.

		APIT	ROCRSSI	ROCRSSI+	ROCRSSI++	PB-ROCRSSI
Anchor	Sent bytes	591	591	591	570	570
	Received bytes	547	547	547	547	547
	Energy Consumption (Tx) [mJ]	12.17	12.17	12.17	11.75	9.83
	Energy Consumption (Rx) [mJ]	10.58	10.58	10.58	10.58	10.58
Sensor	Sent bytes	540	540	540	540	540
	Received bytes	306	306	306	306	306
	Energy Consumption (Tx) [mJ]	11.12	11.12	11.12	11.12	9.35
	Energy Consumption (Rx) [mJ]	16.37	16.37	16.37	16.37	13.93
Localization Time [sec]		4.623136	4.623136	4.623136	4.605664	4.605664

5   Conclusions

This paper follows the current trend in the research on localization systems on obtaining better accuracy not by using dedicated technologies, but by adopting the available technologies in a smart manner. Specifically, we have demonstrated how it is possible to improve the localization accuracy of a well-known range-free algorithm, i.e., ROCRSSI, without requiring additional hardware, and without impacting on the power consumption, but by combining the algorithm executions at multiple levels of PoT. Recently, several efforts are being devoted on multi-modal localization using different technologies. Nevertheless, we believe that research should investigate more on multi-modal localization where only one localization technology can be used. It is more likely for these solutions to be adopted in practice, since they do not require extra hardware nor extra cost. This paper has proposed a possible solution in this sense, and evaluated the proposed algorithms, whose results are summarized in Tables 1 and 2. However, as stated in Sect. 3, further research efforts are needed to investigate how to tune the PoT levels that are to be used for every pair of sensors. In addition, we suppose, also thanks to preliminary simulative results, that also a lightweight cooperative approach can be used to further reduce the localization error. The idea is to exploit already localized unknown nodes (as a sort of *second-level beacons*) when computing the location estimate.

References

1. Al-Karaki, J., Kamal, A.: Routing techniques in wireless sensor networks: a survey. IEEE Wireless Commun. **11**(6), 6–28 (2004)
2. Atmel: Atmel AT86RF230 Datasheet. Retrieved in January 2010 (2009). http://www.atmel.com/Images/doc5131.pdf
3. Liu, C., Wu, K., He, T.: Sensor localization with ring overlapping based on comparison of received signal strength indicator. In: Proceedings of the IEEE International Conference on Mobile Ad-hoc and Sensor Systems, pp. 516–518 (2004)
4. Cinque, M., Cotroneo, D., Di Martino, C.: Automated generation of performance and dependability models for the assessment of wireless sensor networks. IEEE Trans. Comput. **61**(6), 870–884 (2012). http://doi.ieeecomputersociety.org/10.1109/TC.2011.96
5. Cinque, M., Esposito, C., Frattini, F.: Leveraging power of transmission for range-free localization of tiny sensors. In: Di Martino, S., Peron, A., Tezuka, T. (eds.) W2GIS 2012. LNCS, vol. 7236, pp. 239–256. Springer, Heidelberg (2012). https://doi.org/10.1007/978-3-642-29247-7_17
6. Crossbow Technology: Iris OEM Datasheet. Retrieved in January 2010 (2009). www.xbow.com/Products/Product_pdf_files/Wireless_pdf/IRIS_OEM_Datasheet.pdf
7. Gay, D., et al.: The nesC language: a holistic approach to networked embedded systems. In: Proceedings of Programming Language Design and Implementation (PLDI), pp. 1–11 (2003)
8. Esposito, C., Ficco, M.: Deployment of RSS-based indoor positioning systems. Int. J. Wireless Inf. Netw. (IJWIN) **18**(4), 224–242 (2011)
9. Frattini, F., Esposito, C., Russo, S.: ROCRSSI++: an efficient localization algorithm for wireless sensor networks. Int. J. Adapt. Resilient Auton. Syst. (IJARAS) **2**(2), 51–70 (2011)
10. Gobriel, S., Melhem, R., Mosse, D.: A unified interference/collision model for optimal mac transmission power in ad hoc networks. Int. J. Wireless Mob. Comput. **1**(3/4), 179–190 (2006). https://doi.org/10.1504/IJWMC.2006.012554
11. Gu, Y., Lo, A., Niemegeers, I.: A survey of indoor positioning systems for wireless personal networks. IEEE Commun. Surv. Tutorials **11**(1), 13–32 (2009)

12. VanTrees, H.L.: Detection, Estimation, and Modulation Theory, Part I. Wiley, New Jersey (1968)

13. Patwari, N., Ash, J.N., Kyperountas, S., Hero III, A.O., Moses, R.L., Correal, N.S.: Locating the nodes, cooperative localization in wireless sensor networks. IEEE Signal Process. Mag. **22**(4), 54–69 (2005)

14. Polastre, J., Hill, J., Culler, D.: Versatile low power media access for wireless sensor networks. In: Proceedings of the 2nd International Conference on Embedded Networked Sensor Systems, pp. 95–107. SenSys 2004, ACM, New York, NY, USA (2004). https://doi.org/10.1145/1031495.1031508, http://doi.acm.org/10.1145/1031495.1031508

15. Crepaldi, R., Casari, P., Zanella, A., Zorzi, M.: Testbed implementation and refinement of a range-based localization algorithm for wireless sensor networks. In: Proceedings of the 3rd International Conference on Mobile Technology, Applications & Systems (Mobility) (2006)

16. Shi, H., Li, X., Shang, Y., Ma, D.: Cramer-Rao bound analysis of quantized RSSI based localization in wireless sensor networks. In: Proceedings of the 11th International Conference on Parallel and Distributed Systems, vol. 2, pp. 32–36 (2005)

17. Shnayder, V., Hempstead, M., Chen, B.R., Allen, G.W., Welsh, M.: Simulating the power consumption of large-scale sensor network applications. In: Proceedings of the 2nd International Conference on Embedded Networked Sensor Systems, pp. 188–200. SenSys 2004, ACM, New York, NY, USA (2004). https://doi.org/10.1145/1031495.1031518, http://doi.acm.org/10.1145/1031495.1031518

18. He, T., Huang, C., Blum, B.M., Stankovic, J.A., Abdelzaher, T.: Range-free localization schemes for large scale sensor networks. In: Proceedings of the 9th Annual International Conference on Mobile Computing and Networking (MobiCom), pp. 81–95 (2003)

19. Zhang, W., Yin, Q., Chen, H., Gao, F., Ansari, N.: Distributed angle estimation for localization in wireless sensor networks. IEEE Trans. Wireless Commun. **12**(2), 527–537 (2013). https://doi.org/10.1109/TWC.2012.121412.111346

1st International Workshop on High Performance Computing and Applications (IW-HPCA 2019)

Enhance Object Detection Capability with the Object Relation

Mei-Chen Li[1], Lokesh Sharma[1], and Shih-Lin Wu[1,2,3,4](✉)

[1] Department of AI Innovation Research Center, Chang Gung University,
Taoyuan City, Taiwan
slwu@mail.cgu.edu.tw
[2] Department of Computer Science and Information Engineering,
Chang Gung University, Taoyuan City, Taiwan
[3] Department of Cardiology, Chang Gung Memorial Hospital, Taoyuan City, Taiwan
[4] Department of Electrical Engineering, Ming Chi University of Technology,
Taipei City, Taiwan

Abstract. The technique of image recognitions is becoming more and more important to identify objects, places, and people. Currently, several deep learning methods on image recognition have been proposed. To identify multiple targets, the notion of region proposal has proposed which uses multiple resolution methods to improve accuracy, such as R-CNN, Fast R-CNN, Faster R-CNN, Mask R-CNN, SSD, and YOLO. However, these improvements are based on pixel. Still, there are uncertain objects which the human eye observes in the surrounding scene. At this time, we make guesses based on other, more clear objects. In the paper, we propose a method for object recognition using the probability of correlation between the objects. When performing object recognition in an image, we calculate the probability of correlation between the objects to adjust the related parameters and the weight values. Our proposed method improve the overall recognition of objects in the image.

Keywords: Artificial intelligence · Deep learning · Object detection · Bayes classifier · Image detection

1 Introduction

Techniques of image recognition has been developed from many years in which machine learning methods has very essential role. In the review paper [21] the contributions and results of AlexNet [11] in the 2012 ImageNet [1] image recognition competition were mentioned. And their concept accelerated the development of image recognition. With this development, the GPU is used more and more in this kind of research. This greatly enhance the computational efficiency of image recognition, that results in more researchers have started doing research in this field, the benchmark technology such as CNN [7,11,13,18,19], RCNN [3–6,14–17], as well as Semantic Segmentation [2,9,10]. In many research and

© Springer Nature Switzerland AG 2019
C. Esposito et al. (Eds.): I-SPAN 2019, CCIS 1080, pp. 275–282, 2019.
https://doi.org/10.1007/978-3-030-30143-9_21

development, most studies focuses on increasing the speed and improving the identification accuracy as the main research objectives. In order to enhance the recognition rate, most of the available methods has adjust features which is completely based on pixels.

In May 2015, Li Fei-fei in a TED talk, she explain how humans have been receiving visual information in our day today life. The human eye takes one picture in every 200 ms, which is also the average time an eye made a movement. So, in order to learn, our methods needs a huge amount of data set, and that is why they promote the production of ImageNet database. While identifying an object, sometime human eye also need to see at a glance similarly, machines also require number of images to enhance the object accuracy. In our research, we focus on the unidentified objects, we proposed a novel idea to identify the unidentified object by looking the environment objects and calculate the affinity between the number of objects in the image. In our study, by using the connection between the objects we try to identify the unidentified objects with better accuracy.

The remainder of this paper is organized as follows. Section 2 presents the related work; Sect. 3 provides an overview of our method, and in Sect. 4 we discuss the experimental environment and results. Finally, in conclusion, we summarize our method and future direction for our work.

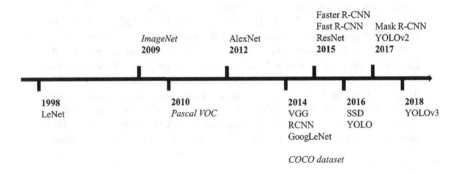

Fig. 1. Timeline of related research.

2   Related Work

In previous studies of image recognition proposed a number of methods as shown in Fig. 1. The CNN take image as an input and classify it whereas, LeNet [13] classify handwritten numeral using the MNIST dataset. Later on, AlexNet [11], VGG [18], GoogLeNet [19], ResNet [7] enhance the performance metrics. In addition to this, researchers also focused more on object detection research such as R-CNN, Fast R-CNN, Faster R-CNN and Mask R-CNN.

In R-CNN, authors has introduced the concept of Selective search (SS) [20] as Region Proposal (RP), the training of the bounding box regression, that increases the accuracy of object detection. However, R-CNN takes a lot of time and space while training and testing. Therefore they proposed Fast R-CNN and Faster R-CNN in order to improve the accuracy and speed of R-CNN. But these method still spent long time in training, and can not be used immediately in testing. Hence, some advertised detection faster multi-target detection methods has proposed classified as one Stage detection such as SSD, YOLO. Even though the overall speed has improved a lot, but still, the accuracy is less than the two Stage detection method in the beginning. In paper [14], Focal loss for dense object detection method of one Stage had a problem with unbalanced sample, so in the loss function step parameter adjustment imbalance problem would be happened.

In study [10], authors use sentences to organize an article by calculating the connection between the things in the sentences. This motivates us to implement the concept in image recognition to find the connection between the region in the images. Therefore, we use the existing method and correlation to achieve our purpose. We are using the concept of Bayes classification [8,12] to find out the correlation between the region in the images.

| (a) | (b) |

Fig. 2. Example describing the Schematic method, (a) In image chair and zebra is marked out with $BayesScore_{Thresh} = 0.2$. (b) In image we set the $BayesScore_{Thresh} = 0.8$.

3   Method

In this paper, we propose a method to improve the connection probability of a region, while considering connection between each region of an image in order to enhance the correlation and accuracy of region. To calculate the connection between each region of image we use Bayesian Classification to identify objects that are less likely to be identified, for example, objects that are uncertain or objects of special shape as shown in Fig. 2. The uncertain objects in region is less discernible or obscured, which make it more difficult to identify. A Naive Bayes classifier is a probabilistic machine learning model that is used for classification. It is used to discriminate different regions based on certain features. It assumes that the presence of a particular feature in a class is unrelated to the presence of any other feature. Among all the datasets COCO is a better choice of selection since it contains more small targets and on an average more number of targets in an image. In COCO dataset there are 80 categories. This makes us to use this dataset for experiments. In training phase, we record the association between the various categories in picture when reading the picture Ground Truth. And then we will get probability of each category appear separately in other categories appear. Whereas in testing phase, we use the probability of association obtained in the previous stage to use Bayes Classification to know the uncertain Region is in which category. In our architecture, we will use the Bayesian Classification for each image to make a score adjustment.

(a)   (b)

Fig. 3. (a) Faster R-CNN results. (b) Faster R-CNN + Bayes results.

4   Experiment and Results

We use an Ubuntu 16.04 operating system, the graphics card is GTX1080Ti, in our experiment, we use Tensorflow to implement Faster R-CNN, and choose VGG16 for neural network. In Fig. 3, we gave more weight adjustment, which obeviously show the bounding box of "table" has changed, and the "person" accuracy has increased. And in Table 1, we didn't using special weighting and it can be found in the small target AP(Average Precision) and AR (Average Recall) have a slight increase. In ours proposal, we only adjust region which has lower original score (uncertain object or Special modeling objects), and these cases most occurs in small target, so we increase at small area And we also made some adjustments to the parameters in same image and shown in Fig. 4, we will find when $BayesScore_{Thresh} = 0.4$, got more target, and result with the position of the box which is better than $BayesScore_{Thresh}$ is 0.3 and 0.2. In $BayesScore_{Thresh} = 0.5$ and 0.6 there had occurs inaccurate positioning problem. We think in this image, $BayesScore_{Thresh} = 0.4$ is best choose.

(a)   (b)   (c)

(d)   (e)   (f)

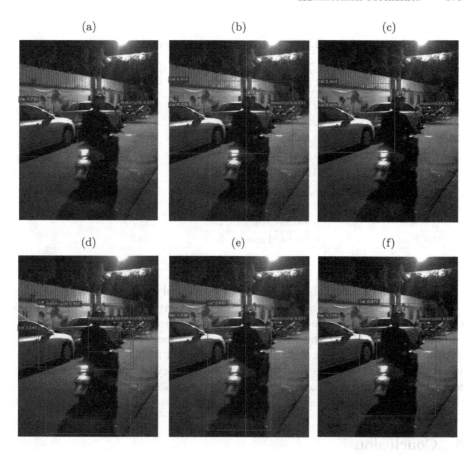

Fig. 4. Comparing the results of 6 different $BayesScore_{Thresh}$ (A) to the original results of Faster R-CNN, when other parameters are fixed in our method, the results of $BayesScore_{Thresh}$ (b) 0.6 (c) 0.5 (d) 0.4 (e) 0.3 (f) 0.2 are shown

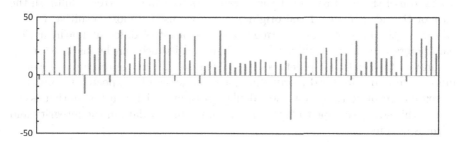

Fig. 5. The number of additional correct candidate boxes per category increases when confidence interval lie in between 0.5–0.95.

Table 1. Performance in the COCO dataset

Performance parameter	IoU	Area	Faster RCNN	Faster RCNN + Bayes
AP(%)	0.5–0.95	All	26.4	26.4
AP(%)	0.5	All	47.0	47.0
AP(%)	0.75	All	26.8	26.8
AP(%)	0.5–0.95	Small	12.4	12.6
AP(%)	0.5–0.95	Medium	30.9	30.9
AP(%)	0.5–0.95	Large	36.1	36.1
AR(%)	0.5–0.95	All	39.2	39.2
AR(%)	0.5–0.95	Small	20.0	20.1
AR(%)	0.5–0.95	Medium	45.7	45.7
AR(%)	0.5–0.95	Large	53.4	53.5

In Fig. 5 which shown the number of the additional correct candidate box can be obtained when using our method in the COCO dataset test 5000 pictures, it can be seen in the figure most of the categories have progress, only a small part of the category is reduced. And we still need to overcome the problem that COCO dataset only 80 categories, even if you can establish a correlation between the various categories, but the correlation in the category in fact is not high, and when a category is just connective only one or two categories, there are also likely to cause bad impact.

5   Conclusion

This method is based on the improvement of Faster R-CNN, the practical change is not troublesome, this method can be used in a variety of methods. Also note that in different data sets, used as a benchmark scores will be different, in the actual use of the need to adjust the parameters to achieve better results. In the part of the adjustment of the original score, we used a more intuitive way to adjust, in the part of the adjustment also has a lot of different mathematical parameters can do fine-tuning on the change. Distance can let us know more accurately the relationship between each item, so that image recognition can be more perfect, but if added more adjustment mode, can be expected to probably increase even more than now the calculation time, which will be another issue, and at this stage we hope to have a more complete test data in the integrity and fairness of come out.

References

1. Deng, J., Dong, W., Socher, R., Li, L.-J., Li, K., Fei-Fei, L.: ImageNet: a large-scale hierarchical image database. In: 2009 IEEE Conference on Computer Vision and Pattern Recognition, pp. 248–255. IEEE (2009)
2. Donahue, J., et al.: Long-term recurrent convolutional networks for visual recognition and description. In: Proceedings of the IEEE Conference on Computer Vision and Pattern Recognition, pp. 2625–2634 (2015)
3. Girshick, R.: Fast R-CNN. In: Proceedings of the IEEE International Conference on Computer Vision, pp. 1440–1448 (2015)
4. Girshick, R., Donahue, J., Darrell, T., Malik, J.: Rich feature hierarchies for accurate object detection and semantic segmentation. In: Proceedings of the IEEE Conference on Computer Vision and Pattern Recognition, pp. 580–587 (2014)
5. Girshick, R., Donahue, J., Darrell, T., Malik, J.: Region-based convolutional networks for accurate object detection and segmentation. IEEE Trans. Pattern Anal. Mach. Intell. **38**(1), 142–158 (2015)
6. He, K., Gkioxari, G., Dollár, P., Girshick, R.: Mask R-CNN. In: Proceedings of the IEEE International Conference on Computer Vision, pp. 2961–2969 (2017)
7. He, K., Zhang, X., Ren, S., Sun, J.: Deep residual learning for image recognition. In: Proceedings of the IEEE Conference on Computer Vision and Pattern Recognition, pp. 770–778 (2016)
8. John, G.H., Langley, P.: Estimating continuous distributions in Bayesian classifiers. In: Proceedings of the Eleventh Conference on Uncertainty in Artificial Intelligence, pp. 338–345. Morgan Kaufmann Publishers Inc. (1995)
9. Johnson, J., Karpathy, A., Fei-Fei, L.: DenseCap: fully convolutional localization networks for dense captioning. In: Proceedings of the IEEE Conference on Computer Vision and Pattern Recognition, pp. 4565–4574 (2016)
10. Krause, J., Johnson, J., Krishna, R., Fei-Fei, L.: A hierarchical approach for generating descriptive image paragraphs. arXiv preprint arXiv:1611.06607 (2016)
11. Krizhevsky, A., Sutskever, I., Hinton, G.E.: ImageNet classification with deep convolutional neural networks. In: Advances in Neural Information Processing Systems, pp. 1097–1105 (2012)
12. Langley, P., Iba, W., Thompson, K., et al.: An analysis of Bayesian classifiers. In: AAAI, vol. 90, pp. 223–228 (1992)
13. LeCun, Y., Bottou, L., Bengio, Y., Haffner, P., et al.: Gradient-based learning applied to document recognition. Proc. IEEE **86**(11), 2278–2324 (1998)
14. Lin, T.-Y., Goyal, P., Girshick, R., He, K., Dollár, P.: Focal loss for dense object detection. In: Proceedings of the IEEE International Conference on Computer Vision, pp. 2980–2988 (2017)
15. Liu, W., et al.: SSD: single shot multibox detector. In: Leibe, B., Matas, J., Sebe, N., Welling, M. (eds.) ECCV 2016. LNCS, vol. 9905, pp. 21–37. Springer, Cham (2016). https://doi.org/10.1007/978-3-319-46448-0_2
16. Redmon, J., Divvala, S., Girshick, R., Farhadi, A.: You only look once: unified, real-time object detection. In: Proceedings of the IEEE Conference on Computer Vision and Pattern Recognition, pp. 779–788 (2016)
17. Ren, S., He, K., Girshick, R., Sun, J.: Faster R-CNN: towards real-time object detection with region proposal networks. In: Advances in Neural Information Processing Systems, pp. 91–99 (2015)
18. Simonyan, K., Zisserman, A.: Very deep convolutional networks for large-scale image recognition. arXiv preprint arXiv:1409.1556 (2014)

19. Szegedy, C., et al.: Going deeper with convolutions. In: Proceedings of the IEEE Conference on Computer Vision and Pattern Recognition, pp. 1–9 (2015)
20. Uijlings, J.R.R., Van De Sande, K.E.A., Gevers, T., Smeulders, A.W.M.: Selective search for object recognition. Int. J. Comput. Vis. **104**(2), 154–171 (2013)
21. Wang, H., Raj, B.: On the origin of deep learning. arXiv preprint arXiv:1702.07800 (2017)

A Simple Algorithm for Oncidium Orchid Cut Flower Grading with Deep Learning

Yin Te Tsai[1(✉)], Hsing Cheng Wu[2], and Shao Ming Zhu[1]

[1] Department of Computer Science and Communication Engineering,
Providence University, Taichung, Taiwan, ROC
yttsai@pu.edu.tw, wgswgswgsl2@gmail.com
[2] Department of Computer Science and Information Engineering,
Providence University, Taichung, Taiwan, ROC
rockuassl235@gmail.com

Abstract. Utilizing emerging information technology in agriculture automation is arisen for reducing human errors and increasing the productivity and quality. This paper proposes a simple algorithm OCG with deep learning network to determine the grading levels of Oncidium orchid cut flowers which are related to the sale prices. The algorithm consists of two phases. The grading criteria about lengths are estimated by image analysis in the first phase, while the grading criteria about counting branches are predicted using deep learning in the second phase. The experimental results show that our algorithm can achieve accuracy of 0.8 and the algorithm is practical.

Keywords: Oncidium orchid cut flower grading · Branch detection · Branch counting · Deep learning

1 Introduction

Orchid flowers are widely popular in the world due to their special colors and shapes. Oncidium orchid flowers, which look like dancing girls, are largely used in western flower arrangements. Over 25 million of Oncidium orchid flowers grown in Taiwan are exported to Japan each year, and this has become a big business for Taiwan's flower farmers. The quality of a flower determines its price, and the flower will be classified into some predefined level for sale. Since the classification process is labor-intensive and easy to make mistakes of classification, an automatic classification system can reduce the required manpower and achieve high accuracy of classification.

An Oncidium orchid cut flower is shown in Fig. 1(a), where L and L_b denote the lengths of main stem and first branch respectively. A typical grading standard for Oncidium orchid cut flowers has four levels: A, B, C and D. The flowers are classified into four levels by L, L_b and the number of branches. The detailed conditions for grading levels are described in Table 1.

Agriculture automation with information technology receives much attention in many related research fields. Especially, image processing technology is widely adopted for plant image segmentation, such as plant branch segmentation and classification using vesselness measure (Mohammed Amean et al. 2013). For harvesting

© Springer Nature Switzerland AG 2019
C. Esposito et al. (Eds.): I-SPAN 2019, CCIS 1080, pp. 283–288, 2019.
https://doi.org/10.1007/978-3-030-30143-9_22

robot research, image segmentation is used to trace stem and detect rose stem branch point and cutting point location (Gürel et al. 2016a; 2016b).

Table 1. A typical grading standard for Oncidium Orchid Cut Flowers

Level	L	# of branches	L_b
A	90 cm	>7	20 cm
B	80 cm	5–6	15 cm
C	70 cm	3–4	10 cm
D	60 cm	2	10 cm

Recently, many such researches use deep leaning to improve automation accuracy. For tomato seedlings, methods combining image processing and deep learning are proposed in Yamamoto et al. (2016) to detect nodes and estimate internode lengths. The StalkNet in Baweja et al. (2018) is an efficient pipeline method with deep learning for counting plant stalk and measuring stalk width. In addition, Liu et al. (2018) proposed a pipeline method with deep learning for counting visible fruits in a sequence of images.

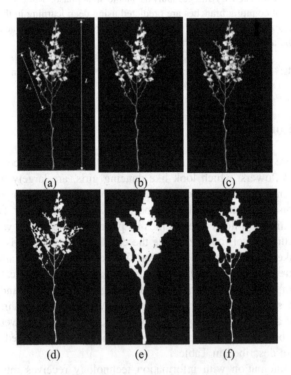

Fig. 1. (a) An Oncidium orchid cut flower. (b) The result image after applying function *GaussianBlur* to (a). (c) The result image after applying function *GreyLevel* to (b). (d) The result image after applying function *Threshold* to (c). (e) The result image after applying function *Dilate* to (d). (f) The result image after applying function *Erode* to (e).

The famous Darknet used in YOLO (Redmon et al. 2018) is a deep learning network based upon convolutional neural networks (CNN). The new YOLOv3 uses Darkent-53 with 53 convolutional layers to get better performance on image recognition than Darkent-19 in YOLOv2. In 2001, a method based upon machine vision developed in Hsi et al. (2001) has accuracy of 0.79 for Oncidium orchid cut flower grading. In this paper, we will propose a new algorithm combining image processing and deep learning to solve this problem.

This paper is organized as follows: Sect. 2 describes algorithm OCG to determine the grading levels for Oncidium orchid cut flowers. The experimental results are reported in Sect. 3 and finally concluding remarks and future research directions are provided in Sect. 4.

2 The Algorithm

This paper proposes a simple algorithm OCG with deep learning network to determine the grading levels of Oncidium orchid cut flowers. The algorithm consists of two phases. The grading criteria about lengths are estimated by image analysis in the first phase, while the grading criteria about counting branches are predicted using deep learning in the second phase.

Algorithm: LenEstimation(I, c)
Input: An image I of oncidium orchid cut flower, and a constant c for the ratio between real distance and pixel distance
Output: the length L of I and the length L_b of first branch of I

// *Finding the top position*
Search I to find the first white pixel position (x_{top}, y_{top}) from top to bottom in row order.
// *Finding the bottom position*
Search I to find the first white pixel position (x_{bottom}, y_{bottom}) from bottom to top in reverse row order.
// *Finding the first branch point*
Search I to find the position (x_{first}, y_{first}) from bottom to top in reverse row order, where pixel at (x_{first}, y_{first}) is white and the pixels at $(x_{first}-a, y_{first})$ and $(x_{first}+b, y_{first})$ are black for some integers a and b.
// *Calculating the length of stem*
$L = c \times \text{sqrt}((x_{top} - x_{bottom})^2 + (y_{top} - y_{bottom})^2)$
// *Finding the end of first branch*
Search I to find the position (x_{end}, y_{end}) along the first branch starting from position (x_{first}, y_{first}), where the pixel at (x_{end}, y_{end}) is white and the number of black neighbors of (x_{end}, y_{end}) is at least 3.
// *Calculating the length of stem*
$L_b = c \times \text{sqrt}((x_{first} - x_{end})^2 + (y_{first} - y_{end})^2)$
Return L and L_b

Fig. 2. Algorithm LenEstimation

Image preprocessing will be performed in the beginning. Let I denote an image of Oncidium orchid cut flower. The following sequence of operations on I is applied: *GaussianBlur* for smoothing, *GreyLevel* for gray leveling, *Threshold* for black & white image, *Dilate* for dilating and *Erode* for thinning. The results for such sequence of operations on the image shown in Fig. 1(a) are depicted in Figs. 1(b)–(f) respectively.

The first phase uses algorithm LenEstimation, described in Fig. 2, to estimate the length of main stem, L, and the length of first branch, L_b, respectively. Then deep learning networks Darcknet-53 is used to predict the number of branches. The complete algorithm OCG is listed in Fig. 3.

Algorithm: OCG(I, c)
Input: An image I of oncidium orchid cut flower, and a constant c for the ratio between real distance and pixel distance
Output: the grading level of I

// *Image Preprocessing*
$I_1 = GaussianBlur(I)$ // Smoothing
$I_2 = GreyLevel(I_1)$ // Gray leveling
$I_3 = Threshold(I_2)$ // Black & White
$I_4 = Dilate(I_3)$ // Dilating
$I_5 = Erode(I_4)$ // Eroding
// *Length estimation*
$(L, L_b) = LenEstimation(I_5, c)$
// *Finding the number of branches*
$R = Darknet(I_5)$
// Return grading level
If (I_5 satisfies conditions of level A) Return A
If (I_5 satisfies conditions of level B) Return B
If (I_5 satisfies conditions of level B) Return C
If (I_5 satisfies conditions of level B) Return D

Fig. 3. Algorithm OCG

3   Experimental Results

We establish a computing environment for evaluating the performance of algorithm OCG. The computing server is equipped with one Intel Xeon E5-2620v4 2.10 GHz CPU, 128 GB memory and Ubuntu 16.04 LTS sever. The server is also attached one GPU accelerator, NVIDIA Tesla P100-PCIE 16 GB HBM2, in 4.7 teraFLOPS of double-precision performance. Docker environment with docker v18.03.0-ce and nvidia-docker v2.0.3 is built and used in our experiments.

OpenCV Python programs are used in the image preprocessing stage. Since the length L_b of first branch is often ignored in field study, we don't consider L_b for grading in our experiments. Algorithm LenEstimation is implemented by Python programs and runs in 0.15 s per image on the server in average. The images of Oncidium orchid cut flower from the Seventh Production and Sales Unit at Xinshe district (Taichung, Taiwan) are used as the datasets used in the second phase.

The training dataset for parameters of Draknet-53 to count the number of branches is composed of 400 flower images (in PNG format), each grading level of 100 images, with 2254 branches in total. For network validation, the training dataset is used as the validation dataset for calibrating the network parameters. Let M_x denote the trained network model by x iterations. Table 2 shows four trained models in our experiment, where batch size is 24. It is easy to know that model M_{40000} behaves better because its detection rate is 0.89 when confidence is 60%. The testing dataset for the trained models contains 192 flower images with 913 branches in total, and the testing results are presented in Table 3. In this case, model M_{40000} also has the high accuracy of 0.8 in 0.19 s per image when confidence is 60%. In summary, for a given image of Oncidium orchid cut flower, it takes $0.15 + 0.19 = 0.34$ s to grade in our experiment environment.

Table 2. Information for network training and validation

Models	M_{2000}	M_{10000}	M_{20000}	M_{40000}
Images	400	400	400	400
Branches	2254	2254	2254	2254
Max_batch(Iterations)	2000	10000	20000	40000
Training time	44 m	6 h	15 h	18 h
Validated branches	566	1087	1165	1995
Validation rate	0.25	0.48	0.52	0.89
Validation time	20 s	21 s	20 s	22 s

Table 3. Information for network testing

Models	M_{2000}	M_{10000}	M_{20000}	M_{40000}
Images	192	192	192	192
Branches	913	913	913	913
Detected branches	371	425	477	725
Accuracy	0.41	0.47	0.52	0.80
Time	32 s	38 s	37 s	37 s

4 Conclusion

This paper gives a simple algorithm OCG with deep learning network to determine the grading levels of Oncidium orchid cut flowers. The algorithm combines image analysis and deep learning. The experimental results show that algorithm OCG can achieve accuracy of 0.8 and the algorithm is practical. One of future research directions is to improve the accuracy of counting the number of branches by better deep learning networks. However, a flower is a 3D object and an image is only a 2D object. How to efficiently grade Oncidium orchid cut flowers in real working fields is a good research direction.

Acknowledgement. This work was supported in part by Ministry of Science and Technology of Republic of China under grants MOST 107-2321-B-055-003 and 108-2321-B-055-002. We express special thanks to Chair B. H. Liao for supporting the field study and providing Oncidium orchid cut flowers. We also appreciate Yi Hsiu Tsai and Yi Yang Chen during setting up the experimental environment.

References

Baweja, H.S., Parhar, T., Mirbod, O., Nuske, S.: StalkNet: a deep learning pipeline for high-throughput measurement of plant stalk count and stalk width. In: Hutter, M., Siegwart, R. (eds.) Field and Service Robotics, pp. 271–284. Springer, Cham (2018). https://doi.org/10.1007/978-3-319-67361-5

Gürel, C., Zadeh, M.H.G., Erden, A.: Rose stem branch point detection and cutting point location for rose harvesting robot. In: The 17th International Conference on Machine Design and Production, UMTIK 2016 (2016a)

Gürel, C., Zadeh, M.H.G., Erden, A.: Development and implementation of rose stem tracing using a stereo vision camera system for rose harvesting robot. In: 8th International Conference on Image Processing, Wavelet and Applications (IWW 2016) (2016b)

Hsi, Y.-L., Lee, F.-F.: Oncidium cut flower grading with machine vision. J. Agric. Mach. **10**(1), 17–30 (2001)

Liu, X., et al.: Robust fruit counting: combining deep learning, tracking, and structure from motion. In: 2018 IEEE/RSJ International Conference on Intelligent Robots and Systems (IROS), pp. 1045–1052 (2018)

Mohammed Amean, Z., Low, T., McCarthy, C., Hancock, N.: Automatic plant branch segmentation and classification using vesselness measure. In: Proceedings of the Australasian Conference on Robotics and Automation (ACRA 2013). Australasian Robotics and Automation Association, pp. 1–9 (2013)

Redmon, J., Farhadi, A.: YOLOv3: An Incremental Improvement. arXiv (2018)

Yamamoto, K., Guo, W., Ninomiya, S.: Node detection and internode length estimation of tomato seedlings based on image analysis and machine learning. Sensors **16**(7), 1044 (2016)

Optimization of GPU Memory Usage for Training Deep Neural Networks

Che-Lun Hung[1,2(✉)], Chine-fu Hsin[1,2], Hsiao-Hsi Wang[1,2], and Chuan Yi Tang[2]

[1] Chang Gung University, Taoyuan 33302, Taiwan
clhung@mail.cgu.edu.tw, mm25712423@gmail.com
[2] Providence University, Taichung 43301, Taiwan
{hhwang, cytang}@pu.edu.tw

Abstract. Recently, Deep Neural Networks have been successfully utilized in many domains; especially in computer vision. Many famous convolutional neural networks, such as VGG, ResNet, Inception, and so forth, are used for image classification, object detection, and so forth. The architecture of these state-of-the-art neural networks has become deeper and complicated than ever. In this paper, we propose a method to solve the problem of large memory requirement in the process of training a model. The experimental result shows that the proposed algorithm is able to reduce the GPU memory significantly.

Keywords: Deep Neural Network · Convolutional Neural Networks · GPU

1 Introduction

Recently, Deep Learning algorithms (DL) have been successfully applied to many scientific domains, such as image recognition, speech recognition, and so forth. Convolutional Neural Networks (CNNs) is one of the DL algorithms for extracting complex features for image recognition. Basically, CNNs are consisting of convolution, max-pooling and fully connected layers, while the number of these layers are alternative. Currently, many complicated CNNs have been proposed to improved accuracy of image recognition on different benchmarks including MNIST, CIFAR 10 or 100, Caltech 101 or 256, ImageNet, and many more [1, 2]. Ba and Rich [3] shows that the deeper network achieves better accuracy than the wider networks. Urban et al. [4] also presents that deeper networks is able to achieve better performance compared to shallow networks with the same number of network parameters.

In General, current CNNs are consisting of multiple layers of nonlinear information processing to extract features for pattern recognition and classification. Due to deep CNNs (DCNNs) are computation-intensive, Graphic Processing Units (GPUs) were brought into the deep learning renaissance for analyzing larger data sets [5–11].

DCNNs have been proved that these networks are capacity of image classification, especially in the ImageNet Large Scale Visual Recognition Challenge (ILSVRC) 2012 [8, 12], achieved a breakthrough over past decade in ILSVRC by using a DCNN to classify approximately 1.2 million images into 1000 classes. Since then, several complicated

© Springer Nature Switzerland AG 2019
C. Esposito et al. (Eds.): I-SPAN 2019, CCIS 1080, pp. 289–293, 2019.
https://doi.org/10.1007/978-3-030-30143-9_23

DCNNs, such as VGG [10], Inception [13], ResNet [2], SENet [14], have successfully reached high accuracy in subsequent versions of the ILSVRC.

DCNN requires GPU memory to train a model, and the use of GPU memory is depended on the size of model and the size of batches. For example, to train an AlexNet model, which contains 7 layers, with batch size of 128 requires over 1 GB of GPU global memory. For the complicated DCNNs, such VGG, ResNet, and so forth, using a batch size of 128 require more than 10 GB of GPU global memory. The use of GPU memory is much smaller than the state-of-the-art DCNNs which contains about one hundred layers. Due to the limitation of GPU memory for training DCNN models, we propose an algorithm to optimize the GPU memory usage by using gradient-checkpointing. The experimental result shows that the proposed algorithm is able to reduce the GPU memory significantly.

2   Method

2.1   Gradient-Checkpointing

DCNNs requires lots of computational resources to train a model; especially huge amount of memory usage of computing the gradient of the loss by backpropagation. Gradient-checkpointing method has been proposed to calculate gradient during back-propagation to reduce memory cost by recomputing the computation graph of network by the defined model. This method is able to reduce the memory consumption to $O(sqrt(n))$ when training deep feed-forward neural networks consisting of n layers, at the cost of performing one additional forward pass [15].

Figure 1 shows the architecture of Gradient-checkpointing method. Node f denotes the forward pass of the neural network layers. During the forward pass all these nodes f are computed in order. Node b denotes the backward pass of the neural network layers. The gradient of the loss and parameters of these layers are calculated in b. During the backward pass, all these nodes b are computed in the reversed order. Generally, all f nodes have to be kept in memory after the forward pass for computing b nodes in backward pass. Hence, the requirement of memory grows linearly with the number of neural net layers n. In the forward pass, all the checkpoint nodes are kept in GPU memory. The remaining nodes are recomputed at most once in backward pass, and these nodes are kept in GPU memory until they are no longer required. However, the checkpoint nodes still occupy memory space when the DCNN is complicated.

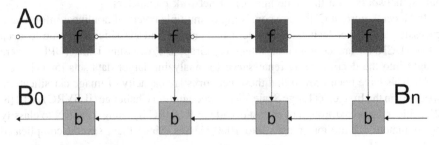

Fig. 1. The architecture of feed-forward neural network with n layers.

2.2   Gradient-Checkpointing Swap Algorithm

To reduce the memory usage of checkpoint nodes, a solution is to move all checkpoint nodes to main memory and release the GPU memory occupied by checkpoint nodes. The strategy used in the proposed algorithm is swapping. Figure 2 shows the process of swapping. According to the Gradient-checkpointing method, the checkpoint is used in backward pass to update the gradient and all network parameters. The proposed algorithm moves the checkpoint to GPU memory corresponding to the current nodes computed.

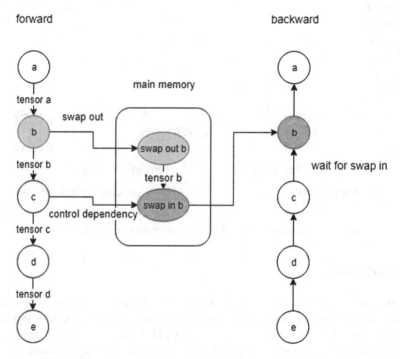

Fig. 2. The strategy of swapping computing nodes in Tensorflow.

3   Experiment

Our implementations are written in Tensorflow 1.11. The experiments were carried out on a computer with operating system Ubuntu 16.04.5- x86_64 with kernel version 4.4.0-131-generic, running on two Intel CPU i7-6850K with 6 processors clocking at 3.6 GHz and 128 GBytes RDIMM main memory. In the meanwhile, a NVIDIA GeForce 1080 11 GB GPUs cooperate to accelerate the experiments. The data set, which is RGB format, is created by using NumPy. To evaluate the proposed algorithm, the batch size is 32. The CNNs used in this experiment are ResNet series.

Figure 3 shows that the proposed algorithm uses the memory. Obviously, the memory usage of the original ResNet grows linearly with the number of neural net layers n. For ResNet-152, the size of the memory usage reaches 7000 Mbytes; ResNet-200 is unable to execute because of leak of memory. ResNet-200 with the proposed algorithm can reduce over 200 Mbytes memory usage than original ResNet-200 with Gradient-checkpointing method.

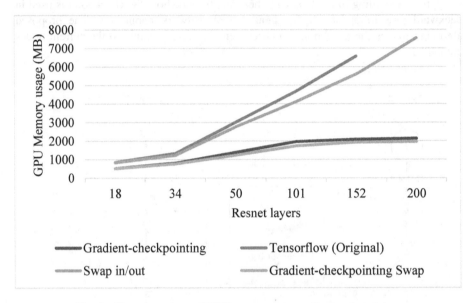

Fig. 3. The comparison of GPU memory usage of network training.

4 Conclusion

Recently, more and more complicated DCNNs have been proposed for image understanding. All of these DCNNs include multiple layers and optimization methods, but most of them are computation-intensive. The GPU device are used to improve the computation performance of these DCNNs. However, the memory limitation of GPU device is the bottleneck of DCNNs. The proposed algorithm is able to significantly reduce memory usage over original network and original network with Gradient-checkpointing method during training model. In the future, the proposed algorithm will be implemented with other famous DCNNs to overcome the limitation of GPU memory.

Acknowledgement. This research was partially supported by the Ministry of Science and Technology under the grants MOST 106-2221-E-126-001-MY2, MOST 108-2221-E-182-031-MY3 and MOST 108-2218-E-126-003.

References

1. Krizhevsky, A., Ilya, S., Hinton, G.E.: ImageNet classification with deep convolutional neural networks. In: Advances in Neural Information Processing Systems, pp. 1097–1105 (2012)
2. He, K., Zhang, X., Ren, S., Sun, J.: Deep residual learning for image recognition. arXiv: 1512.03385 (2015)
3. Ba, J., Rich, C.: Do deep nets really need to be deep? In: Advances in Neural Information Processing Systems (2014)
4. Urban, G., et al.: Do Deep Convolutional Nets Really Need to be Deep and Convolutional? arXiv:1603.05691 (2016)
5. Hinton, G.E., Osindero, S., Teh, Y.: A fast learning algorithm for deep belief nets. Neural Comput. 18(7), 1527–1554 (2006)
6. Hinton, G.E., Salakhutdinov, R.R.: Reducing the dimensionality of data with neural networks. Science 313(5786), 504–507 (2006)
7. Bengio, Y., Lamblin, P., Popovici, D., Larochelle, H.: Greedy layer-wise training of deep networks. In: Platt, J.C., Koller, D., Singer, Y., Roweis, S.T. (eds.) Advances in Neural Information Processing Systems, vol. 19, pp. 2814–2822 (2006)
8. Krizhevsky, A., Sutskever, I., Hinton, G.E.: ImageNet classification with deep convolutional neural networks. In: Pereira, F., Burges, C.J.C., Bottou, L., Weinberger, K.Q. (eds.) Advances in Neural Information Processing Systems, vol. 25, pp. 1097–1105 (2012)
9. Deng, L., Yu, D.: Deep learning: methods and applications. Found. Trends Signal Process. 7(3–4), 197–387 (2014)
10. Simonyan, K., Zisserman, A.: Very deep convolutional networks for large-scale image recognition. arXiv:1409.1556 (2014)
11. Zeiler, M.D., Fergus, R.: Visualizing and understanding convolutional networks. In: Fleet, D., Pajdla, T., Schiele, B., Tuytelaars, T. (eds.) ECCV 2014, Part I. LNCS, vol. 8689, pp. 818–833. Springer, Cham (2014). https://doi.org/10.1007/978-3-319-10590-1_53
12. Russakovsky, O., et al.: ImageNet large scale visual recognition challenge. Int. J. Comput. Vis. 115(3), 211–252 (2015)
13. Szegedy, C., et al.: Going Deeper with Convolutions. arXiv:1409.4842 (2014)
14. Hu, J., Shen, L., Albanie, S., Sun, G., Wu, E.: Squeeze-and-Excitation Networks. arXiv: 1709.01507 (2017)
15. Chen, T., Xu, B., Zhang, C., Guestrin, C.: Training Deep Nets with Sublinear Memory Cost. arXiv:1604.06174 (2016)

Computing Image Intersection and Union Regions for Drosophila Neurons Based on Multi-core CPUs

Ming-Yan Guo[1], Hui-Jun Cheng[2], Chun-Yuan Lin[1,2,3(✉)],
Yen-Jen Lin[4], and Ann-Shyn Chiang[5,6,7,8,9]

[1] Department of Computer Science and Information Engineering,
Chang Gung University, Taoyuan 33302, Taiwan
cyulin@mail.cgu.edu.tw
[2] AI Innovation Research Center, Chang Gung University,
Taoyuan 33302, Taiwan
[3] Division of Rheumatology, Allergy and Immunology,
Chang Gung Memorial Hospital, Taoyuan 33302, Taiwan
[4] National Center for High-Performance Computing, Hsinchu 30076, Taiwan
[5] Brain Research Center, National Tsing Hua University,
Hsinchu 30013, Taiwan
[6] Institute of Biotechnology and Department of Life Science,
National Tsing Hua University, Hsinchu 30013, Taiwan
[7] Kavli Institute for Brain and Mind, University of California at San Diego,
La Jolla, San Diego, CA, USA
[8] Department of Biomedical Science and Environmental Biology,
Kaohsiung Medical University, Kaohsiung 80708, Taiwan
[9] Genomics Research Center, Academia Sinica, Nankang, Taipei 11529, Taiwan

Abstract. With more and more Drosophila Driver and Neuron images, it is an important work to find the similarity relationships among them as the functional inference. There is a general problem that how to find a Drosophila Driver image, which can cover a set of Drosophila Neuron images. In order to solve this problem, the intersection/union region for a set of Drosophila Neuron images should be computed at first, then a comparison work is used to calculate the similarities between the region and Drosophila Driver image(s). In this paper, three encoding schemes, namely Integer, Boolean, Decimal, are proposed to encode each Drosophila Driver and Neuron image as a one-dimensional structure, respectively. Then, the intersection/union region from these images can be computed by using the various operations, such as Boolean operators and lookup-table search method. Finally, the comparison work is done as the union region computation, and the similarity score can be calculated by the definition of Tanimoto coefficient. The above methods for the region computation are also implemented in the multi-core CPUs environment with the OpenMP. From the experimental results, in the encoding phase, the performance by Boolean scheme is the best than that by others; in the region computation phase, the performance by Decimal is the best when the number of images is large. The speedup ratio can achieve 13 based on 16 CPUs.

© Springer Nature Switzerland AG 2019
C. Esposito et al. (Eds.): I-SPAN 2019, CCIS 1080, pp. 294–303, 2019.
https://doi.org/10.1007/978-3-030-30143-9_24

Keywords: Drosophila Driver image · Drosophila Neuron images · Intersection/union computation · Parallel processing · OpenMP

1 Introduction

Since the quantity of neurons in the human brain is very large and complex, Drosophila is chosen as a research material. Drosophila is one kind of model organism, it only has about 130,000 brain nerve cells, which is much simpler than the human brain. However, the Drosophila brain is complex enough to show the specific behavior just like many higher animals, such as learning, memory, and sleep. In the future, we hope to predict the direction of human nerve conduction through the neurotransmission of the Drosophila brain, with this information, we will do the research and develop drugs to treat diseases caused by brain nerve conduction. Drosophila brain images can be divided into two categories: Driver and Neuron. The Drosophila Driver image can be seen as a kind of gene expression forms. For example, when people are watching things, the "watch" function (gene expression) will trigger the nearby Drosophila Neuron to make a "watch" action. These triggered Drosophila Neurons are recorded in the Drosophila Driver image. Therefore, the Drosophila Driver image in general contains several even hundreds of Drosophila Neuron images. To understand that Drosophila Driver triggers those Drosophila Neurons, we can know the difference between them through the comparisons. The main purpose and result of this paper can be explained in Fig. 1. In Fig. 1, we want to know which Drosophila Driver image influences multiple Drosophila Neuron images; there are six Drosophila Neuron images on the left side of the picture, five of which are existing Neuron (fru-F-500555, fru-F-500294, fru-F-500127, fru-F-500510, fru-F-500129). Then the union result among these five Drosophila Neuron images is obtained as the Neuron without the name shown in the lower right corner of Fig. 1. Finally, using this union result to join the database to find the Drosophila Driver image that looks the most similar to him, such as the VT-F-001280 of Fig. 1. Figure 1 also represents that the VT-F-001280 will affect these five Drosophila Neurons. Therefore, the VT-F-001280 may be a suitable target for the next study.

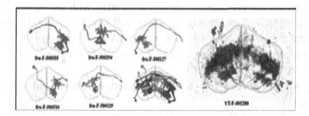

Fig. 1. Five Drosophila Neurons (images) are used to obtain the union region, and then find the most similar Drosophila Driver.

Since the intersection/union region computation needs lots of time, the work in this paper is to speed up the comparison in order to reduce the calculation time. Since the quantity of the Drosophila Neuron images is numerous and each image contains tens of millions of voxels, it is very important to speed up the comparison. For example, assume that the calculation time is 20 s (omitted the time of reading image files) for comparing ten Drosophila Neuron images in a single core CPU. There are currently about 30,000 Neurons in total, therefore, this paper uses multi-core CPUs and GPUs [1] to accelerate the computation phase.

2   Method

In this paper, the main purpose is to do the intersection/union region computation for Drosophila Driver and Neuron images. In addition to using the multi-core CPUs, we also use the GPU to do the acceleration work. The overall development process is divided into four parts: (1) constructing base-map, (2) using single-core CPU to do intersection/union comparison, (3) using multi-core CPUs to do intersection/union comparison, (4) using GPU to do intersection/union comparison.

For the first part, there are three different ways to do this work: (i) convert the original image file (.am) to a binary base-map, (ii) translate the original image file (.am) to a compression file (.CRS, [2]) at first, and then convert the compression file to a binary base-map, (iii) convert the compression file to a decimal base-map in order to reduce the calculation time. According to the difference ways above, there are three comparison types for the second-four parts: (i) Integer type, (ii) Boolean type, (iii) Decimal type. These four parts are explained in the following.

(1) Constructing Base-map: (encoding phase)

In the beginning, we have obtain the original Drosophila Driver and Neuron images (.am file) from the Brain Research Center of National Tsing Hua University (http://brc. life.nthu.edu.tw/) [3]. The .am file contains all the relevant information (non-zero intensity voxels) for Drosophila Driver/Neuron, and the compression file (.CRS) is obtained by compressing.am file to preserve the necessary information of the.am file, especially for non-zero intensity voxels (unpublished method). With these two files (.CRS and.am), we can start to build the base-map, respectively, and we mainly split base-map into three different forms (1) convert.am file to binary base-map, (2) convert . CRS file to binary base-map, (3) convert.CRS file to the decimal base-map. The decimal base-map is converted by the binary base-map with the rule: 8-bits binary/per decimal. For example, binary base-map: 00000000 00000001 00001110 will be converted to decimal base-map: 0 1 14. For the binary base-map, each file size is about 500 MB and the size of the corresponding decimal base-map is only in the range of 123 MB–129 MB.

(2) Using Single core CPU to do intersection/union comparison: (region computation phase)

In this paper, there are three types are used for the comparison: (1) Integer type, (2) Boolean type, (3) Decimal type. The binary base-map is used by the Integer type and the Boolean type, respectively, and the Decimal type is applied into the decimal base-map. After the comparison, the result includes: number of non-zero intensity voxels, the base-map of intersection/union region, and the calculation time. The number of non-zero intensity voxels is mainly used to calculate the Tanimoto coefficient (0–1 range, 1: similar) as the similarity between two images. The calculation time consists of reading (file) time and working (comparison) time. The details of implementation for these three types are descried in the following.

(i) Integer type:

In the Integer type, the INT type of fread function in the C library is used to read the binary base-map at first, and then a Neuron-to-Neuron comparison list is constructed. For example, assume that there are ten Drosophila Neuron images needed to be compared. There are 45 combinations (for each comparison pair) should be determined as a comparison list. We use the comparison list instead of "if-then-else" branch rule in the computation phase. This way can be used to simply the programming code and avoid the branch error in the multi-core environment. Finally, the "if-equal operations" are used to do the comparison for each combination. The matching result is stored as an integer value: 1, otherwise: 0. The pseudo-code of computation phase (omit the reading file step) for Integer type is shown in the following.

===

Pseudo code of region computation phase for Integer type

```
For list ← 0 to 10 //comparison list
  For list_temp ← list+1 to 10
   listname[index][0] = list
   listname[index][1] = list_temp
   index++
  End for loop
End for loop
For index ← 0 to all combinations
  For booleanarray_index ← 0 to max_index
   If( Neuron c0[boolarray_index] == 1 &&
Neuron c1[boolarray_index] == 1 )
//if-equal operations
     nonzero++
     Result[boolarray_index] = 1
   End if
  End for loop
End for loop
```

===

(ii) Boolean type:

In the Boolean type, the BOOL type of fread function in the C library is used to read the binary base-map at first, and then a Neuron-to-Neuron comparison list also is constructed. Finally, the "if-boolean operations" are used to do the comparison for each combination. The matching result is stored as a Boolean value: true (1), otherwise: false (0). Since the reading file functions and comparison operations used in Integer and Boolean types are different, the reading time and working time will be very different.

The pseudo-code of computation phase (omit the reading file step) for Boolean type is shown in the following.

===

Pseudo code of region computation phase for Boolean type

```
For list ← 0 to 10 //comparison list
    For list_temp ← list+1 to 10
        listname[index][0] = list
        listname[index][1] = list_temp
        index++
    End for loop
End for loop
For index ← 0 to all combinations
    For booleanarray_index ← 0 to max_index
        If (Neuron c0[boolarray_index] &&
Neuron c1[boolarray_index] )
//if-boolean operations
        nonzero++
        Result[boolarray_index] = true
        End if
    End for loop
End for loop
```

===

(iii) Decimal type:

In the Decimal type, the INT type of fread function in the C library is used to read the decimal base-map at first, and then a Neuron-to-Neuron comparison list also is constructed. Since the rule: 8-bits binary/per decimal is used to convert the binary base-map to decimal base-map, the range of decimal numbers is 0 to 255. When comparing a decimal number with another decimal number, there are 256×256 possibilities to calculate the comparison results, including the number of non-zero intensity voxels and the binary form. In order to reduce the computation time, a lookup-table with the size of 256×256 is established previously and recorded all of possible matching results. In practice, there are four lookup-tables: two tables (with the number of non-zero intensity voxels and the binary form) for intersection region computation, two tables for union region computation. Finally, the lookup-table search is used to do the comparison for each combination. The pseudo-code of computation phase (omit the reading file step) for Decimal type is shown in the following.

===

Pseudo code of region computation phase for Decimal type

For list ← 0 to 10 //comparison list
For list_temp ← list+1 to 10
  listname[index][0] = list
    listname[index][1] = list_temp
    index++
  End for loop
End for loop

For index ← 0 to all combinations
  For booleanarray_index ← 0 to max_index
    i = Neuron c0[booleanarray_index]
    j = Neuron c1[booleanarray_index]
    nonzero = nonzero + and_nonzero[i][j]
    Result[booleanarray_index] = and_result[i][j]
//lookup-table search
  End for loop
End for loop

===

(3) Using multi-core CPUs to do intersection/union comparison: (accelerate computation phase)

In addition to do intersection/union region computation for single-core CPU, it is very important to optimize the calculating performance. OpenMP [4] is used to implement the parallel programming of computation phase for these three types. It is a job assignment problem to assign all combinations to all CPU cores, and then try to achieve the load-balancing status. It is a simple way to use the comparison list to complete this work.

(4) Using GPU to do intersection/union comparison: (accelerate computation phase)

For GPU implementation [5], there are two major works should be considered: (1) data transfer, (2) thread-job assignment. For data transfer work, the data in host (CPU) should be read into the host memory at first, and then the data should be transferred to device (GPU) memory through the PCI-E channel. For Drosophila Driver and Neuron images, the sizes of binary base-map (500 MB) and decimal base-map (>123 MB) both are large. Therefore, several pairs of binary base-maps and decimal base-maps are read into the host memory at first, and then these base-maps are transferred to device global memory (12 GB for NVIDIA K40m GPU card).

For thread-job assignment work, the jobs should be divided into various parts and then these parts are assigned to different GPU threads. The implementations of multi-core CPUs is to assign all combinations (as jobs) to all CPU cores. Due to the large size of binary base-map and decimal base-map, it is difficult to do many combinations simultaneously in the GPU implementation. Hence, a few of combinations are done by all GPU threads. These binary base-maps or decimal base-maps will be divided into several parts as jobs at first, and then these parts are assigned to various GPU threads. After the computation phase, the results also are transferred from the device global memory to the host memory.

3   Experiment

In this paper, all of works were implemented by C, C+OpenMP and C+CUDA, respectively, on Intel E5-2650 v2 machine and a GPU card. The Intel Xeon E5-2650 v2 machine has 16 Xeon CPUs, each is 2.0 GHz, and 128 GB RAM. The GPU card is NVIDIA Tesla K40m with 2880 cuda cores, each is 745 MHz, and 12 GB RAM.

(1) The encoding phase

There are 950 Drosophila Neuron images (.am file and .CRS files) randomly selected are used to converted to binary base-maps, respectively. The encoding time is shown in Fig. 2. As show in Fig. 2, the encoding time by converting .CRS files is smaller than that by converting .am files under various numbers of images. After the above work, these .CRS files are converted to binary base-maps and decimal base-maps according to three types: Integer, Boolean and Decimal. The average encoding time is shown in Fig. 3. From Fig. 3, the average encoding time by converting .CRS files to binary base-maps (Boolean type) is faster than the other two types (binary base-map (Integer) and decimal base-map).

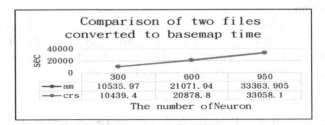

Fig. 2. The encoding time by converting .am and .CRS files to binary base-maps.

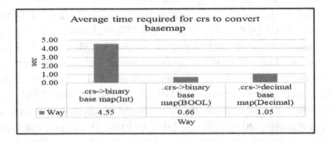

Fig. 3. Average encoding time by converting .CRS files to three types of base-maps.

(2) The computation phase

There are 10 Drosophila Neuron images (.CRS files) randomly selected and are used to converted to binary base-maps (Integer), binary base-maps (Boolean), and decimal base-maps (Decimal), respectively. These base-maps are used to do the union region computations (45 combinations), respectively, based on single-CPU and multi-CPUs (8 and 16 cores). The calculation time, consists of reading time (orange color) and working time (blue color), by these three types and environments is shown in Fig. 4. From Fig. 4, for single CPU environment, the working time by Decimal type is smaller than that by other two types; however, the reading time by the Integer/Boolean type is smaller than that by the Decimal type. Since the number of combinations is small, the calculation time by Boolean type is smallest. For multi-core CPUs environments, we have the same observations. In addition, the calculation time by multi-core CPUs environment is smaller than that by single CPU environment.

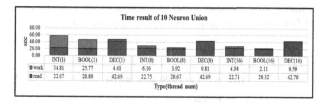

Fig. 4. The calculation time (reading time and working time) by these three types and environments. (10 Drosophila Neuron images) (Color figure online)

There are 40 Drosophila Neuron images (.CRS files) randomly selected and are used to converted to binary base-maps (Integer), binary base-maps (Boolean), and decimal base-maps (Decimal), respectively. These base-maps are used to do the union region computations (780 combinations), respectively, based on single-CPU and multi-CPUs (8 and 16 cores). The calculation time, consists of reading time (orange color) and working time (blue color), by these three types and environments is shown in Fig. 5. From Fig. 5, for single CPU environment, the working time by Decimal type also is smaller than that by other two types. Moreover, the reading time by the Boolean type still is smallest. Since the number of combinations is large, the calculation time by Decimal type is smallest. For multi-core CPUs environments, we have the same observations. However, the calculation time by Integer type based on 16 core CPUs is large (abnormal). The reason is that the memory space is not enough for the computation phase.

In order to compare the calculation time by these three types based on single CPU and GPU, there are 10 Drosophila Neuron images (.CRS files) randomly selected again, and are used to converted to binary base-maps (Integer), binary base-maps (Boolean), and decimal base-maps (Decimal), respectively. These base-maps are used to do the union region computations (45 combinations), respectively, based on single CPU and GPU. The calculation time, consists of reading time (orange color) and working time (blue color), by these three types and environments is shown in Fig. 6. From Fig. 6, the calculation time by these three types based on GPU all are larger than those based on single CPU. There are two reasons: one is that the data transfer time is large, and another is that the number of combinations (can be done simultaneously) is few.

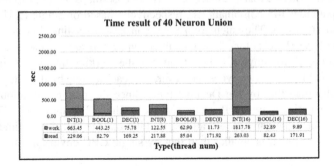

Fig. 5. The calculation time (reading time and working time) by these three types and environments. (40 Drosophila Neuron images) (Color figure online)

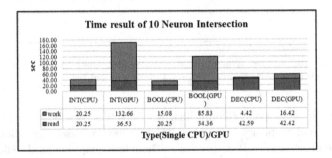

Fig. 6. The calculation time by these three types based on single CPU and GPU environments. (10 Drosophila Neuron images) (Color figure online)

4   Conclusion

In this paper, three encoding schemes, Integer, Boolean, Decimal, were proposed to encode each Drosophila brain images at first. Then, the intersection/union region from these images were computed by using the various operations. Finally, the comparison work was done and the similarity score were calculated according to the Tanimoto coefficient. These methods were also implemented in the multi-core CPUs and GPU environments, respectively. From the experimental results, in the encoding phase, the performance by Boolean scheme is the best than that by others; in the region computation phase, the performance by Decimal is the best when the number of images is large. The speedup ratio can achieve 13 based on 16 CPUs.

Acknowledgement. Part of this work was supported by the Ministry of Science and Technology under the grant MOST 107-2221-E-182-063-MY2 and MOST 107-2218-E-126-001.

References

1. Nickolls, J., Buck, I., Garland, M., Skadron, K.: Scalable parallel programming with CUDA. ACM Queue **6**, 40–53 (2008)
2. Chang, R.G., Chung, T.R., Lee, J.K.: Parallel Sparse Supports for Array Intrinsic Functions of Fortra 90. J. Supercomput. **18**(3), 305–339 (2001)
3. Chiang, A.S., et al.: Three-dimensional reconstruction of brain-wide wiring networks in Drosophila at single-cell resolution. Curr Biol. **21**(1), 1–11 (2011)
4. OpenMP.org. http://openmp.org/
5. Hung, C.-L., Lin, Y.-S., Lin, C.-Y., Chung, Y.-C., Chung, Y.-F.: CUDA ClustalW: an efficient parallel algorithm for progressive multiple sequence alignment on Multi-GPUs. Computat. Biol. Chem. **58**, 62–68 (2015)

Performance Comparison of Lightweight Kubernetes in Edge Devices

Halim Fathoni[1,2,3], Chao-Tung Yang[2], Chih-Hung Chang[4(✉)],
and Chin-Yin Huang[1]

[1] Department Industrial Engineering and Enterprise Information,
Tunghai University, Taichung, Taiwan (R.O.C.)
{D07330701,huangcy}@thu.edu.tw,
fathoni@polinela.ac.id
[2] Department Computer Science, Tunghai University,
Taichung, Taiwan (R.O.C.)
ctyang@thu.edu.tw
[3] Department Ekonomi Dan Bisnis Politeknik Negeri Lampung,
Bandar Lampung, Indonesia
[4] College of Computing and Informatics, Providence University,
Taichung, Taiwan (R.O.C.)
ch.chang@gm.pu.edu.tw

Abstract. Traditional cloud computing has the challenge to serve many clients with many services. Spreading the services to across of edge server will reduce the load of traditional cloud computing. Kubernetes is one of the platforms used for cloud management. Kubernetes helps to deploy, and scaling the application. Nowadays, a lot of communities build a lightweight Kubernetes than suitable for edge device such as Raspberry Pi. This paper Investigate the performance of Kubernetes lightweight that installed in the Raspberry Pi.

Keywords: Lightweight kubernetes · K3s · KubeEdge · Monitoring · Edge computing

1 Introduction

Nowadays, traditional cloud computing has the challenge to serve many clients with many services. With the development of the Internet of things, these challenges predicted will increase exponentially and also increase the load of cloud computing [1]. Edge computing has proposed to keep the minimum quality of services between cloud and user [2].

Edge Computing is extended of the cloud capabilities and services to the edge network. This approach is to reduce the distance between a cloud server and a client, so the cloud services spread to across edge devices, and transmission delay between cloud and client could be decreased [3]. On the other hand, this approach has a limitation. The computation capability of the edge device not good enough compared with a cloud server; this challenge encourages much research to optimize the computation capability of edge devices [4].

© Springer Nature Switzerland AG 2019
C. Esposito et al. (Eds.): I-SPAN 2019, CCIS 1080, pp. 304–309, 2019.
https://doi.org/10.1007/978-3-030-30143-9_25

Biermann et al. designed an edge computing platform running on ARM architecture and HypriotOS as a small data center that represents Edge devices. His research attempt to build a platform that satisfies the computational challenges of Edge devices and to support services and applications, which are needed to successfully manage large data streams and communication of a large number of connected devices. To guarantee high availability and to provide data processing, they used orchestration tools like Docker Swarm and Kubernetes [5].

Kubernetes has been introduced by Google since 2015 [6] as an open-source container management platform. Kubernetes used for automating of manage, deploy, scaling, and operation of application the containers across clusters of hosts [7]. These advantages brought Kubernetes to become a popular container management platform and adapted to many cloud servers. Nowadays, Kubernetes has improved to deploy in a lightweight environment.

In this paper, we inspired [5] and tried to investigate the lightweight Kubernetes, in his paper [5] they do not explain about the type of Kubernetes. Nowadays, Kubernetes has modified by some community to become suitable for a lightweight environment [8]. By understanding the lightweight Kubernetes will bring help us to improve our research in the future.

The paper organized as follows, Sect. 2 We describe the type of Lightweight Kubernetes; Sect. 3 describes the architecture of our environment Sect. 4; we provide our findings of the performance evaluation. Section 5 is discussed.

2 Kubernetes

Kubernetes is a cloud management platform that can help to manage the cloud server to deploy, scaling the application. Kubernetes architecture combines the concept of *Pod,* the abstract form of containers that share resources in a server machine.

2.1 Rancher K3S

Rancher K3s is a lightweight Kubernetes distribution designed for developers [10]. The deprecated API groups and non-essential plug-ins code in the Kubernetes has removed and packaged as a single binary that only 40 MB size and 512 RAM needed. This essential feature is designed to fit with a lightweight environment, such as easy to install. Installing K3s only need three lines of code and it is ready to deploy in the large scale of Kubernetes cluster. When cluster launched all certificates needed to establish TLS between the Kubernetes master and nodes automatically created. In addition, K3s use containers instead of Docker as the runtime container engine. SQLite add as optional to store the data because it has a lower memory footprint, and simple to operate compared with etcd (the feature has responsible for storing the data). Furthermore, Kubelet, Kubeproxy and flannel agent combines become into a single process and it helps to reduce the requirement of RAM. The rancher has successfully made Kubernates become simple and lightweight (Fig. 1).

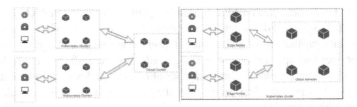

Fig. 1. K3S architecture [10]

2.2 KubeEdge

KubeEdge was launched in December 2018, supported by Huawei [13]. KubEdge designed to provide core infrastructure support for networking, application deployment, and metadata synchronization between the cloud and edge. Based on [9], KubeEdge composed seven components, first *Edged*; an edge node agent that manages the containerized application. Second *EdgeHub*: a web socket client responsible for communication with cloud service. Third *CloudHub*; A web socket server responsible for watching changes at the cloud side, caching and sending messages to EdgeHub. Fourth *EdgeController*; responsible for synchronizing metadata between Edge to the cloud. Fifth *EventBus*; Responsible for interacting with MQTT server. Six *DeviceTwin*: Responsible to synchronize Edge status to the cloud. The last is *MetaManager*; Responsible for store or retrieving metadata to or from the lightweight database (Fig. 2).

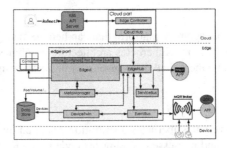

Fig. 2. KubeEdge architecture [11]

3 Architecture

In this paper, we try to implement the simulation position tracker [12] in a lightweight environment. This simulator provided the GPS location of the delivery truck, to simulate communication between the GPS device and server.

The lightweight environment uses 2 units Raspberry Pi 3+ Model B, with 32 GB micro SD Card Samsung EVO and connected to a router with 100 Mbps port speed and provide DHCP service. Each unit of Raspberry Pi installed with RancherOS [14]. This operating system supported Docker 1.14.1. The first unit as Master and the other as a worker. To get a good result, we try with a different scenario: Scenario 1 in this scenario we capture all resources in idle condition. All applications did not install in both Raspberry Pi. In scenario 2 we installed simulator application in Raspberry Pi and monitor resource used by 2 units.

4 Result

Kubernetes scheduler will set up the RAM and CPU resources, when pod launched in Kubernetes [15]. The scheduler will select the best node for deployment, the performance of pod depends on the resource and the workload [16]. From the experiment we found that Raspberry Pi can work stably in the idle condition (see Fig. 3). All resource only used around 14% of CPU, 14% of RAM.

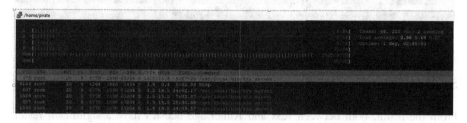

Fig. 3. Rancher K3s resources

In scenario two, CPU resource slightly increases by around 28%, and RAM around 19% (see Fig. 4). All devices has run stable for a week.

Fig. 4. Rancher K3s resources after application deployment

For The KubeEdge almost have a similar result. In the Idle condition only use 10.5% CPU and 8% of RAM (see Fig. 5). This result fluctuates and always change every second, depending on the needed of services. After Installing Application KubeEdge needs 50% of CPU and 19% of RAM (see Fig. 6).

Fig. 5. KubeEdge resources before application deployment

Fig. 6. KubeEdge resources after application deployment

5   Discussion

From the result, both between K3s and KubeEdge doesn't have a significant result. KubeEdge needs more CPU resources than K3s, but this result always fluctuates. It depends on the pod. Kubernetes has automatic scaling to keep the pod works, and will maintain the pod to keep work stable. Compare with the CPU, the needed of RAM not as much as the CPU. The lightweight Kubernetes only spend a few RAM resources. Lightweight Kubernetes (K3s and KubeEdge) still at the beginning of development. Both still have room to improve. KubeEdge more has a communication feature to data synchronization with the master, but in this paper, we are only focusing on CPU and RAM consumption.

Acknowledgment. This work is supported in part by the Ministry of Science and Technology, Taiwan, ROC, under grant number MOST 108-2622-8-029-004-TM1, MOST 108-2221-E-029-010, MOST 106-2221-E-164-009-MY2 and MOST 108-2221-E-126-002.

References

1. Huang, Y., Cai, K., Zong, R., Mao, Y.: Design and implementation of an edge computing platform architecture using Docker and Kubernetes for machine learning, pp. 29–32 (2019)
2. Wang, P., Liu, S., Ye, F., Chen, X.: A Fog-based Architecture and Programming Model for IoT Applications in the Smart Grid (2018)
3. Li, C., Sun, H., Chen, Y., Luo, Y.: Edge cloud resource expansion and shrinkage based on workload for minimizing the cost. Futur. Gener. Comput. Syst. **101**, 327–340 (2019)
4. Cappos, J., Rafetseder, A., Hemmings, M., McGeer, R., Ricart, G.: EdgeNet: a global cloud that spreads by local action. In: Proceedings - 2018 3rd ACM/IEEE Symposium Edge Computer SEC 2018, pp. 359–360 (2018)

5. Eiermann, A., Renner, M., GroBmann, M.: On a Fog Computing Platform Built on ARM Architectures by Docker Container Technology, vol. 863, pp. 71–86 (2018)

6. Santoro, D., Zozin, D., Pizzolli, D., De Pellegrini, F., Cretti, S.: Foggy: a platform for workload orchestration in a fog computing environment. In: Proceedings International Conference Cloud Computing Technology Science CloudCom, vol. 2017-December, pp. 231–234 (2017)

7. Mittermeier, L., Katenbrink, F., Seitz, A., Muller, H., Bruegge, B.: Dynamic scheduling for seamless computing. In: Proceedings - 8th IEEE International Symposium Cloud Service Computing SC2 2018, pp. 41–48 (2018)

8. Abdollahi Vayghan, L., Saied, M.A., Toeroe, M., Khendek, F.: Deploying microservice based applications with kubernetes: experiments and lessons learned. IEEE Int. Conf. Cloud Comput. CLOUD **2018**, 970–973 (2018)

9. Xiong, Y., Sun, Y., Xing, L., Huang, Y.: Extend cloud to edge with KubeEdge. In: Proceedings - 2018 3rd ACM/IEEE Symposium Edge Computing SEC 2018, pp. 373–377 (2018)

10. "K3S". http://k3s.io. Accessed 09 July 2019

11. "KubeEdge". http://KubeEdge.io. Accessed 09 July 2019

12. DockerHub. https://hub.docker.com/u/richardchesterwood. 30 June 2019

13. "Kubernetes". https://kubernetes.io/blog/2019/03/19/kubeedge-k8s-based-edge-intro/. 09 July 2019

14. "RancherOS". https://rancher.com/rancher-os/. Accessed 09 July 2019

15. Chang, C., Yang, S., Yeh, E., Lin, P., Jeng, J.: A kubernetes-based monitoring platform for dynamic cloud resource provisioning. In: GLOBECOM 2017 - 2017 IEEE Global Communications Conference, pp. 1–6. Singapore (2017)

16. Sharma, P., Chaufournier, L., Shenoy, P., Tay, Y.C.: Containers and virtual machines at scale: a comparative study. In: Proceedings of the 17th International Middleware Conference (Middleware 2016), p. 13. ACM, New York, NY, USA, Article 1 (2016)

1st International Workshop on Consumer Cyber Security (IW-ConSec 2019)

Experimental Analysis of the Pixel Non Uniformity (PNU) in SEM for Digital Forensics Purposes

Andrea Bruno$^{(\boxtimes)}$ and Giuseppe Cattaneo

Università degli Studi di Salerno, 83100 Fisciano, SA, Italy
{andbruno,cattaneo}@unisa.it
https://digitalforensics.di.unisa.it

Abstract. Recent years saw an explosion in the number of the counterfeit or stolen images in scientific papers. In particular in the field of biomedical science publication this is becoming a serious problem for the health and economic issues caused by this fraud [1].

In this paper we investigate the possibility to extend a technique commonly used in image forensics to associate a given image with the camera used to take it. The original technique, proposed by *Fridrich et al.* in [3] uses the PNU, a unique fingerprint present in each photo and generated by natural the imperfection in the silicium slice that composes the Charge-Coupled Device (CCD) sensor.

We analyze the quality of the PNU present in the residual noise by evaluating the quality of this noise using its variance. The experimental results shows that some PNU is still present in the residual noise, but is less than the one present in photo from digital cameras.

This technique of evaluation is promisingly because is possible to use also to speedup the source camera identification process in videos by excluding the frames that not preserving enough PNU in the residual noise.

Keywords: Biomedical images · Plagiarism · PNU Noise · Sensor noise

1 Introduction

Fraud in biomedical paper is a problem for health and economy, as shown in [4]. The authors extimated the cost of this fraud in US in the year 1992–2012 in 58 billion of US Dollars. For this reason would be interesting to have a tool that permit to idenbtify the image altered and stolen in biomedical paper.

PNU was widely used for sourse camera identification since its introduction in 2006 by *Fridrich et al.* [3]. Nowadays is a de-facto standard for Source Camera Identification (SCI) with images, but what happens if we try to extend this technique to image source different from standard CCD cameras, such for example Scanning Electron Microscope (SEM) or Magnetic Resonance Image (MRI) device that are the most common source of image in biomedical scientific paper?

© Springer Nature Switzerland AG 2019
C. Esposito et al. (Eds.): I-SPAN 2019, CCIS 1080, pp. 313–320, 2019.
https://doi.org/10.1007/978-3-030-30143-9_26

Recently *Cattaneo et al.*[2] showed that with SEM is possible, under certain condition, to use Photo Response Non-Uniformity (PRNU) based techniques.

It would be useful to have a technique to evaluate the quality of the PNU remained in the Residual Noise (RN).

In this paper we shows the strict correlation between the variation of the RN and the quality of results of application of *Fridrich et al.* technique. This works under the assumption that the source of the noise other than PRNU, temperature variation, magnetism, electric noise etc..., appear less random than PRNU.

Organization of the paper: In Sect. 2 we will analyze the state of the art about PNU in field different than images. In particular in Sect. 2.1 we will provide a short introduction to *Fridrich et al.* technique. In Sect. 3 we will introduce the dataset we created for the experiment we designed and in Sect. 4 will present the result of them, in Sect. 5 we will provide some conclusions for our work and outline the possible future directions.

2   State of the Art

Image forgery and plagiarism in biomedical scientific paper is becoming a serious problem not only for the scientific community. *Bik et al.* in 2016 studied the problem and showed that in the last 20year the number of fraud in scientific paper is constantly increased causing that $\sim 4\%$ of the published paper in this field contains images that are either forged or copied form other sources.

In 2017[2] we proposed a distributed platform with the aim to identify the image copied from other author using the PNU technique proposed by *Fridrich et al.* that we discuss extensively in Sect. 2.1. After this work we noticed that the value of the correlation for the images taken from the SEM were really low, i confronted with the typical results from digital cameras.

As far as we know in literature are not present methodology for evaluation of the quality of the PNU in residual images. Such a methodology can be useful to evaluate the results of the application of the *Fridrich et al.* method, in particular when we try to extend this methodology to digital videos can be used to reduce the number of frame processed, excluding the ones with a poor PNU quality.

2.1   Source Camera Identification

In 2006 *Fridrich et al.* [3] proved that any digital camera sensor based on CCD has a unique fingerprint made by the noise caused by the natural imperfection on the silicium slice used for the sensor and other imperfection introduced by the manufacturing process of the sensor. This noise remains in the final image together with the noise generated by other source, like electromagnetic field, high temperature, etc....

The PNU cannot be directly extracted from the images, but can be estimated by filtering the image, obtaining a noiseless image, that can be subtracted to the original image obtaining the residual noise of the image.

Formally, *Fridrich et al.* technique establish if a device C has benn used to take an image I using the PNU remained in I. Its possible to estimate the PNU in an image I applying a PNU denoising filter F_{PNU} on I and subtracting the resulting filtered image to the original one, obtaining a RN, that contains the PNU, but also noises from other sources. The RN can be estimated this way:

$$RN_I = I - F_{PNU}(I).$$ (1)

The PNU should represent the constant part of the RN, so, given a set of images S_C taken with the same device C, is possible to obtain a better estimation of the PNU od the device C.

$$PNU_C = \frac{\sum_{I \in S_C} RN_I}{|S_C|}$$ (2)

This estimation of the PNU of a camera is generally called Reference Pattern (RP). Formally $RP_C = PNU_C$.

Step 2: Training. In this step a set of acceptance threshold associated each of the cameras (i.e., RPs) under scrutiny must be calculated. This is done by using a set of training images.

Formally, let T be a training image and RN_T the residual noise extracted from T, RP_C is correlated with RN_T using the Bravais-Pearson correlation index as defined in the following formula:

$$corr(RN_T, RP_C) = \frac{(RN_T - \overline{RN_T})(RP_C - \overline{RP_C})}{\|RN_T - \overline{RN_T})(RP_C - \overline{RP_C}\|}.$$ (3)

The result is a value in the range $[-1, 1]$, where higher values implies an higher confidence that T comes from camera C. Using this correlation the threshold t_C for camera C is calculated using the Neyman-Pearson method.

The resulting thresholds are chosen in order to minimize the *False Rejection Rate* (FRR) for images taken by using C, given an upper bound on the *False Acceptance Rate* (FAR) for images taken by using a different camera than C (see [3] for details).

Step 3: Detection. In this step we used the residual noise RN_I extracted from an image under scrutiny I to identify the camera used to acquire it. Formally, if the correlation between the RN_I of an image I and the RP_C of a camera C is greater than corresponding acceptance threshold, then I is marked as taken with that camera.

Formally:

$$I \in C? = \begin{cases} YES, & \text{if } corr(RN_I, RP_C) \geq t_C \\ NO, & \text{otherwise} \end{cases}$$ (4)

3   Dataset

To evaluate the quality of the PNU in the RN of SEM images we built a dataset that includes images from two SEM, previously used in [2] and as a baseline for confrontation the images from 20 Nikon D90, previously used in large scale test with Italian Postal Police. In addition to Nikon D90 cameras, we included photo from a new high resolution Nikon D850 camera and an Apple iPhone Xs. The dataset is composed as in Table 1.

Table 1. Dataset composition

Camera	Resolution (W x H)	Format	Number of images
Zeiss Merlin (SEM)	1024×768	tif	167
Zeiss EVO MA10 (SEM)	1024×768	tif	147
Nikon D90[a]	4288×2848	JPEG	5000
Nikon D850	8256×5504	JPEG	250
Apple iPhone Xs	4032×3024	JPEG	150

[a]The dataset is composed of 20 Nikon D90, each one with 250 images at maximum resolution

The images from the Nikon D90 permit to establish a baseline to compare the results obtained from the analysis of the SEM images. The Nikon D850 is part of a new generation of cameras that not use the Optical Low-Pass Filter (OLPF), commonly present in all the digital camera as an Anti Aliasing filter. The resulting images contains a greater amount of noise than the ones produced with camera that have this filter.

In the end we included in dataset also images taken from a smartphone, the Apple iPhone Xs, to compare the results also with device that always apply artifact to images in order to improve their quality (Figs. 1 and 2).

4   Experimental Results

We designed this experiment with the aim of evaluate the quality of the PNU in the RPs of the SEM. We uesed the intuition that the PNU, in relation to the other source of the noises present in RN and consequently in the RPs, is less predictable because of the intrinsic randomness of the imperfection in the silicium slice that causes it. To prove this intuition we calculated the RPs of all the 5 devices in the dataset, using 100 images for each devices for the enrollment. For each of this device we calculated the variance and the standard variation for the rows and the columns of each RP. All this results are resumed in Tables 2 and 3.

In a second step we confronted each RP with all the images using the correlation in order to check the resulting value of this correlation. In particular we

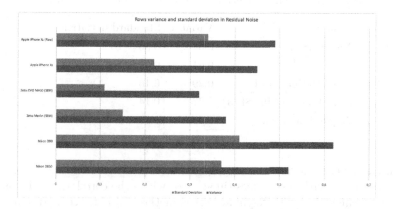

Fig. 1. Row variance for the RP of the devices in dataset

Table 2. Row variance for the RP of the devices in dataset

Device	Variance	Standard deviation
Nikon D850	0.52	0.37
Nikon D90[b]	0.62	0.41
Zeiss Merlin (SEM)	0.38	0.15
Zeiss EVO MA10 (SEM)	0.32	0.11
Apple iPhone Xs	0.45	0.22

[b] Here is reported the average over the results of the 20 RPs of the Nikon D90

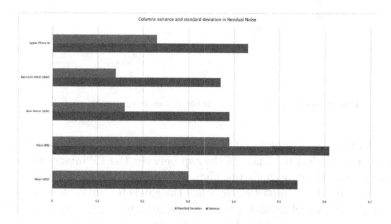

Fig. 2. Column variance for the RP of the devices in dataset

Table 3. Column variance for the RP of the devices in dataset

Device	Variance	Standard deviation
Nikon D850	0.54	0.30
Nikon D90[b]	0.61	0.39
Zeiss Merlin (SEM)	0.39	0.16
Zeiss EVO MA10 (SEM)	0.37	0.14
Apple iPhone Xs	0.43	0.23

computed, for each device, the average of the correlation value the images correctly associated with the devices (images for which the correlation value is over a threshold calculated with Neyman-Person method for a device, and that where taken with this device), lets call them True Positive (TP), and the images that are correctly not associated with the device (images for which the correlation value is under a threshold calculated with Neyman-Person method for a device, and that where not taken with this device), lets call them True Negative (TN) (Table 4).

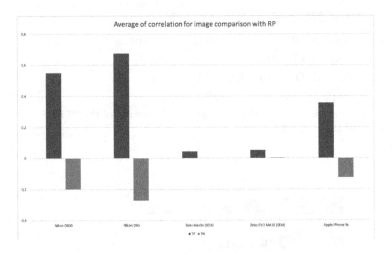

Fig. 3. Average of correlation for image comparison with RP

Is evident by these results that with reduction of value of the row and column variance corresponds a reduction of the gap between the TP images and the TN. This gap is important because the higher is the gap the most reliable are the results of classification. In particular, when the gap is too small the False Positive Rate, the percentage of images wrongly associated to a device grows (Fig. 3).

As we can see from Tables 2 and 3 the images from the two SEMs has a variance sensible lower than the other cameras. This is probably due the post-processing applied to the images from SEM. In-fact from those devices is not

Table 4. Average of correlation for image comparison with RP

Device	TPs correlation value	TNs correlation value
Nikon D850	0.549	−0.198
Nikon D90	0.676	−0.271
Zeiss Merlin (SEM)	0.043	0.002
Zeiss EVO MA10 (SEM)	0.051	0.003
Apple iPhone Xs	0.357	−0.124

possible to obtain a raw images, but only processed images like the one in Fig. 4 to which, p.e. was added a bar with information at the bottom and applied algorithm to enhance contrast.

Fig. 4. Example images from Zeiss Merlin (SEM)

Also the RP from the Apple iPhone Xs has a lowered variance compared to the one from the Nikon cameras, even if is higher than the one from SEM devices. This is probably due the artifacts, in term of electronic image stabilization and color correction applied to the images directly by iOs.

5   Conclusion and Future Works

In this paper we made an experimental analysis of the quality of PNU in RN of images taken with some SEM. We aimed the explore the possibility to use the *Fridrich et al.* technique for SCI even with device different from digital cameras.

The experiment showed us that the PNU in images taken from SEM devices is less effective for this purpose. This is probably due the fact that the images from such devices are higly affected by the artefacts introduced in post-processing phase by those devices, and its analogue to what happens also with the images from Apple iPhone Xs, even if, in this case, with a lower degradation of the PNU.

For the future will be of interest the extension of those experiments to the MRI devices, and to investigate the possibility to obtain the raw image data form those kind of devices to verify the ipothesis that this reduction of the PNU quality is due the introduces artifacts.

References

1. Bik, E.M., Casadevall, A., Fang, F.C.: The prevalence of inappropriate image duplication in biomedical research publications. MBio **7**(3), e00809–16 (2016)
2. Bruno, A., Cattaneo, G., Ferraro Petrillo, U., Narducci, F., Roscigno, G.: Distributed anti-plagiarism checker for biomedical images based on sensor noise. In: Battiato, S., Farinella, G.M., Leo, M., Gallo, G. (eds.) ICIAP 2017. LNCS, vol. 10590, pp. 343–352. Springer, Cham (2017). https://doi.org/10.1007/978-3-319-70742-6_32
3. Fridrich, J., Lukáš, J., Goljan, M.: Digital camera identification from sensor noise. IEEE Trans. Inf. Secur. Forensics **1**(2), 205–214 (2006)
4. Stern, A.M., Casadevall, A., Steen, R.G., Fang, F.C.: Financial costs and personal consequences of research misconduct resulting in retracted publications. Elife **3**, e02956 (2014)

Public WiFi Security Network Protocol Practices in Tourist Destination

Sime Lugovic[1], Leo Mrsic[2(✉)] [iD], and Ljiljana Zekanovic Korona[1]

[1] University of Zadar, Mihovila Pavlinovica, Zadar, Croatia
sime.lugovic@gmail.com, ljkorona@unizd.hr
[2] Algebra University College, Ilica 242, Zagreb, Croatia
leo.mrsic@algebra.hr

Abstract. Paper addresses security issues with public access WiFi networks, with emphasis on networks deployed in touristic places, because of their popularity. Such networks are often poorly administered and guarded whereas tourist-services they support, are massively used by thousands of occasional users daily. With intention to put emphasis on the security awareness of the users, filed research was conducted to investigate current security preferences of wireless computer networks in tourist destination, in the City of Zadar, Croatia. The research was conducted during preparation and early in the tourist season, spring/summer 2018. Hardware research support include AP beacon used a TL-WN722N card with a data rate of 150 Mbps, a 5 db antenna, a chip Atheros AR9271, all powered by Linux operating. Small suite was a passive scan tool for the beacon area. The data set used include the default AP settings that transmits its current SSID every 100 ms. WLAN card was used in the vehicle that was set up in the monitor mode used to collect all the available beacon frames. In addition to field research, we conduct additional survey with aim to investigate the general habits of users of wireless computer networks, from personal perspective. Overall goal was to put attention on WiFi security awareness and to expose security behaviour at router level.

Keywords: Mobile security · Mobile applications security · Domestic appliances security · Identity theft and illicit diffusion of personal data · Law enforcement practices and uses of digital forensics tools · Online frauds

1 Introduction

Public WiFi is a common way for internet access, especially when there is no other easy way of internet access. Paper addresses security issues with public access WiFi networks, with particular emphasis on networks deployed in touristic places, because of their popularity. Such networks are often poorly administered and guarded whereas tourist-services they support, are massively used by thousands of occasional users daily. Being easy to access, users are often not aware that this is not the safest way of internet access. Main challenge, when connecting to public WiFi, is that all information transmitted from your computer is usually available to other devices on that network. That is why such connections can be are extremely dangerous because cyber-attackers can extract usernames, passwords and other information/data from communication stream [1].

© Springer Nature Switzerland AG 2019
C. Esposito et al. (Eds.): I-SPAN 2019, CCIS 1080, pp. 321–332, 2019.
https://doi.org/10.1007/978-3-030-30143-9_27

Considering that, three most common forms of attack are: Man-in-the-Middle Attacks, Malware/ Evil Twins and Fake WiFi Access Points/WiFi Sniffing. In the first form, the attacker is looking to place attack between user and the computer to which one access by creating network through which user will access. The other form is much more dangerous, because the attacker is physically on your computer. The third form is used very often, because it is based on the attacker taking over enormous amounts of data you send and receive and use that data to extract something useful. WiFi Sniffing is not forbidden, user can even use it on its own, because the attacker takes over everything on the network so it's hard to prove that he just attacked someone. Since no great technological knowledge is required for these methods to take place, the best cure is prevention [3–6].

Sensitive information such as bank accounts and passwords are not to be provided or used on public networks. Using a public network should be reduced to entertainment and surfing the web rather than using tools of importance that sometimes sends your passwords to authorization. It's recommended to limit the quantity of background information on your device because apps in the background often send and receive some data without your permission.

2 WiFi Network Setup and Security Basics

The world today cannot be imagined without wireless networks. WiFi is used to connect mobile devices and computers to the Internet and virtually enable permanent connectivity having instant access to the global network. The trend is that cities or local communities, build their wireless networks to provide Internet access to visitors and citizens. All those networks are common and often use the IEEE 802.11 protocol for air communication (radio waves). However, there are serious security risks when using such networks. For end users, it means connecting to the insecure a network or network that is controlled by malicious tools, can provide their confidential information to unwanted persons. In that case, someone can intercept and spy internet user's traffic and extract information like passwords for accessing the web services and other relevant data. Also, most households have a router with a wireless module that lets you connect wired handsets with your wireless waves cell phones, smartphones and other devices on the Internet. All traffic is being served by commercial Internet service provider (ISP). One of the obvious benefits of wireless connectivity is that it is not cable connected neither limited to one location. On the other hand, challenges include fact that waves, by which data is transmitted, are spreading in all directions and cover the wider area. Everyone can try to connect to "user's" connection point within the range of wireless network, and in case it goes hand in hand, it can execute various malicious actions. Routers are required to be adjusted to today's security standards to prevent malicious users from using it. This internet access threatens the security of other internet users, including those who are connected to the same device. Every device connected to the network passes through a set of procedures that either securely use the network traffic or prohibit it [2].

```
▶ Frame 10: 315 bytes on wire (2520 bits), 315 bytes captured (2520 bits) on interface 0
▶ Radiotap Header v0, Length 36
▶ 802.11 radio information
▶ IEEE 802.11 Beacon frame, Flags: .......C
▼ IEEE 802.11 wireless LAN
   ▼ Fixed parameters (12 bytes)
        Timestamp: 0x00000120edbf414c
        Beacon Interval: 0,102400 [Seconds]
      ▶ Capabilities Information: 0x0411
   ▼ Tagged parameters (239 bytes)
      ▶ Tag: SSID parameter set: TP-LINK_59BA6C
      ▶ Tag: Supported Rates 1(B), 2(B), 5.5(B), 11(B), 9, 18, 36, 54, [Mbit/sec]
      ▶ Tag: DS Parameter set: Current Channel: 7
      ▶ Tag: Extended Supported Rates 6, 12, 24, 48, [Mbit/sec]
      ▶ Tag: Country Information: Country Code DE, Environment Any
      ▶ Tag: AP Channel Report: Operating Class 32, Channel List : 1, 2, 3, 4, 5, 6, 7,
      ▶ Tag: AP Channel Report: Operating Class 33, Channel List : 5, 6, 7, 8, 9, 10, 11,
      ▶ Tag: Traffic Indication Map (TIM): DTIM 0 of 0 bitmap
      ▶ Tag: ERP Information
      ▶ Tag: HT Capabilities (802.11n D1.10)
      ▶ Tag: HT Information (802.11n D1.10)
      ▶ Tag: Overlapping BSS Scan Parameters
      ▶ Tag: Extended Capabilities (1 octet)
      ▶ Tag: Vendor Specific: Microsoft Corp.: WPA Information Element
      ▶ Tag: RSN Information
      ▶ Tag: Vendor Specific: Microsoft Corp.: WMM/WME: Parameter Element
      ▶ Tag: QBSS Load Element 802.11e CCA Version
      ▶ Tag: Vendor Specific: Ralink Technology, Corp.
```

Fig. 1. Beacon frame

Figure 1 shows an example of a beacon packet that each Access Point emits approximately every 100 ms (default) during active time, or while SSID broadcasting is enabled. The beacon packet can read different field values. The SSID parameter field detects the network name (if SSID broadcasting is configured), supported rates, and extended support rates, detects supported speeds or data rates that can be used to detect which 802.11 protocol is working. The AP also advertises its current channel where communication takes place (ranging from channel 1 to 14), while optionally we can determine which chipset the AP uses (in our sample case, it is Railink Technology).

```
▶ Frame 1650: 166 bytes on wire (1328 bits), 166 bytes captured (1328 bits) on interface 0
▶ Radiotap Header v0, Length 36
▶ 802.11 radio information
▶ IEEE 802.11 Probe Request, Flags: .......C
▼ IEEE 802.11 wireless LAN
   ▼ Tagged parameters (102 bytes)
      ▶ Tag: SSID parameter set: Wildcard SSID
      ▶ Tag: Supported Rates 1, 2, 5.5, 11, [Mbit/sec]
      ▶ Tag: Extended Supported Rates 6, 9, 12, 18, 24, 36, 48, 54, [Mbit/sec]
      ▶ Tag: DS Parameter set: Current Channel: 12
      ▶ Tag: HT Capabilities (802.11n D1.10)
      ▶ Tag: Extended Capabilities (8 octets)
      ▶ Tag: Interworking
      ▶ Tag: Vendor Specific: Apple, Inc.
      ▶ Tag: Vendor Specific: Microsoft Corp.: Unknown 8
      ▶ Tag: Vendor Specific: Broadcom
```

Fig. 2. Probe request

Beacon frames from AP allow devices (supplicants) to detect when they are within communication reach, and automatically log in to the network if the fields match. User devices that have WiFi enabled send test request packets that are in the service of detecting currently available networks or detecting whether the pre-available networks are still available. Figure 2 shows an example of a device request package that has a wildcard parameter set for the SSID field. The wildcard parameter is actually a parameter that searches for all available networks, or checks which networks are all within the range of the device (because each letter can be a wildcard *). Also, the device announces its available transmission speeds that detect the current 802.1

protocol that it uses. It should be noted that devices that are not connected to any network and have WiFi enabled at time intervals, send test requests to refresh a list of available networks. This is a way of testing requests for all the available channels from 1 to 14 that all APs are listening in range and then AP * and responds with a frame containing SSID and other fields [7]. The schematic view of the probes for the specific SSID and for the null (wildcard) variance is shown in Fig. 3.

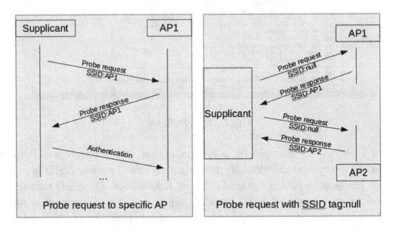

Fig. 3. Probes for the specific SSID/wildcard

3   WEP Security Protocol and Its Vulnerabilities

The WEP security protocol can be simple protection choice, because it is the easiest to implement when it comes to the needs for backward compatibility solutions. WEP disadvantages include usage of RC4 which is a symmetric stream chiper. RC4 uses the OR operator which encodes the message and deliver chipertext [8].

Security protocols for wireless networks can be listed as: WEP, WPA, WPA2. Protocols differ in the level of security they provide. The security level is defined as three different security points known as the "CIA": Confidentiality, Integrity, Authentication. Data privacy is achieved by encryption that ensures that an attacker cannot read packets when he or she analyse network traffic using sniffers. The integrity check verify that the message has not been changed in the transmission by monitoring the integrity check value (ICV) at the end of the packet. Authentication ensures that the recipient accepts messages only from trusted senders [12] (Fig. 4).

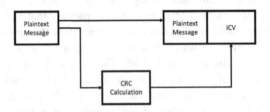

Fig. 4. CRC calculation

WEP, abbreviation for Wired Equivalent Privacy, is a protocol that has copied the level of security on wireless networks to the level that computers have in the network connected to the cable. The implementation of this protocol has opened the door to attackers in the network because of its vulnerability in its application. WEP does not offer any authentication when using the network, which means that there is no identity check or packet source within the network making the network vulnerable to MITM attacks [9] (Fig. 5).

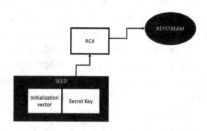

Fig. 5. RC4

Privacy with WEP protocol is achieved by implementing the RC4 encryption algorithm. The RC4 algorithm encrypts the message in a way that uses an initialization vector (IV) as input, which must be 1 higher for each new packet and the key. The output is a stream chipper that encrypts the message so that each bit is inversed using the OR logic. Vulnerability points from the situation where the 802.11 standard for WEP does not prescribe, come from scenario where each packet must have a new IV, meaning that the attacker may, by listening to the traffic, intercept packets that have the same IV (IV are not encrypted but have been added as a plaintext number at the end of the packet). Once the attacker has a duplicate IV, it can easily detect plaintext, since the protocols have a clearly defined structure, and the messages that require, for example, login often look unified.[1] WEP weaknesses can be described as: initialization vector number sent as plaintext in packet, limited rage of diverse IV and no shared key recheck process after initial authentication [14].

The WEP Wireless Encryption Protocol (WEP) is a protocol intended for wireless network security, part of the IEEE 802.11 standard. The WEP protocol encrypts data that travel between a user and an access point with a shared key. The user must have the appropriate WEP key to communicate with the access point. The WEP Encryption Protocol uses a 64-bit or 128-bit RC4 algorithm, and the CRC-32 algorithm is used to provide data integrity. It has been shown that such a security mechanism can be exploited by publicly available tools and is not recommended as an adequate safeguard measure. WPA and WPA2 Wi-Fi Protected Access (WPA) is a security mechanism designed to correct shortcomings in WEP protocol. WPA uses dynamically changing TKIP keys and the "Michael" algorithm for integrity checking. WPA2 as an enhancement instead of RC4 uses a variant of the AES encryption algorithm but is not

---

[1] http://www.isaac.cs.berkeley.edu/isaac/wep-faq.html.

supported on older network interfaces. For authentication, WPA supports 802.1x, but a less secure shared-key system can also be used - users must know a common key to connect to the network [10].

4 WiFi Networks Vulnerabilities: Attack and Protection Tactics and Practices

Using various malicious software, the attacker is able to attack the system, expel users from the network, and hinder the normal operation and attack. After they've been excluded from the network, users are trying to sign back on to the network. The cellular phones are again running the process of association and authentication with AP and are sending packets that contain a shared secret key. After attacking the packets, saving them to the local system and no longer having to risk exposure at the location of the attack, brute-force techniques can break through the password and, if not changed in the meantime, return to the range of the network and sign up as a legitimate user. In addition to the security protocols WPA and WPA2, there are also alternative network protection methods that are not really, but they are important because they are often present in networks. The SSID cloaking technique is used to stop the broadcasting of the network and thus prevent malicious users from entering the network, ie, users can access the network only if they know in advance its name (SSID) and password, and they manually enter and request access [13]. This technique is not particularly effective due to the fact that when a legitimate user reaches the reach of the hidden network, the device sends a request packet while the AP sends a trial response packet, both containing the network name, and if WEP is used together with the cloaking method, the network is extremely vulnerable and exposed to attacks. The network protection technology of MAC protection or router protection so that only devices with a particular MAC address can access the network is also a false security. Deciphering an address is an extremely simple and trivial undertaking, so the question of whether the MAC filtering technique can be placed in network protection techniques [11]. Windows Vista even has the option to send probe request (null) automatically and revert to two categories of networks, those that have both non-configured broadcasts[2].

5 Public Access WiFi Networks Security Protocols Practices in Tourist Destination

With intention to put emphasis on the security awareness of the users, filed research was conducted to investigate current security preferences of wireless computer networks in tourist destination, in the City of Zadar, Croatia. The research was conducted during preparation and early in the tourist season, spring/summer 2018. Hardware research support include AP beacon used a TL-WN722N card with a data rate of

---

[2] https://support.microsoft.com/en-us/help/929661/connecting-to-non-broadcast-wireless-networks-in-windows-vista.

150 Mbps, a 5 db antenna, a chip Atheros AR9271, all powered by Linux operating. Small suite was a passive scan tool for the beacon area. The data set used include the default AP settings that transmits its current SSID every 100 ms. WLAN card was used in the vehicle that was set up in the monitor mode used to collect all the available beacon frames. In addition to field research, we conduct additional survey with aim to investigate the general habits of users of wireless computer networks, from personal perspective. Overall goal was to put attention on WiFi security awareness and to expose security behaviour at router level. The survey had nine questions, of which only one was of an open type, while the rest were closed type. The poll was filled by 64 people and all the polls were taken into account. The first question in the survey was the classification of dependent respondents to which neighbourhood in City of Zadar belonged (Fig. 6).

The second question related to physical access to the router, more than 80% of the

Fig. 6. City of Zadar areas/respondents

respondents answered this question more accurately (Table 1).

The third question was: "If you have access to the router, can you" access "the

Table 1. Router availability

Q1: Do you have physical access to router?	Number of answers
Yes	51
No	13

router? (Logged in as admin/user in router settings …)". 49% of respondents answered positively while 43% answered negatively. Some less than 8% of respondents did not answer this question (Table 2).

Table 2. Router access

Q2: If you have physical access to router, do you have skills to log-on? (admin log-in or similar access to router settings)	Number of answers
Yes	31
No	28

The fourth question was to examine whether network users have changed their settings so far. 39% of respondents answered positively while 59% answered negatively. Some less than 2% of respondents did not answer this question (Table 3).

Table 3. Router settings

Q3: Did you ever changed default router settings?	Number of answers
Yes	25
No	38

The next question was the question of multiple choice through which the habits of changing the default settings were examined. Majority of respondents, 44% of the total number, respond they changed the default settings (25), changed the name of the network and the PSK (Table 4).

Table 4. Router administration

Q4: If you changed router default settings, which one did you change (multiple answers)?	Number of answers
No answer	38
EssID (network name), Password (PSK)	11
EssID (network name), Password (PSK), Security level (WEP, WPA, WPA2)	1
EssID (network name), Password (PSK), Security level (WEP, WPA, WPA2), WiFi Channel	4
EssID (network name), Password (PSK), Security level (WEP, WPA, WPA2), WiFi Channel, MAC filtering, port forwarding	1
Password (PSK)	5
Password (PSK), WiFi Channel	1
Password (PSK), Security level (WEP, WPA, WPA2)	2
Password (PSK), Security level (WEP, WPA, WPA2), WiFi Channel	1

6   Field Research Results

Total number of records collected was 16.982, while only 2.81% networks were without any protection protocol set. Less than 10% of all records indicate cloaked parameter set. WEP protection protocol was set only on 3.07% records (counting 522 records), 33 being cloaked (Fig. 7).

Fig. 7. Router ratio by manufacturer (top rated)

It is noticed that most popular router manufacturers are using default settings which include various kinds of encryption protocols, however most likely not WEP (Figs. 8 and 9).

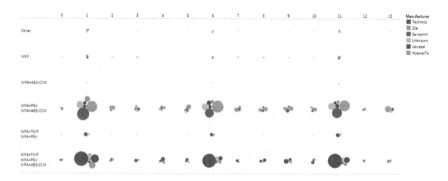

Fig. 8. Channel/router manufacturer/encryption ratio (top manufacturers)

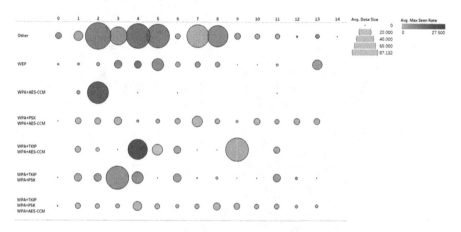

Fig. 9. Channel/encryption/data size/max seen rate ratio (all)

Significant data volumes are related to non-encrypted connection points while most used channels are 1, 6 and 11. In order to put attention on WiFi security awareness and to expose security behaviour at router level, city map was generated showing behaviour patterns and locations covered by WiFi signal (Fig. 10).

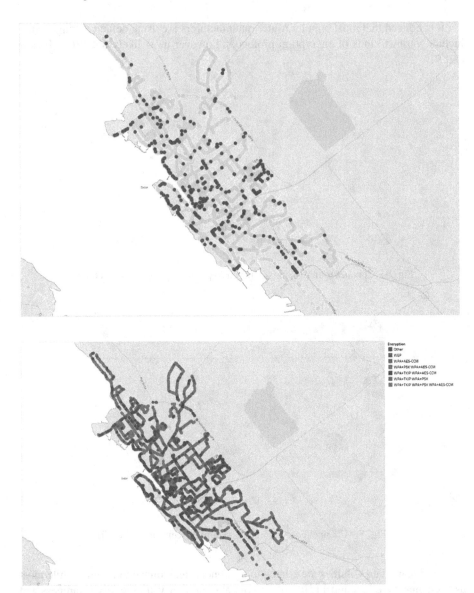

Fig. 10. City of Zadar WiFi/encryption city map (right), access points without encryption (left)

7   Conclusion

Paper addresses security issues with public access WiFi networks, with emphasis on networks deployed in touristic places, because of their popularity. Such networks are often poorly administered and guarded whereas tourist-services they support, are massively used by thousands of occasional users daily. With intention to put emphasis on the security awareness of the users, filed research was conducted to investigate current security preferences of wireless computer networks in tourist destination, in the City of Zadar, Croatia. Overall goal was to put attention on WiFi security awareness and to expose security behaviour at router level.

WiFi security protocols practices in tourist destination based on City of Zadar case, must be monitored carefully and used to engage and motivate access point owners to pay more attention on user behaviour to increase overall access point protection for all users. Large number of owners are relying on default setup for router and management while majority of users are using non encrypted access points.

Wireless networks provide great mobility, while they open new areas of connectivity but are open to various and new security vulnerabilities. The safety of wireless networks due to the properties of wireless media is more sensible and needs to be put in perspective and treated with caution. The speed of wireless network implementation needs to analyse security issues, the level of protection required, and the financial costs needed to achieve that level of protection. Because of the characteristics of wireless networks, they will probably represent the most effective and most vulnerable network segment suitable for cyber-attack. This paper is putting emphasis on the security awareness of the users, showing the most common vulnerability points and ways of reducing risk. Decision on level of protection that will be applied on specific location, primarily depends on the needs and the technical knowledge/possibilities. It is important to emphasize that the security system is dynamic, and that the only way to minimize risk is to keep track of the development of technology, to patch application and upgrade regularly, to apply precise defensive security policies and procedures, and to continuously invest in staff training and administrator recommendations.

References

1. Aime, M.D., Calandriello, G., Lioy, A.: Dependability in wireless networks: can we rely on WiFi? IEEE Secur. Priv. 5(1), 23–29 (2007)
2. Bachman, R., Saltzman, L.E., Thompson, M.P., Carmody, D.C.: Disentangling the effects of selfprotective behaviors on the risk of injury in assaults against women. J. Quant. Criminol. 18(2), 135–157 (2002)
3. BT Wi-fi (n.d.a) Find a Hotspot. https://www.btwifi.co.uk/find/
4. BT Wi-fi (n.d.b) Security when Using BT's Wi-fi Hotspots. https://www.btwifi.co.uk/help/security/index.jsp
5. BT Wi-fi (n.d.c) BT Wi-fi Protect. http://www.btwifi.com/Media/pdf/WIFI_PROTECT_250313_wifi.pdf
6. BT Wi-fi (n.d.d) Terms and Conditions. BT Wi-fi Acceptable Use Policy (including BT Openzone). http://www.btwifi.com/terms-and-conditions/acceptable-use-policy.jsp
7. Cheng, N., Xinlei, W., Wei, C., Prasant, M., Aruna, S.: Characterizing privacy leakage of public wifi networks for users on travel. In: Proceeding of INFOCOM 2013. IEEE (2013)
8. Guerette, R.T., Santana, S.A.: Explaining victim self-protective behavior effects on crime incident outcomes: a test of opportunity theory. Crime Delinq. 56(2), 198–226 (2010)
9. Holt, T.J., Bossler, A.M.: An assessment of the current state of cybercrime scholarship. Deviant Behav. 35(1), 20–40 (2014)

10. Lalonde Lévesque, F., Nsiempba, J., Fernandez, J.M., Chiasson, S., Somayaji, A.: A clinical study of risk factors related to malware infections. In: Proceedings of the 2013 ACM SIGSAC Conference on Computer & Communications Security, pp. 97–108. ACM (2013)

11. Spacey, R., Cooke, L., Muir, A.: Regulating use of the Internet in public libraries: a review. J. Doc. **70**(3), 478–497 (2014)

12. Castiglione, et al.: Virtual lab: a concrete experience in building multi-purpose virtualized labs for Computer Science Education. In: Proceedings of: SoftCOM 2012, 20th International Conference on Software, Telecommunications and Computer Networks, Split (HR), 11–13 September 2012. IEEE (2012)

13. Catuogno, L., Turchi, S.: The Dark Side of the Interconnection: security and Privacy in the Web of Things (2015). https://doi.org/10.1109/imis.2015.86

14. Gast, M.S.: 802.11 Wireless Networks: The Definitive Guide: The Definitive Guide, O'Reilly Media, Sebastopol (2005)

15. Lalonde Lévesque, F.L., Fernandez, J.M., Somayaji, A.: Risk prediction of malware victimization based on user behavior. In: Malicious and Unwanted Software: The Americas (MALWARE) (2014)

1st International Workshop on Vehicular Technology (IWVT 2019)

AEB Control Strategy and Collision Analysis Considering the Human-Vehicle-Road Environment

Xunyi Li, Jinju Shao$^{(\boxtimes)}$, Guo Wei, and Ruhong Hou

Shandong University of Technology, Zibo 255000, China
shaojinju@sdut.edu.cn

Abstract. Automatic emergency braking System (AEB) is one of key technologies of advanced driver assistance systems (ADAS). In order to avoid and reduce the occurrence of rear-end collision accidents. This paper analyzes the motion state of the target vehicle, taking into account the driver's reaction time and real road conditions. And this paper considers the influence of road adhesion coefficient on braking distance. In this paper, the logic rule of AEB is established. Through simulation experiment, the AEB rule is verified for the reliability on different pavements. It enables AEB to adapt to most road conditions and people with different personalities. The performance of traditional autonomous emergency braking system has been improved. The new AEB rule guarantees the safety of longitudinal driving by braking warning and participating in braking at the right time.

Keywords: Autonomous emergency braking · Human-vehicle-road · Vehicle safety braking distance

1 Introduction

With the rapid development of automotive active safety technology in recent years, more and more countries are aware of the importance of active safety. Autonomous emergency braking system (AEB) is one of the key technologies of advanced driver assistance system (ADAS) [1]. As an important part of active safety technology, autonomous emergency braking system (AEB) was formally incorporated into Euro-NCAP scoring rules in 2014. According to the European-NCAP survey, the installation of AEB can reduce traffic accidents by 27% [2]. Literature [3] shows that the incidence of rear-end collision of vehicles equipped with AEB on real roads is 38% lower than that of similar vehicle samples.

As active safety technology, AEB has two main functions: collision warning and autonomous braking. When the subject vehicle is about to collide with the target vehicle, AEB carries out light and sound warnings. This warning can alert drivers to take measures to avoid collisions. When the driver does not take any measures, the system will automatically brake to avoid collision or minimize the degree of collision [4–6].

In order to improve the reliability of AEB, relevant experts have proposed many algorithms: safety braking distance model [7], time-to-collision model (TTC) [8, 9],

© Springer Nature Switzerland AG 2019
C. Esposito et al. (Eds.): I-SPAN 2019, CCIS 1080, pp. 335–346, 2019.
https://doi.org/10.1007/978-3-030-30143-9_28

driver supervisor perception model [10] and so on. Chen et al. proposed an adaptive control system for longitudinal collision avoidance and lateral stability of autonomous vehicles based on MPC [11]. Pei et al. proposed that the reciprocal of collision time TTC^{-1} be used as an evaluation index to adapt to the driver's characteristics, and established a hierarchical safety distance model based on hazard coefficient ε [12]. TTC model depends on time threshold to make logical judgment and the time threshold generally unchanged. Because of vehicle braking performance is related to pavement adhesion coefficient, AEB system needs to consider the availability on different pavements [13]. AEB is difficult to make flexible judgments under different drivers, different vehicles and different road conditions. Therefore, it is necessary to consider the flexibility and stability of AEB from three aspects of people-vehicle-road.

2   Vehicle Front Risk Assessment Based on Distance

The driving process of the two cars on a straight road is shown in Fig. 1.

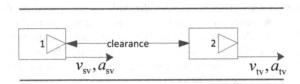

Fig. 1. Two-car straight-line model

Where v_{sv} is velocity of the subject vehicle. a_{sv} is acceleration of the subject vehicle. v_{tv} is velocity of the target vehicle. a_{tv} is acceleration of the target vehicle.

Vladimir et al. proposed a method for fusion of radar sensor measurements and camera images [14]. Han et al. proposed a distance estimation method between two vehicles based on monocular camera [15].

2.1   Brake Dynamics Analysis of Vehicle

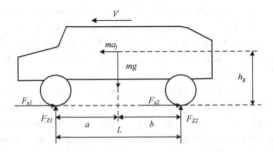

Fig. 2. Forces acting on automobiles during braking

Where F_{x1} is front wheel ground braking force, F_{x2} is rear wheel ground braking force. a_j is brake deceleration. L is the wheel base, a is the distance from car center of mass to front axle, b is the distance from car center of mass to rear axle. F_{z1} is the normal reaction of the ground against the front wheel, F_{z2} is the normal reaction of the ground against the rear wheel. m is the automobile quality, h_g is the vehicle centroid height. The dynamic equation of automobile braking is as follows:

$$\begin{cases} ma_j = Gz = F_{x1} + F_{x2} \\ F_{z1}L = Gb + F_jh_g \\ F_{z2}L = Ga - F_jh_g \end{cases} \tag{1}$$

where G is total gravity of automobile. The normal reaction forces of the front and rear wheels are as follows:

$$\begin{cases} F_{z1} = G(b + zh_g)/L \\ F_{z2} = G(b - zh_g)/L \end{cases} \tag{2}$$

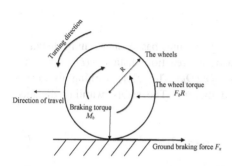

Fig. 3. The wheel is under force when braking

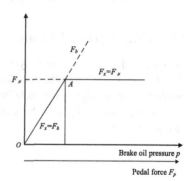

Fig. 4. Relationship between F_x, F_u and F_b

Where F_x is ground braking force, F_u is ground adhesion, F_p is pedal force and F_b is brake braking force.

When subject vehicle brakes on a good road surface, the wheel stress is shown in Fig. 3. In the process of braking, the relationship between ground braking force F_x, brake braking force F_b and adhesion F_u is shown in Fig. 4. If the friction moment of the brake is small, the ground braking force equals the braking force of the brake. However, because the ground braking force is limited by the adhesion coefficient between wheel and ground, the ground braking force cannot exceed the adhesion force.

$$F_x \leq F_u = \mu F_z \tag{3}$$

When the front and rear wheels are locked at the same time, the formula of ground braking force is as follows:

$$\begin{cases} F_{x1} = F_{\mu1} = F_{z1}\mu \\ F_{x2} = F_{\mu2} = F_{z2}\mu \end{cases} \tag{4}$$

where F_z is vertical ground reaction, μ is road adhesion coefficient.

When the front and rear wheels of the car are locked at the same time, the maximum braking deceleration is as follows:

$$a_{jmax} = \mu_s g \tag{5}$$

If the car is equipped with an ideal ABS position to control the braking of the car, the maximum braking deceleration is as follows:

$$a_{jmax} = \mu_p g \tag{6}$$

Where μ_s is sliding adhesion coefficient, μ_p is peak Adhesion Coefficient.

2.2   Safety Warning Distance

Chen et al. [16] developed a system of braking warning based on warning distance. Warning distance includes the following aspects: reaction distance (D_r), pressure buildup distance (D_p) and vehicle braking distance (D_b). The safety warning distance is the distance traveled from the current speed to zero, The safety warning distance formula is as follows:

$$D_{w,min} = D_{r,min} + D_{p,min} + D_{min} \tag{7}$$

$$D_{w,max} = D_{r,max} + D_{p,max} + D_{max} \tag{8}$$

$$D_{r,min} = v_{sv}t_{r,min} \tag{9}$$

$$D_{r,max} = v_{sv}t_{r,max} \tag{10}$$

$$D_{p,min} = v_{sv}t_{p,min} \tag{11}$$

$$D_{p,max} = v_{SV}t_{p,max} \tag{12}$$

$$D(x) = \frac{\gamma W}{2gC_{ae}} In \left(1 + \frac{C_{ae}v_{sv}^2}{\eta_b(\mu + f_r)Wcos\theta_s \pm Wsin\theta_s} \right) \tag{13}$$

where $D(x)$ is the braking distance when the speed of the subject vehicle decreases to zero. γ is the equivalent mass factor. W is the vehicle weight. ρ is the mass density of the air. g is the gravity speed. A_f is the characteristic area of the vehicle. C_d is the coefficient of aerodynamic resistance. v_{sv} is the vehicle speed. η_b is the brake efficiency. μ is the road adhesion coefficient. f_r is the rolling resistance coefficient. θ_s is the angle of the road slope with the horizontal. $\pm$ is the slope of the road. $C_{ae} = (\rho * A_f * C_d)/2$.

2.3   Safety Braking Distance

When the clearance between two vehicles is less than the safety clearance, the forced braking is carried out. It is composed of delay distance and brake distance. In order to avoid emergency braking resulting in rear-end collision, the vehicle only needs to slow down to the same speed as the target vehicle to avoid collision.

$$V_r(t) = v_{tv}(t) - v_{sv}(t) \tag{14}$$

$$v_{sv} + a_{sv}t = v_{tv} + a_{tv}t \tag{15}$$

$$v_{sv}t_d + v_{sv}t + \frac{1}{2}a_{sv}t^2 = v_{tv}t + \frac{1}{2}a_{tv}t^2 + D_b - d \tag{16}$$

Safe braking distance Eq. 17 can be obtained by Eqs. 6, 15 and 16.

$$D_b = v_{sv}t_d + d - \frac{v_r^2}{2(\mu g - a_{tv})} \tag{17}$$

where, t_d is the system delay time, d is reserved for a safe distance of 3 m. v_r is the relative velocity.

3   AEB Rules and Experimental Testing

3.1   Establishment of AEB Rules

Figure 5 shows the AEB rule. When the data measured by the sensor is calculated, the safety warning distance D_w, the safety braking distance D_b and the relative distance L between the two vehicles and are obtained. When the relative distance is less than the warning distance, the driver is warned and the driver is judged to take measures. At the same time, data calculation and warning update are carried out. When the relative distance reaches the braking distance, the system carries out forced braking to avoid collision.

According to this logic rule, the corresponding Simulink model can be established. Next, the correctness of this rule will be tested in real vehicles.

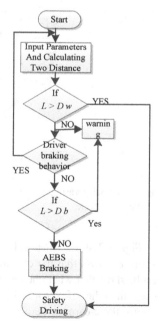

Fig. 5. Algorithm of AEB

3.2   Vehicle Real Road Test

This AEB logic rule test platform is Harvard H7 automobile. Sensors include radar, mobileye, etc. Vehicle positioning is carried out by GPS and IMU. The AEB logic rule model is established by Simulink, and the model is imported into the dSPACE controller. The dSPACE controller transmits the signal to the bottom controller through the CAN Bus of the whole vehicle. Bottom controller controls vehicle braking. Figure 6 shows the test vehicle and signal transmission route. This test is based on good road surface.

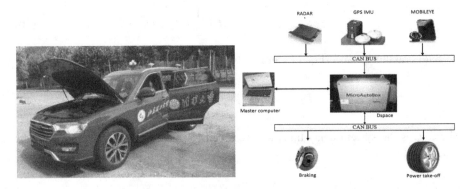

Fig. 6. Test vehicle and Signal flow chart

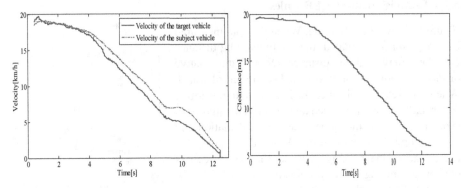

Fig. 7. Velocity variation of subject and target vehicles with time

Fig. 8. The clearance between subject and target vehicles with time

Figure 7 shows that Velocity variation of subject and target vehicles with Time. Figure 8 shows that the clearance between subject and target vehicles with time. The results show that when the target vehicle brakes, the clearance between the two vehicles is less than the safe clearance, and the AEB triggers. When the velocity of the two cars is zero, the clearance between the two vehicles is 6 m.

Next, we will analyze different drivers' reaction time and braking conditions on different roads. The reliability of AEB under different pavement conditions is verified by simulation.

4   Braking Distance Analysis Based on Driver Reaction Time and Road Adhesion Coefficient

4.1   Analysis of Driver's Response Time

Driver's response time includes observation time, judgment time and action time. The response time will be affected by age, identity and mood [17, 18].

Driver's response time is crucial for the AEBS warning system, and the AEBS warning system determines whether to remind the driver at the right time, so as not to advance or delay. This paper analyzed the reaction time mainly from age. Table 1 shows the reaction time of different age groups. The two cases with the shortest and longest response times were selected as 0.74 and 1.17 s respectively for the warning braking distance analysis. Figure 9 shows the warning braking distance with the change of speed in the two extreme times.

Table 1. Reaction time of driver

Age of driver	Reaction time
18–33	0.74–1.10
34–47	0.75–1.12
48–57	0.77–1.13
58–70	0.78–1.17

4.2   Analysis of Adhesion Coefficient

The adhesion coefficients of several different road surfaces are given in Table 2. Figure 3 shows the relationship between speed and safe braking distance under different road surfaces. When all the wheels are locked, the adhesion coefficient is slip adhesion coefficient [19]. It is assumed that the subject vehicle ABS performance is good and other factors are certain. Figure 5 shows that the safety warning distance decreases with the increase of road adhesion coefficient at a certain initial speed. In the simulation, the road surface adhesion coefficient provided by the peak adhesion coefficient.

Table 2. Average adhesion coefficient on different road surfaces.

Pavement type	Peak adhesion coefficient	Slip adhesion coefficient
Asphalt (dry)	0.8–0.9	0.75
Asphalt (wet)	0.5–0.7	0.45–0.6
Dirt road (dry)	0.68	0.65
Dirt road (wet)	0.55	0.4–0.5
Snow road (compact)	0.2	0.15
Ice	0.1	0.07

According to Figs. 2 and 3, with the increase of vehicle speed, the driver's reaction time and road condition have a greater impact on the warning distance (Figs. 10, 11 and 12).

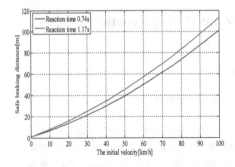

Fig. 9. Safety warning distance and speed under two reaction time

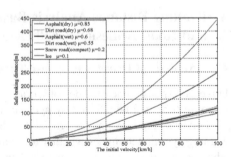

Fig. 10. Safety braking distance and speed under different road surfaces

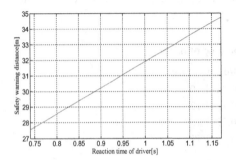

Fig. 11. Safety warning distance under different reaction time

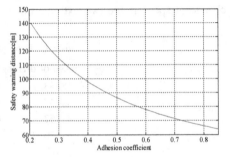

Fig. 12. Safety warning distance under different road surfaces

5   Simulation Results

This simulation selects three working conditions: Car-to-Car Rear Stationary (CCRs), Car-to-Car Rear Moving (CCRm), Car-to-Car Rear Braking (CCRb). Assume that the driver response time is an average of 0.95 s and the initial speed of the vehicle is 60 km/h. Simulation verifies the validity of AEB logic rule based on three different roads.

5.1   Car-to-Car Rear Stationary

The subject vehicle is stationary and tested on 3 different road surfaces. Asphalt (dry), Asphalt (wet) and Snow road. Figures 13 and 15 show the change of acceleration and velocity respectively. Figure 14 shows the change of clearance between the two cars. On different roads, the shortest clearance between two cars is 2–7 m. Figure 16 shows the opening of the brake pedal.

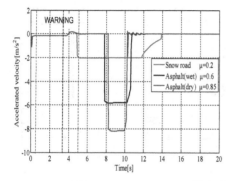

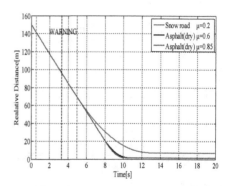

Fig. 13. Acceleration under different pavement conditions

Fig. 14. Relative distance under different pavement conditions

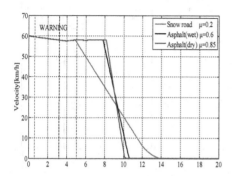

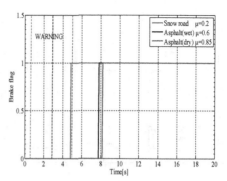

Fig. 15. Velocity under different pavement conditions

Fig. 16. Brake flag under pavement conditions

The simulation results show that AEB can give a warning and braking at a reasonable time to avoid collision on different roads when target vehicle is stationary.

5.2 Car-to-Car Rear Moving

Set the front car running at a constant speed of 30 km/h. The subject vehicle travels at a speed of 60 km/h. Figure 17 shows the change of clearance between the two cars. Figures 18 and 19 show the change of velocity respectively and acceleration. Figure 20 shows the change of the brake pedal in the operation.

It can be seen from Figs. 17 and 19 that the vehicle speed finally drops to 30 km/h without any collision with the target vehicle. And the minimum clearance between the two cars on different roads is 1.5 m.

According to the simulation result, AEB warning time and braking time are different on three different roads under two working conditions. And AEBS can prevent vehicles from colliding with vehicles in front.

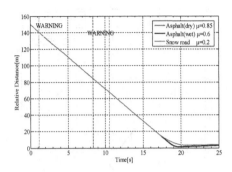

Fig. 17. Relative distance under different pavement conditions

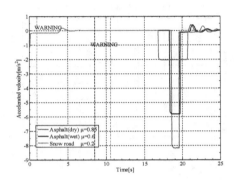

Fig. 18. Acceleration under different pavement conditions

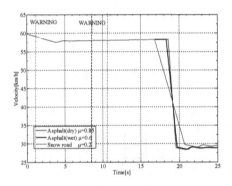

Fig. 19. Velocity under different pavement conditions

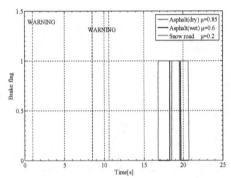

Fig. 20. Brake flag under different pavement conditions

5.3   Car-to-Car Rear Breaking

When the target vehicle decelerates rapidly, simulation results as shown above. Figure 21 shows the change of velocity of subject vehicle on three different roads. Figure 23 shows the clearance of workshop distance over time on three different roads. From the results, it can be concluded that the AEB braking rules can avoid collisions on dry and wet pavement. On the snow road with low road adhesion coefficient, the subject vehicle collides with the target vehicle. But the subject car has obviously adopted braking (Figs. 22 and 24).

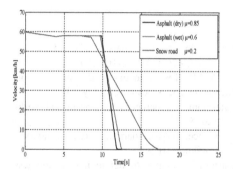

Fig. 21. Velocity under different pavement conditions

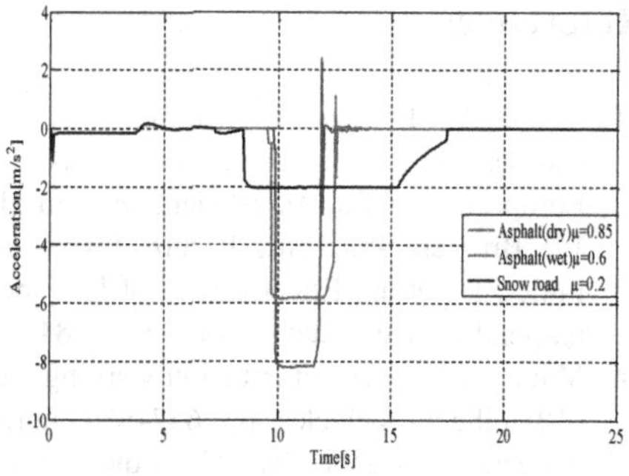

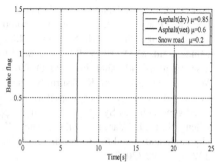

Fig. 22. Acceleration under different pavement conditions

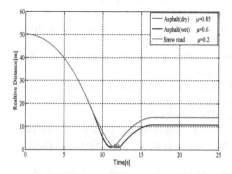

Fig. 23. Relative distance under different pavement conditions

Fig. 24. Brake flag under different conditions

6   Conclusion

The AEB logic rule is proposed in this paper. It has been verified to be feasible by real vehicle test. It effectively avoids collision accidents and reduces the degree of collision to ensure safer driving of vehicles. At the same time, the AEB system specified in this paper can also set different safe distances according to different road conditions. And the system can make timely collision alarm according to the different reaction time of drivers through simulation. The simulation results show that the system can adapt to more complex pavement and is more flexible than the traditional AEB system. However, in this system, the adhesion coefficient of different pavement is artificially calibrated. It is a future research topic to realize more accurate braking control for vehicle self-determination of road adhesion coefficient.

References

1. Segata, M., Locigno, R.: Automatic emergency braking: realistic analysis of car dynamics and network performance. IEEE Trans. Veh. Technol. **62**(9), 4150–4161 (2013)
2. European New Car Assessment Program (Euro-NCAP). Test protocol - AEB system version 1.0. Brussels: Euro-NCAP. https://www.euroncap.com/zh. Accessed 25 May 2019
3. Fildes, B., et al.: Effectiveness of low speed autonomous emergency braking in real-world rear-end crashes. Accid. Anal. Prev. **81**, 24–29 (2015)
4. Maurer, M.: Forward collision warning and avoidance. In: Eskandarian, A. (ed.) Handbook of Intelligent Vehicles, pp. 657–687. Springer, London (2012)
5. Sander, U., Lubbe, N.: The potential of clustering methods to define intersection test scenarios: assessing real-life performance of AEB. Accid. Anal. Prev. **113**, 1–11 (2018)
6. Ando, K., Matsui, Y., Tanaka, N.: Pedestrian accidents and expectations for AEB. J. Soc. Mech. Eng. **118**(1157), 192–195 (2015)
7. Lee, W., Chen, Y.: Safety distance warning system with a novel algorithm for vehicle safety braking distance calculating. Int. J. Veh. Saf. **5**(3), 213–231 (2011)
8. Lee, K., Peng, H.: Evaluation of automotive forward collision warning and collision avoidance algorithms. Veh. Syst. Dyn. **43**(10), 735–751 (2018)
9. Minderhoud, M.M., Bovy, P.H.: Extended time-to-collision measures for road traffic safety assessment. Accid. Anal. Prev. **33**(1), 89–97 (2015)
10. Wada, T., Doi, S., Imai, K., Tsuru, N., Isaji, K., Kaneko, H.: Analysis of braking behaviors in car following based on a performance index for approach and alienation. In: IEEE Intelligent Vehicles Symposium, Istanbul, pp. 547–552 (2007)
11. Cheng, S., Li, L., Yan, B., Liu, C., Wang, X., Fang, J.: Simultaneous estimation of tire side-slip angle and lateral tire force for vehicle lateral stability control. Mech. Syst. Sig. Process. **132**, 168–182 (2019)
12. Pei, X., Liu, Z., Ma, G., et al.: Research on test scenarios of automatic emergency braking system. J. Autom. Safe Energ. **3**(1), 26–33 (2012)
13. Panáček, V., Semela, M., Adamec, V., Schüllerová, B.: Impact of usable coefficient of adhesion between tyre and road surface by modern vehicle on its dynamics while driving and braking in the curve. Transport **31**(2), 142–146 (2016)
14. Lekic, V., Babic, Z.: Automotive radar and camera fusion using generative adversarial networks. Comput. Vis. Image Underst. **184**, 1–8 (2019)
15. Han, J., Heo, O., Park, M., Kee, S., Sunwoo, M.: Vehicle distance estimation using a mono-camera for FCW/AEB systems. Int. J. Autom. Technol. **17**(3), 483–491 (2016)
16. Chen, Y., Shen, K., Wang, S.: Forward collision warning system considering both time-to-collision and safety braking distance. In: 2013 IEEE 8th Conference on Industrial Electronics and Applications (ICIEA), Melbourne, VIC, pp. 972–977 (2013)
17. Stanisław Jurecki, R., Lech Stańczyk, T., Jacek Jaśkiewicz, M.: Driver's reaction time in a simulated, complex road incident. Transport **32**(1), 44–45 (2017)
18. Sena, P., d'Amore, M., Brandimonte, M.A., Squitieri, R., Fiorentino, A.: Experimental framework for simulators to study driver cognitive distraction: brake reaction time in different levels of arousal. Transp. Res. Procedia **14**, 4410–4419 (2016)
19. Novikov, I., Lazarev, D.: Experimental installation for calculation of road adhesion coefficient of locked car wheel. Transp. Res. Procedia **20**, 463–467 (2017)

Context-Awareness Enhances 5G MEC Resource Allocation

Shihyang Lin[✉] and Jieqin Wan

Shandong University of Technology, Zibo 255049, China
shihyang@sdut.edu.cn

Abstract. The concept of MEC is to smoothly integrate cloud capabilities into the mobile network architecture. It enables multi-operator operation for V2X mobiles/users to provide convenience service continuity across access network coverage and across borders of different operators' networks. Based on the requirements of traffic prediction and adaptive traffic control system, some computational tasks can offload to MEC server. Considering the network bandwidth, storage capacity, and processor performance, we need a resource allocation mechanism to distribute tasks to MEC server in balance. Otherwise, some tasks may be queued on a MEC server for a moment because there are too many tasks allocated to the same MEC serve at the same time. In order to resolve the problem, the Context-Awareness MEC Resource Allocation (CARA) mechanism is proposed in this paper. The evaluated results show that the CARA can balance resource allocation to every MEC server.

Keywords: 5G · MEC · Offloading · Resource allocation

1 Introduction

The concept of Mobile/Multi-access Edge Computing (MEC) was defined by the European Telecommunications Standards Institute (ETSI) in 2014. It provides cloud-computing capabilities within the Radio Access Network (RAN) in close proximity to mobile subscribers to lower propagation delay and computing latency. The ETSI MEC Industry Specification Group (ISG) has already published a set of specifications focusing on use case and requirement [1], architecture [2], and service scenarios [3], platform and requirements management of MEC applications [4, 5], application enablement Application Programming Interface (API) [6], service APIs [7–10] and the User Equipment (UE) application interface [11]. Referring to [2], MEC host architecture is shown in Fig. 1.

In Fig. 1, the MEC host contains the MEC platform and a virtualization infrastructure which provides compute, storage, and network resources for MEC applications. The virtualization infrastructure includes a data plane that executes the traffic rules received by the MEC platform, and routes the traffic among applications, services, DNS server/proxy, 3GPP network, other access networks, local networks and external networks. The MEC platform offers an environment and services, receives traffic rules

© Springer Nature Switzerland AG 2019
C. Esposito et al. (Eds.): I-SPAN 2019, CCIS 1080, pp. 347–358, 2019.
https://doi.org/10.1007/978-3-030-30143-9_29

and DNS records from the MEC platform manager, hosts MEC services, and provides access to persistent storage and time of day information. The MEC application can interact with the MEC platform to consume and provide MEC services via reference point Mp1, in which the Mp1 provides service registration, service discovery, and communication support for services. It also provides other functionality such as application availability, session state relocation support procedures, traffic rules and DNS rules activation, access to persistent storage and time of day information. The Mp2 reference point is used to instruct the data plane on how to route traffic among applications, networks, services, and the Mp3 reference point is used for control communication between MEC platforms [2].

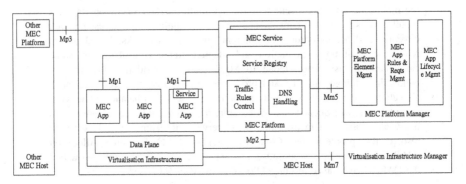

Fig. 1. The architecture of MEC host level.

The concept of MEC is to smoothly integrate cloud capabilities into the mobile network architecture. The article [13] briefs five fundamental principles of its implementation as follows. (1) The principle of Small Cell Cloud (SCC) has been firstly introduced in [14, 15], which adds additional components to enhance small cells (SCeNBs) computation and storage capabilities. (2) The principle of Mobile Micro Clouds (MMC) has been firstly introduced in [16], which allows users to have instantaneous access to the cloud services. The MMCs can directly interconnect or through backhaul in order to guarantee service continuity if the UEs move within the network to enable smooth virtual machine (VM) migration among the MMCs. (3) The principle of Fast Moving Personal Cloud (MobiScud) [17] integrates the cloud services into the mobile networks by means of Software Defined Network (SDN) and Network Function Virtualization (NFV) technologies. In the MobiScud, the cloud resources are not located directly at the LTE base stations (e.g., SCeNB or E-UTRAN Node B (eNB)). They are located at operator's clouds within RAN or close to RAN. (4) In the principle of Follow Me Cloud (FMC), cloud services run at distributed data centers, which follow the UEs roam throughout the network using the same way as in the case of the MobiScud [18, 19]. (5) The principle of CONCERT has been proposed in [20]. In CONCERT, the computing and storage resources are presented as virtual resources to converge cloud and cellular systems.

Various applications and use cases employ MEC architecture to enhance computation and storage capabilities. For the application in the connected car, four V2X use cases based on MEC for driving safety, convenience, advanced driving assistance, and vulnerable road user are discussed in [12]. The use case of driving safety includes several different types to support road safety. Intersection movement assist is used to warn drivers of vehicles approaching from a lateral direction at an intersection, which is designed to avoid intersection crossing crashes. The queue warning information is used to inform drivers beforehand for the purpose of potential danger and delay of traffic avoidance. The use case of convenience can technically be implemented with existing access technology and are partly already supported by car manufacturers. It enables multi-operator operation for V2X mobiles/users to provide convenience service continuity across access network coverage and across borders of different operators' networks. Advanced driving assistance includes two use cases. (1) The case of real time situational awareness and high definition maps should be extended to distribute and aggregate locally available information in real time to the traffic participants. (2) The case of see-through (or high definition sensor sharing) uses shared camera images or sensor data of road conditions ahead in platoons to vehicles behind them. The use case of vulnerable road user utilizes the accurate positioning information of traffic participants to improve traffic safety and to avoid accidents.

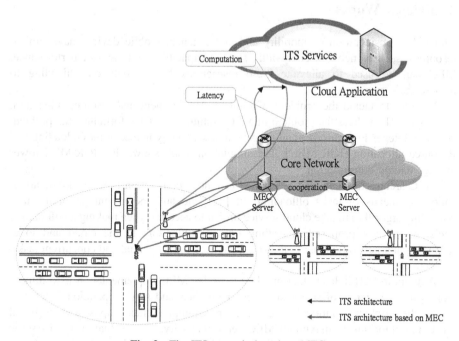

Fig. 2. The ITS scenario based on MEC.

The concept of MEC is to offload the network controlling, storage, and mobile computing towards the edges of network to lower latency. It enables new business, use cases, applications and services for not only mobile end user but also telecommunication operators. Use cases include, but not limited to, video analytics, location services, Internet-of-Things (IoT), augmented reality, optimized local content distribution and data caching, etc. It can also be applied to the Intelligent Transportation System (ITS) to create computation intensive. Figure 2 depicts the concept of ITS scenario based on MEC application. In Fig. 2, vehicles provide some related information (e.g. location, speed, heading…) to the MEC server across road side units (RSUs) for particular applications, e.g. traffic prediction. The MEC server connects RSU to local control traffic lights based on the predicted traffic information for the purpose of adaptive traffic signal control. Also, MEC servers exchange data with each other to get more information for the traffic prediction.

In order to achieve aforementioned ITS application, MEC application has to overcome a challenge: how to enhance MECs resource allocation based on data exchanging among MEC servers. This paper proposes a Context-Awareness MEC Resource Allocation (CARA) scheme to overcome some related problems. The rest of the paper is organized as follows. Section 2 introduces some related works. Section 3 introduces the proposed CARA. Section 4 describes the simulation environment and results. Finally, the conclusion remarks are given in Sect. 5.

2   Related Works

Under the consideration of mobility and convenience, mobile devices have limited resources, such as network bandwidth, storage capacity, and processor performance. MEC can be used to alleviate these restrictions by computation offloading to resourceful servers.

In order to tackle the problem of joint task assignment and resource allocation, authors in [21] address the problem in MEC architecture. They formulate the problem as a new Integer Program (IP) and propose a new strategy named Joint Offloading and Resource allocation (JOR-MEC). The simulation result shows that JOR-MEC lower average energy consumption.

MEC architecture can also be applied to reduce completion time of mobile application by means of tasks offloading. In [22], the authors present an online task offloading algorithm to take cloud service time into account when making an offloading decision. In their proposed algorithm, optimal offloading to the cloud and load-balancing heuristic offloading to the cloud are used for sequential and concurrent tasks, respectively.

Authors in [23] indicate that one key issue for MEC implementation is to dimension systems in terms of server size, server number, and server operation. They formulate the problem as a mixed integer linear program, and then propose a graph-based clustering algorithm to maximum MEC server capacity. The evaluation results show that the core network can be largely offloaded, and the algorithm provides MEC get well-balanced in terms of workload.

MEC offloads vehicular applications to proximal MEC servers to decrease heavy computation on vehicular devices. In [24], the authors consider a cognitive vehicular network to formulate a dual-side optimization problem for the purpose cost minimization of vehicular devices and MEC servers at the same time. It guarantees network stability through jointly optimizing the offloading decision and local CPU frequency on the VT side, and the radio resource allocation and server provisioning on the server side. They propose a dual-side dynamic joint task offloading and resource allocation algorithm in vehicular networks (DDORV), it only needs a little information to operate well, such as channel states and traffic arrivals. Simulation results show that DDORV converges faster, can balance the cost-delay trade-off flexibly, and can obtain more performance gains in cost reduction.

3GPP allowing a MEC system and a 5G system to collaboratively interact in traffic routing and policy control related operations. Based on the requirements of traffic prediction and adaptive traffic control system, some computational tasks can offload to MEC server. Considering the network bandwidth, storage capacity, and processor performance, we need a resource allocation mechanism to distribute tasks to the MEC server in balance. Otherwise, some tasks may be queued on a MEC server for a moment because there are too many tasks allocate to the same MEC serve at the same time. In order to resolve the problem, the Context-Awareness MEC Resource Allocation (CARA) mechanism is proposed in this paper.

3   Context-Awareness MEC Resource Allocation (CARA)

In order to balance computation resource among MEC servers, we propose the CARA mechanism, in which the CARA mechanism gathers relevant information from vehicular devices to allocate tasks to the suitable MEC server. Figure 3 depicts the scenario. The procedure of CARA is described in detail as follows.

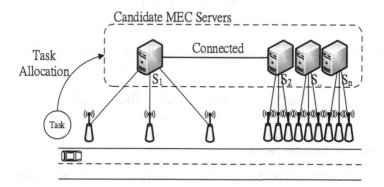

Fig. 3. The scenario of task allocation.

3.1   Exchange Data Periodically

The CARA needs some relevant information of every MEC server to select a suitable server for the task allocation. The information contain its available computing resource C_t, available memory M_t, and available bandwidth B_t, at time t. MEC servers exchange the relevant information periodically among each other to maintain the latest information of neighboring servers.

3.2 Reserve Computational Resource

In order to let MEC servers provide computing resource for specific events, it has to reserve some computing resource. In the CARA, the MEC server will keep 10% available computing resource for specific events. To achieve it, let:

$$\begin{cases} C_{pr} = C_t - 10\% \\ M_{pr} = M_t - 10\%, \ where \\ B_{pr} = B_t - 10\% \end{cases} \begin{cases} C_{pr} = \text{proper resource for computing} \\ M_{pr} = \text{proper resource for memory} \\ B_{pr} = \text{proper resource for bandwidth} \end{cases} \quad (1)$$

3.3 Filter Unsatisfied Servers

If any of the following equations is unsatisfied, it will not be a candidate server to serve the task.

$$\begin{cases} C_{pr} > 0 \\ M_{pr} > 0 \\ B_{pr} > 0 \end{cases} \quad (2)$$

Let the vehicle i needs computing resource C_{ni}, memory M_{ni}, and bandwidth B_{ni} to finish its task, hence the ratios of total task requirement are:

$$\begin{cases} C_{pn} = \sum C_{n_i}/C_r \\ M_{pn} = \sum M_{n_i}/M_r \\ B_{pn} = \sum B_{n_i}/B_r \end{cases} \quad (3)$$

If any of the following equations is satisfied, it will not be a candidate server to serve the task.

$$\left(C_{pn} \geq C_{pr}\right) \cup \left(M_{pn} \geq M_{pr}\right) \cup \left(B_{pn} \geq B_{pr}\right) \quad (4)$$

3.4 Select the Suitable Server

For those MEC servers who pass the filter will be further calculated to select the best one for task allocation. The selection procedure in the CARA considers four parameters: computing, memory, bandwidth, and distance between vehicles and MEC servers. Summation of the distance between vehicle i and the MEC server is represented as the following equation.

$$\sum_1^i d_{(i, MEC \ server)} \quad (5)$$

And, summation of the distance between vehicles and MEC servers is represented as the following equation.

$$\sum_1^j \sum_1^i d_{(i,j)} \tag{6}$$

Next, we adapt Analytic Hierarchy Process (AHP) to decide weight value for every parameter, in which elements A_1 to A_4 denote computing, memory, bandwidth, and distance, respectively. Assuming A_1 is of equal importance to A_2, A_1 is of week importance to A_3, A_1 is of essential importance to A_4, A_3 is of week importance to A_4, we can get quantitative results as follow.

$$A_1 : A_1 = 1 : 1; A_1 : A_2 = 1 : 1; A_1 : A_3 = 3 : 1; A_1 : A_4 = 5 : 1;$$
$$A_2 : A_1 = 1 : 1; A_2 : A_2 = 1 : 1; A_2 : A_3 = 3 : 1; A_2 : A_4 = 5 : 1;$$
$$A_3 : A_1 = 1 : 3; A_3 : A_2 = 1 : 3; A_3 : A_3 = 1 : 1; A_3 : A_4 = 3 : 1;$$
$$A_4 : A_1 = 1 : 5; A_4 : A_2 = 1 : 5; A_4 : A_3 = 1 : 3; A_4 : A_4 = 5 : 1;$$

And, the judgment matrix is as follow.

$$M = \begin{array}{c} \\ A_1 \\ A_2 \\ A_3 \\ A_4 \end{array} \begin{array}{cccc} A_1 & A_2 & A_3 & A_4 \\ \begin{pmatrix} 1 & 1 & 3 & 5 \\ 1 & 1 & 3 & 5 \\ 1/3 & 1/3 & 1 & 3 \\ 1/5 & 1/5 & 1/3 & 1 \end{pmatrix} \end{array} \tag{7}$$

We can get four roots of each element product are $L_1 = 1.9680$, $L_2 = 1.9680$, $L_3 = 0.7598$, and $L_4 = 0.3398$, respectively. Their weights can be got by orthonormalization as follows.

$$W = \begin{pmatrix} \alpha_1 \\ \alpha_2 \\ \alpha_{.3} \\ \alpha_4 \end{pmatrix} = \begin{pmatrix} 0.3908 \\ 0.3908 \\ 0.1509 \\ 0.0675 \end{pmatrix} \tag{8}$$

And the matrix is:

$$MW = \begin{pmatrix} 1 & 1 & 3 & 5 \\ 1 & 1 & 3 & 5 \\ 1/3 & 1/3 & 1 & 3 \\ 1/5 & 1/5 & 1/3 & 1 \end{pmatrix} \begin{pmatrix} 0.3908 \\ 0.3908 \\ 0.1509 \\ 0.0675 \end{pmatrix} = \begin{pmatrix} 1.5718 \\ 1.5718 \\ 0.6139 \\ 0.2741 \end{pmatrix} \tag{9}$$

Its largest eigenvalue can be got as follows.

$$\lambda_{max} = \frac{1}{4} \left(\frac{1.5718}{0.3908} + \frac{1.5718}{0.3908} + \frac{0.6139}{0.1509} + \frac{0.2741}{0.0675} \right) = 4.0433 \tag{10}$$

The Random Index (R.I.) can be got from the Table 1.

Table 1. Table of random index.

N	1	2	3	4	5	6	7
R.I.	0	0	0.58	0.9	1.12	1.24	1.32

We can use Consistency Index (C.I.) and Consistency Ratio (C.R.) to verify whether it satisfy the consistency or not.

$$C.I. = \frac{\lambda_{max} - n}{n-1} = \frac{4.0433 - 4}{4 - 1} = 0.0144 \tag{11}$$

$$C.R. = \frac{C.I.}{R.I.} = \frac{0.0144}{0.9} = 0.016, < 0.1 \tag{12}$$

Since C.R. is less than 0.1, we can say that it satisfies the consistency check, and the weight value for every element is trusty.

Finally, we use Eq. 13 to calculate summation of every candidate MEC server, where the minimum value of the summation is the best choose. It will be selected to provide computing resource for the specific task.

$$\text{where} \begin{cases} \text{Min}(Sum_1, Sum_2, \ldots, Sum_n), \\ \quad n = \text{number of MEC server} \\ \quad Sum_i = 0.3908 \left(\frac{C_{pn}}{C_{pr}} \right) + 0.3908 \left(\frac{M_{pn}}{M_{pr}} \right) \\ \quad + 0.1509 \left(\frac{B_{pn}}{B_{pr}} \right) + 0.0675 \left(\frac{\sum_1^i d_{(i, \text{MEC server})}}{\sum_1^j \sum_1^i d_{(i,j)}} \right), \end{cases} \tag{13}$$

4   Evaluation of CARA

We consider a typical grid road environment. There are 6 horizontal roads across 6 vertical roads in the evaluation. And, there are totally 36 RSUs deployed at every intersection. Each MEC Server manages 4 RSUs, and they can communicate with each other by wire connection. Figure 4 depicts the scenario.

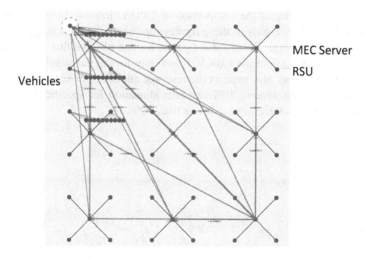

Fig. 4. The diagram of evaluated scenario.

We allocate 50 vehicles in the evaluate scenario. Every vehicle has a task to offload to MEC server with different requirements of computing resource, memory, bandwidth, etc. When the task reaches to the connected MEC server, it will trigger CARA to select the optimal MEC server for the computation. We compare the proposed CARA with Location-Based Resource Allocation (LBRA) mechanism, in which the LBRA only selects the closest MCE serve for the task allocation.

Figure 5 depicts the evaluation result. In Fig. 5, we can observe that the LBRA selects the server MEC5 to serve many tasks. Because there are many vehicles nearby the server MEC5 at a given time, their tasks are allocated to the MEC5 through the LBRA. If these tasks simultaneous reach the server MEC5, they may be queued for a moment because there are too many tasks allocated to the same MEC server. Comparatively speaking, the CARA gets balance performance for the task allocation for each MEC server. Even though these vehicles locate nearby the same MEC server, the CARA allocates their tasks to MEC servers in balance.

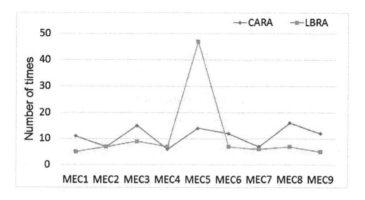

Fig. 5. The comparison of MEC server selection.

Figures 6, 7 and 8 depict the comparison of CPU utilization, memory, and bandwidth, respectively. The Y-axis in these figures represents the percentage value of all the MEC servers in average. From these figures, we can observe that wave motion of the CARA always lower than the LBRA. It not only means the stability of CARA is higher than the LBRA but also appears the resource allocation of CARA is better than LBRA. Since the CARA reserve 10% resource allocation for specific situation, saturation of the utilized resource always lower than 90%.

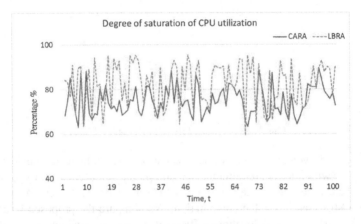

Fig. 6. The comparison of CPU utilization.

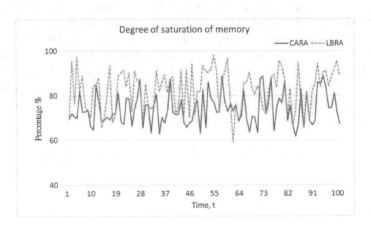

Fig. 7. The comparison of memory.

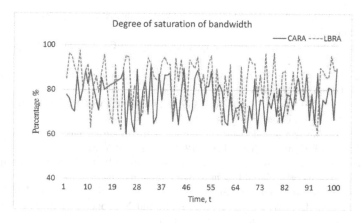

Fig. 8. The comparison of bandwidth.

5 Conclusion

Computation offloading in MEC provides an alternative opportunity to adapt to the 5G mobile communication network. Considering ITS application in the near future, MEC server has to provide context-aware resource allocation mechanism for some specific purposes. This paper proposes the CARA mechanism to fit its requirement, and evaluates the performances of the CARA. The evaluated results shown that the CARE can balance resource allocation to every MEC server. Hence, the problem of many tasks allocate to the same MEC serve can be solved.

References

1. ETSI ISG.: MEC 002 V2.1.1 Multi-access Edge Computing (MEC); Phase 2: Use Cases and Requirements. Group specification (2018)
2. ETSI ISG.: MEC 003 V2.1.1 Multi-access Edge Computing (MEC); Framework and Reference Architecture. Group specification (2019)
3. ETSI ISG.: MEC-IEG 004 V1.1.1 Mobile-Edge Computing (MEC); Service Scenarios. Group specification (2015)
4. ETSI ISG.: MEC 010-1 V1.1.1 Mobile Edge Computing (MEC); Mobile Edge Management; Part 1: System host and platform management. Group specification (2017)
5. ETSI ISG.: MEC 010-2 V1.1.1 Mobile Edge Computing (MEC); Mobile Edge Management; Part 2: Application lifecycle, rules and requirements management. Group specification (2017)
6. ETSI ISG.: MEC 011 V1.1.1 Mobile Edge Computing (MEC); Mobile Edge Platform Application Enablement. Group specification (2017)
7. ETSI ISG.: MEC 012 V1.1.1 2Mobile Edge Computing (MEC); Radio Network Information. Group specification (2017)
8. ETSI ISG.: MEC 013 V1.1.1 Mobile Edge Computing (MEC); Location API. Group specification (2018)

9. ETSI ISG.: MEC 014 V1.1.1 Mobile Edge Computing (MEC); UE Identity API. Group specification (2018)

10. ETSI ISG.: MEC 015 V1.1.1 Mobile Edge Computing (MEC); Bandwidth Management API. Group specification (2017)

11. ETSI ISG.: MEC 016 V2.1.1 Multi-access Edge Computing (MEC); UE application interface. Group specification (2019)

12. ETSI ISG.: MEC 022 V2.1.1 Multi-access Edge Computing (MEC); Study on MEC Support for V2X Use Cases. Group report (2018)

13. Mach, P., Becvar, Z.: Mobile edge computing: a survey on architecture and computation offloading. IEEE Commun. Surv. Tutor. 19(3), 1628–1656 (2017)

14. FP7 European Project, Distributed Computing, Storage and Radio Resource Allocation Over Cooperative Femtocells (TROPIC). http://www.ict-tropic.eu/

15. Lobillo, F., et al.: An architecture for mobile computation offloading on cloud-enabled LTE small cells. In: IEEE Wireless Communications and Networking Conference Workshops (WCNCW), Istanbul, pp. 1–6. IEEE Press (2014)

16. Wang, S., et al.: Mobile micro-cloud: application classification, mapping, and deployment. In: Fall Meeting ITA (AMITA), New York (2013)

17. Wang, K., Shen, M., Cho, J.: MobiScud: a fast moving personal cloud in the mobile network. In: 5th Workshop on All Things Cellular: Operations, Applications and Challenges, London, pp. 19–24. ACM (2015)

18. Taleb, T., Ksentini, A.: Follow me cloud: interworking federated clouds and distributed mobile networks. IEEE Netw. Mag. 27(5), 12–19 (2013)

19. Taleb, T., Ksentini, A., Frangoudis, P.A.: Follow-me cloud: when cloud services follow mobile users. IEEE Trans. Cloud Comput. 7(2), 369–382 (2019)

20. Liu, J., Zhao, T., Zhou, S., Cheng, Y., Niu, Z.: CONCERT: a cloud based architecture for next-generation cellular systems. IEEE Wirel. Commun. Mag. 21(6), 14–22 (2014)

21. Dab, B., Aitsaadi, N., Langar, R.: A novel joint offloading and resource allocation scheme for mobile edge computing. In: 16th IEEE Annual Consumer Communications & Networking Conference (CCNC), Las Vegas. IEEE Press (2019)

22. Jia, M., Cao, J., Yang, L.: Heuristic offloading of concurrent tasks for computation-intensive applications in mobile cloud computing. In: 2014 IEEE Conference on Computer Communications Workshops, Toronto, pp. 352–357. IEEE Press (2014)

23. Bouet, M., Conan, V.: Mobile edge computing resources optimization: a geo-clustering approach. IEEE Trans. Netw. Serv. Manag. 15(2), 787–796 (2018)

24. Du, J., Yu, F.R., Chu, X., Feng, J., Lu, G.: Computation offloading and resource allocation in vehicular networks based on dual-side cost minimization. IEEE Trans. Veh. Technol. 68(2), 1079–1092 (2019)

Optimal Hybrid Path Planning Considering Dynamic and Static Characteristics of Intelligent Vehicles

Gang Shen, Jinju Shao, Derong Tan, Yaming Niu, and Song Gao$^{(\boxtimes)}$

Shandong University of Technology, Zibo 255049, China
gs6510@163.com

Abstract. Aiming at the global path planning of intelligent vehicles, an optimal hybrid path planning algorithm considering the dynamic and static characteristics of intelligent vehicles is proposed. On the grid map with known static information of the environment, the improved A* algorithm is used for global path planning, and the obstacles in the path are expanded according to the static characteristics of the intelligent vehicle itself. Combined with the dynamic characteristics of the intelligent vehicles, dynamic window approach is used to carry out the local obstacle avoidance and path planning of the vehicle according to the unknown and varied environmental information around the vehicle. On this basis, the key turning point in the global path is used as the sub-target point correction of Dynamic Window Approach (DWA). The simulation results show that the proposed method can be used to avoid dynamic and static obstacles by guiding the vehicle to the target ending. Additionally, the dynamic constraints of the vehicle are satisfied during the journey without collision with the road boundary, which ensures the stability and safety of the vehicle.

Keywords: Intelligent vehicle · Path planning · A* algorithm · Dynamic obstacle avoidance

1 Introduction

In recent years, intelligent vehicles have become hot research issues so that more and more research scholars have started to develop related technologies for intelligent vehicles. Path planning technology is the basis and key of navigation [1–3]. How to get the optimal planning path under the premise of safe obstacle avoidance is even more difficult. Path planning techniques based on environmental information can be broadly classified into two categories: global path planning based on known environmental information [4, 5] and local path planning based on local environment known or non-static environment information [6, 7].

For mobile robots, the path planning technique is to complete the path planning between the defects on the static map with known environmental information. The most common planning methods are traditional grid method and artificial potential field method [8, 9], based on heuristic genetic formula. Ant colony algorithm [10–12] and particle swarm algorithm, as well as A* algorithm and dynamic window approach based on node search. In [13], an improved A* algorithm is proposed, which can calculate the

© Springer Nature Switzerland AG 2019
C. Esposito et al. (Eds.): I-SPAN 2019, CCIS 1080, pp. 359–370, 2019.
https://doi.org/10.1007/978-3-030-30143-9_30

rotation angle and direction of the mobile robot at the inflection point of the path on the basis of the simplified path, but does not have the ability to avoid obstacles in the dynamic environment. The dynamic window approach [14] can perform path planning in real time, and is suitable for robot autonomous navigation in a local dynamic environment, but this method cannot satisfy the global path optimization.

Different from mobile robots, when the intelligent vehicle is planning the path, the environmental information of the scene is relatively complex and changeable, which is mainly reflected in the fact that the environmental information is not completely static during the real driving process of the intelligent vehicle, inevitably other unknown people or environmental changes have occurred [15]. Document 16 introduces virtual force field into path planning and establishes virtual force field model to generate random point set to verify collision [16]. At the same time, the intelligent vehicle itself is very different from the mobile robot. When the mobile robot performs path planning, it does not need to consider the influence of its own volume on obstacle avoidance and the influence of kinematics related factors, which may easily cause obstacle avoidance failure of intelligent vehicle or affect the efficiency and adaptability of path planning [17].

In order to solve the above problems, this paper uses the static information of the prior environment to establish the grid map. By improving the A* path finding algorithm, considering the influence of the width of the intelligent vehicle, the obstacles are expanded, and then the path turning points are extracted, and the path is obtained according to the connected turning points. Whether the redundant turning point is judged by the obstacle and eliminated; based on the dynamic characteristics of the vehicle, the steering angle and stationarity of the vehicle are taken into account in the path evaluation index based on the dynamic window method; finally, the turning point obtained under the global path planning is taken as the sub-goal Click to complete the partial path planning. The method fully considers the static and dynamic characteristics of the vehicle, overcomes the shortcomings that the robot path planning is difficult to apply to the actual scene, and can obtain a safer, smoother and smoother optimal path.

2 Improved A* Algorithm

2.1 Introduction to A* Algorithm

A* algorithm is a heuristic path search algorithm, which can effectively solve the path planning problem in static environment. By setting the valuation function, the cost of the path search process from the start position to the end position of the target is estimated, and the best search direction is selected preferentially. Its cost estimation function is:

$$f(n) = c(n) + h(n) \tag{1}$$

where $f(n)$ is the total cost estimate from the starting node to the ending node; $c(n)$ is the actual cost of the starting node to the current node; $h(n)$ is the valuation cost of the current node to the ending node.

2.2   Obstacles Expansion

The optimal path planned by A* algorithm can ensure that the smart car can quickly and accurately reach the destination along the path. However, the driving environment of the smart car is complex, there are many fixed obstacles, and obstacles will inevitably appear. Close to the driving path and even close to the driving path. It can be found from Fig. 1 that a general mobile robot can be approximated as a particle point when performing path planning, without considering the risk of collision with a corner obstacle during traveling; however, in Fig. 2, when the smart car performs path planning And when the path reaches the corner of the obstacle, due to the existence of the width of the vehicle itself, it is easy to cause the smart car to rub or collide with the obstacle. Aiming at this problem, considering the static characteristics of the smart car itself, an obstacle expansion strategy is proposed. The specific ideas are as follows:

The obstacle is expanded and the radius of expansion is half of the width of the intelligent vehicle. The planned minimum distance between the path and the obstacle is half of the width of the vehicle, which can protect the intelligent vehicle from the danger of collision with surrounding obstacles during travel.

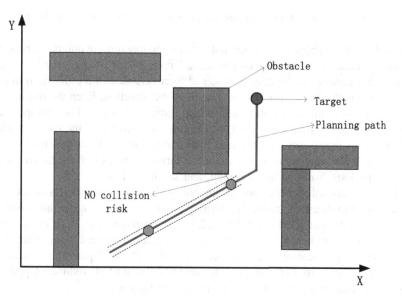

Fig. 1. Collision risk of mobile robot with obstacles during path planning

2.3   Track Smoothing

On the other hand, A* algorithm searches for the optimal path by hierarchical traversal, which inevitably leads to the planned path containing many redundant turning points, which will be detrimental to the subsequent partial path planning.

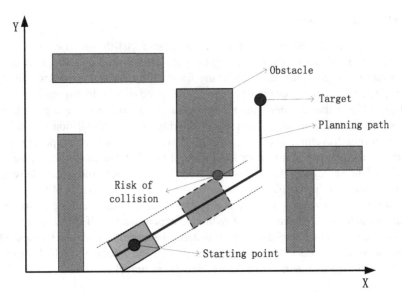

Fig. 2. Collision risk of intelligent vehicle with obstacles during path planning

Based on this problem, this paper first extracts the key turning points. Starting from the starting point, the direction of the second node relative to the starting point is determined according to the coordinates, and then extended in the direction until the nodes on the path start to turn and deviate from the direction. Keep the turning point and starting point and delete the intermediate redundant points. For example, if the coordinates of the starting point are (3, 2) and the coordinates of the second node are (3, 5), then the abscissa of the backward node can be judged. Until the abscissa of the node is not 3, the previous node is used as the turning point. Continue looking for the next turning point from the turning point, and so on until the end.

Since there are still unnecessary turning points after the turning points are extracted, it is necessary to delete the redundant turning points. Assume that the path point after the turning point is extracted is $\{P_k | k = 1, 2, \cdots, n\}$, connecting P_1P_3. If P_1P_3 does not pass the obstacle, it means that P_2 between them is a redundant turning point, which can be deleted and continue to connect P_1P_4; if P_1P_3 Will pass the obstacle and continue to connect to P_2P_4. Repeat the above steps until all redundant points are deleted and retain the critical turning points on the final path.

3   Dynamic Window Approach

The A* algorithm solves the global path planning problem of the intelligent vehicle in the known initial static environment. However, in the actual driving environment, other unknown moving obstacles will inevitably appear. If the moving obstacle pass the driving path, it will lead to collision. Aiming at this problem, this paper proposes to use the dynamic window approach to complete the local path planning of the smart car, and realize the collision avoidance between the smart car and the moving obstacle.

The core of dynamic window approach is based on the dynamics and kinematics of the robot. During a certain sampling time period, the trajectory is predicted based on the velocity space composed of the moving speed and the rotating speed of the robot, and the motion is premised on the trajectory. Optimally, the optimal motion state under the optimal trajectory is extracted for the target.

3.1 Search Speed Vector Space

To predict the trajectory of a smart car, it is necessary to know the speed state of the smart car. Considering the difference between the smart car and the robot motion model, in reality, the robot is constrained by its maximum moving speed and rotational speed, and the actual motion control of the smart car is the vehicle speed and the vehicle steering angle, thus constituting the smart car dynamic window approach search. The speed constraint space is:

$$V_S = \{v \in [-v_{max}, v_{max}], \alpha \in [-a_{max}, a_{max}]\} \tag{2}$$

During a sampling time period, the smart car is actually subject to the maximum acceleration and the maximum steering speed, so that the range of variation of the vehicle speed and the steering angle is limited. The constraint interval is:

$$V_d = \{(v, \alpha)| \in [v_0 - a_{dmax}Vt, v_0 + a_{dmax}Vt] \cap [a_0 - \omega_{max}Vt, a_0 + \omega_{max}Vt]\} \tag{3}$$

where v_0 is the speed of the smart car at the current time and α_0 is the steering angle of the smart car at the current time, a_{dmax} is the maximum brake deceleration, ω_{max} is the maximum steering speed.

In order to ensure that the smart car can avoid obstacles and pass safely, the dynamic window method needs to ensure that the smart car can stop before it hits the obstacle, so the minimum distance between the smart car and the obstacle can be calculated to determine whether the smart car can stop under the condition of maximum deceleration. In this case, the speed constraint space of the smart car is:

$$V_a = \{(v, \alpha)|v \le \sqrt{2distant(v, a) \cdot a_{dmax}} \cap a \le \sqrt{2distant(v, a) \cdot \omega_{max}}\} \tag{4}$$

where $distant(v, \alpha)$ is the closest distance of the robot to the obstacle on the path at time (v, α).

Finally, by solving the intersection of the above three speed constrained spaces, the final speed constraint space of the smart car searching under the dynamic window method is:

$$V_r = V_s \cap V_d \cap V_a \tag{5}$$

3.2 Search Speed Vector Space

When we obtain different trajectories of a certain sampling period through the velocity vector set, we need to evaluate and analyze the velocity vector corresponding to each trajectory, and select the one with the highest score as the velocity vector in the sampling period. Considering that in order to avoid the smart car turning to brake frequently and improving its comfort, the objective function selected in this paper considers five evaluation indicators: azimuth deviation, obstacle avoidance distance, moving speed, speed change and corner change. Among them, the evaluation indicators of speed change and steering angle change are:

$$variation\_v = \frac{1}{|v_{k+1} - v_k|} \tag{6}$$

$$variation\_\alpha = \frac{1}{|\alpha_{k+1} - \alpha_k|} \tag{7}$$

where v_k is the current speed of the smart car, v_{k+1} is the speed of the smart car at the next moment, α_k is the current steering angle of the smart car, α_{k+1} is the steering angle of the smart car at the next moment.

According to these five evaluation indicators, the objective function of the dynamic window approach is:

$$G(v, \alpha) = \lambda_1 \cdot heading(v, \omega) + \lambda_2 \cdot dist(v, \omega) + \lambda_3 \cdot vel(v, \omega) + \lambda_4 \cdot$$
$$variation\_v + \lambda_5 \cdot variation\_\alpha \tag{8}$$

where $heading(v, \omega)$ represents the degree of the smart car toward the target point at the next moment, and is evaluated by $180 - \theta$, that is, the smaller the θ is, the higher the evaluation index score is; $dist(v, \omega)$ represents the proximity of the predicted trajectory at the next moment to the obstacle, and reflects the smart car. Obstacle avoidance ability, the larger the value, the less likely the smart car will collide. If there is no obstacle on the trajectory, set it to a constant value; $vel(v, \omega)$ represents the moving speed of the smart car on the corresponding trajectory; $variation\_v$ and $variation\_\alpha$ represent the speed and angle of change of the smart car.

According to the score of different paths obtained by the target evaluation function, the optimal local path to be executed by the smart car can be determined.

3.3   Optimal Path Planning

Although DWA has taken into account the dynamic characteristics of the smart car and the surrounding environment, it is not the global optimal path. In this paper, combined with improved A* algorithm, after obtaining the global path, the smart car is used as the center, the local map is obtained with the detection distance of the vehicle sensor as the radius, and the local path planning is carried out with the key turning point on the global path as the target point. The specific steps of the algorithm are as follows (Fig. 3):

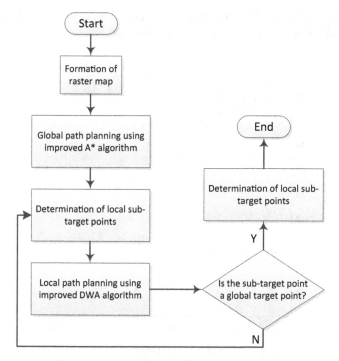

Fig. 3. Hybrid path planning process

4   Experimental Simulation

In order to verify the effectiveness of the improved algorithm, simulations were performed on a 20 * 20 planar raster map based on MATLAB R2016a. The experiment was carried out in two groups. The width of the smart car is set to 1.5 m, the maximum speed is 33.3 m/s (120 km/h), the maximum acceleration is 2 m/s^2, the maximum steering angle is 35°, and the maximum steering speed is 20°/s. The starting point of the experiment was set to $(1.5, 2)$ and the endpoints were set to $(18, 19)$. The second group of experiments added dynamic obstacles based on the static environment of the first group of experiments to verify the obstacle avoidance of smart cars.

4.1   Improved A* Algorithm Verification

In the first set of experiments, in order to verify the improved A* algorithm, A* algorithm, A* algorithm after the obstacle expansion process, A* algorithm after extracting the key turning point, and the improved elimination of the redundant turning point were adopted. The path planning results of various algorithms are shown in Fig. 4. As can be seen from Fig. 4, A* algorithm can plan a global optimal path. The path planned after the obstacle is expanded obviously maintains a certain safe distance from the obstacle, extracts the key turning point and eliminates the path after the redundant turning point. Obviously improved, the path length is smaller than A* algorithm, and the path trajectory is relatively smoother.

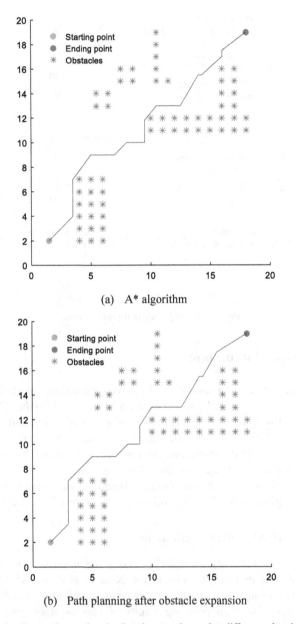

(a)   A* algorithm

(b)   Path planning after obstacle expansion

Fig. 4. Comparison of path planning results under different algorithms

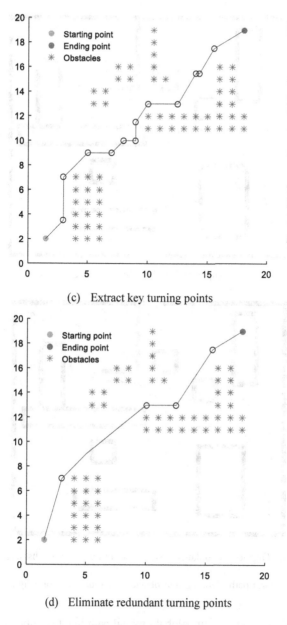

(c) Extract key turning points

(d) Eliminate redundant turning points

Fig. 4. (*continued*)

4.2 Hybrid Path Planning

Based on the first set of experiments, the second set of experiments added dynamic obstacles to the static map. The dynamic obstacle avoidance experiment results of the algorithm are shown in Fig. 5.

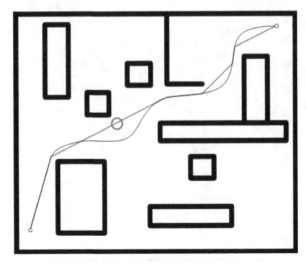

(a)   Comparison of obstacle avoidance results

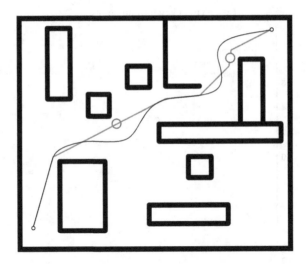

(b)   Obstacles avoidance result under more dynamic obstacles

Fig. 5. Hybrid path planning and obstacles avoidance (Color figure online)

The red solid line indicates the global optimal path that the improved A* algorithm plans in the static map, and the black solid line indicates the optimal path by improved A* algorithm and improved DWA algorithm. The green circle represents a dynamic obstacle. As can be seen from the Fig. 5, the red path obtained by improved A* algorithm cannot avoid the smart car hitting the dynamic obstacle, but the black path obtained by combining improved DWA algorithm perfectly avoids the dynamic obstacle. When the ending point is near, dynamic obstacles appear. Smart car can safely avoid it and re-plan the best path. At the same time, the path obtained by the algorithm is very smooth, and the curvature of the path changes continuously. On the basis of achieving the global optimality, it is more in line with the dynamic control and comfort requirements of the smart car. The intended purpose of the design algorithm is basically achieved.

5 Conclusion

Aiming at the problem of smart car path planning, a global dynamic optimal hybrid path planning method based on the fusion improved A* algorithm and improved DWA algorithm of smart car dynamic and static features is proposed. Based on the static characteristics of smart cars, a strategy of obstacle expansion is designed. Based on A* algorithm, key turning points and redundant turning points are eliminated, which makes the path trajectory smoother and improves the performance of path planning. The dynamic characteristics of the car improve the DWA algorithm, taking full account of the speed and steering limits of the smart car, ensuring that the vehicle can run smoothly and the comfort requirements are also met. The path planned by the proposed algorithm can achieve global optimization and dynamic obstacle avoidance, and also ensure the comfort and smoothness of the smart car.

The proposed algorithm is simulated under low-dimensional grid map, and the computational complexity of the improved A* algorithm increases with the increase of spatial dimension, and the real-time performance will also decrease. Therefore, for real-time path planning of high-dimensional large scenes, more in-depth research is needed.

References

1. Eele, A.J., Richards, A.: Path-planning with avoidance using nonlinear branch-and-bound optimization. J. Guid. Control Dyn. **32**(2), 384–394 (2015)
2. Fakoor, M., Kosari, A., Jafarzadeh, M.: Humanoid robot path planning with fuzzy markov decision processes. J. Appl. Res. Technol. **14**(5), 300–310 (2016)
3. Cobano, J.A., Conde, R., Alejo, D.: Path planning based on genetic algorithms and the Monte-Carlo method to avoid aerial vehicle collisions under uncertainties. In: 2011 International Conference on Robotics and Automation, pp. 4429–4434 (2011)
4. Chen, Y., Wang, Y., Tan, J., Mao, J.: Incremental sampling path planning for service robot based on local environments. Chin. J. Sci. Instrum. **38**(05), 1093–1100 (2017)
5. Zhan, W., Qu, J., Lu, X., Hou, L.: Global path planning based on improved ant colony algorithm for mobile robot. Modern Electron. Tech. **41**(24), 170–173 (2018)
6. Zhuge, C., Xu, J., Tang, Z.: A local path planning method based on support vector machine. J. Harbin Eng. Univ. **40**(02), 323–330 (2019)
7. Wu, L., Yang, J.: Research on global path planning for intelligent vehicles based on optimized AWA* algorithm. J. Chongqing Univ. Technol. (Nat. Sci.) **36**(8), 39–46 (2018)
8. Xu, X., Zhu, Q.: Multi-artificial fish-swarm algorithm and a rule library based dynamic collision avoidance algorithm for robot path planning in a dynamic environment. Acta Electronic Sinica **40**(8), 1694–1700 (2012)
9. Khatib, O.: Real-time obstacle avoidance for manipulators and mobile robots. Int. J. Robot. Res. **5**(1), 90–98 (1986)

10. Zhou, Z., Nie, Y., Gao, M.: Enhanced ant colony optimization algorithm for global path planning of mobile robots. In: 2013 5th International Conference on Computational and Information Sciences, pp. 698–701 (2016)
11. Zhu, D., Sun, B., Li, L.: Algorithm for AUV's 3D path planning and safe obstacle avoidance based on biological inspired model. Control Decis. **30**(5), 798–806 (2015)
12. Pan, J., Wang, X., Cheng, Y.: Improved ant colony algorithm for mobile robot path planning. J. China Univ. Min. Technol. **41**(1), 108–113 (2012)
13. Wang, D.: Indoor mobile-robot path planning based on an improved A* algorithm. J. Tsinghua Univ. (Sci. Technol.) **52**(8), 1085–1089 (2012)
14. Liu, J., Yang, J., Liu, H.: Robot global path planning based on ant colony optimization with artificial potential field. Trans. Chin. Soc. Agric. Mach. **46**(9), 18–27 (2015)
15. Chen, H., Shen, C., Guo, H., Liu, J.: Moving horizon path planning for intelligent vehicle considering dynamic obstacle avoidance. China J. Highw. Transp. **32**(1), 162–172 (2019)
16. Golan, Y., Edelman, S., Shapiro, A.: Hybrid dynamic moving obstacle avoidance using a stochastic reachable set-based potential field. IEEE Trans. Robot. **33**(5), 1124–1138 (2017)
17. An, L., Chen, T., Cheng, A., Fang, W.: A simulation on the path planning of intelligent vehicles based on artificial potential field algorithm. Autom. Eng. **39**(12), 1451–1456 (2017)

Single-Binocular Vision Conversion Strategy for Obstacle Detection at Non-signalized Intersections

Xiaotian Ma, Xiaoqing Sang, Yehui Sun, Xiaotong Gong,
Shanshang Gao, Yi Xu, and Derong Tan[✉]

Shandong University of Technology, Zibo 255049, China
150032773@qq.com

Abstract. Taking full account of the advantages and disadvantages of monocular vision and binocular vision in environmental perception, this paper proposes a single-binocular vision conversion strategy based on monocular camera for obstacle detection at non-signalized intersections. Using this strategy we can get fast and accurate identification of obstacles on the lateral anterior of the vehicle, and achieve fast and accurate detection for subsequent distances and speeds of obstacles. To ensure driving safety at the intersections on the premise of effectively detecting cross-conflict, first, the monocular camera conversion model, the number of cameras and the installation position are determined. Second, a single-binocular vision conversion strategy is made: the single-binocular visual composition is determined in real time according to the distance parameter and the angle parameter, and the obstacle information on the lateral anterior of the vehicle is acquired. In the end, compared with the complete monocular vision and complete binocular visual environmental perception method, the comparison results prove the rationality of the conversion strategy, and prove that the strategy is efficient and accurate in environmental perception and obstacle recognition, ranging, and speed measurement.

Keywords: Monocular vision · Binocular vision · Conversion strategy · Obstacle recognition · Ranging · Speed measurement

1 Introduction

In the fields of Advanced Driver Assistant System (ADAS) and Intelligent Traffic System (ITS), environmental perception is the prerequisite of safety status assessment, intelligent collision avoidance and safe driving [1, 2]. It is also a key issue in traffic status assessment, path planning, etc. In the fields, machine vision-based environmental perception has been widely used [3, 4].

Machine vision includes monocular vision and binocular vision. Monocular vision uses only one camera to complete the positioning work [5, 6]. Monocular vision only requires one vision sensor, so the advantage of this method is that the camera calibration is simple. At the same time, it has the fast sensing speed and high sensing efficiency, but it is difficult to adapt to complex environmental conditions, and the measurement accuracy is lower than binocular vision [7, 8]. Binocular stereo vision

© Springer Nature Switzerland AG 2019
C. Esposito et al. (Eds.): I-SPAN 2019, CCIS 1080, pp. 371–380, 2019.
https://doi.org/10.1007/978-3-030-30143-9_31

technology is a technique that simulates the human eyes to process scene images. The cameras are used to image the same target object from different locations, and the disparity map is used to achieve depth information acquisition of the obstacle. The advantage of monocular vision is that the distance measurement of obstacle is relatively accurate, and the characteristics of the world coordinates can be flexibly extracted in various environments, but there are disadvantages of high system cost and high calculation speed requirement [9, 10].

The traditional vision-based environmental perception method is mostly based on monocular vision or binocular vision. Although they can achieve obstacle recognition, speed measurement, ranging and other goals, the detection method based on monocular vision is prone to get low perceived efficiency in complex environments, the accuracy rate is not as good as binocular vision [11, 12]. Moreover, the perception results of the environment based on binocular vision are not as fast as the perception results based on monocular vision. Many researchers use binocular cameras directly as sensors, which leads to high detection costs and waste [13, 14].

The lateral anterior of the vehicle is a high-risk zone of the crossing conflict. The Wayne diagram model considers that traffic conflicts and accidents are continuous and unified. As shown in Fig. 1, there will be serious traffic conflicts before the accidents [15, 16]. Taking fast and accurate traffic conflict detection in advance can effectively avoid traffic accidents and ensure driving safety.

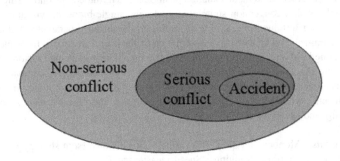

Fig. 1. Wayne diagram of conflict and accident.

Taking full account of the advantages and disadvantages of monocular vision and binocular vision in obstacle detection and distance measurement, this paper proposes a single-binocular vision conversion strategy based on monocular camera for obstacle detection at non-signalized intersections. According to the distance parameter d and the angle parameter α, the single-binocular visual composition is determined in real time, and the image information acquired by the monocular camera is processed. The monocular vision can quickly realize the rapid recognition of the obstacle, the binocular vision can accurately detect the obstacle. The conversion strategy improve the speed and accuracy of environmental perception and obstacle detection. The linear distance from the centroid of the obstacle to the centroid of the vehicle is denoted as d, the angle between the line connecting the centroid of the obstacle to the centroid of the vehicle and the longitudinal axis of the vehicle is denoted as α, The distance parameter d and the angle parameter α are as shown in Fig. 2.

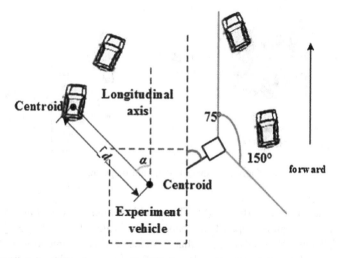

Fig. 2. Schematic diagram of distance parameter and angle parameter.

2 Single-Binocular Vision Conversion Strategy

2.1 Number of Cameras, Layout and Installation

The crossing conflict mainly occurs in the lateral anterior of the vehicle. According to the data analysis, the range of the cross-accident occurred was about 135° symmetrical about the longitudinal axis of the vehicle. Therefore, based on the above situation, this paper determines the number of cameras, and designs the camera installation and layout scheme.

In this paper, the sensor of the visual perception system includes three cameras that are fixed in place. In order to realize the perception of the environmental information on the lateral anterior of the vehicle, the camera field of view covers the area prone to collision, three cameras are mounted on the hood. The camera visual angle used in this paper is 150°. The optical axis of camera 2 is collinear with the longitudinal axis of the vehicle. The camera 1 and camera 3 are symmetrically distributed with respect to camera 2, and the optical axis is at an angle of 75° to the longitudinal axis of the vehicle. In the overlapping visual area of the two monocular cameras, the combination of the two cameras can play the binocular vision function, which makes the information collection more efficient and accurate, and can improve the accuracy of the subsequent ranging speed measurement. The cameras are installed as shown in Fig. 3. The number of cameras and the layout schemes can meet the environmental sensing needs of the lateral anterior of the vehicle.

2.2 Single-Binocular Vision Transformation Architecture

Defining the distance between the obstacle and the vehicle is d, the unit is meter (m), the angle between the running direction of the obstacle and the longitudinal axis of the

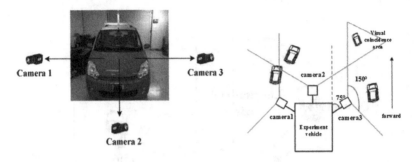

Fig. 3. Camera installation diagram.

vehicle is α, and the unit is degree (°). The specific expressions of d and α are given above. The main research scope of this paper is the range of d $\leq$ 55, α $\leq$ 150.

Taking full use of the advantages that monocular visual perception is faster and more sensitive to long-distance obstacle perception than binocular vision; giving full play to the advantages that the higher accurate of binocular vision in distance measurement relative to monocular vision, according to distance parameter d and angle parameters α develops a single-binocular visual real-time conversion strategy.

A. Three monocular cameras firstly play the monocular vision function to collect environmental information. Using density clustering algorithm to distinguish obstacles, and detect the height of each obstacle, the distance parameter d and angle parameter α are detected of the space obstacle. The value d of each conversion node is defined based on the data.

B. When d > 40, monocular vision is used to identify and detect obstacles, and then Kalman filter is used to track obstacles. Tracking is abandoned when it is predicted that an obstacle is unlikely to collide with the vehicle; when the probability of collision is large, monocular vision is used to measure the obstacle distance parameter d to achieve fast ranging.

C. When 15 m $\leq$ d $\leq$ 40, 0 $\leq$ α $\leq$ 75, the binocular vision is used to track the obstacle firstly. When the tracking predicts that the obstacle is likely to collide with the vehicle, the image control unit automatically combines the Image information of two cameras. The image information acquired by the two monocular cameras is used to perform binocular visual stereo matching, then by quickly and accurately measuring to the distance and the running angle of the obstacle, so as to find the danger in time. When α is another value, proceed to strategy B and use monocular vision to implement subsequent operations.

D. When d < 15, in the range of 0 $\leq$ α $\leq$ 75, the image control unit automatically combines the image information acquired by two adjacent monocular cameras to perform binocular visual stereo matching, then by accurately measuring to the distance and the running angle of the obstacle, so as to find the danger in time. when α is other, continues to execute strategy B and use monocular vision to implement subsequent operations.

E. Execute strategies B, C, and D at the same time, repeat step A every 10 s.

The conversion process is shown in Figs. 4. and 5.

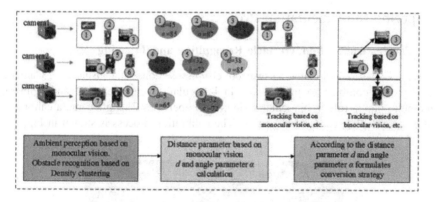

Fig. 4. Schematic diagram of the conversion process

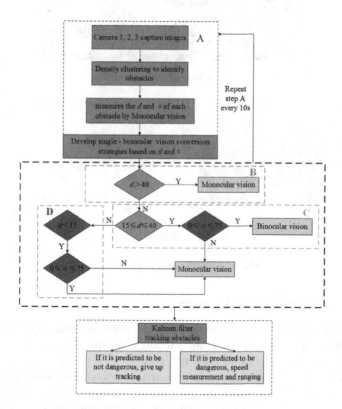

Fig. 5. The flow chart of the conversion process

3   Specific Implementation Process

3.1   Camera Calibration, Obstacle Recognition and Tracking

Camera1, Camera2 and Camera3 respectively play a monocular visual role, Camera1 and Camera2 combine to play a role in binocular vision, Camera2 and Camera3 combine to play a role in binocular vision, this paper uses Zhang's camera calibration method to complete camera calibration. The calibration process is shown in Fig. 6.

(a)   Camera calibration process

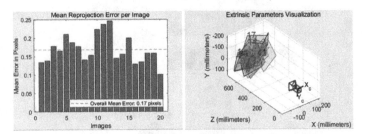

(b)   Camera calibration results

Fig. 6.   Camera calibration process.

3.2   Obstacle Recognition and Tracking

In order to improve the speed of recognition and detection, this paper uses density clustering algorithm instead of machine learning algorithm to distinguish obstacles. The density clustering algorithm does not need to give the partition number k in advance, and is suitable for clustering data sets of unknown content, and can find clusters of arbitrary shapes, which can meet the recognition requirements of unknown obstacles in reality [17]. Compared with machine learning, the density clustering algorithm does not need to process a large amount of image data, and the calculation speed is fast and the space-time complexity is low [18]. In this paper, the density clustering method is used to cluster the obstacle pixels in the image to distinguish different obstacles and mark the center of mass of the obstacle. The density clustering effect is shown in Fig. 7.

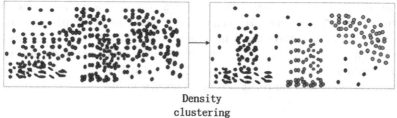

Density
clustering

Fig. 7. Schematic diagram of density clustering.

After density clustering distinguishes each obstacle in the image, establish a monocular vision and a binocular vision ranging model respectively, measure the distance parameter d and the angle parameter α for each obstacle, develop a single-binocular visual conversion strategy based on parameter d and parameter α, the whole process uses Kalman filter for obstacle tracking. The tracking process is shown in Fig. 8.

Fig. 8. Kalman filter tracking process diagram.

3.3 Principle of Visual Transformation Strategy

1. When d > 40, the requirement for distance accuracy is low, and the reaction speed is the first consideration of the system. The value of α is not considered. At this time, All subsequent tracking or speed measurement are based on monocular vision. When the probability of collision between the obstacle and the self-vehicle is small, the tracking is abandoned; when the probability of the collision is large, the distance parameter d of the obstacle is measured by the monocular vision to realize fast ranging.

2. When $15 \leq d \leq 40$, the reaction speed in this range needs to be considered. When $0 \leq \alpha \leq 75$, this range of viewing angle is the best scene for binocular vision, which helps to achieve stereo matching quickly and accurately. And the probability of collision in this range is large, so in this case, the detection accuracy is considered at the same time. Therefore, in this area, binocular visual stereo matching is performed by combining image information acquired by two adjacent monocular cameras. Binocular vision is used to track or perform the tasks of subsequent ranging and velocity measurements and to detect hazards in time. When α is other values, only the detection speed is considered at this time, so strategy A is continued for subsequent operations.

3. When d < 15, the distance between the vehicle and the obstacle is already very small. While ensuring the accuracy of the inspection, the speed of identification and detection must be ensured. However, the coverage of the two adjacent cameras may

be small, and binocular vision blind spots may occur, it is difficult to grasp the whole situation by binocular vision alone, it is necessary to complete the cooperation of Monocular vision and binocular vision. When $0 \leq \alpha \leq 75$, tracking, ranging and speed measurement based on binocular vision are performed on the corresponding obstacles, and when α is others, step B is repeated, tracking and subsequent operations are performed by monocular vision.

4 Experimental Comparison

Using the single-binocular vision conversion strategy described above to conduct experiments on obstacle detection on the lateral anterior of the vehicle at non-signalized intersections. In the same environment, the experimental results were compared with simple monocular visual inspection and simple binocular visual inspection results. The feasibility of this paper conversion strategy is verified by comparing the overall perception recognition speed, obstacle identification accuracy and ranging, speed measurement accuracy. The type of obstacles per unit time is three: motor vehicles, nonmotor vehicles, pedestrians. Express the overall perceived speed in units of 30 s, 10 is the number of obstacles. Obstacle identification accuracy rate is determined by manually identifying obstacles in a unit time and comparing with machine identification. The ranging accuracy is determined by comparing the field measurement data.

The experimental results show that the perceptual recognition speed based on the single-binocular visual conversion strategy is almost the same as the perceptual recognition speed based on monocular vision, the identification accuracy is 5% points higher, the distance measurement accuracy is 8% points higher, and the single-binocular conversion is based on The perceived recognition speed of the strategy is 8% points higher than the perceived speed based on binocular vision, the identification accuracy is 2% points higher, and the speed measurement accuracy is almost the same.

Obstacle recognition and detection results are shown in Fig. 9.

The overall recognition speed, identification accuracy, ranging speed accuracy results are shown in Tables 1, 2, and 3.

Fig. 9. Experimental comparison results.

Table 1. Percentage comparison table for identifying the number of obstacles per unit time

Visual composition	Motor vehicle	Non-motor vehicle	Pedestrian
Monocular vision	89.0%	78.0%	59.0%
Binocular vision	81.0%	69.0%	52.0%
Single-binocular vision	88.4%	78.2%	59.0%

Table 2. Identification accuracy comparison table

Visual composition	Motor vehicle	Non-motor vehicle	Pedestrian
Monocular vision	88.2%	88.0%	82.2%
Binocular vision	91.2%	90.9%	85.0%
Single-binocular vision	93.2%	92.8%	87.2%

Table 3. Comparison of distance measurement accuracy

Visual composition	Motor vehicle	Non-motor vehicle	Pedestrian
Monocular vision	88.0%	88.2%	86.5%
Binocular vision	96.0%	96.2%	93.6%
Single-binocular vision	96.2%	95.8%	94.0%

5 Conclusion

This paper considers the non-signalized intersections with a high crossing accident rate, combines the advantages and disadvantages of monocular vision and binocular vision in environmental perception, ranging, and speed measurement, proposed a single-binocular vision conversion strategy based on monocular camera to detect the obstacles on the lateral anterior of the vehicle. The density clustering algorithm is used to distinguish obstacles, which can effectively reduce the space-time complexity based on machine learning algorithms. The obstacle tracking is performed by Kalman filter; the conversion visual strategy is formulated by the distance parameter d and the angle parameter α to ensure effective tracking, fast and accurate identification and detection of obstacles.

Finally, compared with the complete monocular visual environment perception method and complete binocular visual environment perception method. The experimental results show that the single-binocular vision conversion strategy based on the obstacle detection on the lateral anterior of the vehicle has high speed, high precision, high accuracy and has low environmentally perceived cost, it is of great significance to improve the detection speed and detection efficiency of obstacles on the road.

References

1. Bengler, K., Dietmayer, K., Farber, B., et al.: Three decades of driver assistance systems: review and future perspectives. IEEE Intell. Transp. Syst. Mag. **6**(4), 6–22 (2014)
2. Monreal, C.O.: Intelligent vehicle technology R&D group [ITS research lab]. IEEE Intell. Transp. Syst. Mag. **10**(3), 200–203 (2018)
3. Cai, Y., Li, D., Zhou, X., et al.: Robust drivable road region detection for fixed-route autonomous vehicles using map-fusion images. Sensors **18**(12), 4158 (2018)
4. Pan, J., Chen, W., Peng, W.: A new moving objects detection method based on improved SURF algorithm. In: 2013 25th Chinese Control and Decision Conference (CCDC), pp. 901–906. IEEE (2013)
5. Royer, E., Bom, J., Dhome, M., et al.: Outdoor autonomous navigation using monocular visio. In: 2005 IEEE/RSJ International Conference on Intelligent Robots and Systems (2005)
6. Zhuge, C., Xu, F., Jinsong, S., Tang, Z.: A local path planning method based on support vector machine. J. Harbin Eng. Univ. **40**(02), 323–330 (2019)
7. Zhu, A., Cao, Z., Xiao, Y.: Real-time stereo matching system. In: Chen, Z., Mendes, A., Yan, Y., Chen, S. (eds.) ICIRA 2018. LNCS (LNAI), vol. 10985, pp. 377–386. Springer, Cham (2018). https://doi.org/10.1007/978-3-319-97589-4_32
8. Bensrhair, A., Bertozzi, M., Broggi, A., et al.: A cooperative approach to vision-based vehicle detection. In: 2001 IEEE Intelligent Transportation Systems, 2001, Proceedings, pp. 207–212. IEEE (2001)
9. Guindel, C., Martín, D., Armingol, J.M.: Traffic scene awareness for intelligent vehicles using ConvNets and stereo vision. Robot. Auton. Syst. **112**, 109–122 (2019)
10. Dehnavi, M., Eshghi, M.: FPGA based real-time on-road stereo vision system. J. Syst. Archit. **81**, 32–43 (2017)
11. Aguilar, W.G., Casaliglla, V.P., Pólit, J.L.: Obstacle avoidance based-visual navigation for micro aerial vehicles. Electronics **6**(1), 10 (2017)
12. Yi, X., Song, G., Derong, T., et al.: Fast road obstacle detection method based on maximally stable extremal regions. Int. J. Adv. Robot. Syst. **15**(1), 1729881418759118 (2018)
13. Isotalo, E., Kapoula, Z., Feret, P.H., et al.: Monocular versus binocular vision in postural control. Auris Nasus Larynx **31**(1), 11–17 (2003)
14. Blake, R., Camisa, J.: Is binocular vision always monocular? Science **200**, 1497–1499 (1978)
15. Sayed, T., Zein, S.: Traffic conflict standards for intersections. Transp. Plan. Technol. **22**, 309–323 (1998)
16. Glauz, W.D., Migletz, D.J.: Application of traffic conflict analysis at intersections. Shaping Transport Future **02**, 123–126 (1980)
17. Fraley, C., Raftery, A.E.: Model-based clustering, discriminant analysis, and density estimation. J. Am. Stat. Assoc. **97**, 611–631 (2002)
18. Mateus, A., Ribeiro, D., Miraldo, P., et al.: Efficient and robust pedestrian detection using deep learning for human-aware navigation. Robot. Auton. Syst. **113**, 23–37 (2019)

The Research on Intelligent Vehicle Trajectory Tracking Based on Model Predictive Control

Yaming Niu, Di Tan$^{(\boxtimes)}$, Jinju Shao, Gang Shen, Xunyi Li,
and Guo Wei

Shandong University of Technology, Zibo 255000, China
Tandi@sdut.edu.cn

Abstract. In order to complete the trajectory tracking of smart cars, a trajectory tracking method based on model predictive control is proposed. The linear linearization scheme of kinematics model is used to obtain the necessary linear time-varying system, and the three elements of model predictive control are adopted to design the controller. And based on the advantages of MPC in the control process can increase the constraints, establish the constraints based on the vehicle kinematics model, Simultaneous trajectory tracking simulation experiment of simulink and Carsim after writing corresponding algorithm with MATLAB. The trajectory is designed based on the premise that there is an obstacle in front of the vehicle. The experimental results show that the controller based on MPC algorithm can track the desired trajectory quickly and stably.

Keywords: Model predictive control · Linearization · Trajectory tracking

1 Introduction

The rolling optimization strategy is one of the advantages of Model Predictive Control (MPC), so it has a stable and a good control effect on the time variation of the system, and MPC can feedback correction of the system output to minimize the error to improve the system' Robustness [1–3]. The unmanned vehicle needs to establish the vehicle dynamics model during planning and control, A large number of tests have shown, if the vehicle kinematics and dynamic constraints can be calculated during the planning period, the controller tracking performance will be better [4]. Therefore, when establishing the model predictive controller, the appropriate control increment must be selected according to the actual driving condition of the vehicle, and a kinematic model that can accurately describe the relationship between the smart car and a dynamic model describing the dynamic constraints can be established [5–7].

However, the dynamic process of the car is extremely complicated especially during driving. Therefore, in order to ensure the real-time performance of the control tracking algorithm, various constraints are often simplified and approximated [8, 9]. Therefore, this paper first establishes the kinematics model of the vehicle, and then It linearizes to obtain the corresponding linear model, and then uses the three elements of model predictive control: predictive equation establishment, rolling optimization and feedback correction to design the controller; finally, use MATLAB/simulink and Carsim to have test simulation to verify the control effect [10, 11].

© Springer Nature Switzerland AG 2019
C. Esposito et al. (Eds.): I-SPAN 2019, CCIS 1080, pp. 381–391, 2019.
https://doi.org/10.1007/978-3-030-30143-9_32

2   Establishment of Vehicle Kinematics Model

Before establishing a vehicle kinematics model, it is necessary to take the lead in simplifying the car movement so that the model is simple and easy to use, and can basically reflect the vehicle characteristics and performance [8, 12]. For this reason, the Bicycle Model is our preferred method. Make a few assumptions before using the bicycle model:

The movement of the vehicle in the Z-axis direction is not taken into account, and only the motion in the X Y aspect is considered (That is, the described vehicle is on a two-dimensional plane) as shown in Fig. 1; Think of the two front wheels and the two rear wheels of the car as one wheel, so that it is convenient to build the car model, as shown in Fig. 2; In the case of a very low speed, the change of the front and rear axle loads is ignored; The body and suspension system are rigid [13, 14].

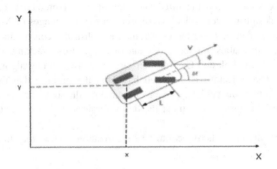

Fig. 1.   Vehicle two-dimensional motion model

Where v is the speed of the vehicle, which is in the φ direction. L is the wheelbase of the car (the length between the center of the front and rear tires), φ is the heading angle of the vehicle, and (x, y) is the current position of the vehicle.

The bicycle model combines the two wheels in front of the car into one point, assuming A; combining the two wheels behind the car into one point, assuming B; the vehicle's centroid is assumed to be C.

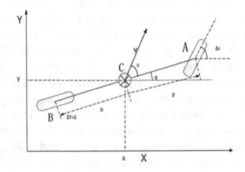

Fig. 2.   Kinematic bicycle model

Among them, (x, y) is the current position of the vehicle, a is the direction of the vehicle speed V, also known as the slip angle, and φ is the heading angle; δ_f, δ_r respectively refers to the yaw angle of the front and rear wheels of the vehicle, that is, the clip between the vehicle and the X-axis's Angle; l_f, l_r is the total control input, which can be reduced to (a, δ_f).

When the driver steps on the accelerator pedal, the vehicle accelerates. On the other hand, when the brake pedal is pressed, the vehicle performs the deceleration motion, δ_f which is the angle when the steering the wheel. It is assumed that the angle of the steering wheel is the current angle of the front tire. In this way, the control inputs of the vehicle can be described using two quantities.

In the model, four quantities are generally used to describe the current state of the vehicle:

X: the current X coordinate of the vehicle. Y: the current Y coordinate of the vehicle. φ: current yaw of the vehicle (yaw angle in Y direction, often described in radians, counterclockwise is positive). v: the speed of the vehicle.

Then based on the bicycle model, as shown in Fig. 2, the vehicle Kinematic model is built. Available from the sine law:

$$\frac{\sin(\delta_f - \beta)}{l_f} = \frac{\sin(\frac{\pi}{2} - \delta_f)}{R} \tag{1}$$

$$\frac{\sin(\beta - \delta_f)}{l_r} = \frac{\sin(\frac{\pi}{2} + \delta_r)}{R} \tag{2}$$

Combine Eqs. (1) and (2):

$$\dot{\varphi} = \frac{v \cos \beta}{l_f + l_r} \left(\tan \delta_f - \tan \delta_r \right) \tag{3}$$

Where a is the angular velocity of the vehicle. Then according to the Kinematics principle, the update formula for several state quantities in the model is as follows:

$$\begin{cases} \dot{x} = v \cos(\varphi + \beta) \\ \dot{y} = v \sin(\varphi + \beta) \\ \dot{\varphi} = \frac{v \cos \beta}{l_f + l_r} \left(\tan \delta_f - \tan \delta_r \right) \\ \dot{v} = v_t + at \end{cases} \tag{4}$$

$$\beta = \arctan \left(\frac{l_f \tan \delta_r + l_r \tan \delta_f}{l_f + l_r} \right) \tag{5}$$

Equation (5) is all the formulas of the model.

Because most of the rear wheels of the car can't be deflected, as shown in Fig. 2, when the car is turning, only the front wheel is deflected, the rear wheel deflection angle δ_r at this time can be considered as 0. So the bicycle model assumes the steering angle input of the rear wheel $\delta_r = 0$. On the other hand, the corner input on the steering wheel is transplanted to the corner of the front wheel. So at this point the formula (5) becomes:

$$\beta = \arctan\left(\frac{l_r \tan \delta_f}{l_f + l_r}\right) \tag{6}$$

At this point, the car kinematics model can be obtained, and the center of the axis can be used as the reference point. (x_r, y_r) is the position of the center of the rear axle, φ is the angle of the navigation direction. v_r is the vehicle's speed, δ_f is the front wheel's steering angle. The front wheel steering angle δ_r was assumed 0, ω for the yaw rate, β, the slip angle can be ignored, assuming 0. At this time, the state quantity of the car is $\zeta = [x_r, y_r, \varphi]^T$, and the control amount is $\mu = (v_r, \delta_f)^T$, at this point, formula (4) can be transformed into the following form:

$$\begin{bmatrix} \dot{x}_r \\ \dot{y}_r \\ \dot{\varphi} \end{bmatrix} = \begin{bmatrix} \cos \varphi \\ \sin \varphi \\ \frac{\tan \delta_f}{l} \end{bmatrix} v_r \tag{7}$$

In the control of the unmanned vehicle, it is generally used ω to replace the front wheel yaw angle δ_f. so, the formula (7) can be converted into the following form (Fig. 3):

$$\begin{bmatrix} \dot{x}_r \\ \dot{y}_r \\ \dot{\varphi} \end{bmatrix} = \begin{bmatrix} \cos \varphi \\ \sin \varphi \\ 0 \end{bmatrix} v_r + \begin{bmatrix} 0 \\ 0 \\ 1 \end{bmatrix} \omega \tag{8}$$

uild the above model in simulink, as shown below:

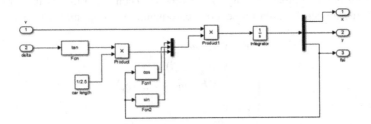

Fig. 3. Vehicle kinematics simulink simulation modeling

When the speed v of the car and the wheel angle delta are input, the position x, y and heading angle fai of the car can be obtained by the formula (7). Lay the foundation for the overall modeling.

3 Controller Design

3.1 Linearization of Nonlinear Systems

The car is a strong nonlinear system, and the Kinematics model established above is not linear and needs to be linearized. There are many methods, which are roughly divided into two categories: approximation and precision. Accurate linearity is generally not universal. It is usually analyzed for a separate system. Therefore, an approximate linear method is generally adopted. However, after obtaining a continuous linear time-varying model, it is not possible to design the controller directly. First, we must use approximate discretization:

$$\dot{\tilde{\varepsilon}} = A(t)\tilde{\varepsilon} + B(t)\tilde{u}$$
$$\tilde{\varepsilon}(q+1) = A_{q,t}\tilde{\varepsilon}(q) + B_{q,t}\tilde{u}(q) \tag{9}$$

Combine the two formulas of Eq. (9):

$$\begin{cases} A_{q,t} = I + TA(t) \\ B_{q,t} = TB(t) \end{cases} \tag{10}$$

Among them, $A(t) = J_f(\varepsilon)$, $J_f(\varepsilon)$ is the Jacobi matrix for f to ε; $B(t) = J_f(\mu)$, $J_f(\mu)$ is the Jacobi matrix for f to u.

At this time, the previous nonlinear system is transformed into a linear system at any reference point, which also lays a foundation for the implementation of the MPC algorithm.

3.2 Prediction Equation

Convert the linear model of Eq. (10) into the following equation:

$$x(q+1) = A_{q,t}x(q) + B_{q,t}u(q) \tag{11}$$

Then assume:

$$\xi(q|q) = \begin{bmatrix} x(q|q) \\ u(q-1|q) \end{bmatrix} \tag{12}$$

Then the state equation at q+1 is as follows:

$$\begin{cases} \xi(q+1|q) = \tilde{A}_q\xi(q|q) + \tilde{B}_q\Delta u(q|q) \\ \eta(q|q) = \tilde{C}_q\xi(q|q) \end{cases} \tag{13}$$

The matrix in the formula is defined as follows:

$$\tilde{A}_q = \begin{bmatrix} \tilde{A}_q & \tilde{B}_q \\ 0_{m \times n} & I_m \end{bmatrix}, \quad \tilde{B}_q = \begin{bmatrix} B_q \\ I_m \end{bmatrix}, \quad \tilde{C}_q = [C_q \quad 0]$$

Set the domain value of the system prediction time is N_p, the domain value of the control time is N_c, expressions for state vectors and system outputs in the predicted time domain are known. Usually, when describing the future output of a system, it is expressed in a matrix:

$$Y(q) = \Psi_q \xi(q|q) + \theta_q \Delta u(q) \tag{14}$$

among them:

$$Y(q) = \begin{bmatrix} \eta(q+1)|q \\ \eta(q+2)|q \\ \cdots \\ \eta(q+N_c)|q \\ \cdots \\ \eta(q+N_p)|q \end{bmatrix} \quad \Psi_q = \begin{bmatrix} \tilde{C}_q \tilde{A}_q \\ \tilde{C}_q \tilde{A}_q^2 \\ \cdots \\ \tilde{C}_q \tilde{A}_q^{Nc} \\ \cdots \\ \tilde{C}_q \tilde{A}_q^{Np} \end{bmatrix} \quad \Delta u(q) = \begin{bmatrix} \Delta u(q|q) \\ \Delta u(q+1|q) \\ \cdots \\ \Delta u(q+N_c|q) \end{bmatrix}$$

$$\theta_q = \begin{bmatrix} \tilde{C}_q \tilde{B}_q & 0 & 0 & 0 \\ \tilde{C}_q \tilde{A}_q \tilde{B}_q & \tilde{C}_q \tilde{B}_q & 0 & 0 \\ \cdots & \cdots & \ddots & \cdots \\ \tilde{C}_q \tilde{A}_q^{Nc-1} \tilde{B}_q & \tilde{C}_q \tilde{A}_q^{Nc-2} \tilde{B}_q & \cdots & \tilde{C}_q \tilde{B}_q \\ \tilde{C}_q \tilde{A}_q^{Nc} \tilde{B}_q & \tilde{C}_q \tilde{A}_q^{Nc-1} \tilde{B}_q & \cdots & \tilde{C}_q \tilde{A}_q \tilde{B}_q \\ \vdots & \vdots & \ddots & \vdots \\ \tilde{C}_q \tilde{A}_q^{Np-1} \tilde{B}_q & \tilde{C}_q \tilde{A}_q^{Np-2} \tilde{B}_q & \cdots & \tilde{C}_q \tilde{A}_q^{Np-Nc-1} \tilde{B}_q \end{bmatrix}$$

According to Eq. (15), the current state transition quantity of the system is known, and the control input quantity in the control time domain is known. Through both, the state quantity and output quantity of the system in the predicted time domain can be separately calculated. At this point, the predictive function in the MPC, that is, the predictive function will play its role.

3.3   Rolling Optimization

Generally, it is not known in advance when setting the control input. Therefore, before this, an appropriate optimization target needs to be set first, and then it will be solved, and the control sequence in the corresponding control time domain will be obtained:

Has the following objective function:

$$\psi(q) = \sum_{j=1}^{N} \tilde{X}^T(q+j|q)Q\tilde{X}(q+j|q) + \tilde{u}^T(q+j-1|q)R\tilde{u}(q+j-1|q) \quad (15)$$

Where Q is the weight matrix of the state vector and R is the weight matrix of the control vector.

Cause the nature of the problem at this time can be called the optimization problem. The above formula has set the penalty function (that is, the objective function), but this function has a significant disadvantage that it cannot accurately constrain the control amount. Avoid situations where the penalty function is not working when the system is strict. Therefore, to change the shape, it is not difficult to consider a cost function, that is, the "distance" between the trajectory predicted by the model and the reference path, and then take into account other control quantities, so the optimized objective function is:

$$J(\xi(q), u(q-1), \Delta u(q)) = \sum_{i=1}^{Np} \|\eta(q+i|q) - \eta_{ref}(q+i|q)\|_Q^2 + \sum_{i=1}^{Nc-1} \|\Delta u(q+i|q)\|_R^2 \quad (16)$$

Among them, the first expression means the distance between the predicted path and the actual reference trajectory, reflecting the tracking performance of the system on the reference trajectory; the second term reflects the system's ability to control the control input. At the same time, some constraints on state quantity and control quantity are also necessary to be added in the actual control system, such as control quantity and control increment constraint:

$$\Delta u_{min}(q+i) \leq \Delta u(q+i) \leq \Delta u_{max}(q+i), i = 0, 1, \ldots N_c - 1$$
$$u_{min}(q+i) \leq u(q+i) \leq u_{max}(q+i), i = 0, 1, \ldots, N_c - 1$$

For the optimization goal, you can choose a scheme to transform it into a quadratic programming problem, and write Eq. (16) as a matrix:

$$\varphi(q) = \frac{\Delta U^T(q)H(q)\Delta U(q)}{2} + f^T(q)\Delta U(q) + d(q) \quad (17)$$

Among them:

$$H(q) = \theta_q^T Q\theta_q + R, \, f^T(q) = 2E(q)^T Q\theta_q$$
$$d(q) = E(q)^T QE(q), \quad E(q) = \varphi_q \xi(q|q) - Y(q)$$

3.4   Feedback Control

Solve the quadratic programming problem written in the form of a matrix and get the desired control input:

$$\Delta U_t^* = \left[\Delta u_t^*, \Delta u_{t+1}^*, \ldots, \Delta u_{t+1+N_c-1}^*\right] \quad (18)$$

It can be obtained by the basic principles of MPC:

$$u(t) = u(t-1) + \Delta u_t^*   \tag{19}$$

The system starts to operate from the last moment when the control input comes in, until the control input of the next moment is entered. Next, the system will predict the state of the next moment from the current state, and then continue to optimize, get new output, repeat this process, until the system can complete the entire control process.

4 Selection of Tracking Trajectory

When there are obstacles in the environment, the path planning control system will be highly uncertain. When the smart car is driving on the road, there will be a situation where the faulty car in front is parked in the middle of the road. At this time, the main car has to actively avoid the faulty car, while driving on the two-way road, the main car will be avoiding the obstacle car. In the process, the car in the opposite direction will come. If the main car cannot drive normally in the driving lane due to the faulty car, it will have to occupy the lane of the other party. Therefore, it is especially important to design a reasonable and safe driving track for the situation of the main car and the incoming car.

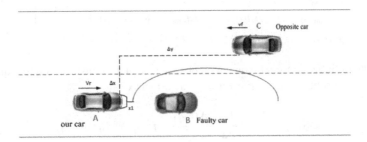

Fig. 4. Emergency obstacle avoidance and car route map

In Fig. 4, A is the main vehicle. When there is a faulty vehicle B in the driving route, it is safely avoided. Considering the rear-end collision, it is also necessary to consider the adjacent lane between the vehicle c and the main vehicle. Safety distance constraints. The red solid line is the self-planning road map of the vehicle when it is in the obstacle avoidance and when it comes to the opposite side. The consideration of this scenario is to prepare for the desired trajectory establishment after the simulation.

The following figure shows the flow of the entire trajectory tracking (Fig. 5).

For the designed MPC algorithm, it is mainly composed of linear error model, system constraints, and objective function.

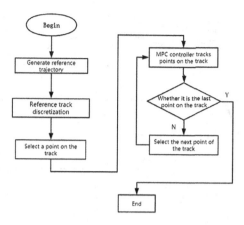

Fig. 5. Trajectory tracking flowchart

5 Simulation Experiment

In order to achieve the control purpose of the MPC controller based on MATLAB/Simulink and Carsim software for trajectory tracking, based on the establishment of the controller, the selected and set reference trajectory is the unmanned vehicle in the obstacle avoidance meeting. A semi-elliptical curve similar to that of a car.

Because carsim software can flexibly define the experimental environment and experimental process,in the complete vehicle model database of Carsim software, there are many models to choose from, and any parameters on the car can also be set.

In the simulation, under the premise that the road surface adhesion coefficient is constant, the simulation speed is set at 10 m/s, the sampling time is set to 0.05 s, the domain value of the prediction time is 15, and the domain value of the control time is 3. The weight matrix Q is set to $\begin{bmatrix} 20 & 0 & 0 \\ 0 & 15 & 0 \\ 0 & 0 & 300 \end{bmatrix}$, and the matrix R of the control vector is set to 400. The trajectory tracking control test is performed on the smart car under the premise that the road surface adhesion coefficient is constant, and the simulation result is shown in Fig. 6.

In Fig. 6, the red line segment is the reference track to be tracked by the smart car, also called the desired track, and the blue line segment is the track where the car actually travels during the tracking process. (a) and (b) are the curves of system state quantities and system control quantities over time, respectively.

Therefore, the control logic based on MATLAB/Simulink is used to model the control system and the more accurate model of the overall vehicle designed in Carsim. The joint simulation can achieve the simulation results, so that the smart car can follow the expected trajectory to achieve stable driving and reach the desired state.

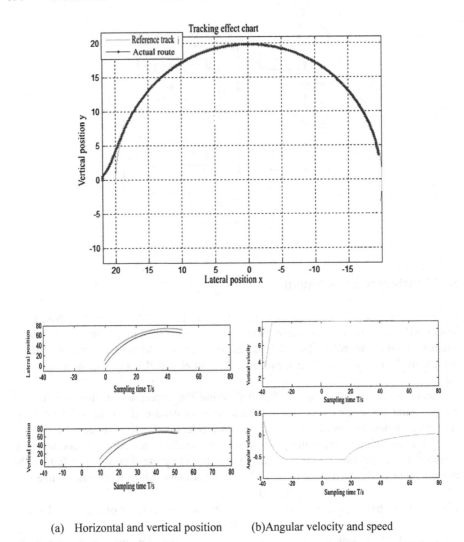

(a) Horizontal and vertical position   (b) Angular velocity and speed

Fig. 6. Trajectory tracking effect diagram (color figure online)

6   Conclusion

The results show that the model predictive controller based on MATLAB/simulink and Carsim designed in this paper can make the vehicle have good robustness at medium and low speeds. Because the controller is continuously rolling optimization, the tracking error is small and the control is small. The device thus enables faster tracking of the desired trajectory. However, this simulation is carried out at a lower speed, trajectory follow-up test for obstacle avoidance conditions at 10 m/s,therefore, it can be seen from the figure that the actual tracking trajectory and the reference trajectory error are not large. Because the advantage of model control is that it can take into account the situation in the future to obtain the current optimal solution of the system, which is achieved through a limited prediction time domain. But generally the car is driven at a medium and high speed, so that a better control effect at a relatively high speed is one of the contents to be studied in the future.

References

1. Xu, Y.T., Chen, H., Ji, D., Xu, F.: Design of vehicle start-up MPC controller and FPGA implementation. Control Eng. **22**(05), 785–792 (2015)
2. Sun, Y.J.: Research on Trajectory Tracking Control Algorithm for Unmanned Vehicles based on Model Predictive Control. Beijing Institute of Technology, Beijing (2015)
3. Falcone, P., Borrelli, F.: Multi-objective control synthesis: an application to 4WS passenger vehicles. Mechatronics **9**(4), 363–390 (1999)
4. Chunhong, W., Jinchun, H., Xi, Z., Wensheng, Y.: Optimal synchronous trajectory tracking control of wafer and reticle stages. Tsinghua Sci. Technol. **14**(3), 287–292 (2009)
5. Zhao, J.: Research on Path Tracking and Underlying Control of Intelligent Vehicles. Jilin University, Jilin (2018)
6. Wang, Y., Cai, Y., Chen, L., Wang, H., He, Y., Li, J.: Design of intelligent networked vehicle path tracking controller based on model predictive control. J. Mech. Eng. **55**(08), 136–144 + 153 (2019)
7. Duan, J., Tian, X.S., Song, Z.X.: Study on the tracking method of intelligent vehicle target path based on model predictive control. Automobile Technol. **08**, 6–11 (2017)
8. Gong, P., Yang, J., Ma, C.: Research on multi-point monitoring anti-collision system for vehicle auxiliary driving. Optik – Int. J. Light Electron. Optics **127**(18), 7121–7127 (2016)
9. Wender, S., Dietmayer, K.: 3D vehicle detection using a laser scanner and a video camera. IET Intell. Transp. Syst. **2**(2), 105–112 (2008)
10. Falcone, P., Borrelli, F.H., Tseng, E., Asgari, J., Hrovat, D.: Linear time-varying model predictive control and its application to active steering systems: stability analysis and experimental validation. Int. J. Robust Nonlinear Control **18**(8), 862–875 (2008)
11. Yoon, Y., Shin, J., Jin Kim, H., Park, Y., Sastry, S.: Model-predictive active steering and obstacle avoidance for autonomous ground vehicles. Control Eng. Pract. **17**, 741–750 (2008)
12. Ho, M.L., Chan, P.T., Rad, A.B., Shirazi, M., Cina, M.A.: Novel fused neural network controller for lateral control of autonomous vehicles. Appl. Soft Comput. J. **12**(11), 514–525 (2012)
13. Jia, L., Yumin, Z., Lei, G., Xiaoying, G.: Multi-objective antidisturbance robust filter for SINS/GPS navigation systems. Int. J. Intell. Comput. Cybernetics **6**(3), 216–231 (2013)
14. Jo, K., Chu, Y., Sunwoo, M.: Interacting multiple model filter-based sensor fusion of GPS with in-vehicle sensors for real-time vehicle positioning. IEEE Trans. Intell. Transp. Syst. **13**(1), 329–343 (2012)

Author Index

Printed in the United States
By Bookmasters

Printed in the United States
By Bookmasters